D0151429

JAPANESE AND
AMERICAN EDUCATION

JAPANESE AND AMERICAN EDUCATION

Attitudes and Practices

Harry Wray

BERGIN & GARVEY
Westport, Connecticut • London

Library of Congress Cataloging-in-Publication Data

Wray, Harry, 1931–
    Japanese and American education : attitudes and practices / Harry
Wray.
        p.   cm.
    Includes bibliographical references and index.
    ISBN 0–89789–652–1 (alk. paper)
    1. Education—Japan.   2. Education—United States.   3. Comparative
education.   I. Title.
    LA1312.W73   1999
    370'.952—dc21   98–44209

British Library Cataloguing in Publication Data is available.

Copyright © 1999 by Harry Wray

All rights reserved. No portion of this book may be
reproduced, by any process or technique, without the
express written consent of the publisher.

Library of Congress Catalog Card Number: 98–44209
ISBN: 0–89789–652–1

First published in 1999

Bergin & Garvey, 88 Post Road West, Westport, CT 06881
An imprint of Greenwood Publishing Group, Inc.
www.greenwood.com

Printed in the United States of America

The paper used in this book complies with the
Permanent Paper Standard issued by the National
Information Standards Organization (Z39.48–1984).

10   9   8   7   6   5   4   3   2   1

To my wife, Miyuki,
whose support gives me peace of mind for productive work
and whose humor, insights, and companionship are my treasures

Contents

Acknowledgments

I would like to express my deep gratitude to colleagues at Nanzan University who read and commented on one or more chapters: Charles Wordell, Thomas Bauerle, David Rines, Philip Rush, James Vincenti, Linda Woo, Mark Wright, Tom Bauerle, Gabriel Yardley, and Fathers Jack Seland, Dave Mayer, and Jan Swyngedow. I am especially grateful to colleagues Edward Skrypzcak and John Lenihan who read the entire draft and made excellent suggestions to reduce verbiage and redundancies from a draft that at one time reached nine-hundred typed pages. John also took on the burden of helping me with proof-reading and the index. Helpful comments were also made on Chapters 2 and 5 by David Plath, University of Illinois. Jim Huffman, Wittenburg University, and his late wife, Judith, a Springfield, Ohio elementary school teacher added constructive criticisms to Chapters 2, 6, 7, and 8. Vicki Downs of the American School of Japan and Jack Nicholson of Anderson High School made constructive comments on Chapters 2, 3, 5, 6, and 7 based upon their many years of teaching and reflection on two different cultures. David Dycus of Aichi Shukutoku University, Wayne McWilliams of Towson State University, Roger Danielson of Stayton Union High School, and Wright Cowger of Williamette University, the latter two former high school teaching colleagues, commented on Chapters 2, 5, and 6. Robert Edwards, now of Sacramento State University but once a colleague of mine at Lake Washington High School, made helpful comments on Chapter 6. My former advisor, George Akita, Professor Emeritus of the University of Hawaii, offered helpful criticisms on Japanese education. Professor Nobuo Shimahara of Rutgers University read the entire manuscript. His recent manuscripts and comparative education insights proved very beneficial. David Slater, a Ph.D. Candidate at the University of Chicago now teaching at Sophia University, made excellent suggestions to improve all my chapters, especially those dealing with Japanese education. I am grateful to Reiko Yamamoto for many suggestions and information regarding her own *juku* (children) and grandchildren's experiences. I would like to express thanks to my four children, Marceline, Jennifer, Stephen, and David, whose experiences with Japanese education and American education provided me with more insights than they realize. Finally, I wish to express gratitude to my Greenwood Publishing editors, Jane Garry and Lynn Taylor and to acknowledge the work of John Beck, who produced the book, and Sharon Pabst, who copy edited it so thoroughly. Of course, I accept full responsibility for errors of fact and interpretation.

CHAPTER 1

Japanese Schools' Higher Achievement, Literacy, Efficiency, Discipline, Classroom Management, and Strengths of Centralization

In 1984 Thomas Rohlen concluded from his study of Japanese high schools that the top 50 percent of Japanese high school students entering two-year or four-year colleges already possess the knowledge and analytical skills that the average American graduating from college possesses. He wrote, "The great accomplishment of Japanese primary and secondary education lies not in its creation of a brilliant elite (Western industrial nations do better with their top students) but in its generation of such a high average level of capability. The profoundly impressive fact is that it is shaping a whole population, workers as well as managers, to a standard inconceivable in the United States."[1] Can such startling judgments be supported?

International test comparisons show that Japanese students' mean achievement is much higher than students in the United States for all age groups and for all areas, and that their academic achievement ranks them among the top nations in almost every category. A math test covering algebra, geometry, modern mathematics, and probability for 950 American students and 1,700 Japanese students aged 15, 16, and 17 resulted in the average Japanese student scoring better than 98 percent of American high school students for all three age groups. In the 1995 Third International Mathematics and Science Study (TIMSS), a study to examine the math and science knowledge of a half-million students from forty-one nations at five different grade levels, American eighth graders scored below the international average in math and slightly above the international average overall. At first glance, it sounds as if American schools are doing better, but a more careful analysis of the TIMSS countries for the mathematics tests shows two striking facts. First, the American eighth graders score of 500 compared poorly to Singapore (643), Korea (607), Japan (605), Hong Kong (588), and twelve European countries and Canada, which ranged from 20 to 65 points higher. Second, most of the countries scoring "significantly lower" than the United States were developing nations. In the science test, the U.S. score of 534 was 73 points below Singapore and 36 points behind Japan. Again, with the exception of France, Belgium (French sector), and Denmark, most nations who scored lower than the United States were not noted for their high economic development.[2] The National Goals Panel's seventh annual report showed as "many areas of decline as improvement."[3]

The Japanese achievement in educating all students to a higher academic standard counteracts some Americans' efforts to argue that American society cannot simultaneously achieve excellence and democratic egalitarianism. American educational standards did decline in the late 1950s through the 1980s because of the massive positive efforts to integrate African American students, to inaugurate such programs as "Head Start," to compensate for a poor educational environment in low income homes, and to mainstream special education children. At the same time, the Japanese increased enrollments and educational equality spectacularly, due to two occupation forces reforms and the remarkable improvement in the Japanese economy. The two reforms were, first, compulsory education was extended from six to nine years in 1947, and second, a reform to achieve equal educational opportunity increased high school attendance from approximately 2 percent in 1947 to 40 percent in 1950, and then to over 95 percent by 1992.[4] Students enrolled in higher education increased from 2.9 percent in 1947 to approximately 14.6 percent in 1965, 30.3 in 1975, and 39 percent in 1992.[5] In addition, Japan, a poor country in the 1950s, did not achieve the spectacular economic growth that made the financing of education a lesser burden until the 1970s. Notwithstanding, tests in four subjects in the period of 1982 to 1983 showed that scores of fifth and sixth graders had improved between 10 to 17 percent in Japanese language, social studies, and science and a whopping 20 to 30 percent in mathematics, over those of students in the early 1960s.[6]

Some may argue that international tests are invalid comparisons because other countries are only educating the top 20 to 30 percent. But this criticism is not valid for Japanese or Korean students because (1) their education for students age eight, thirteen, and fourteen is single-tracked and compulsory; and (2) 20 percent more Japanese students attend secondary school than in the United States. The Japanese have managed to avoid what occurs in most egalitarian societies, namely a reduction in quality standards by an inevitable trend to focus on the least common denominator.

JAPANESE SCHOOLS DO A BETTER JOB ON LITERACY

Only about 3 percent of Japanese are labeled as functionally illiterate. The high academic achievement and literacy rate achieved by Japanese schools is achieved through traditional methods of drill (often in imaginative ways), rote memory, group effort, systematic and sequential learning, and repeated testing that American progressive educators labeled old-fashioned, authoritarian, and unscientific. Japanese schools limit the extent of functional literacy by the coordination of mothers, teachers, textbook writers, and the Ministry of Education to ensure learning a prescribed number of *kanji* at the end of each school year. Because students are expected to know how to combine these *kanji* in many ways to make other vocabulary, all but approximately the lowest 25 percent will have achieved enough literacy to be able to read blueprints, consumer information, and easier newspaper articles. The Japanese achievement is made despite large classes of thirty-five to fifty students.

Benjamin Duke's high praise for Japanese literacy, however, has been qualified by two studies.[7] One concluded, "There are Japanese children with serious difficulties in learning to read, and the severity of their problems is at least as great as that of American children."[8] Stevenson and Stigler demonstrated that 21 percent of fifth graders were only reading at a third-grade level.[9] The discrepancy between the Japanese claim that there are few language problems and no dyslexia in Japan and the high literacy rate can be explained by important school and cultural differences. First, although Japanese schools and society have a strong tendency to hide unpleasant facts, the numbers of illiterate and only functionally literate in Japan are much lower than in the United States. Second, Japanese parents and teachers do not recognize dyslexia or poor results. By methodically pushing and persuading students to exert effort and to persevere, a much larger percentage of Japanese students learn to read and write satisfactorily in the elementary grades.

One indication of this high literacy rate is the subscription rate to newspapers in Japan. Many households subscribe to two newspapers. The Ministry of Education reported in 1984 that the combined morning and evening daily circulation of major national newspapers was over 40 million in a nation of 120 million plus.[10] Another index is the amazing profusion of general and special interest magazines in bookstores, even in small cities.[11]

Jonathan Kozol wrote that Americans think of themselves as an educated people, but the reality is that the United States ranks only twenty-fourth in the world in books published per capita, and 37 percent of eighteen to twenty-one-year-olds are reading no books at all. Among adults, 45 percent do not read newspapers. Even famous magazines such as *Time*, *Newsweek*, and *The New Republic* are now aimed at a twelfth-grade reading level, and *U.S.A. Today* at a tenth-grade reading level.[12]

Although by tradition a good percentage of enlisted recruits have come from the lower 50 percent of high school classes, the U.S. Department of Defense testing of military recruits' reading skills in the 1980s is sobering. It demonstrates convincingly that we cannot assume that many of the structural reforms of the 1980 reform movement to increase the number of years in high school have resulted in a bona fide higher academic achievement. Even though the percentage of high school graduates in the military services increased from 81 percent in 1981 to 92 percent in 1987, the reading grade level of recruits only increased from a grade level of 9.8 to one of 10.2. Furthermore, although the U.S. Navy is more selective than the Army, about 25 percent of its recruits could not read at the ninth-grade level. Thirty percent of naval recruits have been characterized as "a danger to themselves and to costly naval equipment" because of their low reading competency.[13]

JAPANESE USE THEIR SCHOOLS MORE CHEAPLY AND EFFECTIVELY

Japanese schools are more efficient and effective in the use of human energy, time, and space. Savings that could be made by adopting these practices selectively could be applied to other areas to improve the performance of American schools.

Time

The American school year runs between 175 and 180 school days, and a school day approximately consists of a nine-to-three weekday schedule. The Japanese Ministry of Education requires a 210-day school year, but local school boards are free to increase the number of days. The Japanese trimester school year runs from approximately 1 April to 20 July, the first week in September to 23 December, and from 7 January through mid-March, or about 220 to 225 school days.[14] Japanese students spend approximately seven hours at school on weekdays. In progression, Japan eliminated one half-day on Saturday in 1993, two half-days in 1995, and in 2003 will eliminate all Saturdays, a controversial decision.

A study by the U.S. Department of Education concluded that when adjustments were made for half-days on Saturdays, the Japanese school year is about 195 days of classroom instruction rather than the often touted 240 day school year because: 20 to 30 days of the Japanese school year may be consumed by various nonacademic events such as Sports Day, Culture Day, and graduation and opening day ceremonies; on some days, mere greetings are exchanged and students return home; several days are used for school excursions (field trips); half-days are the norm for elementary school children in July; and during days at the end of each semester high school students take comprehensive exams for a week, but only attend school a half-day.[15] Catherine Lewis also thinks the Japanese school year is overstated because it is calculated on the number of days attending school, not instructional time.[16]

Both of these studies are misleading. Why? Japanese schools' usage of noninstructional times for class meetings, self-reflection time, recesses, cleaning, and special activities are considered an integral part of the curricular goal to build character. By local schools' semiformal practices, Japanese students go to school longer than these calculations allow. Most schools schedule another thirty days beyond the legally required 210 days precisely to compensate for the above academic and nonacademic school activities. At some schools, particularly at private and rural public schools in Honshu and the other islands (where generally public schools have higher prestige than private schools), and at some lower ranking schools eager to increase their school ranking, one or two fifty-minute special classes will be held in the morning before regular classes, and again in the afternoon on every school day (some schools have even two extra afternoon classes) for students who want to take university entrance examinations.

During the short six-week summer vacation eighth and ninth graders and eleventh and twelfth graders meet several days for formal classes to prepare for entrance examinations. More specifically, ninth and twelfth graders preparing for entrance examinations will meet at least a half-day for ten days to study English, Japanese, mathematics, science, and social studies. In fact, the complaint of many young junior high school teachers is that they really enjoy only one week of vacation between school years, one to two weeks during the summer vacation, and one-day-a-month leave during the school year. Most telling, however, is the scramble by many schools, even elementary schools, to substitute for the recent loss of two Saturdays a month by holding week-long compensatory classes during the summer vacation. Because the amount of learning material has not been reduced, teachers and administrators complain that they cannot cover the required material unless compensatory classes are held.

Research shows that American students forget a significant amount of what they have learned over the long, three-month vacation period.[17] For this reason Japanese schools schedule only a six-week summer vacation, and students are generally given homework for all their subjects over their summer vacation. Elementary school students receive a winter booklet and a much thicker summer booklet for recording their homework for all subjects. Secondary high school students receive homework assignments from individual teachers. Students must turn in their homework at the beginning of the new semester in September and take tests covering all subjects at the commencement of school. Examinations serve the dual function of ensuring that students have done their homework and test their knowledge of subject matter. We may conclude safely that by the time Japanese students graduate from high school they have attended school at least one and one-half years more than an American student.[18]

We must add to these calculations the greater actual time on task of Japanese students.[19] Japanese educators keep interruptions that interfere with class time to an absolute minimum. Rohlen's description of the senior high level is outstanding:

Time is thoroughly segmented and defined, with the curriculum serving as the central gear in a complex machine of time-activities. Because time is precious, order is reinforced, and social organization achieves a high level of immutability. . . . The high uniformity greatly simplifies the task of coordination. Teachers easily keep together because they follow a fixed national curriculum. . . . The lack of variation and surprises makes for a monotony that Americans would find oppressive, yet the orderliness of Japanese schooling is a crucial source of their efficiency in preparing for exams. . . .

During class periods students do not . . . sign out of school or engage in individual tasks or do administrative errands. . . . The school day is not complicated by short periods or by classes getting out early or field trips or classes outside on the lawn. . . . As socialization in orderliness, nothing could be more effective.[20]

Ten-year-olds and fourteen-year-olds spend at least 30 percent more in time on task than American students.[21] If we calculate according to a 210-school-day year, Japanese children spend approximately 1,330 hours doing academic work compared to approximately 710 hours for the Americans. The National Association of American School Principals comparative research on American, South Korean, and West German schools made this strong statement:

Research makes clear, however, that student time on task affects achievement; it constitutes one of the few unqualified statements that educators can make about learning. A positive correlation exists between time and learning. The American school year is at the bottom 10 percent of industrialized nations. Perhaps that has some impact on the low international test scores of American students.[22]

The conclusion is not debatable: Japanese use their schools longer, more efficiently, and more effectively than Americans.

In the United States, teachers' associations and unions have fought against any increase beyond a 180-day school year. They deny that a longer school day and school year would raise schools' achievement. Teacher associations and unions should abandon forthwith such a self-serving argument and selfish attitude. By the same foolish logic it could be concluded that conducting a six-hour day and 180-day school year is not really any more significant than a five-hour school day and a 150-day school year.

Think of how much more subject matter and character formation activities could be taught with an extension of the school year by only one more month. Spread out over students' twelve years of schooling, they would receive one more year of actual instruction. In addition, if an eleventh month is added to the school year for students who are not achieving competency for their grade level, this could assist them in achieving a required minimum standard. Special enrichment programs for gifted or ambitious students could also be taught during this eleventh month. Can anyone doubt the potential for a great improvement in academic achievement?

But here again is where we run head-on with an attitude problem. In 1983, a reforming Polk County, North Carolina superintendent extended the school year for a month for a trial two-year period. Although test scores rose, the community strongly opposed the longer school year, elected a new school board, reinstated the old school year, and the superintendent fled to a job in another state. He said, "Educationally, it was a real success, but politically it was a failure." Chester Finn argues for a 300-day school year, six days a week, and from 7 A.M. to 7 P.M. "both as a safe harbor from the hazards of the street and a place where teachers, tutors, and counselors are ready to advance the learning process."[23] Of course, all students would not go to school for that many days or that many hours, but they would attend school at least one more month a year.

Three questions need to be asked in respect to school usage. Are the schools sacred institutions that can only be used during the traditional nine months of the year and only from nine to five or six by traditional students?[24] Are school custodians' rigid labor contracts limiting school usage and regulating wages more important than making schools available to local taxpayers for constructive community activities? Are bussing programs supposed to dictate school scheduling practices, or should they be subservient to society's and students' needs? Educators would be surprised at the good will and the greater support the general public would give them if they showed greater flexibility and imagination in scheduling longer school days, school years, and opening the schools to the general public for community activities. Patricia Graham criticizes the schools for alienating parents from a sharing teacher–student–parent relationship by practices that are "antithetical to family routines."[25] She complains that present scheduling discourages teacher meetings with parents and denies school use as a community center to many volunteer programs and social welfare agencies in the late afternoons and evenings. Conversely, some Japanese schools that have suffered declining enrollments are now using part of the building(s) for housing senior citizens, or have been recently authorized to construct high rise buildings that will be jointly used by senior citizen groups.

Although farmers today constitute less than 10 percent of the population, Americans still operate schools as if students had to return home each day for chores, or as if the summer vacation and fall schedule had to be used to help parents with planting, cultivating, and harvesting crops.[26] Today, most American mothers work full-time and children have much more free time and live in less secure urban conditions. The school day should be lengthened to provide a safer, more secure, and better educational environment. (Of course, teachers should not be expected to work longer hours and additional teachers would be needed to staff such a program.)

Two sisters from the relatively rural area of Ibaraki prefecture are Yukiko, a university graduate, and Akiko, a college sophomore. They provide specific examples to substantiate my view that the Japanese school year can be calculated at least as 210 days. Their experiences are not unusual for students planning to attend college. Both of them in the junior year were expected by their teachers to study during the forty-day summer vacation. For the first two weeks, Yukiko studied Japanese at home 5½ hours a day (her weakest subject) and other subjects for another 2½ hours. Subsequently, she spent another ten-day period at school attending lectures for all her subjects from 8:30 to 3:10 P.M. (with forty minutes off for lunch). Since she was a *bunkei* (literature student), she studied Japanese, world history, biology, English, and math each for ten class periods. She also studied art, physical education, and home economics four times during this ten-day period. Akiko's experience was virtually the same. Even though Japan is very hot and humid in late July and August, air conditioners are not used in the schools at this time. Yukiko's parents, however, could afford cooler study conditions and a more professional cramming school. Hence, as a senior approaching the difficult entrance examinations in February, she spent another ten days in the Nagano Alps cramming with students from other prefectures under the tutelage of teachers from a prestigious Tokyo cramming school.

As ninth and twelfth graders, Yukiko and Akiko, similar to other college-bound students, were not allowed to participate in their favorite after-school club activity, tennis, after the first semester ended. The reason is it interferes with preparations for the senior high school and college entrance examinations. As a ninth grader, Akiko prepared for the next spring's high school entrance examinations by studying with her teachers at least three hours a day for two weeks during the first part of the short summer vacation. Thereafter, she spent the period from 30 July through 21 August studying social studies, Japanese, mathematics, science, and English daily from 8:15 to 12:15.

Because Akiko was anxious to be admitted to the area's best public school, her daily after-school schedule changed markedly during the second and third quarters of the ninth grade. She returned from school at 4 P.M., slept under the warm *futon kotatsu* (an electrically heated, low-level table with a warm blanket covering for retaining the heat) for almost two hours, ate her dinner, and then studied in her room until 1 or 2 A.M. with occasional breaks for snacks and telephone calls. This regimen proved successful. Akiko successfully passed the high school's entrance examination. She then enjoyed her sophomore year more leisurely before pressure built up again in her junior year to study intensively for university examinations.

If Americans changed their attitudes regarding the use of schools for the school day and school year, significant improvements could be made. A computerized, modular system could be created to meet students' different needs and to ensure higher academic performance for all. Schools could offer academic subjects from 9 A.M. to 3 P.M., and arts, crafts, vocational courses, and special interest classes from 3 P.M. to 5 or 6 P.M. In addition, schools could be used as sites for countless community organizations and needs. Huge savings could be applied elsewhere in schools by this step.

Space

Since the mid-1980s some beautiful and slightly more spacious new schools have been built at all levels throughout Japan to take advantage of Japan's greater affluence, as well as Mombusho educational subsidies to encourage more open education. But some rural schools are still utilitarian, plain, unadorned, wooden, or unattractive concrete structures built forty years ago. The size of the physical plant and campus of most Japanese schools cannot compare with American ones. The best secondary school in Japan, Nada (rated so by the dubious distinction of getting almost one of every two students into Japan's premier institution, Tokyo University), possesses school facilities, supplies, and audio–visual materials equal to only those of our poorer American schools. In a nation where land is incredibly expensive, campuses remain small and lawns are almost nonexistent. (These same conditions prevail at many Japanese universities.)[27]

During the Allied Occupation, the Ministry of Education developed uniform buildings and floor plans in detail that reflected a poor country's limited resources. Secondary schools continue to accommodate about 1,200 students and a faculty of forty to fifty in plain, three-story classroom buildings where grade levels are separated at each floor level. The density of student desks in a classroom is at least one-and-a-half times greater than in the United States. The campus usually consists of a small, dirt athletic field, one or two tennis courts, a gymnasium, and a swimming pool. One typical private school, *Meisei Gakuen*, accommodates on one block of land a separate coeducational kindergarten and elementary school, separate girls' and boys' junior high schools, and separate girls' and boys' senior high schools. These students manage to use the athletic field, tennis courts, and the swimming pool efficiently and cooperatively. Although most American schools are not being used by their communities on the weekends, Japanese school facilities and campus are often used for club activities and sports on Saturdays and Sundays and during the spring and summer vacations.

To the delight of many foreign visitors, Japanese elementary schools are often richly decorated with posters, plants, and artwork.[28] Still, with the exception of some of our inner-city and older, large, urban schools, American elementary and secondary schools are superior in lighting, heating, audio–visual aids, classroom facilities, supplementary textbooks, teaching materials, physical education or sports facilities, and computer and music equipment. The campus area is vastly larger. In 1985, only 1,245 of Japan's 46,827 elementary and secondary schools had baseball and softball grounds.[29] It has always astonished me that most Japanese classrooms at the secondary and university levels lack maps, globes, and other audio–visual aids for the classrooms. Most schools, even new ones, lack air conditioning and central heating (although the teachers' room may be air conditioned).[30] Hallways, gymnasiums, and toilets are generally not heated, and few Japanese schools have showers for students to wash themselves after a physical education class or sport club activity. The one exception to the above Spartan depiction is the prevalence of swimming pools at elementary schools (75%).[31] This condition reflects the greater importance to which Japanese schools value physical activity for the young. Consequently, elementary school teacher-candidates must pass a swimming examination to obtain a teaching license.[32]

A peculiar feature of Japanese schools is that older means better. Almost universally, older schools (generally meaning prewar), especially at the secondary level, are ranked at the top in their local areas. This phenomenon reflects the fact that such schools in the prewar period were usually a prestigious technical school, middle school, or higher school. Although renovation of most of these prewar school buildings has occurred, most lack air conditioning and central heating. Individual classrooms are heated by a kerosene space heater. In the United States, newer means better. Furthermore, lack of American students' pride in older buildings invites students' indifference and property damage. Proud Japanese teachers and students in these older schools may envy the newer facilities, but ordinarily never think of transferring to them simply to enjoy superior amenities.

Efficiency

America may have the world's most bloated administrative school bureaucracy. In 1959, 56 percent of school expenditures went for teachers salaries, compared with only 40.4 percent in 1989.[33] In 1950, elementary and secondary classroom teachers comprised 70.3 percent of the instructional staff, but in 1992 they comprised only 53.3 percent. Support staff made up 20.4 percent of school personnel.[34] Much of that difference went toward an increased number of specialists and administrators at the central administrative office and special activities staff. Schools need to bring superior teachers back from administrative jobs into the classrooms and to supervise young teachers. In no other corporate activity is so little attention paid to developing personnel as in American schools. Here is where America needs more effective school-principal leadership, untrammelled by the bureaucratic superintendent's office. A by-product of these reforms would be monies saved for use elsewhere in schools.

Japanese teachers work under much more crowded but efficient conditions that facilitate coordination. The entire teaching staff is accommodated in one room where all teachers are seated by subject matter, grade level, and home room under the leadership of a vice principal. Greater efforts must be made in American schools to improve teacher efficiency. Schools need to break down the concept that once a teacher is hired, his or her classroom is a sacred area. In most American schools teaching is a lonely job because teachers are largely confined to their own classrooms throughout the working day. According to Shimahara and Sakai's observation of one teacher, "This individualist view of (elementary) classroom management required her to develop her own coping strategies, and classroom management remained Ellen's personal struggle for most of the year."[35]

American administrators need to create arrangements for greater supervision of classrooms in the early years of a teacher's career and periodically thereafter, when reports of a teacher's ineffectiveness surface. This procedure will help teachers improve teaching and disciplinary skills. To accomplish those goals schools need to hire competent teachers at the outset, to assign young teachers to a competent, veteran teacher for assistance and supervision for at least one year, and to institute a system of warnings, penalties, suspension, and fines for older teachers who are failing to achieve greater time on task.

Many other Japanese school practices could be adopted selectively to improve efficiency and time on task. At their secondary school level students do not move from classroom to classroom; teachers do. Admittedly, this arrangement is possible because the curriculum is standardized and the number of elective courses is limited. Still, if most American schools would adopt a core curriculum, reduce electives, and make greater scheduling efforts, more classes could meet in this manner. There are many advantages to the Japanese practice of students remaining largely in the same classroom throughout the day. Little time is lost by students moving from class to class. The disorder of American students milling through the hallways, slamming lockers, occasionally fighting, and disrupting classes by tardy arrivals does not occur in the top-ranked 80 percent of Japanese schools. Usually there are no lockers; students keep their books in their desks. And because they own their own textbooks and the texts are much more compact than American ones, they carry them home at the end of the day in knapsacks at the elementary school level and in briefcases at the secondary school level.

Is there also any reason, other than custodians' labor union opposition, why American schools cannot adopt Japanese schools' practices of having students clean their classrooms and hallways? Two advantages would occur: less physical damage to the school and custodial savings that could be plowed back into salaries and learning materials. Japanese students generally write graffiti on walls and in toilets only in pencil because they are the ones who will have to clean them.[36]

The Japanese practice of having students study under relatively Spartan conditions achieves greater student recognition of limited human resources. A deep-seated Japanese attitude is that if you don't suffer, achievement lacks merit and satisfaction.[37] For example, "Japanese folk theories of health hold that developing resistance to the cold and stimulating the skin by contact with the natural elements develops resistance to disease and strength of character."[38] These attitudes can be seen in the practice at many preschools and elementary schools of boys wearing only shorts and a short-sleeved shirt during the winter. My oldest daughter, Marceline, used to grind her teeth when the teacher would ask the children whether a space heater should be lit on a cold winter day. Macho male students would invariably give a negative reply.[39] (One cannot help noticing, however, the large number of pupils with colds.)

American students wear inadequate winter clothing and complain if classrooms are not sufficiently heated. The attitude is one of, "Turn up the thermostat! What do you mean, 'wear a sweater'?" Here is another area where schools could reverse an attitude. On the surface it seems to be a small thing, but by working with parents and students schools could turn thermostats down a couple degrees and bring about cooperation by wearing warmer clothes. Students would obtain a greater awareness of the need to husband precious national resources and save the environment, as well as society's considerable sacrifice for their education. Schools could also save precious monies for financing other areas more central to education.

I do not advocate crowded or frigid classrooms, hallways, and gymnasiums. I also have reservations about the ascetic conditions the Japanese favor at school. But two things need to be stressed. Frugal circumstances create an attitude among students that education is a serious business. Furthermore, Japanese conditions nullify the American views that more money, an outstanding school environment, and low student–teacher ratios are essential to good student and teacher performances.

COMPARATIVE JAPANESE AND U.S. EDUCATIONAL EXPENDITURES

Americans educators have been inclined in the postwar period to believe that the solution to our educational problems is more money. America's educational woes do not lie fundamentally in the amount of money spent. It is the inefficiency, selfishness, prejudice, and sometimes, crookedness, with which it is distributed that blights the American effort. Good schools and good teachers require adequate financing, but most American schools are academically poor and ethically weak, less from money than excessive bureaucracy, indifferent students and parents, and poor attitudes.[40]

In fact, American taxpayers generally have been generous. In Secretary Bennett's last report to President Reagan in April 1988, he wrote that per capita spending for elementary and secondary education had increased nationally between 1981 and 1986 by more than 40 percent and that education had become the largest budget item in forty-eight of the fifty states.[41] The amount of public expenditures for education as a percentage of government expenditures increased from 15.1 percent in 1960 to 18.2 percent in 1989.[42] Among the G-7 countries (Canada, France, former West Germany, Italy, Japan, the United Kingdom, and the United States), only Canada has a higher level of public expenditure as a percentage of GDP for elementary and secondary education than the United States, 3.5 percent compared to 2.3 percent for Japan. The combined annual spending of American local, state, and national government funds for education over the past thirty years as a portion of the GNP has been greater than in Japan; yet, Japan gets a higher performance.[43] America's public expenditures on elementary and secondary education as a percentage of GNP has been greater than Japan's: 5.8 percent and 4.7 percent.[44] In public expenditures per student for elementary and secondary students for 1993, respectively the United States spent $5,942 and $6,541, compared to Japan's expenditures of $3,960 and $4,356; yet, American school results have been poorer.[45] The conservative economist Eric Hanushek wrote emphatically, "Since the mid-sixties, there have been around 200 studies looking at the relationship between the inputs to schools, the resources spent on schools, and the performance of studies. . . . Result 1 is that there is no systematic relationship between expenditures on schools and students' performance. Result 2 is that there is no systematic relationship between the major ingredients of instructional expenditures per student . . . and student performance."[46]

Table 1.1 demonstrates that American public education revenue for elementary and secondary schools and students (in 1994 constant dollars) in three categories has constantly increased from 1930 to 1993, except for the national index of public effort to fund education (revenue per student in relation to per capita personal income).[47]

The Japanese experience should demonstrate that lack of money is not an obstacle to higher standards. Nor do schools have to dismiss large numbers of teachers because of greater emphasis on adopting the core curriculum recommended by *A Nation at Risk* and the James Madison Curriculum. They can return some of the educational specialists to the classrooms and cut down on truly extracurricular frills. The Japanese send slightly more than 20 percent of their students than Americans to high school and graduate 95 percent of them, and they send more males and females to colleges and universities.

Table 1.1
National Index of Public Effort (Public Education Revenues per Student in Relation to per Capita Personal Income)

School year	National Index	Revenue Spent per Student	Revenue as Percentage of GDP	Per Capita Personal Income
1930	10.6	$ 639	2.0	$6,017
1940	14.6	856	2.5	5,871
1950	3.9	1,196	2.1	8,623
1960	16.2	1,823	3.0	11,328
1970	20.0	3,095	4.2	15,443
1976	22.9	3.827	4.5	16,691
1980	21.5	3,970	3.9	18,472
1986	23.1	4,522	3.7	19,553
1990	25.0	5,290	4.0	21,200
1993	25.3	5,379	4.1	21,302

They get a more competent student at the elementary and secondary levels than America does. Money is not the answer to the nation's total educational problem, though continued reliance on local property taxes and unequal state funding among the fifty states perpetuates unequal educational opportunity for hundreds of thousands of children.

DISCIPLINE AND EFFECTIVE
CLASSROOM MANAGEMENT

Poor discipline and ineffective classroom management are major contributors to America's low academic standards and unsatisfactory character formation. Failure to maintain a reasonable standard of discipline results in a poor academic performance for the class as a whole, and in a lack of respect for teachers, school property, and antisocial conduct outside the school. Much of America's poor classroom management results simply from bad housekeeping practices and casual attitudes that limit time on task every hour and day of the school year, such as tardiness, skipping of classes, frequent absenteeism, office messages, public address announcements, poor study habits, students failing to bring appropriate learning materials to class, and being excused from class to leave early or enter late. These administrative inefficiencies and sloppy student habits must be corrected by fostering better student attitudes and practices, improved administrative procedures, and a higher appreciation for achieving maximum classroom time on task.[48]

Three reflections of a lack of discipline are school absenteeism, tardiness, and cutting classes. A comparative survey of school absenteeism showed that American students were absent from school twenty days a year, but Japanese students only three days a year. Nationwide, the absenteeism rate in America's larger urban schools was at least 15 percent daily in 1983.[49] In 1991, the situation had not improved. On a typical day 8 percent of public high school students were absent, with 12 percent in central cities.[50] The Detroit public schools officially reported a 20-percent absence rate, but teachers gave a more accurate figure of almost 30 percent, a common discrepancy.[51] The reasons for this discrepancy are simple: Administrators are inclined to report a high attendance rate to obtain maximum state funding, and students come to school, but attend only some classes and spend the rest of the time in other parts of the building. Accordingly, they are marked absent by classroom teachers.[52] Although 27.1 percent of all public school teachers and 44 percent of central city public high school teachers considered student absenteeism a serious problem in 1993 and 1994, only 4 percent of the general public in 1993 viewed "public lack of interest/truancy" as a major problem.[53] The same survey found that 34.5 percent of teachers of public school secondary students view parental indifference as the third most important problem facing their schools. Student apathy was cited by 38 percent, and "students come unprepared to learn" by 36 percent.[54]

Serious Disciplinary Problems

The erosion of discipline in the American schools between the 1940s and 1970s is illustrated dramatically by the following contrasts. In 1940 the five most frequent school discipline problems were talking, chewing gum, making noise, running in the halls, and getting out of turn in line. Seven of the seventeen most frequent discipline problems in the public high schools in the same year were vandalism, extortion, drug abuse, alcohol abuse, pregnancy, abortion, and venereal disease.[55] In 1982 the five most serious ones were rape, robbery, assault, burglary, and arson! Gerald Grant wrote of Hamilton High School in Media City (fictitious names), a New York upstate school, that a newly hired high school principal found "vandalism high, thefts from school lockers averaged $350 a week, teacher morale was low, drug use was wide-spread . . . absenteeism had increased . . . three students were indicted by a grand jury for substantial drug trafficking . . . sixty . . . [were] identified as heavy users . . . and an average of fifty-five windows [were] broken per year."[56] To deal with a 60-percent increase in crime from the previous year a retired Army general as superintendent of Washington, D.C. schools hired 223 guards to provide greater security and was contemplating a security system of armed guards, cameras, and metal detectors to prevent students attending schools with weapons.[57] National surveys from 1980 to 1996 cited "use of drugs" as one of the three biggest problems, and for twenty-four of the past twenty-six years, "lack of discipline" as the biggest problem facing American schools. In fact, the percentage of teachers at two schools who thought the number of students requiring constant discipline and using drugs and alcohol was "very serious" at their school, was 14 percent and 33 percent, respectively.[58] A 1995 National Center for Health Statistics study based on a survey of 10,645 twelve to twenty-one-year-olds warned that "a substantial number of U.S. youth are engaging in risk taking behaviors that can lead to chronic disease, injury and death" including pervasive tobacco and alcohol use, unprotected sex, unsafe driving, staying out overnight without parental possession, and carrying a weapon.[59] A conclusion was that teenagers lack the self-esteem and negotiation skills to say no.

Though New York City's school discipline problems exaggerate rural and private schools' conditions, they generally reflect conditions in most urban schools. A *New York Times* poll of over 5,000 randomly selected New York City teachers showed that one-third of them had been assaulted. City school officials confiscated 6,920 weapons, including 129 handguns in the 1995–1996 school year.[60] In 1995, approximately 4 to 5 percent of New York State's students were suspended, 40,000 of them from New York City alone.[61] George Westinghouse Senior High School reported 5.1 violent incidents per one-hundred students.[62] In the Boston area three out of every ten students were reported carrying a weapon to school.

Metropolitan violence and discipline problems have spread even to smaller midwestern cities such as Wichita and Omaha and to rural communities. In Antioch, California, a high school student walked into a class and poured gasoline on a fifteen-year-old girl, stabbed her repeatedly, and attempted to set her on fire with a cigarette lighter. In Newark, New Jersey, two teenage girls fighting in a high school cafeteria spawned gang neighborhood clashes that resulted in one girl receiving a punctured lung from a stabbing. Two million violent crimes occur on or near American school campuses every year.[63] According to the National Urban League, violent crimes have doubled during the last decade and are expected to double again in the next one. For African American males aged 5 to 9, 10 to 14, and 14 to 18 years, homicide accounted for 30, 41, and 62 percent of total deaths, respectively.[64] Students are being "acclimatized to violence" similar to combat soldiers.

In February 1993 the National Education Association and American Federation of Teachers requested $100,000,000 to provide safety in the nation's schools because 100,000 to 130,000 students take guns to schools daily. This request seemed to be a typical example of a pressure group's exaggeration, but it is not. In 1993, 13.8 percent of white students and 23.5 percent of black high school seniors reported being threatened with a weapon and 4.3 percent and 6.4 percent respectively reported being injured with a weapon.[65] Twenty-four percent of black high school senior males and 14 percent of white seniors reported being threatened with a weapon in 1993. To cope with a deteriorating situation the Clinton administration asked Congress in the Safe Schools Act of 1993 to authorize a $175 million appropriation for two years. These conditions make a travesty of the sixth national educational goal, namely, "Every school will be free of drugs and violence by the year 2000."

Teacher and Student Views of Discipline

National surveys confirm teacher dissatisfaction with poor discipline. In 1987, 53 percent of elementary school, 42 percent of junior high school, and 34 percent of high school teachers believed that the incidence of disruptive classroom behavior had increased since 1982. An amazing 87 percent of all teachers reported disruptive behavior in their schools, and 24 percent of them reported cases of violence against teachers.[66] Forty-four percent of surveyed public school teachers in 1994 reported that the "level of student misbehavior in this school interferes with my teaching."[67] Teachers listed these obstacles to maintaining order: lack of student interest in learning (38%), school or district restrictions on the use of strict penalties (27%), lack of administrative support (20%), likelihood of complaint from parents (19%), and fear of being sued by parents (18%).[68] These anxieties deeply affect teacher morale and retention. Indeed, 31 percent of public school and 20 percent of private school teachers responded to a 1990–1991 survey by saying that "if I had the chance to exchange my job for another kind of job, I would."[69]

Students' perceptions regarding discipline do not differ greatly. Thirty-three percent of twelfth graders in 1992 reported that disruptions by other students interfered with their learning; 22.7 percent said that fights often occurred between different racial and ethnic groups; and 10.4 percent that they did not feel safe at their school.[70] An astounding 40 percent of eighth grade students thought "disruptions by other students interfere with my learning" and 80 percent of all students thought other students "often disrupt class."[71] One survey showed that 58 percent of students had stayed home from school "at least once because they were bullied," and another by the American Medical Association reported that 33 to 44 percent of male teens said they had been slapped, hit, or punched at school.[72]

A Qualification of My Characterizations of School Discipline

Some may complain that my portrayal of American schools describes all schools as if they are replicas of large urban and inner-city schools. There is a disciplinary difference between inner-city schools and suburban and rural public schools and private schools, but in general it is a difference in degree, not in kind. An analysis of the U.S. Department of Education's annual statistics demonstrates that there is only a difference in degree in many categories. For example, on the topic of personal safety, 7.6 percent of students at Catholic schools and 5.8 percent of those at other private schools "feel unsafe" at their schools. Almost 70 percent of private school students also say that "other students often disrupt class," and 30 percent of them say that "disruption by other students interferes with my learning."[73] Even at small schools of less than 400 students, 46 percent of teachers polled think that disruptive behavior has increased in the last five years (this figure is only 7 percent lower than urban school teachers and 3 percent lower than suburban schools).[74] When teachers were asked in various surveys between 1986 and 1989 to rate selected factors that limited their ability to maintain order, the differences between rural, suburban, and urban schools were relatively minimal (see Table 1.2).

When we look at the incidence of student infractions, disciplinary actions, and perceived changes in amount of classroom disruption in public secondary schools for other categories according to "percentages of schools with occurrences," the gaps are also relatively small, except for drug selling (Table 1.3). An examination of statistics for eighth graders also shows that differences in discipline are only in degree (Table 1.4). To be accurate, however, the gap is one of kind when we include the inner cities in the categories for the percent of teachers who say the discipline problem is "very serious at their school" (Table 1.5). Looked at in another way there is also one other difference. America's best private and public schools understand the bad effects of absenteeism. Their stricter practices achieve benefits. Even when we include Catholic students of the inner cities, only 5.1 percent of them in 1988 missed five or more school days, 8.1 percent were late three or more days, and 4.2 percent cut classes sometimes.[75]

Table 1.2
Factors Limiting Teachers' Ability to Maintain Order (in Percentage of Teachers Agreeing)

	Rural	Suburban	Urban
Lack of student interest in learning	36	36	52
Fear of student reprisal	4	5	11
Likelihood of complaint from parents	18	18	23
School or district restrictions on the use of strict penalties	17	21	34

Source: NCES, *Digest of Education Statistics, 1991* (Washington, D.C.: U.S. Government Printing Office, 1991), 135.

Table 1.3
Incidence of Disruptive Behavior (in Percentage of Occurrence)

	Rural	Suburban	Urban
Students caught selling illegal drugs at school	21	46	51
Theft of personal item reported to school	70	84	89
Suspension for disciplinary reasons	92	98	100
Student caught selling illegal drugs at school (in terms of occurrences per 100 students)	(0.1)	(9.2)	(0.5)
Expulsion (per 100 students)	(0.2)	(0.2)	(0.6)
Teacher's perceptions of changes in disruptive student behavior over 5 years ago			
"somewhat more"	26	26	23
"much more now"	16	18	26

Source: NCES, *Digest of Education Statistics, 1991* (Washington, D.C.: U.S. Government Printing Office, 1991), 135.

The Meaning of These Statistics for American Schools and Students

Two conclusions are that society and schools are failing in character formation and that teachers, especially those at the secondary level and in inner cities, are devoting an inordinate amount of time trying to achieve classroom order at the expense of actual teaching of skills and content. A national tragedy is that precious physical and fiscal resources for achieving the post-1983

Table 1.4
Differences in Disruptive Behavior for Eighth Graders (in Percentage of Occurrence)

	Public	Catholic	Other private
Cut classes	9.4	4.2	5.8
Number of times late over the past 4 weeks for three days or more	11.9	8.1	13.3
Number of days missed over the past 4 weeks for 4 or more days	8.1	5.1	5.1

Source: NCES, *Digest of Education Statistics, 1991* (Washington, D.C.: U.S. Government Printing Office, 1991), 138.

Table 1.5
Number of Students Involved in Aberrant Behavior

	Inner-city	Rural	Suburban	Urban
Number of students requiring constant discipline	27	11*	11	19
Number of students who lack basic skills	38	13.5 *	12	16
Number of teenage pregnancies	28	12.5*	12	9
Number of students using drugs	26	13.5*	14	11
Number of incidents involving violence	10	5 *	3	4
Number of dropouts	30	7.5*	6	11

Source: NCES, *Digest of Education Statistics, 1992* (Washington, D.C.: U.S. Government Printing Office, 1992), 31.

*Indicates an averaging of small town and rural categories polled by Metropolitan Life–Louis Harris and Associates, Inc., May 1989.

national goal of Educational Excellence for All are being used instead to achieve order and safety.[76] A third conclusion is that hundreds of thousands of students' psyche and their academic achievement are being affected adversely. What is it like for students to attend classes where they "do not feel safe," where some students require "constant discipline," and where other students "often interfere with my learning?" It reflects a poorer teaching and learning environment than 80 percent of Japanese teachers' and students' experience.[77]

A fourth conclusion is that American public schools have not been able to raise academic standards because classroom teachers confront discipline problems every day that defeat their objective. In 1980, William K. Cummings could only conjecture that American teachers spent at least twice as much time establishing order in the elementary schools as Japanese teachers.[78] Five recent studies, one by John Goodlad, one of classroom behavior in Sendai, Taipei, and Minneapolis by Stevenson's group, one by Grant, another by Nancy Karweit, and another by the National Education Commission on Time and Learning have concretely substantiated Cummings' suspicions. The Stevenson study showed that American first graders and fifth graders only spent 70 percent and 65 percent of their time on academic activities in academic classes, compared to 85 and 92 percent figures for Chinese children and 79 percent and 87 percent figures for Japanese students.[79] Goodlad's study of thirteen American high schools showed that in good schools 84 percent of class time was spent in real instruction, but in poorer schools a figure of only 68 percent was attained.[80] A 1994 report by the National Education Commission on Time and Learning concluded that students spent about 41 percent of their school day, or 1,460 hours during a four-year high school, on basic academics, while Japanese spent 3,170 hours, French students 3,280 hours, and German students 3,528 hours.[81]

Why America Has Serious Discipline Problems

The breakdown of school discipline is the harvest Americans reap from the larger societal attitudes of self-indulgence, family breakdown, permissiveness, lack of respect for authority, and excessive individualism. The late Albert Shanker, President of the American Federation of Teachers, said, "The amount of disruption in our schools is much larger than it needs to be because it is tolerated. . . . If the schools aren't seen as taking it seriously when a kid comes to school with a gun, you'll soon see other kids coming to school with guns—in self-defense, of course."[82]

From the elementary through the secondary school levels, mischievous, rebellious, and frustrated students do not face enough censure from their peers, teachers, administrators, and parents for disruption of classes, violence, and damage to school property. When my Tsukuba University students read a chapter in Boyer's *High School* profiling a fictitious midwestern school, they thought the schools' permissive manner and low level of academic expectation demonstrated only an upper elementary or junior high school quality.[83] As one result of excessive individualism, students and parents have objected to school uniforms, but student uniforms can bring group ethos and camaraderie as well as remove excessive competition in dress that leads to school violence. Coupled with this are the courts' and students' attitude that the latter's individual rights are more important than the school community. In other words, as in the famous New York City Juan C———, a court case where a boy who was failing all his classes and roaming the hall with what appeared to two school aides to be a pistol, it is a student's right not to be searched for weapons when there is doubt.[84] The entire school's safety is compromised because of one troubled youth. This thinking defies common sense.

The attitude of too many Americans is that high schools exist as a socializing institution—a place "to let off steam." Attitudes are twofold: (1) youth should have its day, because serious study can take place later at college or a trade school, and (2) unruly behavior by the noncollege bound will be tamed by the discipline of employment. Scott Thompson wrote, "One anomaly of the American culture is that a high school senior will cut up in class, but three months later as a college freshman he never interrupts class. Perhaps this phenomenon reflects that students and parents consider high school class work to be less serious than college. Perhaps it reflects a subtle but devastating view of the importance of the high school teacher's work."[85]

Why should society's expectations of behavior be lower for secondary school students than for college freshmen? At the college level, where a serious learning environment exists, professors immediately remove a student interfering with lectures, discussion, or a laboratory class. Similarly, college students themselves will not tolerate student behavior that interferes with learning because it is more important to them, and because they may be paying part or all of their tuition and living expenses to attend college. The same attitudes should prevail in secondary schools.

How important these differing high school and college attitudes are in shaping student behavior is corroborated by what happens in Japanese universities. In them we do not find serious discipline problems, but rather a permissive faculty, administration, and societal attitude toward students' lack of commitment to rigorous academic standards, particularly for nonscience students. The assumption is that student sacrifices made earlier to enter university should be compensated by low academic expectations. These attitudes create an environment congenial to "youth having their day" and a view that a university should be a place where students learn to become social beings. Students exploit this permissive attitude to the fullest extent.

DRUGS: CATASTROPHIC IN THE UNITED STATES, THREATENING IN JAPAN

America's excessive drug consumption may have originally been a symptom of many things wrong with current American society, but now it is both effect and cause of discipline problems. It is a grievous cancer debilitating American society and contributing to unprecedented violence. Although American students' high drug consumption decreased modestly in the late 1980s, it is on the rise again, and at a younger age. According to a survey of the University of Michigan's Institute for Social Research, drug consumption increased for high school seniors from 33.3 percent in 1955 to 37.5 percent in 1996, by sophomores from 21.4 to 23.6 percent for the same years, and by eighth graders up from 11 percent in 1991 to 21 percent in 1995.[86] Although Americans comprise only 5 percent of the world's population, in the 1980s they consumed 50 percent of the world's cocaine. In 1993, the percentage of high school students who reported using drugs or alcohol at any time during the previous year by type of drug was as follows: alcohol (76%), marijuana (26%), LSD (6.8%), and cocaine (3.3%).[87] One report declared that the annual cost of caring for our cocaine-exposed babies is more than $1.4 billion, for alcohol-exposed newborn infants $375 million, and for treatment of tobacco-exposed newborn infants a whopping $1,652 million.

In the past three years I have visited Malaysia, Singapore, and Taiwan. Many airport signs informed foreign travelers that "drug dealing is punishable by death." They have no serious drug problems! America has let the drug problem get so far out of control that it cannot resort to such draconian standards, but America must get deadly serious about protecting its youth and future society by taking severer disciplinary measures in schools and society. A survey of 567 school counselors in Pennsylvania and New York, however, "showed that 38 percent of school counselors said they would not 'break confidentiality' to tell a parent that a child was in possession of drugs, 29 percent did not answer the question, and 29 percent would not inform a parent even when the child was selling drugs."[88]

Japanese have had a relatively limited drug problem until very recently. Schools and society have cooperated with the police to prevent the increase of drugs. Japanese do not have the attitude that it is up to the individual to "do his or her own thing," or because the problem exists, it should be made legal in order to control it better.

THE LINK BETWEEN COURT RULINGS
AND POOR DISCIPLINE

The American Bill of Rights, the continual expansion of democracy, the protection of individuals, and the desirable response of the courts to sociological changes to extend the meaning of democracy and individual rights are vitally important. But they have been applied excessively. Judicial rulings and excessive interpretation of state child-abuse laws of the late 1960s played a contributing role to the decline in school discipline. The broad shift in relations between adults and children of the 1970s raised new questions about what defined children's status. By the Gault (1967) and Winship (1970) decisions the Supreme Court applied to schools the legal protections and rights that had been limited to adult society. The Gault decision declared that juvenile court proceedings must provide all the essentials of "due process and fair treatment." The Winship ruling stated that juvenile courts hearing school cases must meet the standard of proving the guilt of a juvenile "beyond a reasonable doubt." The broad interpretation of new child-abuse laws in the 1960s to protect children from parental physical violence was applied also to teachers to include vague "emotional abuse." Grant wrote that Hamilton High School students quickly realized that "suits could be brought against teachers as well as against parents, and some pupils taunted, 'Don't you touch me or I'll have you arrested.' A social studies teacher said he began to feel, 'Watch out, stay out of the way, don't get yourself in a situation where these people can falsely accuse you.'" This climate limited school officials' authority to promulgate dress and conduct codes. In the 1970s Hamilton teenagers could obtain birth control devices over parental objection and force parents to support them at age sixteen when they chose to live outside their parental home.[89]

The impact of these court decisions has created a climate where teachers feel reluctant to impose discipline. Accusations of student cheating, destruction of school property, sexual harassment, and physical violence at the hands of a student end in protracted court cases that can damage a teacher's reputation, create stress, and cost the school district expensive legal fees to prove the validity of disciplinary actions. As a results, more teachers are inclined to turn their back on discipline infractions. Principals and school boards fearful of bad publicity and litigation costs undermine teacher morale by failing to give support to teachers. According to a U.S. Department of Education survey in 1986 and 1987, 18 percent of all teachers feared being sued for disciplining students, 15 percent of them thought court decisions on student misconduct limited their ability to maintain order, 22 percent of elementary teachers feared being sued for disciplining students, and 18 percent of teachers thought that principal–administrator fear of being sued for disciplining students was a factor limiting teachers "much" or "very much" in maintaining order.[90] (To protect themselves and their schools from legal actions some administrators tape all conferences involving themselves, teachers, and students.)[91]

The need for schools to have discretionary disciplinary powers to maintain school and classroom order has been severely handicapped by social changes and a breakdown in consensus that have had a negative influence on students' acceptance of authority relationships in schools.[92] Public schools have become legalistic, contractual, and bureaucratic, and students more impersonal, legalistic, and manipulative. Fairness and decent respect for others is abandoned in favor of a fatuous, legal casuistry. And when the affluent can obstruct justice, the effect on all students' respect for law, courts, and schools is undermined. Adversarial relations occur between the school administration and teachers' unions. Secondary school teachers are inclined to see themselves only as subject matter specialists rather than persons with a holistic, moral modeling relationship with students. Here again are examples of good attitudes and civil rights taken to extremes.

IMPACT OF PART-TIME WORK ON DISCIPLINE AND STUDY HABITS

The American belief that students who work part time learn the value of money and become more independent, resourceful, mature, and responsible must be challenged. Parents permitting part-time work teach their children to place a high value on material goods and instant gratification and accelerate adult activities too rapidly at the expense of good discipline and academic performance. In the early 1980s a former high school principal at Illinois State University's laboratory school in Normal, Illinois, Dr. Dennis Kelly, shocked his PTA audience with a candid talk in which he said a staff study led the school to serious doubts about the value of students working part time. He noted they were caught up in a vicious cycle of buying and supporting a car, paying exorbitant insurance premiums because of teenagers' high accident rates, wasting a great deal of time enjoying the car with friends and on dates, studying little, and being tardy or absent. Those who worked fifteen to thirty hours a week either were at the bottom of their classes academically or showed a marked decline in academic performance after accepting part-time employment.

Kelly's tentative conclusions are being validated by recent research. In 1993, 30.5 percent of all students in the sixteen to twenty-four age bracket were working part time, 11.4 percent more than 20 hours, and 1.4 percent were employed thirty-five or more hours per week.[93] Paradoxically, students from middle and upper income groups were working more than lower income students. A 1988 survey of North Carolina high school students revealed that one-half of the juniors were working, and 67 percent of them held jobs of twenty hours or more a week. Only 5 percent of these students were helping support their families. Not surprising, the same survey showed that those most likely to drop out of school worked the most hours.[94]

One reason some American students have poor study habits and get into trouble is because they have too much spending money available.[95] For most students who work part time, or who receive too much of an allowance from their parents, surplus money is a means to buy drugs and cars and to neglect school. In Japan, these problems occurring from part-time work are much less serious because private schools do not allow it. Although public schools have become less successful in forbidding it in the past five years, students who work part time are much fewer than in the United States.

Many American parents won't cooperate with the schools because they cannot say no or find themselves caught in a vexing dilemma. They may have a strong belief in the value of part-time work because of their own high school experiences and the existing consensus that part-time work helps children to become independent and resourceful. They have lectured to their children on maturity and responsibility; the implication for many youths is that they should earn their own money. Others, particularly single parents, who can little afford the clothing, school lunches, or expenses required by their children to enjoy student social and sports activities, feel they cannot deny them the additional income gained from part-time work.

Oddly enough, the impact of part-time work on students' academic performance and school attendance can be corroborated by looking at a similar phenomenon in Japanese universities. There, many male and female students cut classes frequently (and do little studying) in order to drive nice cars, buy more clothes, travel within or outside the country, and enjoy leisure activities. Four juniors in my diplomatic history course at Yokohama National University with mediocre academic records and poor attendance had gone skiing that season fifteen times and missed classes frequently on Fridays and Mondays. To afford skiing they were working part time.

BUDGET CUTS AND EARLY SCHOOL DISMISSAL

Two interrelated factors that have caused an increase in student violence is the closing of American schools at approximately 3 P.M. and the curtailment of many extracurricular activities from a generation ago by severe budget cuts. The National Center for Juvenile Justice showed that peak hours for juvenile crime was 3 to 6 P.M.[96]

THE RELATIVELY HIGH LEVEL OF JAPANESE SCHOOL DISCIPLINE

Four generalizations can be made regarding Japanese school discipline. First, school violence and poor school discipline are distinctly minimal compared to American schools despite large classes.[97] Japanese schools and society will not accept a lack of discipline, particularly in the top 80 percent of Japanese secondary schools. When school bullying increased dramatically by Japanese standards between 1980 and 1985 to reach a figure of 150,000 cases in one six-month period alone and was accompanied by related student suicides, a concerned Japanese society engaged in an intensive discussion of the causes and the cures. Bullying still remains a serious problem, but as a result of various steps taken inside and outside the schools, the Ministry of Education and the National Police Agency reported that bullying had decreased by over 40 percent in 1986, to 30,000 cases in 1989, and to approximately 20,000 cases between 1992 and 1994.[98] When bullying soared again to 56,000 cases in the 1994 to 1995 school year and to 60,000 in 1996, the Ministry of Education summoned all prefectural superintendents of education to Tokyo for a discussion of the gravity of the issue, ordered surveys and inspections of school conditions, allocated a larger sum of money for preventive measures, and created a ministry task force headed by the Vice Minister of Education to prevent bullying.[99] Over seventy books were published on the subject in 1996.[100] The problem is inherent in an exclusive and conformist society, but actions are being taken. The National Police Agency also revealed that nationwide there were 2,125 cases of school violence over a one-year period; less than one-half of such violence was directed at teachers. I do not completely trust these statistics because of the the tendency of Japanese society to conceal embarrassing conditions affecting public relations. But when we compare them with the 280,000 cases of physical attacks on students by their peers and one thousand cases of student violence against teachers in a single month in the United States at the junior high level alone, it can be seen that Japanese schools are more successful at achieving a better learning climate and safer environment.[101]

Second, this low level of Japanese school discipline infractions prevails even though approximately 20 percent more Japanese students graduate from high school than in America. If that 20 percent of less-motivated students did not drop out, a more unfavorable comparison with Japanese schools would result, since many could be potential discipline problems.[102] Third, most discipline infractions are not as serious as in the United States. They tend to be smoking, cutting classes, reading comic books or sleeping during classes, dress code violations, and pretending to be sick to avoid a teacher or a particular subject. The one disgusting and inhumane exception is prolonged and severe bullying of an unfortunate classmate. In most cases, however, the bullying is minor. For example, students may avoid or act cold for one or two days toward a student who is too conspicuous by his or her grade performance, accomplishments, or behavior. Fourth, discipline problems are generally less serious in rural areas, where students cannot be anonymous, and in Kyushu, Shikoku, and Hokkaido, where public schools generally have a better reputation.

EXPLANATIONS FOR JAPAN'S BETTER DISCIPLINE

Early Childhood School Practices and Attitudes

I want to stress strongly that the high priority that Japanese early education places on character formation is a significant reason that Japan experiences fewer discipline problems and greater time on task. Peak's research led her to the conclusion that "by investing much time and patience during the beginning of the year in establishing good classroom habits, Japanese teachers ultimately accomplish a great savings in the time and energy required for classroom management. Although these techniques may not work with all American students, they are worthy of serious consideration."[103]

Attendance Practices

Although truancy, absenteeism, and school violence and delinquency are increasing in Japanese schools, they most often occur in Japan's lowest-ranking schools, the poorest private and vocational schools, and junior high schools. From kindergarten days pupils learn that attendance is highly valued as a reflection of character. They are taught to respond vigorously when their name is called for attendance and to walk to the front of the room to receive a small sticker for placement in their calendar attendance book. Even though this exercise is time consuming, Japanese preschool teachers believe it important for the personal attention and encouragement a child receives. At the end of the year prizes are given for good attendance.[104] Because of the continued emphasis on good attendance at elementary school, children become proud of their attendance. A few even attend classes when they do not feel well or when parents might wish them to miss school for family-related reasons.

Japanese Students Are Made Responsible for Classroom Management

Sometimes Japanese are stereotyped as passive and immature, while American society is generalized as creating independent, responsible, mature students.[105] Yet many times American school clubs at all levels of education prosper or fail on the basis of faculty advisors' leadership. In Japan, however, the higher the educational level the more the students run their own clubs. By the time students reach high school, advisor input is often limited to the signing of names to authorize or to accept official responsibility for a club action.[106]

Differences between Japanese and American secondary schools' discipline problems reflect the greater emphasis that Japanese schools place upon creating a teacher–student partnership for classroom management. Discipline is more student-centered. Through the *toban* (class monitor) system, every student in class will have several opportunities throughout the year to be a class monitor. So much significance is attached to the role of the class monitor in Japanese preschools that 55 percent of them responded to a Mombusho survey that it was the most important activity undertaken.[107] In Japanese schools from elementary grades two new *toban* usually are chosen every day. They fulfil such purposes as taking attendance, calling the class to order in the morning and afternoon, bringing lunch from the cafeteria and distributing it, taking ultimate responsibility for a clean classroom, cleaning hallways and assigned parts of the whole school with other classes, acting as liaison with other teachers and the administration, cleaning the blackboard after a lecture, and, in some classrooms, decorating the classroom with flowers. The class monitor practice gives all students an opportunity to gain some recognition. All students learn responsibility and the importance of gaining cooperation and disciplined behavior to achieve classroom and school objectives. Students' repeated experience as *toban* over the years gives them a better idea of the bad consequences of a disorderly classroom.[108]

One Nanzan University student told me that in her junior high school the physical education teacher did not emerge from the teachers' room until he was summoned by that day's *toban*—not a rare practice. When that teacher arrived and found the students not ready for the lesson, he either left the room until the *toban* had achieved order or scolded the monitor rather severely for failure to achieve it. Stevenson and Stigler wrote:

Consider the following scene, which we observed in a Japanese first-grade classroom. The teacher tried to begin the daily mathematics lesson. The children were noisy and continued their loud conversations. The teacher paused, looked at the class, and then called on the child who was the day's classroom leader: "The children are too noisy. Until they are quiet, I cannot teach," she said matter-of-factly. The young leader went into action. She stood, faced the class, and announced, "Please stand up. We are so noisy, teacher can't teach." The children quickly became quiet. The leader turned to the teacher and reported: "We are quiet now." The children bowed to their teacher and sat down, attentive, as the teacher announced, "We will begin."[109]

Students as an entire group are made responsible for rearranging a classroom or physical education facility for different scheduled activities throughout the day. This can be observed after students' lunch hour (taken in their own classrooms), different classroom activities, physical education activity in the gymnasium, or on the playing field. This cooperative group approach is a delightful experience when one hosts a group of university students or adults, because they pitch in to help prepare a meal or to clean up afterward.

Japanese teachers minimize future potential problems by discouraging children from seeing themselves as unique. Instead of the American overemphasis on self-esteem and unique identity, students are encouraged to see how much they have in common with other students. This curtails attention-getting, excessive competition, and antisocial behavior. In American schools the pressures to be different and unique can be fulfilled for many students by sports, scholarship, and extracurricular activities, but when school material cannot be mastered, and the channels to self-identity and self-esteem are thought by students to be closed, the shorter persistence level of American students leads many youth to express themselves in exceptionally unconventional language, dress, hairstyles, and behavior, and to ignore school and community rules.

Another practice that could be adopted in American schools in a modified form is the *han* system, composed of five or six groups comprising four to seven pupils. Teachers use this system for organizing group academic work, school calendar events, and club activities. For example, a *han* may be made responsible for a class newspaper or for coordination with other *han* within and outside the classroom to prepare school activities. The *hancho* (group leaders) and *han* membership are usually appointed for one semester and made responsible for directing the activity of their group. Each group leader holds members of the group responsible for completing the activity. This system achieves classroom management efficiency and produces cooperation and division of responsibility. Disadvantages of the group leader and group system are that it creates too much hierarchy, conformity, and pressure. There may be too much pressure on slower students to keep up academically. American teachers could use the system by shortening the period of group leadership, and by sometimes making communications directly to the entire class rather than only through the leader.[110]

Impact of Entrance Examinations

It cannot be overemphasized that Japanese schools enjoy an enormous advantage over American schools in imposing disipline because of the pervasive impact of entrance examinations. They are a powerful club over secondary school students compelling them to cooperate with teachers. Students know there are no other options for entering high school, university, or employment except absorption of subject-matter and a good conduct record. The pressure of the prescribed curricular material is such that the misbehaving student usually finds himself isolated and censured by his peers. Rebellious and slow students gradually learn to be quiet, to daydream, to doodle, to read a comic book surreptitiously, and in other ways not to interfere with class progress.

NATIONAL DIFFERENCES IN GROWING UP

Although more Japanese high school teachers look the other way, most Japanese teachers feel they are responsible to society for censuring discipline problems inside and outside the schools. Since Japanese junior high school students are not supposed to enter coffee houses, teachers remove students from their premises. Coffee houses remove senior high school students for smoking. McDonald's managers instruct staff to remove students who smoke. Some schools do not allow high school students to attend discos or to frequent *pachinkos* (pinball parlors). Junior high school students are not supposed to frequent restaurants, coffee houses, game parlors, *karaoke*, or game centers. At one famous roadside noodle shop in Yokohama a sign proclaims, "All middle and high school students who do not smoke will receive a 15 percent price reduction." Drug consumption is relatively easy to control because drugs are much more difficult to obtain. PTAs nationwide have instituted three campaigns, two against alcohol and another against the availability of pornography to minors. One is the "must not campaign": minors must not drink alcohol, students must not buy it from vending machines, and adults must not let children drink alcohol.[111] The other is an effort to prevent the sale of beer at Japan's 130,000 vending machines. Both campaigns are relatively ineffective yet, but gains are being made. At the bottom 20 percent of the schools, especially night schools, teachers are not able to control student smoking and inhaling paint thinner or glue, and rebellious youth tend to wear rough, baggy clothes, and dye their hair.

Japanese schools operate from an advantage in that they enjoy a societal consensus that students through high school are children and should be kept innocent and unsophisticated. There is no confusion administratively that they are dealing with anyone other than children. This consensus results in Japanese schools delaying premature adult activities that encourage dress competition, premature and distracting heterosexual social activities, and excessive independence. Some examples are that Japanese students cannot drive automobiles until they are eighteen. There also are no school dances or social activities to encourage premature dating or poor study habits. Generally, students feel a resonsibility for the school's reputation and observe school rules.

Americans visiting Japanese secondary schools and colleges are struck by the childlike activities, naive behavior, and social inexperience of Japanese students. Americans adoration of youth allowed TV entertainment to ridicule delayed maturation as old-fashioned and unsophisticated. Some Americans view singing of school songs as corny, and limiting the use of cosmetics, form-enhancing clothes and shoes, bizarre hair, and clothing styles, as restricting students' individuality and independence. One Nanzan University 1994 senior female, however, commented in a composition, "I went to the U.S.A. at 15. I was really surprised to see junior high school students wearing sexy clothes, makeup, jewelry, long and colorful nails, and various hairstyles. Though I was surprised at the differences between their and my junior high school days, I did not envy them. I wondered why such young girls felt the need to dress in such an adult manner."

The slower maturation process nurtured by the Japanese schools helps parents reduce the tensions that manifest themselves in many American homes. Japanese and Americans possess widely different views on independence. Americans think of themselves as independent entities for whom fulfilment of personal goals is imperative. Individualism and independence are closely associated with self-reliance, personal identity, free will, and maturity.[112] Consequently, these qualities are strongly cultivated in children by parents and schools. On graduating from high school and finding employment, most American noncollege youth fulfill their goal of independence by renting apartments. College students will often live in a dormitory or an apartment at a distant university, often with parental encouragement, rather than attending one within commutable distance. Parents view them as adults and refrain as much as possible from interfering in their personal lives. This emphasis for 20 percent of the student body produces remarkably mature students.[113]

In reality, however, most teenagers are not mature and are only pseudo-sophisticated. They confuse maturity and sophistication with moral neutrality and tolerance with a view that everyone has the right to do their own thing. They become too independent too early in life; hence, parental and school tasks of managing them are made more difficult. A North Carolinian teacher said, "Our children are jaded by the time they reach sixteen by drinking, drugs, sex, and other adult activities. What is there left?"

Japanese students may be more childlike, but they are socialized by the schools and their parents to show more mature responsibility for their minds, bodies, and future employment. Although 60 percent of Japanese teenagers approve of sexual relations with their peers, the pregnancy and abortion rates are among the lowest in the world.[114]

JAPAN'S CENTRALIZED EDUCATION PRODUCES HIGH STANDARDS

Modern Japanese education has benefited greatly from the jurisdictional authority of the Ministry of Education (Mombusho). The Mombusho makes educational policy and decides standards for such things as textbooks, courses of study, and curricula; teachers' qualifications, salaries, internships, and in-service education; school financing, building specifications, class sizes, and university entrance examinations.

One illustration of how more centralized controls at the metropolitan and state level can achieve better-quality education is demonstrated by Japanese administrative practices regarding teacher placement. Most Japanese metropolitan and prefectural areas rotate teachers to prevent the highest ranked schools from always having the best teachers. Rural areas are ensured competent young teachers by prefectures requiring young Japanese elementary and junior high teachers to teach in rural areas for six to eight years and senior high school teachers for approximately ten years before they are eligible for assignment to another school district within the prefecture. This practice explains why the median age of teachers in rural schools is approximately thirty-five, but teachers in prefectural capitals may average approximately forty-five to fifty years of age.[115]

MORE EQUITABLE FISCAL SCHOOL SUPPORT

In contrast to the U.S. federal government's indirect subsidies (16 percent of all government expenditures for education), the Japanese national government provides approximately 43 percent of all public expenditures for education. More specifically, the Ministry of Education provides one-half of the total expenditures for compulsory elementary and junior high school; total costs for publication and distribution of elementary and junior high school textbooks; one-half to two-thirds of the subsidy for construction of school buildings; one-half the cost of teachers' salaries, instructional materials, and equipment; financial assistance for school attendance, lunches, and medical care; equalization subsidies to schools and school children suffering from poverty or discrimination (such as the outcast people known as *burakumin*); and for those located in remote mountain areas or on isolated islands. These subsidies can increase per capita expenditures to twice the amount of those for children in typical schools.[116] As a result, gaps in the financial support of education and academic competence at the prefectural and local levels are minimal compared to the United States. The per capita variation in expenditure for public school children is very small.[117]

CONCLUSION

Nurturing social skills, students' self-esteem, and independence are secondary concerns in Japan. Self-esteem is considered to result from achievement—a more logical conception than many American educators' view that self-esteem precedes achievement. How can one feel good about one's self when there is little achievement to feel good about? What should cause romantic educators and parents to ponder whether self-esteem or achievement comes first? Despite the strong emphasis in the schools on developing self-esteem and self-identity for the past seventy years, there is little evidence that it has borne good fruit; quite the contrary seems to be true in that the National Center for Health report mentioned earlier emphasized that today's youth still lack self-esteem. Is it not in great part because Americans have tried to make children feel good about themselves by praise for mediocre performance and behavior that students themselves know is mediocre?

Japanese schools allow children to enjoy childhood more and place less strain on growing up. They create school pride and a sense of shame about betraying their peers and school by misbehavior. Schools become a child's primary identification. Wherever they go they identify themselves from kindergarten through the university as being from such-and-such a school.

American schools can greatly reduce their discipline problems by changing some attitudes and practices concerning what are allowable. One recommendation is to follow the Japanese practice of not issuing drivers licenses to youth until they are eighteen. At the very least, states should enact legislation that empowers schools to deprive students of their licenses when grades fall; an automobile, scooter, or motorcycle traffic violation occurs; more than twelve hours are spent on part-time work; disciplinary infractions occur at school; or students in any way abuse their privilege to drive. Indiana has taken a positive step by enacting legislation that allows principals the authority to take away a student's license for a driving violation. In short, if parents find it difficult to say no to their children about the purchase or the use of an automobile when their school conduct and academic performance do not warrant the privilege, state legislatures and schools should assist them by enacting appropriate legislation and rules. Americans should make the privilege of driving one that is earned rather than grabbed as an automatic right. These measures would send two very important messages to students: (1) schoolwork has priority and (2) students have the responsibility to school and to society to adopt the cooperative attitudes that are essential to community. A Seattle school superintendent wants to deny licenses to any student who is a member of a gang, to require students to wear a uniform, and to have parents graded on how well they encourage their children.[118]

Students should be made responsible for cleaning their own classrooms, toilets, and hallways, and for maintaining the playing condition of the schoolground areas allotted to their clubs. These practices teach responsibility, respect for public property, cleanliness, the dignity of labor, and they blur class lines. Students are less likely to destroy, deface, or dirty what they are responsible for. Schools and community will be saved the enormous expense of employing custodial personnel and repairing damaged property.

Americans need to create schools where effective teaching and study can take place by improved classroom management and stricter rules regarding part-time work, attendance, and disciplinary infractions. Students must learn from preschool and elementary school pedagogical practices to avoid wasting classroom time, be responsible for classroom behavior, and cooperate with teachers to increase time on task. Schools need help from the mass media and the community to publicize and reward good student behavior.

The excessive emphasis on individualism of American society since the late 1960s and 1970s ignores both the individual and society's long-range interests. A society cannot preserve itself and the rights of others if its individual components fail to assume responsibility for being cooperative, compassionate, and peaceful.

TWO RECOMMENDATIONS TO IMPROVE
AMERICAN SCHOOLS AND SOCIETY

Community Service

One way for American schools to produce more humane and disciplined youths is to develop programs where students perform community service. Youth need to be exposed to those who suffer through no fault of their own and to those who have paid the consequences of undisciplined lives. And in large cities where budget cuts have gutted extracurricular activities and city recreational and cultural programs, children would be off the streets from 3:00 to 6:00 P.M., during the peak hours of juvenile crime.[119] These objectives can be accomplished by secondary schools and communities requiring students to perform community service once or twice a week. Secondary students who spend two to four hours a week at different grade levels working alternatively at such places as hospitals, drug and alcohol clinics, senior citizen homes, AIDS clinics, homes for unwed mothers, abortion clinics, orphanages, fire stations, or some other service- and corrective-oriented institution will understand the value of community service. They will comprehend the results of excessive individualism and instant gratification for those who use drugs, tobacco, alcohol, sex, violence, and other people's possessions indiscriminately. They will learn to have a deeper meaning of human dignity, the importance of individual self-discipline to a community, and the immense satisfaction that comes from doing service for others. Healthy senior citizens should be enlisted to work with youth. They can give leadership, a steadying hand, and confidence to the youth working at the same institutions. Generation gaps will be narrowed and greater mutual respect will occur through working together.

Service-oriented programs should become number-one priorities for schools and communities. Four important by-products will be generated by them: Schools and communities will forge better working relationships; great private, local, state, and national savings for our taxpayers could result from volunteer activity; communities will be more stable and less prone to violence; and youth and senior citizens' personal lives will take on greater meaning from doing service for others.

The Need for an Ethics Course to Improve
Discipline and Community

A major difference between Japanese and American schools is that moral education (*dotoku*) is required by Japan during the nine years of compulsory education. I recommend the adoption of a roughly similar moral course in the United States. Why? I used to be a staunch believer in the American view that ethics and morality should be taught at home and at religious institutions, and at schools only indirectly by a democratic and ethical process that pervades the entire school. Teaching ethics smelled of indoctrination. I now feel compelled to advocate the teaching of an ethics or morals course in our schools for two reasons.

First, the Japanese postwar experience shows that a course emphasizing basic values such as honesty, compassion, duty, diligence, justice, community consciousness, responsibility, respect, sensitivity, cooperation, and value for human dignity can be taught through democratic discussion methods and superior audio–visual aids. Second, I have changed my mind because of the sheer deterioration of universal ethical values and family system, the lessenened impact of organized religions on children's (and adults') behavior, and the disorder, violence, and materialism of contemporary life. The failure of too many homes to teach values demands that schools must play a more active role in teaching universal ethical values.

It was precisely for some of the same reasons that post-1868 Japanese leaders instituted a moral education course in their schools. They argued that (1) unlike in the West, Buddhism and Shintoism did not penetrate Japanese society sufficiently to exert a strong influential role on daily Japanese moral behavior; and (2) public ethical values were not taught adequately in the home. Consequently, prewar moral education courses offered many examples of Western, Chinese, and Japanese heroes who embodied a particular ethical quality or moral value. Unfortunately, Japan's increasing nationalism and imperialism led to moral education becoming indoctrination to serve state ends.

There is no reason, however, why the earlier prewar and postwar Japanese moral education experience cannot be adapted to American cultural values to produce a better society. An ethics course teaching desirable universal values can be developed through a year-long effort in every community and school district to reach consensus on them by fair-minded citizens representing differing ethnic, religious, political, cultural, and social views. Textbooks, films, and supplementary materials designed to provoke thought and real discussion of the ethical and moral issues faced by the human condition can be developed by local, state, and national groups of caring citizens and educators.

What must permeate such courses is a respect for the dignity of one's fellow human beings. American schools must impress upon students that ethical and moral foundations and civil rights are the glue of a society, and without them mankind descends into disorder, divisive prejudices, psychological and physical loneliness, and insecurity.[120] It is in the interest of all Americans to unite and to forge a consensus on attitudes and values that should be taught in the schools and practiced at home and in society. The time to start is now.

NOTES

1. Thomas Rohlen, *Japan's High Schools* (Berkeley and Los Angeles: University of California Press, 1984), 160, 321, 322.

2. U.S. Department of Education, National Center for Education Statistics (U.S. DOE, NCES), *Pursuing Excellence: A Study of U.S. Eighth-Grade Mathematics and Science Teaching, Learning, Curriculum, and Achievement in International Context* (Washington, D.C.: U.S. Government Printing Office, 1996), 19–21.

3. "Mixed report for U.S. Schools' Goals," *Asahi Evening News*, 16 November 1997.

4. Japan, Ministry of Education, Sciences, and Culture (Japan, MESC), *Outline of Education in Japan, 1987* (Tokyo: Government of Japan, 1986), 16; idem, *Education in Japan 1994: A Graphic Presentation*, rev. ed. (Tokyo: Gyosei, 1994), 18–20.

5. Ushiogi Morikazu, "Transition from School to Work: The Japanese Case" in *Educational Policies in Crisis*, ed. William K. Cummings, Edward R. Beauchamp, Shogo Ichikawa, Victor N. Kobayashi, and Morikazu Ushiogi (Westport, Conn.: Praeger, 1986), 28; Japan, Ministry of Education, Sciences, and Culture (Japan, MESC), *Education in Japan 1994*, 18–20, 24. Higher education includes the last two years of five-year technical schools (colleges of technology), junior colleges, universities, special training schools, and miscellaneous schools.

6. "School Children Are Brainier in Math These Days," *Asahi Evening News*, 29 September 1984.

7. Benjamin Duke, *The Japanese School: Lessons for Industrial America* (Westport, Conn.: Praeger, 1986), 60.

8. T. Hirose and T. Hatta, "Reading Disabilities in Modern Japanese Children," *Journal of Research in Reading* 11, no. 2 (1988): 152–160.

9. Harold W. Stevenson and James Stigler, *The Learning Gap: Why Our Schools Are Failing and What We Can Learn from Japanese and Chinese Education* (New York: Summit, 1992), 48.

10. U.S. Department of Education (U.S. DOE), *Japanese Education Today* (Washington, D.C.: U.S. Government Printing Office, 1987), 10; Japan, Ministry of Education, Science, and Culture (Japan, MESC), *Development of Education in Japan, 1981–84*, Report for submission to the 39th session of the International Conference on Education (Tokyo: The Ministry, 1984), 54–60. The morning edition of *Yomiuri Shimbun* alone is read by almost 10 million readers.

11. Recently, in a small convenience store, I counted over two hundred magazines. Of course, some reading materials were only comic books and pornographic and sadistic trash.

12. Jonathan Kozol, *Illiterate America* (New York: Doubleday, 1985), 17.

13. William J. Bennett, *American Education: Making It Work* (Washington, D.C.: U.S. Government Printing Office, 1988), 10.

14. Japan, MESC, *Education in Japan*, 68.

15. U.S. DOE, *Japanese Education Today*, 10.

16. Catherine C. Lewis, *Educating Hearts and Minds* (Cambridge: Cambridge University Press, 1995), 62–63.

17. E. W. Turner, "The Effect of Long Summer Holidays on Children's Literacy," *Educational Research* (June 1972): 182–186.

18. Lynn argues that the Japanese spend three more years in school than British and American students. Richard Lynn, *Educational Achievement in Japan* (Armonk, N.Y.: M. E. Sharpe, 1988), 128, 143.

19. Stevenson and Stigler, *Learning Gap*, 141–143.

20. Rohlen, *Japan's High Schools*, 155–156, 158, 179.

21. Ibid., 53, 144–148; Nancy Karweit, "Time on Task: A Research Review," Report of the U.S. National Commission on Excellence in Education, 1983.

22. Scott D. Thomson, "Report Card USA: How Much Do Americans Value Schooling?" *National Association of Secondary School Principals Bulletin* 73, no. 519 (October 1989): 60.

23. Chester E. Finn, Jr., *We Must Take Charge* (New York: Free Press, 1991), 30, 260.

24. Ibid., 28–30, 67.

25. Patricia Alberg Graham, *S.O.S.: Sustain Our Schools* (New York: Hill and Wang, 1992), 54–56.

26. Two percent of American families still live on farms. Ibid., 53; Finn, *Take Charge*, 29; "Clinton Favors Longer School Year to Compete," *The Japan Times*, 24 May 1997.

27. In the last five years private universities are competing for students by building newer buildings. Even national universities are adding new ones. Rohlen, *Japan's High Schools*, 145–146.

28. Merry White, *The Japanese Educational Challenge* (New York: Free Press, 1987), 67.

29. U.S. DOE, *Japanese Education Today*, 16–25.

30. Lois Peak, *Learning to Go to School in Japan* (Berkeley and Los Angeles: University of California Press, 1991), 46. Peak's experience was that room temperatures were kept at 55 to 60 degrees Fahrenheit.

31. In 1985, 28,707 of 46,821 schools had swimming pools.

32. Duke, *Japanese School*, 182.

33. Stevenson and Stigler, *Learning Gap*, 206.

34. U.S. Department of Education, National Center for Education Statistics (U.S. DOE, NCES), *Digest of Education Statistics 1994* (Washington D.C.: U.S. Government Printing Office, 1994), 89.

35. Nobuo K. Shimahara and Akira Sakai, *Learning to Teach in Two Cultures: Japan and the United States* (New York: Garland, 1985), 109, 163.

36. Nicholas D. Kristof, "Japanese Schools Stand Out, but Not Always for the Best." *The New York Times*, 24 July 1995.

37. Two proverbs epitomize this thinking: "One cannot rise above mediocrity, if one does not suffer" and "Adversity makes a person wise."

38. Peak, *Learning in Japan*, 19.

39. Nagoya University and Nanzan University students, however, believe today's youth would have a negative reaction to these practices.

40. U.S. Department of Education, National Center for Education Statistics (U.S. DOE, NCES), *The Condition of Education 1991*, Vol. 1, *Elementary and Secondary Education* (Washington, D.C.: U.S. Government Printing Office, 1991), 152; Stevenson and Stigler, *Learning Gap*, 205.

41. Bennett, *Making It Work*, 45–46; Finn, *We Must Take Charge*, 38.

42. U.S. DOE, NCES, *Digest 1992*, 419–420. Finn, *We Must Take Charge*, 36.

43. In 1988 Japan spent 16.5 percent of its government expenditures for education while the United States spent 17.2 percent. U.S. DOE, NCES, *Digest 1992*, 419–420; U.S. DOE, NCES, *Condition 1995*, 152–153.

44. U.S. DOE, NCES, *Digest 1994*, 419, 429–430; U.S. DOE, NCES, *Condition 1991*, 90–91.

45. U.S. DOE, NCES, *Digest 1997*, 454.

46. Eric Hanushek, "How Business Can Save Education: A State Agenda for Reform," Heritage Foundation Conference, 24 April 1991, as cited in Charles Sykes, *Dumbing Down Our Kids* (New York: St. Martin's Press, 1945), 23.

47. Ibid., 148.

48. Duke, *Japanese School*, 229–230; Stevenson and Stigler, *Learning Gap*, 170.

49. U.S. DOE, NCES, *Digest 1989*, 133.

50. U.S. DOE, NCES, *Condition 1995*, 130–131.

51. Arthur G. Powell, Eleanor Farrar, and David K. Cohen, *The Shopping Mall High School* (Boston: Houghton Mifflin, 1985), 142; U.S. DOE, NCES, *Digest 1994*, 143.

52. Gerald Grant, *The World of Hamilton High* (Cambridge: Harvard University Press, 1988), 205.

53. U.S. DOE, NCES, *Digest 1994*, 30, 31, 32; U.S. DOE, NCES, *Condition 1995*, 130–131.

54. U.S. DOE, NCES, *Digest 1997,* 31.

55. Philip N. Marcus, "Evidence of Decline in Educational Standards," in William Johnston, ed., *Education on Trial* (San Francisco: Institute for Contemporary Studies, 1985), 20.

56. Grant, *Hamilton High*, 196–199.

57. "Armed Guards to Patrol Washington Schools?" *Asahi Evening News*, 8 December 1996; "Incidents of Bullying on the Rise," *Asahi Evening News*, 18 December 1995.

58. U.S. DOE, NCES, *Digest 1997*, 25, 28–30.

59. Christine Russell, "Clueless about What's Good for Them," *The Japan Times*, 4 October 1995.

60. James Dao, "Court Upholds Suspension of Student Carrying a Gun," *The New York Times*, 2 April 1997.

61. "Suspend the Right to Suspend," *Asahi Evening News*, 9 March 1996.

62. Jacques Steinberg, "School Crime Is Down, Chancellor Says," *The New York Times*, 19 September 1996.

63. Bob Herbert, "A Way to Head Off Teen Violence," *Asahi Evening News*, 7 March 1996.

64. Sean Jensen, "Forum Aims Big Guns at Youth Victims," *Black Issues in Higher Education*, 12 August 1993, 12–13.

65. U.S. DOE, NCES, *Condition 1995*, 134.

66. U.S. DOE, NCES, *Digest 1991*, 28, 135; Bennett, *Making It Work*, 19–20.

67. U.S. DOE, NCES, *Digest 1994*, 33.

68. U.S. DOE, NCES, *Digest 1989*, 135; U.S. DOE, NCES, *Digest 1994*, 32–33.

69. U.S. DOE, NCES, *Digest 1994*, 32–33.

70. U.S. DOE, NCES, *Digest 1997*, 142; U.S. DOE, NCES, *Digest 1992*, 31.

71. U.S. DOE, NCES, *Condition 1990*, vol. 1, 70.

72. "Incidents of Bullying on the Rise in U.S.," *Asahi Evening News*, 18 December 1995.

73. U.S. DOE, NCES, *Condition 1990*, 70.

74. U.S. DOE, NCES, *Digest 1991*, 135, 138; U.S. DOE, NCES, *Digest 1992*, 30, 31.

75. U.S. DOE, NCES, *Digest 1992*, 142.

76. David S. Broder, "Progress in the Fight to Rescue American Schools," *Asahi Evening News*, 20 October 1997.

77. U.S. DOE, NCES, *Condition 1990*, 70.

78. William K. Cummings, *Education and Equality in Japan* (Princeton, N.J.: Princeton University Press, 1980), 111, 153.

79. Stevenson and Stigler, *Learning Gap*, 147.

80. John Goodlad, *A Place Called School: Prospect for the Future* (New York: McGraw-Hill, 1984), 99, 105–106. Nancy Karweit, "Time on Task: A Research Review," Report to the National Commission on Excellence in Education, 1983.

81. Catherine S. Manegold, "41% of School Day Is Spent on Academic Subjects, Study Says," *The New York Times*, 5 May 1994; Neil MacFarquhar, "Newark Schools Struggle to Contain Anarchy," *Asahi Evening News*, 2 October 1995.

82. William Raspberry, "What Went Wrong with Schools? Discipline," *The Herald-Sun*, Durham, N.C., 31 September 1995.

83. Ernest L. Boyer, *High School* (New York: Harper Colophon Books, 1983), 11–15.

84. "Gun Ruling Raises Furor on Searches at Schools," *The New York Times*, 19 September 1996; David Kocieniewski, "Student at Center of Case is Nowhere to Be Found," *The New York Times*, 19 September 1996.

85. Thompson, "Report Card USA," 64.

86. "Adolescent Drug Use Still Rising in U.S.," *Asahi Evening News*, 27 December 1996; "Experts Divided in Teen Drug Fight," *The New York Times*, 30 September 1996.

87. U.S. DOE, NCES, *Condition 1990*, 72–73; U.S. DOE, NCES, *Condition 1995*, 136–137.

88. Grant, *Hamilton High*, 260.

89. Ibid., 50–56, 56–57.

90. U.S. DOE, NCES, *Digest 1989*, 135.

91. Boyer, *High School*, 15.

92. Christoper Hurn, "Changes in Authority Relationships in Schools," *Research in Sociology of Education and Socialization* (Greenwich, Conn.: JAI, 1985), 5: 40–42.

93. U.S. DOE, NCES, *Condition 1995*, 384; Thompson, "Report Card USA," 56–57.

94. Noah Lewin-Epstein, "Youth Employment during High School," as cited in Gerald Grant, *The World of Hamilton High* (Cambridge: Harvard University Press, 1988), 206.

95. Chicago National Opinion Research Center, 1981, 8, as cited in Gerald Grant, *The World of Hamilton High* (Cambridge: Harvard University Press, 1988), 206; Thomson, "Report Card USA," 63.

96. Herbert, "A Way to Head Off."

97. Mamoru Tsukada, "A Factual Overview of Japanese and American Education," in *Educational Policies in Crisis*, ed. William K. Cummings, Edward R. Beauchamp, Shogo Ichikawa, Victor N. Kobayashi, and Morikazu Ushiogi (Westport, Conn.: Praeger, 1986), 108.

98. "Lessons from a Schoolboy's Suicide," *The Japan Times*, 31 March 1991.

99. "Lost Innocence," *Asahi Evening News*, 6 March 1996; "Bullying Cases Top 60,000," *Asahi Evening News*, 25 December 1996.

100. Kunihiro Yamada, "Critical New Books on School Bullying Epidemic," *Asahi Evening News*, 8 December 1996.

101. "Preparing to Wield the Rod," *Time*, 23 January 1984, 41.

102. Duke, *Japanese School*, 87.

103. Peak, *Learning in Japan*, 191.

104. Ibid., 95–96.

105. Lewis, *Educating Hearts and Minds*, 126–128.

106. But Rohlen thought that the success of Japanese high school clubs depended on an active faculty sponsor. Rohlen, *Japan's High Schools*, 189–193.

107. Peak, *Learning in Japan*, 76.

108. Lewis, *Educating Hearts and Minds*, 106–109.

109. Stevenson and Stigler, *Learning Gap*, 171.

110. For other limitations, see Lewis, *Educating Hearts and Minds*, 96–98, 186.

111. "Residents Begin War against Smut," *Asahi Evening News*, 21 May 1996; "Parents Take Aim at Alcohol Vending Machines," *Asahi Evening News*, 19 July 1994.

112. Tsuneyoshi Ryoko, *Ningen keisei no Nichi-Bei hikaku* (A comparison of Japanese and American character formation) (Tokyo: Chuo Koron, 1992), 20–32.

113. Benjamin Duke, *Education and Leadership for the Twenty-First Century: Japan, Britain, and America* (Westport, Conn.: Praeger, 1992), 15.

114. Ibid., 186. Abortions are not rare as a means of birth control. Also, 59 percent of Japanese males and 14.8 percent of all females in Japan smoke. Lily Matsubara, "Japan Is Still a Smoker's Paradise," *Asahi Evening News*, 11 May 1994; "Smoking Issue Clouded Over," *The Japan Times*, 23 July 1992.

115. The American confidence that a decentralized educational system is superior can be seen in George C. Bereday and Shigeo Masui, *American Education through Japanese Eyes* (Honolulu: University Press of Hawaii, 1973).

116. Estelle James and Gail Benjamin, *Public Policy and Private Education in Japan* (London: Macmillan, 1988), 168–174; Shogo Ichikawa, "Financing Japanese Education," in Edward R. Beauchamp, ed., *Windows on Japanese Education* (Westport, Conn.: Greenwood Press, 1991), 82–84; Gail R. Benjamin and Estelle James, "Public and Private Schools and Educational Opportunity in Japan," in *Japanese Schooling*, ed. James J. Shields, Jr. (University Park: Pennsylvania State University Press, 1989), 157.

117. Cummings, *Educational Policies in Crisis*, 124, 126–127; William K. Cummings, "Japan's Science and Engineering Pipeline," in Edward R. Beauchamp, ed., *Windows on Japanese Education* (Westport, Conn.: Greenwood Press, 1991), 180. Ichikawa shows that the coefficient of variation of unit cost per public primary and public secondary schools across Japan's forty-seven prefectures is only from 0.12 to 0.18, and per class is even lower. Ichikawa, "Financing Japanese Education," in *Educational Policies in Crisis*, ed. William K. Cummings, Edward R. Beauchamp, Shogo Ichikawa, Victor N. Kobayashi, and Morikazu Ushiogi (Westport, Conn.: Praeger, 1986), 87.

118. Timothy Egan, "Boot Camp for Seattle Schools," *International Herald Tribune*, 2 November 1995; William Damon, *Greater Expectations: Overcoming the Culture of Indulgence in Our Schools* (New York: Free Press, 1995), ch. 9.

119. Herbert, "A Way to Head Off."

120. Damon, *Greater Expectations*, ch. 10.

CHAPTER 2

Factors Shaping Current Japanese Education

By the early 1980s some Americans envied high Japanese educational standards and economic performance. They failed, however, to understand that they came from three positive attitudes: (1) higher societal expectations and greater societal support of schools; (2) stronger emphasis on character formation; and (3) an understanding that cultivating good attitudes is a prerequisite for a vigorous economy and an orderly society. Traditionally in Japan character formation has received priority over scholarship. Most serious Western scholars of Japanese society understand that this emphasis is related to Japan's achievements in other fields besides education.[1] Japan's priorities have been shaped by its historical legacy.

CONFUCIANISM

Confucianism was introduced to Japan by the beginning of the seventh century but only became pervasive and influential in a modified form during the long Tokugawa Shogunate (1600–1868). Chinese Confucianism taught that education which did not produce good character was worthless and that men became virtuous officials or scholars by intensive study, disciplined repetition of proper forms, and observance of Confucian values. Virtuous human beings in turn were important for the purposes of loyally and fearlessly advising the emperor and for acting as social models of the Way (i.e., correct living). Accordingly, the hero of Confucian society was the omnicompetent scholar, not the athlete or specialist. In Confucian circular thinking knowledge created good character, good character led to good study habits, and good study habits produced good academic achievement.[2] This thinking translates in current Japanese beliefs to the idea that individuals are a neutral, malleable element that can be made good or bad depending on their environment, and generalists are more important than specialists. Today's graduates from the most outstanding Japanese universities and their professors are to conduct themselves as models for current Japanese students.

Confucianism emphasized that the "good society" was orderly and harmonious. It could be achieved by (1) maintaining an agricultural society; (2) observing a hierarchical class structure of scholar–gentry, farmers, artisans, merchants, warriors, and "mean" people (outcasts); (3) fulfilling scrupulously role duties within the famous five social relationships (all of which were hierarchical and three familial in nature: sovereign to subject, husband to wife, father to son, elder brother to younger brother, and friend to friend); and (4) observing a litany of Confucian virtues such as sincerity, loyalty, effort, courtesy, respect for authority, parents, and elders, benevolence, cooperation, obedience, selflessness, duty, harmony, and propriety. To create hard workers and loyal and obedient subjects to the emperor and state, the post-1868 Meiji leaders deliberately revived and promoted Confucian values in the schools as state ideology. Current Japan is still characterized by a hierarchical (vertical) society, male dominance, and nostalgia for rural, agrarian life. To its credit in all of those modern East and Southeast Asian countries where Confucianism held sway, a more orderly social life exists than in urbanized, industrialized Western societies.

BUSHIDO AND THE SPREAD OF LITERACY

During Japan's long feudal period (1180–1868) the samurai class constituted approximately 5 percent of the population. Though lowly warriors in the Confucian hierarchy, the samurai co-opted the teachings of Confucianism and arrogated to themselves the role of moral leadership of the masses. They supplemented Confucianism with the code of the warrior: Bushido. That meant stressing Spartan qualities such as a strong will, bravery, honor, endurance of pain, and duty and loyalty—not to family first, as in China, but rather to one's feudal lord. Paralleling Bushido thought and behavior, secular, commercial, and hedonistic values, alien to Confucianism, flourished in urban areas without government patronage from approximately 1670 to 1868.

By 1700 every one of Japan's approximately 270 fiefdoms (*han*) possessed schools for teaching Chinese classics and moral education to the samurai class.[3] The samurai model of learning and the greater commercialization and secularization of society between 1670–1868 gave rise to private academies and *terakoya* (temple schools) open to all who could afford them, primarily, merchants, artisans, and rich farmers. The former taught "various nonorthodox branches of Confucianism, nativist studies (*kokugaku*), and areas of practical value" related to military medical, and engineering needs.[4] In the latter, education was a mixture of the practical and moral. These conditions stimulated publishing and literacy. By 1868, an amazing 40 percent (some say 50%) of males and 17 percent of females could read and write, a level that compared favorably with the most advanced Western nations.[5]

The Meiji leaders deliberately used the schools to indoctrinate students in those commercial and samurai virtues considered important for modern Japan's military needs. In prewar Japan these virtues endowed the Japanese military with prestige—and a loyalty, courage, and stoicism that sometimes approached fanaticism.

BUDDHISM

Buddhism provided a third legacy for modern Japanese education. One Buddhist sect, Zen, particularly appealed to the samurai class. Zen taught that one could master nothing until one had mastered one's self. Mastery of self could only be achieved by relentless concentration, self-denial, strong will, self-discipline, intuition, and persevering repetition of a difficult task until it had been perfected through effort. Another Buddhist sect proved to be Japan's rough equivalent of Protestant Calvinism. By emphasizing service, hard work, and saving, it fostered values favorable to capitalism.[6] The general Buddhist and Shinto emphasis upon cleanliness as a means of purifying the mind and instilling discipline continues today by the practice of students cleaning their own schools. The Japanese leadership also co-opted these values to shape post-1868 education and students' character.

PREWAR JAPANESE EDUCATION

Nationalism

Post-1868 Meiji education was strongly influenced by leaders' consensus in the early Meiji period (1868–1912) that long-range national needs took precedence over individual needs, and that Japan's priorities should be the preservation of Japanese independence, modernization, and catching up with the West. Mori Arinori, Minister of Education from 1885 to 1889, told students in 1885 that "our country must move from its third-class position to being second-class, and from being second-class to being first-class; and ultimately to the leading position among all the countries of the world. The best way to do that is [by laying] the foundations of education." Two weeks before his death, Mori repeated a frequent refrain, "In the administration of schools, it must be kept in mind that what is to be done is not for the sake of the pupils but for the sake of the country."[7]

It was an uphill struggle to educate most children in the first three decades of the Meiji period.[8] Japanese parents tried to avoid public education. Since the Ministry of Education's support of elementary school education did not exceed 10 percent of local school income and tuition rates were not abolished until 1900, farming communities considered tuition and military conscription as blood taxes.[9] The Meiji leaders succeeded in achieving only a 70-percent compulsory elementary school attendance rate to the fourth grade in 1900 and to the sixth grade only in 1907.[10] This was accomplished by a generous allocation of fiscal resources, sacrifice, and exhorting the populace that schooling was important for them and the national interest.

Although Meiji leaders were united on national goals, they were divided over ideology and methods to shape and to achieve that goal. Accordingly, education became a battleground among Confucian, Western, and State Shinto advocates. Westernizers wanted an educational system suffused with Western ethics and studies: emphasis on the individual, human dignity, Pestalozzian ethics, and French centralization practices. Already by 1880, however, Confucianists had succeeded in making *Shushin* (moral education based primarily on traditional Japanese values) the most important course in the elementary school curriculum.[11] By the time of the famous Imperial Rescript on Education of 1890 (IRE), traditional Confucian, Buddhist, and Bushido ethics, and nationalism won the struggle for the shaping of Japanese minds and character by a highly centralized education system. The IRE intensified traditional values and nationalistic education by stressing subjects' obligations (*on*) to the emperor and the enhancement of the Imperial Way. It enjoined students during peacetime to serve the country diligently in their future vocations and in wartime by literally "throwing away their bodies." "Life," pupils were taught, "is as light as a feather, but duty is as heavy as a mountain."[12]

After the Russo–Japanese War of 1904–1905, Japan became a committed imperialistic power, and nationalistic and militaristic thought gradually distorted Japanese education. By 1910 *Shushin* textbooks taught an ideologically crafted nationalism and State Shintoism stressed that subjects were to be as filial and loyal to the emperor as they were to parents and ancestral will. Gradually education at the elementary school level changed from a healthy emphasis upon character formation to an ideological instrument for indoctrination. By the 1920s moral education and history textbooks justified Japan's growing imperialistic goals.[13]

Utilitarianism

One document that characterized the effort of early Meiji leaders to catch up with the West by introducing as many Western institutions and thoughts as possible was the famous preamble to the Education Code of 1872. It stated

It is only by building up his character, developing his mind, and cultivating his talents that a man may make his way up in the world, employ his wealth wisely, make his business prosper, and thus attain the goal of life. . . . Learning is the key to success in life, and no man can afford to neglect it . . . there shall, in the future, be no community with an illiterate family, nor a family with an illiterate person.[14]

By four education decrees of 1885, Minister Mori designed a multitrack system to fit Japan's needs. Elementary schools would produce obedient, loyal, conforming, and reasonably literate subjects. Normal schools would train Spartan, nationalistic, and orthodox teachers.[15] *Semmon gakko* (technical schools) would produce the necessary technicians to serve agricultural, fishing, technical, and commercial needs. Male graduates of the academic track selected meritocratically would staff the government bureaucracy, the upper levels of business, and the military. Education would harness and rein the energies and ambitions of individual's search for wealth and fame to societal and national goals of order, wealth, and power.

Most Japanese value education for practical benefits and social status. Private individuals want employment commensurate with their abilities and effort. Industrialists want loyal, competent, diligent workers; the government wants the best graduates to staff the bureaucracy and to fuel Japan's goal of being wealthy; and Japanese mothers want their sons on the fast track in either the bureaucracy or industry.

Elitism

Prewar education was definitely elitist. Approximately 80 percent of prewar Japanese ended their education after six years of compulsory education. Only 5 percent of elementary school graduates made their way into the normal schools, *semmon gakko*, and academic-track schools. Not quite 1 percent of prewar elementary school graduates graduated from a college or university. Elitism still underlines the prestige of Japan's best high schools and universities. Competent but domineering elite bureaucrats are protected from serious supervision.

Sexism

Prewar education was sexist. In prewar Japan only one in ten girls advanced beyond elementary school education and only one in ten graduates of an upper school attended post-secondary education. Women were considered morally and intellectually inferior to men. Since women could not vote and would not pursue a professional career, women in secondary and higher education were considered unnecessary. From the fourth grade, boys and girls either received schooling in separate classrooms, or, where that was impractical, used separate textbooks.[16]

Gradually, people like Yukichi Fukuzawa maintained that post-elementary education for women was desirable because they had to be "good wives and wise mothers" (*ryosai kenbo*).[17] By 1875 girls graduating from higher elementary school (eighth grade) could attend normal schools, and in 1889 higher women's schools were opened to graduates of elementary school. Higher women's schools corresponded roughly to prewar men's middle schools, but unlike them did not lead to a three-year higher school followed by university studies. The vacuum at the secondary level was filled by private, primarily mission, schools. Wealthy parents, often Christian, could only send their daughters to universities abroad or to a few private colleges within Japan because "a common argument was that academic study would make a young woman . . . conceited."[18] Overcoming this mind-set was one of the most difficult tasks the Civil Information and Education Section (CI&E) confronted during the Occupation period.[19]

These prewar influences on Japan's educational system produced high academic standards and orderly, loyal subjects. They continue to influence current Japanese education. While Jefferson thought the salvation of the state lied in the active vigilance of its citizens, Japanese leaders have wanted docile, diligent subjects who cooperate with the leaders' goals. In today's schools, students still hear Confucian, Bushido, and Buddhist virtues dressed in modern language. When I was a visiting professor at Meisei University, I thought its motto, "Health, Sincerity, and Effort," was banal for an institution of higher education. "Where is there any mention of scholarship?" I said to Reiko Yamamoto, a colleague. She countered, "It is taken for granted that universities will teach scholarship, but society also wants them to cultivate these three essential qualities among students."

TRADITIONAL ATTITUDES THAT STILL SHAPE MODERN JAPANESE EDUCATION

Centralization and Vertical Thinking

After World War II, the Allied Occupation's efforts to decentralize education permanently collided directly with strong traditional Japanese attitudes. One attitude is the "catch up" syndrome, which results in the belief that centralized education is more effective. For almost 150 years Japanese leaders have struggled to raise the standard of living and culture of the people to catch up with the West. That quest has meant continued control by the state of almost every sector of Japanese life and sacrifices by the Japanese public. Japanese attitudes centering around trust, order, and safety provide a second explanation for Japan's centralization. They fear men acting without detailed guidelines will exceed orders and make costly and embarrassing mistakes.[20] Long meetings, elaborate planning, painstakingly cautious experimentation, and detailed rules are believed to limit independent, capricious, and mistaken actions—good practices that carried to an extreme severely limit schools' innovation and Japan's capacities to deal with emergencies such as the Kobe earthquake of 1994 and the oil spill crisis of 1997. After three years of study (1984–1987) the blue ribbon National Council on Educational Reform (NCER) concluded that local educational officials and educators are "negative to reforms with the excuse that education needs stability and continuity."[21]

A third Japanese attitude is that all wisdom comes from the top. Underneath the modern Japanese state lies a blend of over two centuries of Tokugawa

Shogunate (1600–1868) regimented feudalism and post-1868 German and Meiji statist theory and practice, posited on the premise that the individual and society are to be controlled to achieve order. The bureaucrats' paternalistic attitude continues to be that they know what is best for the people. For them active participation of political parties is too partisan; citizens' input is meddling; teachers should serve national needs; and students should adapt themselves to group goals and eschew rights in favor of order and harmony.

Japanese centralization reflects a fourth attitude stemming from the preceding one. Japanese have a historic habit of looking upward for answers and orders. Traditionally, they have been weak and passive before authority, rank, hereditary, and educational pedigree. Prewar Japanese accorded the bureaucrats, graduates of Japan's best schools, great respect and obedience because they were viewed both as experts and emperor's servants. Currently, local and prefectural officers boards of education, administrators, and teachers still look to the center for advice and permission to act. On any working day they can be seen docilely waiting in the corridors of the Ministry of Education. The NCER concluded that the attitude that education is a task of the national government is too "deeply rooted in the minds of educators and educational administrators;" hence they "seek uniform judgement or directives from above."[22]

And finally a fifth attitude shaping Japanese education is a minimum emphasis upon individualism and independence. Adherence to one's principles and insistence on personal autonomy are characteristically considered to be signs of a stubborn, uncooperative, righteous, and excessively aggressive person. Indeed, "individualism" was initially translated in nineteenth-century China and Japan as selfishness or egoism. In the early Meiji period, however, Fukuzawa Yukichi stressed the importance of individualism, independence, and self-assertion to become modern and civilized. But these values did not take root because they are alien and viewed as causes for America's social ills.

Japanese and Americans who criticize Japanese schools for failing to develop individuals with an independent spirit are going against a strong Japanese value. Westerners relate to a supreme God, ideology, or some ultimate principle as an absolute standard, but Japanese identity is found within the group and learning through imitating a senior, teacher, or master.[23] Society and experience are god, that is to say, its standards, rather than individual norms, commandments or abstract principles restrict individuals' behavior. Moral and ethical standards are relative to time, place, and situation; however, individuals are not free to do as they please. Society inhibits action and restricts choice. Japanese schools reinforce the value that group judgment is the ultimate standard, and that learning will occur best in shared group activity or by imitation of a superior.[24] Mothers' indulgent and self-sacrificing practices make children dependent on them for everything—what child psychologist, Hiroshi Azuma, referred to as "maternalistic protection and indulgence on the one hand and pressure to conform to the group on the other."[25] Children, particularly males, learn that in return for benefits gained at home, their mothers expect them to conform to public and school practices, to avoid making mistakes, and to narrow their interests and activities to enter the best possible high schools and universities.[26]

SHAPING POSITIVE ATTITUDES FOR EFFECTIVE SCHOOLING IN CURRENT JAPAN

Education has been a permanent, central concern of Japanese society since the beginning of the modern period. Prewar Japanese governments allocated a greater percentage of national income to public educational expenditure than many Western countries. Postwar support has been good. In 1992, Japan's public expenditures for education as a percent of GDP for elementary and secondary schools was 2.3 percent, or $2,707 per student compared to 3.5 percent and $4,909 in the United States. When this is added to the large amount of money that Japanese spend on cram schools, private tutors, traditional arts and activities, and adult education, the Japanese expenditure on education may be the highest in the world.[27]

Anyone who has lived in Japan becomes aware of the great interest (bordering on obsession) that Japanese have in education. Unlike the situation in the United States, where interest in education waxes and wanes periodically, it is the central focus of school children and mothers' daily lives. It is discussed extensively by political, business, and other opinion leaders.[28] For males, educational concerns are even manifest in mate choice. William Cummings noted that when Japanese men were surveyed for the qualities they preferred in a spouse, they indicated a clear preference for a woman devoted to children's education, a point verified by the research of Donald Spence, an educator at East Carolina University.[29] Education occupies far more time and space in the Japanese media than in the United States. Nihon Hoso Kaisha (NHK) (radio station) and the University of the Air (television station) daily broadcast nationwide programs devoted solely to education. One NHK television station broadcasts many programs of an educational nature.[30] Many more education journals, magazines, and newspapers are published than in the United States.

The Japanese attitude toward education can be demonstrated by looking at post-formal education. Although American society fosters a more desirable climate for nontraditional students to return to a university for undergraduate or graduate education, Japanese schools and society nurture an attitude more favorable to post-formal education. It is carried on by millions of Japanese to improve cooking, learn a craft, study conversational English, improve the efficiency of the manufacturing, marketing, and delivery of a product, study an assortment of national and international subjects, and, particularly, to train high school and university graduates in medium and large industries. Literally thousands of study groups link businessmen, journalists, politicians, scholars, and members of the legal and medical profession. One of the three largest nationwide business associations, Keizai Doyukai, spent a year researching what type of person and educational system should be forged for the twenty-first century. The Japanese attitudes are that personal responsibility and the need to conform to what others are doing requires continued learning to be a good housewife, company employee, scholar, or labor union member. This favorable attitude toward learning is generated by a recognition of Japan's imperative need to be diligent in an economically competitive international arena.

DEVELOPING GROUP CONSCIOUSNESS, ORDER, AND RESPONSIBILITY FOR DEVELOPING STUDENTS' CHARACTER AND CLASSROOM MANAGEMENT

Unlike in America, there is a greater Japanese consensus on methodology and goals. Japanese educators believe that effective classroom management can only be achieved by molding attitudes and behavior appropriate to shaping individuals into orderly members of a group, what Japanese call whole-person education (*zenjin kyoiku*). That means not only transmitting knowledge, but also having classroom teachers be responsible for guiding, counseling, and disciplining students.[31] Early Japanese education emphasizes development of character more than intellectual development. Paradoxically, however, this whole-child approach produces a higher academic performance than the narrower American one emphasizing cognitive learning, yet teachers themselves do not seem to grasp this point. One survey demonstrated that 60 percent of American teachers believe that "building basic literary skills" and "encouraging academic excellence" were schools' most important goals.[32] Only 13.2 percent believed that "promoting good work habits" and self-discipline were the most important goals for education, and a mere 1.6 percent thought "promoting human relations" was. Conversely, none of the nineteen Japanese first-grade teachers Catherine C. Lewis interviewed mentioned academic skills as most important for children to learn during the first month of first grade.[33] Among eight goals of education, Japanese elementary school teachers ranked students "personal growth, fulfillment, and self-understanding" and "human relations skills" first and second, but academic skills only seventh.[34]

Parents expect schools to teach the values and attitudes necessary to learn group life and public behavior. Schools assume that both group life and academic objectives can be best achieved by learning through shared group activities. The eight words most frequently spoken to Japanese students from kindergarten through university are cooperation, perseverance, responsibility, effort, sincerity, self-restraint in dealing with others, self-denial or self-discipline, and *sunao* (amenable or docile).[35] Children (and adults) who are said to be *sunao* are praised not only because they are trainable but also because their cooperation will benefit the student and entire class. This attitude makes children and adults easier to teach than Americans because they are willingly disposed to be taught. It is as if they are an open vessel waiting to be filled.

Two concrete preschool examples demonstrate the current emphasis on adjusting pupils to group life. At the kindergarten level, the prevailing attitude is that it is better for children to be taught in large groups of thirty rather than the American ratio of ten or fifteen. In large classes children are believed to be better able to relate to many different kinds of children and to study in an atmosphere that reflects the complexity of the outer world.[36] Preschool teachers think American preschools' emphasis on small classes encourages too much independence and individuality, and cultivation of self-esteem and individual identity at the expense of group cooperation.[37] The other preschool practice is deliberately to limit the number of toys available for play to encourage children to learn to share and to help children develop their social skills in groups. They want them to solve academic problems and quarrels among themselves as much as possible. One teacher said, "I understand how this kind of small [American] class size can help young children become very self-reliant and independent. But I can't help feeling that there is something kind of sad or lonely about a class that size. Don't American teachers worry that children may become too independent?" Americans assume that groups are unspontaneous, repressive, and restrictive of human feeling, but Japanese teachers emphasize that "groupism" brings about camaraderie and unity, a point understood by American coaches and extracurricular advisors.[38]

Preschools take their role of character formation seriously. In fact, 71 percent of Mombusho-surveyed preschools chose "basic habits of daily life" and a healthy body as their most important instructional objectives. Basic habits refers not only to toilet training or eating habits, but also to learning "that their own desires and goals are secondary to those of the group."[39] When five hundred parents were asked what were the three most important things to be learned in preschool, over 50 percent of American mothers answered, "To give children a good start academically"; paradoxically, only 2 percent of Japanese mothers answered in that manner. Conversely, where only 39 percent of American mothers chose sympathy, empathy, and concern for others, 80 percent of Japanese parents chose that option. Other preschool objectives include "being responsible for doing one's own things for oneself," "kindness," "wholesome sentiments," and "social life." Tobin, Wu, and Davidson learned that preschool teachers valued empathy, gentleness, harmony, social consciousness, kindness, cooperation, amenability, cheerfulness, liveliness, perseverance, patience, and generosity. In striking contrast, no American teachers listed harmony among the qualities they wanted most to develop. Rather honesty, self-confidence, and independence were most valued.[40] Significantly, only a minority of Japanese teachers and administrators, often progressive, Christian, or Western-trained, value independence, individuality, and creativity.[41]

Elementary and secondary level schools work diligently at building a sense of community and solidarity through the use of posted goals and participation in many extracurricular activities where all children are included. At the end of each school day (and once a week for a slightly longer period) in most elementary schools, children spend ten minutes or more in "self-reflection, a time when they discuss behavior which has advanced or prevented the accomplishment of classroom and school goals."[42] To achieve harmony children learn to share, play, settle disputes, avoid blaming others, and assume responsibility for themselves and classroom. They also develop a sense of loyalty and responsibility to the group for academic performance and school rules and are taught to respect authority and complete relatively detailed tasks. Pupils are taught that noncompliance is antisocial. It is labeled slovenly, uncooperative, immature, selfish, rude, irresponsible, and lacking in self-discipline.

We can see how successful Japanese schools are at producing a cooperative group attitude by observing Japanese school grounds during physical education classes and after school. Despite ten or more different boys' and girls' physical education classes and sports clubs cooperatively sharing school grounds (which may be one-fourth the size of American elementary and secondary school playgrounds), the quarrels seen on Japanese school playgrounds are minimal.[43]

At the middle school level students are expected to conform to a single ideal and image of student behavior. That means to be lively and cheerful, to internalize school rules, and to study hard. Middle schools achieve social control by subjecting students to writing notebooks and diaries in which they discuss their daily activities, study routine, feelings, and problems as well as by self-criticism reflection meetings during scheduled times, or at specially convened times when a serious disciplinary infraction has occurred within the class or school. Through them students learn that they are measured by school and peer norms emphasizing group life, obeying seniors, the acceptance and internalization of school rules, the appeal to school identification and loyalty, responsibility, and avoiding being a nuisance to other students or to adjoining classrooms by exercising self-restraint. Teachers may punish an entire class for an individual or small groups transgressions; charge group leaders to take responsibility for solving a problem; emphasize that small infractions lead to major crimes; shame the students by the allegation that the general public will associate their school with other schools that have a poor reputation; and threaten that good high schools will not accept students from their own school because of the poor reputation brought on the school by unacceptable student behavior.[44]

Middle schools allow senior club leaders considerable control in teaching juniors hierarchical relationships and stress the importance of following orders, correcting misbehavior that interferes with classroom teaching, and enduring personal disadvantage for the greater good of the group. In the Japanese way of thinking this activity is called learning common sense and group life (*shudan seikatsu*) to achieve success for all. Student committees corresponding to teacher committees supervise and manage "every aspect of the students' lives—from the milk they drink to the clothes they wear."[45]

A final way in which Japanese schools cultivate group consciousness is to promote a strong student identity with their school by various techniques. They try as much as possible to fashion their own unique and attractive uniforms. Students also have their own badges, student identification labels, winter, spring, and fall coats, briefcases, and sturdy knapsacks. Schools try to encourage students to feel a homeroom identity by being identified as such over the school's public address system. At preschools students wear caps with emblems, sometimes with an attached ribbon or feather. In addition, pupils carry identification labels indicating their school, school year, and homeroom. For the "All Sports Day" or special outings students may also wear special hats or uniforms to distinguish them from other schools.

MOTIVATION, UNITY, COOPERATION, AND EMOTIONAL BONDING

American elementary schools reflect a learning process in which activity centers on the teacher as an authority figure.[46] In Japanese elementary schools the emphasis is upon the whole class, even if it is organized into five or six groupings (*han*) of four to seven students each for study and other class activities. *Han* members cooperate and compete with other *han*.[47] Teachers believe that children can learn much by themselves under skillful management that keeps all groups on unified goals and uses peer groups to achieve leadership and class management. An International Association for the Evaluation of Academic Achievement survey showed that in the teaching of math for the category of "work together as a class and teacher teaches whole class," the corresponding figures for Japanese and American teachers were 78 and 49 percent respectively.[48]

The validity of this approach has been substantiated by several studies.[49] For example, a British study of the elementary level learned that more important than size for effective learning was the extent to which the teacher was able to spend time in "communication with the class as a whole."[50] Conversely, research shows that many American teachers of lowest ability students in smaller classes fail to have significant interaction with an entire class.

In dealing with individuals, as much as possible Japanese teachers avoid direct confrontation with pupils and making absolute judgments of right and wrong. As one Japanese teacher said, "The moment a teacher raises her voice or begins to argue or plead with a child, the battle is already lost." Teachers' strategy is to gain influence over children by benevolence and avoiding unpleasant "showdowns." They (and mothers) often manage a difficult child by an "affectively neutral approach." Indeed, they may drive pupils to more frustrated rage and crying because the latter cannot find a target against which to vent their anger.[51] Lois Peak wrote

Japanese teachers' approach . . . usually focuses on trying to understand their [students'] confused and unhappy feelings and going to considerable lengths to communicate with them. . . . Rather than using their authority to force or coerce a child to exhibit proper behavior in the absence of a genuine desire to behave, Japanese teachers repeatedly explain to the child the behavior expected of him and arrange the environment so that through other agents he experiences the negative consequences of his own behavior.[52]

A foreigner's remedy might be that of giving the child a good whack on the behind or isolating it. But Japanese teachers wait children out, and, then, comfort them by showing concern and love.

A difference in Japanese and American preschool and elementary school teachers' approach is that the former place a great deal of emphasis on the ideal of motivating children through an *explicit* emotive and bonding relationship. According to Lewis, they try to build a thread "to connect teacher and child and allow each to know what the other was feeling."[53] The objective of the Japanese teacher is to foster *kizuna*, empathy and "touching of the hearts." Some teachers may spend as much as the first two weeks of school primarily getting acquainted with their pupils in an emotive manner to establish the role they believe necessary to form students' character and to teach subjects effectively. One veteran sixth-grade teacher told a beginning teacher

I am not concerned with how to teach children; rather I try to understand them first by developing personal relations, *kakawari*. When I get a new class I do not teach subject matter immediately. Instead I play with the children intensely for a week to gain a good understanding of them. Then I will begin to know what kinds of children they are and gradually direct them toward the goals of learning on the basis of a happy and trustful *kakawari* [relationship] with them.[54]

At the crucial stage for forming good habits and attitudes, Japanese elementary school teachers also get to know their pupils better because they teach the same students two years (occasionally three years) and teach them all subjects through at least the first three grades (with the exception of music, from the fourth to sixth grade). They eat and chat with their classroom students at lunch time, direct daily school meetings, and plan and carry out the special activities program: a minimum of two school hours a week for home room, clubs, student council, and planning for school events.[55] Japanese schools should have more counselors, but they need fewer than American schools because teachers know their students better.

Recent significant research on teaching and learning by a group of scholars demonstrate that emotional bonding continues to play an important role in secondary school guidance, especially by homeroom teachers.[56] The assumption is that homeroom teachers are most effective in achieving good student discipline because they are closest to the student. One method practiced to achieve the goal is that of requiring daily diaries at the middle school level that encourage students to record how much they have studied, activities they have undertaken, and problems that they are experiencing. Teachers learn students' character and personal problems through reading them.[57] Ideally, they establish a personal, caring relationship by their comments in the diaries. In their response students may confide in teachers or even joke with them. Homeroom teachers attend morning and end-of-the-day meetings, accompany students on class or school outings, and hold parent conferences, and younger teachers may eat with the class and join in the cleaning. When serious disciplinary problems occur, the homeroom teacher (sometimes in concert with the designated all-grade level teacher and school nurse) may spend hours dealing with a student or students in an effort to correct student behavior by counseling and written self-criticsm essays that are to lead students to understand and to feel remorse, rather than just compliance. Club advisors also play an important role in guidance and bonding because they meet students daily and get to know students well on a more informal and personal basis. The head nurse also is expected to be a sympathetic listener to students' problems, to watch for physical signs of poor health, head or stomach aches, insufficient sleep, or first menstruation. They report these conditions daily to teachers. A reflection of the importance of character formation and emotional bonding is that teacher guidance and teacher and student committees are organized to relate to an entire grade level rather than a department as in America.[58]

American elementary teachers work on a more objective, impersonal, and controlling relationship stressing cognition and students' individuality. Beginning teachers may be admonished, "Don't make the mistake of trying to be friends with the kids."[59] One beginning teacher said, "I feel it is important to maintain formal relationships with kids. I need to be in power. I do not have to be liked, I do not need to be in a popularity contest. The rapport I would have with kids must be professional and appropriate."[60]

EFFORT, PERSEVERANCE, SUFFERING, AND HIGH EXPECTATIONS

Japanese teachers and parents expect a good performance of students and minimize their IQ and aptitude. Unlike American students they do not establish unrealistic expectations that learning will be fun, interesting, or exciting, but rather that it will be difficult and require some suffering. Students are taught to exert maximum effort, to persevere, and to be responsible with the assumption that they will become better and more intelligent persons. They gradually become socialized to the view that anything learned that is easy and enjoyable may not be worth the effort. Enduring discomfort by strenuous effort to discipline character is a strongly respected behavior. This thinking about learning underscores what every reader has experienced, namely, that those who have ability and aptitude do not always excel. The reason: They lack self-discipline and persistence. Self-discipline to master a subject, suffering, and subordinating one's personal autonomy and identity are highly valued at all stages of Japanese life. Foreign graduate students and professors are surprised when they find out that they are evaluated by how long the lights are on in their office at night.[61]

Academic Ability Is Related to Effort and Character

Why do Japanese schools and society emphasize effort and persistence so strongly and minimize IQ scores?[62] One reason is that Japanese assume academic ability is related to good character and effort; therefore, all students, even poor ones, can become stronger persons and more intelligent by persistent effort, cooperation with others, and self-management.[63] They believe that children possess equal abilities at birth. Success or failure in life and in preserving one's "original goodness" are considered to be almost entirely dependent on how hard a child tries.[64] Accordingly, all schools and individual classrooms try to motivate effort, imitation, and good character by posting yearly goals; elementary schools post weekly ones. Schools integrate them into academic lessons, class meetings, reflection time, and extracurricular activities. Lewis recorded ninety-four banners and posters at nineteen elementary schools. She categorized them into socioemotional, health and nutrition, physical energy and exercise, neatness and punctuality, persistence, and academic goals. Most significant, 90 percent of the goals were in a strict sense nonacademic and almost one-half were socioemotional in nature, such as friendship, cooperation, consideration, listening well, keeping promises, responsibility for self, greetings, being calm, and having a beautiful heart. She found four goals particularly stressed in all fifty schools she studied: friendship, persistence, energy, and self-management.[65]

The Japanese attitude emphasizing effort recognizes the human potential to raise performance, reduces the potential for teacher discrimination, and encourages students to work more diligently. A British team after a four-year survey of 2,000 English pupils of age seven through eleven in fifty schools concluded

Children's performance changes over time. Given an effective school, children make greater progress. Greater progress leads to greater capability and, if handled sensitively, to greater confidence. In this way children's ability grows. . . . The responsibility of teachers is to ensure that their pupils do not adopt fixed views of their own abilities. . . . We believe that, in the right circumstances, children can become more intelligent.[66]

Similarly, Japanese mothers are more successful than American mothers in insisting on effort and persistence as important.[67] American teachers are inclined to conclude that a student will only be able to achieve at a certain level—anything beyond is labeled "over achievement." Japanese children learn to be much more enduring in concentrating on a task.

The Japanese attitudes regarding effort, perseverance, and suffering contrast markedly with American ones, which state that innate ability or aptitude is more significant for subject mastery and university admission. Theresa Kneckt Dozier, a National Teacher of the Year in 1985, later experienced teaching in the American School in Singapore. She concluded that Singapore students were not smarter than American students; instead, the difference occurred when her American students had trouble. "They immediately took the attitude the course was too difficult for them. They just didn't have the academic ability to do well and they needed to drop down to a lower level. By contrast my Asian students never took that attitude. They would simply say, 'I must try harder.'"[68] Dozier's impressions are corroborated by solid research on Chicago, Taiwan, and Sendai children that showed American children gave up much quicker than their Asian cohorts.[69] Similarly, Japanese language teachers note that American university students assume that their lack of comprehension of subject matter is the teacher's fault. Asian students believe that they themselves are the problem.

Part of the fault for the continued use of the aptitude tests is that runaway grade inflation resulting from educators' permissiveness and excessive emphasis on helping students achieve self-esteem over the past thirty years has meant that college admission boards cannot really trust students' transcripts. Studies by UCLA announced in 1996 show that 31.5 percent of college freshmen nationwide reported average grades of A– or higher, twice the level of thirty years ago. Only one-fourth of college applicants average less than a B, down from 35 percent in 1990 and 45 percent in 1966.[70] From the late 1950s American colleges and universities admitted students on the basis of their aptitude scores on either the nationally administered American College Test (ACT) or Scholastic Achievement Test (SAT).[71] The former test measures aptitude of a student to do college work. The ACT test measures the ability of a student to work at college level in English, mathematics, natural science, and social studies. Neither test adequately examines students on their acquisition of subject matter. A sample survey of 200 four-year colleges in 1980 demonstrated that 80 percent of U.S. colleges granted admission on the basis of SAT scores.[72] Many universities still admit students who achieve above-average scores on these tests despite poor scholastic achievement in junior and senior high schools.

Aptitude tests influence students to think "Why study? One either has the ability or one does not"; and, "Sustained study for mastery of subject matter is unrelated to how well I will do in college."[73] Students cultivate the optimistic attitude that earnest study after entering college will compensate for past poor performance. Three studies came to the same conclusion. A well-balanced Japanese research team's study in 1987 on American education concluded, "Isn't it possible that this emphasis diminishes the desire of high school students to learn, and is . . . contributing to declining standards? Faced with a precipitous decline both in educational standards in the high schools . . . and in the academic standards of high school graduates, the U.S. system of university admissions . . . must be reviewed."[74] A study by Lynne V. Cheney, former chairwoman of the National Endowment for the Humanities, revealed that national tests in European Community countries and Japan only tested students' mastery of subject matter. Japanese students were asked to identify

European thinkers such as Euclid, Bacon, Newton, and Locke. British students had to write an essay on whether Woodrow Wilson was "unbelievably naive" or a "dogged man of principle." Cheney complained that both the SAT and the ACT tests were fundamentally multiple-choice, had an "arm's-length relationship to curricula," did not test students over classroom study, and did "little to advance the notion that hard work in school matters."[75] Third, as Gardner noted, "SAT tests don't measure zeal, character, judgment, staying power, and so on."[76]

Children Are Good and Good Children Are Intelligent

A second reason that Japanese minimize IQ scores is that they succeed by continuous positive reinforcement in getting children to associate a good mind with moral character, and failure to cooperate with group goals as a character deficiency. In a cynical way it seems like an effective way of brainwashing children into acceptable behavior. If pupils are obedient, cooperative, and gentle, they are praised as intelligent or clever. Because children are viewed as inherently good, misbehavior is viewed as occurring only because children do not understand, have not learned to control their desires, and need guidance. Misbehavior may only be labeled as strange or odd, rather than bad.[77] An assessment of a boisterous, selfish, and aggressive preschool Japanese child by American researchers was that he was so intelligent that he was bored. The Japanese kindergarten staff, however replied, if the child were so intelligent why did he not behave better?[78]

Maternal Expectations of Children

Various researchers have observed striking differences between Asian and American mothers' expectations and children's attitudes toward achievement, study, and homework. Harold Stevenson's research team shows striking differences in five areas. Despite their children's lower performance, 42 percent of American mothers rated their academic performance as "very satisfactory." But only 5 percent of Japanese mothers did so. American mothers were also more satisfied with their children's poorer math achievement than Taiwanese or Japanese mothers. Although 91 percent of American mothers believed their elementary schools were doing a "good job," only 39 percent of Japanese mothers believed similarly. American mothers were also much more inclined to believe that school success is the result of innate ability rather than effort. A fifth result was that American mothers were more willing to accept a child's low performance. In fact, they prefer standards not to be set too high to prevent children losing self-esteem. The Stevenson group thought these American attitudes provided an excuse for offering some children less challenging curricula, making fewer demands for their mastery of material, and holding lower expectations about "what can be accomplished through hard work."[79]

Effort and Homework

Stevenson and Stigler's research also demonstrated that Sendai mothers' estimates of the amount of time their first-grade children spent on homework were three times greater than the time spent by American first graders. (Taipei mothers' estimates were seven times more, and Beijing mothers estimates' two times.) At the fifth-grade level Sendai and Taipei mothers believed their children spent 6 hours and 13 hours a week respectively doing homework; Minneapolis mothers estimated that their children only spent four hours a week doing homework.[80] Minneapolis teachers gave 79 minutes of homework a week to six-year-olds compared to 2 hours and 57 minutes by Japanese teachers. At the ten-year-old level, Taipei teachers gave 13 hours of homework a week, Japanese teachers slightly more than 6 hours, and American teachers slightly more than 4 hours a week. According to the 1994 NAEP report, 29 percent of American seventeen-year-olds say that they do less than 1 hour of homework on a daily basis and 22 percent do none.[81] The same research showed that 21 percent of American thirteen-year-olds say they do no homework, 4 percent "don't do assignments," and 36 percent do less than 1 hour of homework. Two-thirds of American high school seniors and juniors spend less than 1 hour daily on homework; about one high school junior in three does almost no homework; another third spent an hour a day studying at home; and the remaining third devoted two or more hours a day to doing homework.[82]

All Taiwan teachers gave their elementary school students homework during the winter vacation, but only 12 percent of Minneapolis teachers did. Two-thirds of the Sendai teachers gave homework during the six-week summer vacation.[83] In the United States, students and some parents consider it almost a violation of children's human rights to be given homework over the three-month summer vacation.

We don't have to go to Japan, however, to learn that America's outstanding students study diligently. Benjamin Duke made a study of over 3,000 American, British, and Japanese students at sixteen of each country's outstanding private and public schools. His research showed that 37.1 percent of the American students studied 2 to 3 hours on weekdays and 26.6 percent studied 4 or more hours weekdays. This performance was even higher than the corresponding figure for the equivalent Japanese students—43.3 percent and 16.3 percent, respectively.[84]

By the time Japanese students, especially males, enter junior high school they have been socialized to believe that study and preparing for a future carry a heavy responsibility. Most children do their homework for six reasons:

1. Children understand it is their responsibility and may not be able to go out to play until they have finished their homework.

2. Children understand that their teacher will keep them after school or double their homework for failure to do it. Students who want to enter secondary schools are conscientious because they need recommendations.

3. Children feel responsible to their *han* at the elementary and junior high school level for doing assigned homework.

4. Children may be given a note asking parents to help children with schoolwork or to supervise study hours.

5. Many mothers arrange home life in such a way as not to interfere with children's study and may deny themselves TV viewing time during children's study hours.[85]

The British researcher, Cyril Simmons, did a survey of Japanese and British students, which revealed different attitudes toward the importance of education. He asked Japanese and English ninth graders to respond to the question, "What matters to me more than anything else?" The six categories were "family," "friends," "getting a job," "studying," "entering high school," and "exams." No British students answered studying, entering high school, or exams, but of the 187 Japanese students' responses "studying" ranked highest (21%), "entering high school" ranked third (15%), and exams ranked somewhat lower (5%). One girl added, "And I will never forget the final words of a teacher when he retired from my high school last year: 'Life, until death, is study.'" To two other questions regarding what students thought were "the best" and "the worst" things that could happen to them, 22 percent of the Japanese students wrote that the best thing was entering high school, while 10 percent wrote "passing exams." Not a single English student chose these two categories. Twenty-five percent of Japanese students thought the worst thing that could happen was "failing exams"; only 13 percent of British students chose this category.[86] I believe the British responses are comparable to how American students might have responded.

Americans might be inclined to seize on these statistics as an example of excessive anxieties that Japanese society and schools foster. Yet, not one Japanese chose "school" as "the worst thing about life." By contrast, 13 percent of the British students did. More than 80 percent of Japanese fifth and sixth graders are completely satisfied or mostly satisfied with school.[87] All these attributes contrast with the judgment of an English author who wrote, "It [Japanese education] fails to develop the mind or logical thinking, suppresses originality and discourages pupils from asking questions. The main objective is to impart huge quantities of information."[88] It is not true that elementary school children are suffering from rote learning, psychological stress, suicide, pushy mothers, and excessive emphasis on academics. Stevenson and Stigler's research showed that neither Chinese nor Japanese elementary school pupils were suffering from anxiety and hypertension as a result of higher expectations. They stated, "If anything, Asian children's frank enthusiasm about school . . . would suggest that studying hard may lead to a feeling of accomplishment and mastery that actually enhances their self-image and their adjustment to school."[89] Conversely, American teachers complained more frequently about their students' inattentiveness, hyperactivity, headaches, and stomachaches. Another study by Tsuchida Ineko of American and Japanese fourth graders showed a greater fondness for school by Japanese elementary school pupils.[90] Unchallenged students are bored students. If school is easy, the pleasure of attending it wears off quickly.

Study Halls Reflect Unsatisfactory American Effort

Japanese society does not expect secondary schools to build study periods (one-class-period study halls) for homework into the school day, an option that all but the most ambitious Americans students selected as a part of their daily schedule from 1945 to the early 1960s. Japanese schools do not want to surrender this precious hour of instruction to provide class time for doing homework and do not want to utilize precious staff and financial resources for this unnecessary supervisory function. Japanese parents and teachers expect students to do homework where the word implies: at home.

POSITIVE PARENTAL ATTITUDES
SUPPORTING EDUCATION

When fifty mothers who had lived abroad for an extensive period were asked "What was most important to you in the return to Japan?" they answered most frequently "their children's education."[91] I have always been impressed on visiting Japanese homes, one-half the size of American homes, to observe that children have their own study desks, workbooks, and various study references.[92] The purchase of a study desk sends a message to children that school is important and a student's role is to study. But how prevalent is the Asian practice of purchasing study desks? Stevenson and Stigler showed that 80 percent of Sendai and Taipei children already have desks in the first grade and 95 percent of them by the fifth grade. Only 63 percent of American fifth graders have one—a much higher level than I can believe from my own American experience.[93] Stevenson and Stigler's research showed that an anxious 50 percent of Japanese parents purchased elementary school pupils' supplementary workbooks for mathematics and 29 percent for science. Conversely, only 28.9 percent of American parents had purchased math workbooks and only 1 percent of them science workbooks.[94]

Not so incidentally, Stigler and Stevenson's research proved indirectly that students who can read well also will read more. Sendai children spent 5.7 hours a week reading for pleasure, compared to 4.3 hours for Taipei children, and 3.8 hours for Minneapolis students. Beijing fifth graders read two hours more a week than Chicago children.

American mothers expect their children to help much more at home with domestic chores or to run more errands than Asian mothers. On the one hand, this American practice admirably teaches children to be responsible for helping with housework and to respect their mothers' work. On the other hand, the attitudes expressed in the different demands made by American and Asian mothers are revealing. American mothers rarely ever said that they demanded fewer chores from their children so the latter could do school-related tasks. Most Asian mothers, however, gave study responsibilities as the most important reason. The American maternal attitude produces a more desirable socialization, but the Asian mothers' attitude tells a child that school is important.[95]

American and Japanese students have the same bad habit of watching too much TV. The Third International Mathematics and Science Study (TIMSS) showed that the amount of American and Japanese students watching more than three hours of TV or video a day was almost the same, 38 and 39 percent respectively. But the difference is that Japanese parents are more successful in making "television viewing dependent on the completion of homework." They do a better job of monitoring what and how much their children watch.[96] Ravitch and Finn's research showed that only 12 percent of American students reported any family rules about how much television they watched. Forty-four percent of American high school juniors and 64 percent of eighth graders are watching three to five hours of television a day.[97] A 1992 report of the National Center for Education Statistics showed that 13 percent of eighth grade students were watching TV 6 or more hours a day and three to eight-year-olds an average of 2.5 hours daily. In 1994, 8.4 percent of high school seniors said they watched TV 5 or more hours a week and 13 percent said they played video games more than an hour a day. An international comparison that did not include Japanese students was conducted in 1991 for science and mathematics of nine and thirteen-year-olds. Twenty-five percent of the American nine-year-olds watched TV more than 5 hours a day, the highest percentage rate, or 17 percent and 18 percent more than Taiwanese and Korean children, and among thirteen-year olds only Scottish children watched TV more.[98] Paradoxically, a 1987 survey showed that 79 percent of American parents believed that limiting television viewing until all homework had been finished was desirable.[99] A 1991 survey, however, showed that only 56 percent of three to eight-year-olds experienced rules for how long they could watch TV.[100] Here is a clear example of the gap between what parents say is desirable for their children and what they actually enforce.

Furthermore, the amount of American television time devoted to educational programs is much lower than in Japan and other "advanced" industrial countries. A report of the National Association of Secondary School Principals, which compared America, South Korea, and Germany in how much their societies value schools, gave Americans three "Cs" on a report card for "TV programs aimed at educating youth," "content of late afternoon/early evening TV programming," and "values expressed by the popular culture." Seventy-one percent of thirteen-year-old Korean students regularly watched science programs on TV, compared to only 37 percent of their American counterparts.[101]

Japanese parents and society are stricter about play outside the home after school and are aided in helping high school students establish good study habits by national law that does not allow a driving license until age eighteen. Including Sundays, Japanese children spend only about five hours a week in social relations. Most Japanese students not attending a *juku* (cram school) will not venture outside the home in the evening. By contrast, some American high school seniors own a car, while many other seniors, juniors, and a few sophomores will have access to their parents' car because they have a driver's license.[102] Further, many secondary school students after dinner will spend two or three hours playing outside or talking on the phone.

RITUALS

Japanese pupils learn to do a task well and proper attitudes and forms must precede it at every step of the process and it must be practiced over and over with due attention to mastering the basic skills. This is true of play as well as study. Japanese practice what Confucius taught over two thousand years ago, namely, that constant repetition of forms creates both good habits and greater achievement. Children who learn to bow from the time they are carried on their mothers' backs gradually internalize societal values concerning civility, respect, and, less fortunately, status in a vertical society. Japanese believe that exact observance of routine produces a better person because they will learn that effort, persistence, imitation, and suffering will develop their inner strengths—will power, self-discipline, and respect—that are necessary for coping, competing, and excelling. Observing forms helps to account for the smoothness of social interaction and effective classroom management.[103] In fact, one of the greatest concerns today is the failure of many youth to observe forms because many parents are not insisting upon them.

All classes in Japan begin the day (and at the secondary level begin each period) with a designated class monitor (*toban*) calling the students to stand to attention. The teacher and students formally greet each other with a "Good Morning" and bow to each other. At a few schools and most school physical education classes and private sports clubs, the students also cry out in unison "*onegaishimasu*," literally, "We beg of you (to teach us)." After the students sit down the monitors make and request announcements, and at elementary schools the teacher may spend a minute praising some ethical behavior or goal accomplishment. The monitor notes that the morning meeting is finished and tells the students to take out the supplies for the first class of the day. At the end of the school day students will once again stand at attention and say good-bye. True enough, students being somewhat similar the world over, these rituals may become a mere mouthing of words, but over the years rituals set the mood for a class period or a day's learning activity.

In preschools and the first years of elementary school, teachers patiently take children methodically through activities. Unlike American schools, where variety, innovation, and unpredictability are valued, all Japanese schools follow rigidly the same daily routine to provide the predictability, efficiency, and order that Japanese society treasures. Pupils learn to follow proper behavior by observing modeled behavior, by repeated reminders of what is expected, and by group pressure that may be brought into play by the teacher's delaying an activity or class dismissal until every student complies with a request in the prescribed way.

One example of how attitudes are created at preschools can be seen in the orchestrated, ritualistic group practices that bring individualistic youngsters into line.[104] When kindergarteners arrive at school they are responsible for placing their shoes, coat, knapsack, lunch, and school supplies all in their proper place. They learn to select in accord with need; outdoor shoes, indoor slippers, and toilet slippers, and to change their clothes frequently for appropriate activities throughout the school day. Peak observed that preschool teachers spent almost half of the class time in the first few weeks simply helping children change clothing, putting slippers, bags, and other items in their proper order, and teaching what clothing and what slippers and shoes were proper for various situations. These practices are supposed to teach children the moral discipline necessary for discriminating (*kejime o tsukeru*) between appropriate behavior and language inside and outside the home and for learning proper habits for harmonious group life.[105]

Pupil's lunches (*bento*) prepared by their mothers provide another example of socialized ritual.[106] (In elementary and secondary schools similar ritualized patterns are instilled via the school lunch program.) At preschools each food item is arranged to conform to molded patterns in a rectangular box. The children remove their lunch box from their knapsack and the special drawstring bag, arrange the box, chopsticks, and cup on a special napkin in a prescribed fashion and return the cup and chopstick bags to the drawstring bag underneath the table. No one, however, begins to eat until everyone finishes their toilet, takes a seat, sings a luncheon song under the class monitor's supervision, bows their heads, and thanks their "honorable" father and mother. Then the pupils utter in unison the expression *itadakimasu* (roughly translated, "We thankfully receive this meal," or simply, "I am going to eat").[107] At the conclusion of a meal, everyone expresses gratitude in unison for the meal and the pupils place their lunch accoutrements in a prescribed fashion within their knapsacks. All knapsack contents are also neatly arranged for carrying pupils' textbooks and school supplies between school and home.

In preschool and elementary school days children are made to feel responsible for the cleanliness of their school and assigned classrooms. This means cleaning the blackboards, erasers, floors, and desks. Periodically, a special time period is set aside for mopping, waxing, or oiling the floors and hallways, and tidying the school yard. These activities make pupils feel responsible for school property.

Japanese college students returning from home-stay in the United States are sensitive to these cultural differences. One of them described her six week home-stay experience in the United States in this way:

I was shocked at the different expressions used daily in the two societies regarding the attitude one should take toward schoolwork, one's job, and interaction with others. In America I repeatedly heard: "Take it easy," "Be cool," "Don't sweat it," "Who cares?" "Relax," "Don't worry about the details," "That's all right. You don't have to be perfect," and "If you don't take care of number one, who will?" I was always thinking about what I should be doing for others, but my host family said, "Relax!" "Take it easy, and make yourself at home." But in Japan I continually heard at school and home: "Hang tough," "Do your best always," "You must have a sense of responsibility and shame," "Be sensitive to others," "You must not be a stickler for principle; cooperate," "Don't be selfish," "You can do anything, if you work hard enough," "What a good child!" "That's bad," "Practice self-restraint in dealing with others," "You can't do such a thing. What will other people think?"

By the third grade of elementary school, children have acquired considerable skill in group activities and music and art. Group effort, attention to detail, and forms are said to account for adult Japanese being "masters of quality mass production."[108]

Influenced by the frontier spirit, Americans believe forms and authority to be unnecessary, too ritualistic, and, sometimes, hypocritical. Self-identity, integrity, individual creativity, and personal autonomy are believed to be more important than observing meaningless societal conventions. In contrast, much of Japanese learning is based on imitation of upper classmates, a teacher, or a master. Students learn by persistent imitation of proper form and adapting themselves to their experience and material "rather than by controlling or subordinating the material to oneself."[109]

In an ethnocentric article on Japanese education, an American high school teacher who had spent merely two weeks visiting Japanese schools demonstrated the American emphasis on being original and individualistic. She correctly noted that the art curriculum was very standardized and that students were expected to draw and paint exactly as their teacher prescribed based on forms handed down through the centuries. She took umbrage when the Japanese teacher corrected American students' drawings according to traditional methods, or took their painting hands and guided them in the "correct" manner. She failed to appreciate the need for students to master the basic elements of art before emphasizing their originality.[110]

The Japanese method stifles interests and originality and results in a lesser number of creative geniuses in art in Japan than in the West. But it also spawns a higher level of ability to draw and paint. Japanese understand what every coach or athlete knows: Imitation of models, constant repetition of basic forms, and persistence lead to achievement, skill, and satisfaction. At that point, one merits self-esteem. Rohlen and LeTendre wrote that Americans "assume almost automatically that, to improve, we have to 'break out of,' our old ways of doing things and forge a new way. We see—in our seemingly endless cycles of educational reform in this country, for example—a tremendous emphasis on finding a new and better way that makes old ways obsolete."[111]

SPORTS AS AN EXAMPLE OF JAPANESE SOCIALIZATION PROCESSES

Although Japanese athletes' attention to detail and incessant repetition of prescribed form is often ridiculed by Americans, it produces good results in performance and attitudes. On a five-day ski excursion, elementary and secondary students are likely to spend four and a half days methodically repeating teachers' instructions on the fundamentals of skiing. Only in the last half day will the students be allowed free skiing time. Most Americans, however, will spend one-half day learning to fall, stop, and a few other basic fundamentals, then spend the remaining time perfecting their own technique and enjoying their freedom. Japanese will express their pleasure less explicitly. The Japanese method pays off. After five days, they look professional.

Students of most Japanese sports believe Japan's weaker performance in international athletic competition stems from an overemphasis on form and excessively long practice sessions. It is probably true. American baseball players playing in Japan's professional leagues insist that the Japanese wear themselves out with three- and four-hour practice sessions prior to actual games and a "spring" training program that begins in December. Similarly, for a club activity such as cheerleading or choral singing, it is common to see members of such clubs running long distances—chanting all the time "*Faito! Faito!*" (fight)—to achieve self-discipline and group unity. These criticisms miss the point. Japanese athletes' and students' characters are judged for how well they follow expectations, achieve self-discipline, persevere, and suffer to achieve perfection. This is the major reason why Japan's most famous industries give priority to employing members of sports clubs, especially club captains, even though their academic achievement may be mediocre.

THE ROLES OF THE JAPANESE MOTHER AND SCHOOLS

Japanese society actually achieves for its children at the time of entry into elementary school the "readiness for school" that former President Bush and the nation's governors declared to be an American goal by 2000. In fact, despite the earnest effort of the Ministry of Education and the preschools to avoid teaching academic subjects, anxious parents prepare kindergarten pupils for elementary schools both academically and emotionally. Among surveyed preschools, 90 percent of them noted that most students could write their names, recite numbers up to twenty, and count correctly ten objects. Two-thirds of the same preschools reported that approximately one-half of their children could read simple storybooks.[112] By the time most children reach first grade they can read and write the phonetic script, count to a hundred, do arithmetic problems under ten, and sing several songs and poems.[113]

Japanese kindergarten authorities believe they can only achieve their socialization objectives if there is complete parental cooperation. Accordingly, they work very hard at creating two supportive attitudes among parents: (1) that cooperation with the schools is essential for achieving school objectives, and (2) that mothers' most important responsibility is their children's education. Peak wrote, "By . . . requiring daily practice of supportive behavior and attitudes, the preschool accustoms mothers to providing sustained, intensive support for the child's educational activities, which will be maintained throughout the child's school career."[114] Some tangible evidence of the Japanese attitude is that kindergartens (supervised by the Ministry of Education, as opposed to nursery schools supervised by the Welfare Ministry) try to avoid accepting children of working mothers.[115]

Kindergartens expect that mothers should participate in school excursions, monthly PTA meetings, work groups associated with PTA activities, and mothers' clubs organized for group singing, hiking, and needle craft. Mothers are also expected to prepare "loving and nutritious" lunches that will move a child, upon removing the lunch box lid, to feel "his mother's love . . . pop out of the box." They are personally to escort their children to the school or the bus stop and to meet them at the same places at the end of the school day. Asking another mother to substitute or being tardy to meet a child are believed to be evidence that a parent does not fully support the school's activities and the child's psychological needs.[116]

At most preschools a mother is expected to make by hand a long-sleeved, button-down painting smock; a cloth bag lined with vinyl for modeling clay; an appliquéd bag to take home monthly subscription magazines and books; a wrapper for the lunch box with a velcro closure; separate drawstring bags for a drinking cup and a toothbrush; and a special flame-retardant hooded cape for use in case of fire. They are to place sewn or inked name-labels on the child's lunch box, seat cushion, school uniforms, every item of regular clothing, and every piece of equipment used at school. Mothers must be sure to put a pocket handkerchief and a small packet of facial tissue in the uniform pocket, and to place the daily attendance record and parent–teacher message book in the shoulder bag.

Via the parent–teacher message book, preschool teachers convey to the parents daily information about each child. Mothers are expected to read it and return daily remarks to teachers about their children's behavior and health. In addition, they are to meet the school's expectations by observing a detailed monthly schedule and carefully reading the frequent mimeographed sheets brought home by the children.[117] Peak noted that preschool authorities' high expectations of mothers to help collect tuition fees, produce newsletters, hold festivals, plan excursions, and help with clerical duties was less for the purpose of operating with a limited support staff than to inculcate a sense of parent responsibility and to demonstrate "respect for the teachers and activities of the preschool."[118] One foreign mother told me all these expectations were exhausting. But she failed to comprehend that the beleaguered kindergarten teacher has these responsibilities for thirty to forty pupils. Elementary and middle schools continue these practices, but with less frequency.

Preschool authorities create a favorable impression of school by scheduling several mother–child visits to the school six months prior to the opening day. On the first occasion mothers' and children's fears are allayed by speeches given by teachers and older students, and sometimes by a mother of currently attending children. The second time children are warmly initiated into the routine of many activities by the current students. Mothers and new students hear more speeches, witness children's presentations, and experience a typical school day.[119] Most impressive are parents' and schools' effort to create a positive attitude toward schooling by talking about the forthcoming entrance as a major event for months before the opening day, by impressive formal ceremonies on the first and last day, and by sixth graders assuming special responsibilities on opening days. Anxious incoming students want models; in Japan's schools they get them.

Throughout the school year, especially in elementary school, family members, relatives, and others create the attitude in children that they have a serious and important role they are expected to fulfill. Parents, usually the mother, and sometimes her mother, sustain enthusiasm for school by shopping with their children for the school uniform, knapsack, educational supplies, study desk and chair, and other items necessary for attendance. Expensive knapsacks that may cost between $350 to $500 and serve children through all six elementary school grades are often purchased by the father's parents.[120] New clothes are often purchased when a child is about to start preschool, elementary school, secondary school, and even university. On opening days, presents may be given to the children, and the children may be treated to a special lunch or dinner at home or a restaurant. On the closing day and graduation day, formal ceremonies again lend much dignity to the occasion.

CONCLUSION

Americans are often looking for the one thing to explain why American educational standards have deteriorated. There is no one explanation or quick fix for overcoming this condition, nor is there one magic solution that can be borrowed from Japanese education to correct America's educational woes. Americans arrived at the present unsatisfactory educational standard by a host of poor attitudes and practices, or good ones carried to excess. They can only extricate themselves from this condition by correcting them and borrowing selectively better attitudes and practices toward education from Japan and other nations.

University professors and administrators must assume a greater responsibility for imposing higher college entrance standards. Stricter college entrance requirements reduce the degree of need for a greater national government role. Nationally administered tests also will let each school and its community know where it is failing.

The need for all American post-secondary institutions, rather than 5 percent of them (as of 1985), to use the Educational Testing Service Achievement Test (ACH) is imperative. Because the ACH measures mastery of subject matter content, the impact on secondary schools would be profound. Students in a democratic society should be able to overcome poor academic performance by attending public junior or community colleges where requirements are lower. But an increase in these institutions requirements for the number of years applicants must study the basic courses and the establishing of a minimum GPA for full-time students would have an immediate salutary effect on high school curriculums and students. Some Americans fear that achievement tests will introduce harmful test-oriented education. That need not be a concern, however, if they are combined with aptitude tests, teacher recommendations, increased basic course requirements, grade point averages, and students' talents as an important "mix" in universities' selection procedures.

NOTES

1. William K. Cummings, *Education and Equality in Japan* (Princeton, N.J.: Princeton University Press, 1980); Benjamin Duke, *The Japanese School: Lessons for Industrial America* (Westport, Conn.: Praeger, 1986), 20–24; Thomas P. Rohlen, *Japan's High Schools* (Berkeley and Los Angeles: University of California Press, 1983); Ronald Dore, *Education in Tokugawa Japan* (Berkeley and Los Angeles: University of California Press, 1965); Nobuo K. Shimahara and Akika Sakai, *Learning to Teach in Cultures: Japan and the United States* (New York: Garland, 1995); Herbert Passin, *Society and Education in Japan* (New York: Teachers College Press, Columbia University, 1965); Catherine C. Lewis, *Educating Hearts and Minds* (New York: Cambridge University Press, 1995); Ezra Vogel, *Japan as Number One: Lessons for America* (Tokyo: Charles E. Tuttle, 1979); Merry White, *The Japanese Educational Challenge* (New York: Free Press, 1987).

2. John K. Fairbank, *The United States and China* (Cambridge: Harvard University Press, 1958), 56–59, 65–66, 88–89.

3. Passin, *Society and Education*, 273–274; Richard Rubinger, *Private Academies of Tokugawa Japan* (Princeton, N.J.: Princeton University Press, 1982), 4; Dore, *Education*, 42–44, 291–316.

4. Richard Rubinger, "Continuity and Change in Mid-Nineteenth-Century Japanese Education," in *Japanese Schooling*, ed. James J. Shields, Jr. (University Park: Pennsylvania State University Press, 1989), 225; Passin, *Society and Education*, 50–61.

5. Passin, *Society and Education*, 56–60.

6. Robert N. Bellah, *Tokugawa Religion: The Values of Pre-Industrial Japan* (Glencoe, Ill.: Free Press, 1957).

7. Karasawa Tomitaro, *Nihon kyoiku shi* (History of Japanese education) (Tokyo: Sobunsho, 1962), 22; Passin, *Society and Education*, 68, 88.

8. Mark Linicome, "The Historical Context of Japanese Education to 1945," in *Windows on Japanese Education*, ed. Edward R. Beauchamp (Westport, Conn.: Greenwood Press, 1991), 17–19.

9. Rubinger, "Continuity and Change," 229–230.

10. Kaigo Tokiomi and Arata Naka, *Nihon no kyoiku* (Japanese education) (Tokyo: Tosho Sensho, 1979), 30, 54, 90, 92.

11. Passin, *Society and Education*, 82–84, 225–232; Kaigo Tokiomi and Naka Arata, *Kindai Nihon no kyoiku* (Modern Japanese education) (Tokyo: Tokyo Shosen,

1983), 53–69; Karasawa Tomitaro, *Kyokasho no rekishi* (A history of textbooks) (Tokyo: Sobunsha, 1960).

12. Harry Wray, "Militarism in Japanese Textbooks, 1903–1945," in *China–Japanese Relations: The Search for Balance*, ed. Hilary Conroy and Alvin Coox (Santa Barbara: A.B.C. Clio Press, 1977).

13. Japanese language and *Shushin* textbooks published immediately after World War I introduced limited aspects of internationalism, pacifism, and democracy. Harry Wray, "A Temporary Balance between Internationalism and the *Kokutai*, 1918–1931," *Asian Forum* 5, no. 4 (1973): 49–69; Takiomi and Naka, *Nihon no kyoiku*, 53–69; Kaigo Tokiomi and Naka Arata, *Nihon kyokasho taikei kindai hen* (A compilation of Japanese textbooks: Modern edition) (Tokyo: Kodansha, 1962); Harry Wray, "Change and Continuity in Images of the *Kokutai* and Attitudes and Roles towards the Outside World: A Content Analysis of Japanese Textbooks, 1903–1945," Ph.D. diss., University of Hawaii, 1971.

14. Passin, *Society and Education*, 69, 209–211.

15. Ivan Parker Hall, *Mori Arinori* (Cambridge: Harvard University Press, 1973), 390–447.

16. Kumiko Fujimura-Faneslow and Anne E. Imamura, "The Education of Women in Japan," in *Windows on Japanese Education*, ed. Edward R. Beauchamp (Westport, Conn.: Greenwood Press, 1991), 230. Between 1888 and 1904, girls' elementary school attendance increased from 30 to 90 percent.

17. Fukuzawa's wife and daughter learned English at a Christian school in Yokohama. Haru Reischauer, *Samurai and Silk* (Tokyo: Charles E. Tuttle, 1986), 182.

18. National universities admitted women only as auditors. Fujimura-Faneslow and Imamura, "Education of Women," 233.

19. Joseph C. Trainor, *Educational Reform in Occupied Japan: Trainor's Memoir* (Tokyo: Meisei University Press, 1983), 147–148.

20. This attitude is especially prominent where ideological differences are strong. In the Faculty of Economics at Yokohama National University every item had to be discussed in detail at faculty meetings lasting a minimum of five hours.

21. Japan, National Council on Educational Reform (Japan, NCER), *Second Report on Education Reform* (Tokyo: Government of Japan, 1986), 200.

22. Ibid.

23. Takie Sugiyama Lebra, *Japanese Patterns of Behavior* (Honolulu: University of Hawaii Press, 1976), 11–14.

24. Joseph J. Tobin, David Y. H. Wu, and Dana H. Davidson, *Preschool in Three Cultures: Japan, China, and the United States* (New Haven: Yale University Press, 1989), 57–59, 71; Ryoko Tsuneyoshi, *Ningen keisei no Nichi-Bei hikaku* (A comparison of Japanese and American character formation) (Tokyo: Chuo Koron, 1992), 28–32.

25. Hiroshi Azuma, "Why Study Child Development in Japan?" in *Child Development and Education in Japan*, ed. Harold Stevenson, Hiroshi Azuma, and Keaji Hakata (New York: W. H. Freeman, 1986), 10.

26. George A. De Vos, "Achievement Orientation, Social Self-Identity, and Japanese Economic Growth," *Asian Survey* 15, no. 12 (1965): 583–586; Fujita Mariko, "It's All Mother's Fault: Child Care and the Socialization of Working Mothers in Japan," *The Journal of Japanese Studies* 15, no. 1 (1989): 67–91.

27. Shogo Ichikawa, "Financing Japanese Education," in *Windows on Japanese Education*, ed. Edward R. Beauchamp (Westport, Conn.: Greenwood Press, 1991), 78, 79.

28. Patricia Alberg Graham, *S.O.S.: Save Our Schools* (New York: Hillard Wang, 1992), 9.

29. Cummings, *Education and Equality*, 88. Spence's remark was made at an International House of Japan Seminar, 4 November 1991.

30. Vogel, *Japan as Number One*, 180–181.

31. Lewis, *Educating Hearts and Minds*, 28–31; Rebecca Irwin Fukuzawa, "The Path to Adulthood," in *Teaching and Learning in Japan*, ed. Thomas P. Rohlen and Gerald K. LeTendre (Cambridge: Cambridge University Press, 1996), 295.

32. Tobin, Wu, and Davidson, *Preschool*, 190–194; Lewis, *Educating Hearts and Minds*, 31–32, 66; Lois Peak, *Learning to Go to School in Japan* (Berkeley and Los Angeles: University of California Press, 1991), 72–74.

33. Lewis, *Educating Hearts and Minds*, 54–55.

34. Y. Ito, *Kyoshi bunka gakko bunka no nichibei hikaku* (A comparison of teacher and school culture in Japan and the United States) in *Nihon no kyoshi bunka* (The culture of Japanese teachers), ed. T. Inagaki and Y. Kudoni (Tokyo: University of Tokyo Press, 1994), 140–156, as cited in Lewis, *Educating Hearts and Minds*, 66.

35. Merry White and R. Levine, "What Is an *Ii Ko* (good child)?" in *Child Development and Education in Japan*, ed. Harold Stevenson, Hiroshi Azuma, and Kenji Hakuta (New York: W. H. Freeman, 1986), 58; Takie Sugiyama Lebra, *Japanese Women* (Honolulu: University of Hawaii Press, 1984), 187.

36. Lewis, *Educating Hearts and Minds*, 9; Tobin, Wu, Davidson, *Preschool*, 38; Fukuzawa, "The Path to Adulthood," 298.

37. My conclusion on large class sizes differs some from Tobin's view that Japanese teachers prefer larger classroom numbers. I agree with Professor Umakoshi Toru who thinks they are more likely to accept them from economic considerations, cultural emphasis on group consciousness, and a preference for fewer classroom teaching hours. His comments were made at my seminar at Nagoya University, 10 January 1995.

38. Tobin, Wu, and Davidson, *Preschool*, 38; Peak, *Learning in Japan*, 38–39, 48; Tsuneyoshi, *Ningen keisei*, 41–47. After witnessing three grandchildren fight over one toy from among hundreds of toys and stuffed animals, I concede to preschool administrators' wisdom.

39. Tobin, Wu, and Davidson, *Preschool*, 38; Peak, *Learning in Japan*, 11–12, 67–68.

40. Tobin, Wu, and Davidson, *Preschool*, 6–7, 17, 191–193; Irene S. Shigaki, "Child Care Practice in Japan and the United States: How Do They Reflect Cultural Values in Young Children?" *Young Children* 38 (May 1983): 13–24, 38; John Singleton, "Gambare: A Japanese Cultural Theory of Learning," in *Japanese Schooling*, ed. James J. Shields, Jr. (University Park: Pennsylvania State University Press, 1989), 11.

41. Tobin, Wu, and Davidson, *Preschool*, 30–31. Fifteen percent of Japanese preschools are Christian. Ibid., 50.

42. Lewis, *Educating Hearts and Minds*, 37–42, 170–172.

43. Walter Enloe and Philip Lewin, "The Cooperative Spirit in Japanese Primary Education," *The Educational Forum* 51, no. 3 (Spring 1987): 233–247.

44. Fukuzawa, "Path to Adulthood," 303–317.

45. Ibid., 312–317; Gerald K. LeTendre, "*Shido*: The Concept of Guidance," in *Teaching and Learning in Japan*, ed. Thomas Rohlen and Gerald LeTendre (Cambridge: Cambridge University Press, 1996), 275–294.

46. Shimahara and Sakai, *Learning to Teach*, ch. 2.

47. Lewis, *Educating Hearts and Minds*, 94–98.

48. U.S. Department of Education, National Center for Education Statistics (U.S. DOE, NCES), *Digest of Education Statistics 1994* (Washington D.C.: U.S. Government Printing Office, 1994), 444.

49. Harold W. Stevenson and James Stigler, *The Learning Gap: Why Our Schools Are Failing and What We Can Learn from Jananese and Chinese Education* (New York: Summit, 1992), 69–70.

50. Peter Mortimore, Pamela Sammons, Louise Stoll, David Lewis, and Russell Ecob, *School Matters* (Berkeley and Los Angeles: University of California Press, 1988), 188–189, 228–229, 252–253.

51. Tobin, Wu, Davidson, *Preschool*, 25–28; Peak, *Learning in Japan*, 155–156; Catherine Lewis, "Cooperation and Control in Japanese Nursery Schools," *Comparative Education Review* 28 (1984): 69–84.

52. Peak, *Learning in Japan*, 156.

53. Lewis, *Educating Hearts and Minds*, 54–55.

54. Shimahara and Sakai, "Teacher Internship and the Culture of Teaching in Japan," *British Journal of Sociology* 13, no. 2 (1992): 157.

55. T. Kataoka, "Class Management and Student Guidance in Japanese Elementary and Lower Secondary Schools," in *Japanese Educational Productivity*, ed. R. Leestma and H. J. Walberg (Ann Arbor: University of Michigan Press, 1992), 69–100.

56. Thomas P. Rohlen and Gerald K. LeTendre, eds., *Teaching and Learning in Japan* (Cambridge: Cambridge University Press, 1996).

57. Shimahara and Sakai, *Learning to Teach*, 85.

58. LeTendre, "Shido," 278–288; Fukuzawa, "The Path to Adulthood," 305–307.

59. White, *Japanese Educational Challenge*, 181–182. Shimahara and Sakai, *Learning to Teach*, 71–73, 79–85; Tobin, Wu, and Davidson, *Preschool*, 25.

60. Shimahara and Sakai, *Learning to Teach*, 82.

61. A frequently rerun scene on Japanese TV of the 1992 Olympics was that of an African athlete who doggedly finished a 400-meter race despite limping through the last 200 meters because of an excruciating muscle cramp.

62. Singleton, "Gambare," 11.

63. Lewis, *Educating Hearts and Minds*, 44–46, 48; Harold W. Stevenson, "The Asian Advantage: The Case of Mathematics," in *Japanese Schooling*, ed. James J. Shields, Jr. (University Park: Pennsylvania State University Press, 1989), 93.

64. Yoshiaki Yamamura, "The Child in Japanese Society," in *Child Development and Education in Japan*, ed. Harold Stevenson, Hiroshi Azuma, and Kenji Hakuta (New York: W. H. Freeman, 1986), 28–37; Tsuneyoshi, *Ningen keisei*, 58–60.

65. Lewis, *Educating Hearts and Minds*, 45–50.

66. Mortimore et al., *School Matters*, 264.

67. Priscilla N. Blinco, "Task Persistence in Japanese Elementary Schools," in *Windows on Japanese Education*, ed. Edward R. Beauchamp (Westport, Conn.: Greenwood Press, 1991), 128–130, 136; Robert D. Hess et al., "Family Influences on School Readiness and Achievement in Japan and the United States: An Overview of a Longitudinal Study," in *Child Development and Education in Japan*, ed. Harold Stevenson, Hiroshi Azuma, and Kenji Hakuta (New York: W. H. Freeman, 1986).

68. Theresa Kneckt Dozier, "The Next Education Reform: Restructuring Student and Parent Attitudes," *Paideia* (Winter 1993): 2–9.

69. Stevenson and Stigler, *Learning Gap*, 106.

70. "When Everyone Gets an A, Grades Are Meaningless," *USA Today*, 25 March 1997; Charles Sykes, *Dumbing Down Our Kids* (New York: St. Martin's Press, 1995), 30–32.

71. Lynne V. Cheyney, *Tyrannical Machines* (Washington, D.C.: National Endowment for the Humanities, 1990), 16–20; Japanese Study Group, "Educational Reforms in the United States," in *A Report of the Japan–United States Cooperative Study on Education in Tokyo* (January 1987), 16–20.

72. R. F. Harnett and R. A. Feldmesser, "College Admissions Testing and the Myth of Selectivity," *APHE Bulletin* 32 (1980): 3–6, cited in Richard Lynn, *Educational Achievement in Japan* (Armonk, N.Y.: M. E. Sharpe, 1988), 77.

73. Arthur G. Powell, Eleanor Farrar, and David K. Cohen, *The Shopping Mall High School* (Boston: Houghton Mifflin, 1985), 43.

74. Japanese Study Group, "Educational Reforms," 64.

75. Cheyney, *Tyrannical Machines*, 16–20. For an opposing view see Tamara Hendry, "Study: U.S. Achievement Tests Are No Measure of Mastery," *The Daily Yomiuri*, 30 April 1991.

76. John Gardner, *Excellence* (New York: Norton, 1987), 64–65.

77. Lewis, *Educating Hearts and Minds*, 131–133; LeTendre, "Shido," 276–278, 288, 292.

78. Tobin, Wu, and Davidson, *Preschool*, 24.

79. Harold W. Stevenson, Shin-ying Lee, and James Stigler, "Math Achievement of Chinese, Japanese, and American Children," *Science,* 14 February 1986; Stevenson and Stigler, *Learning Gap*, 100, 113–129.

80. Stevenson and Stigler, *Learning Gap*, 55–56.

81. U.S. DOE, NCES, *Digest 1994*, 114.

82. Diane Ravitch and Chester E. Finn, Jr., *What Do Our 17-Year-Olds Know?* (New York: Harper & Row, 1987), 14.

83. Stevenson and Stigler, *Learning Gap*, 56.

84. Benjamin Duke, *Education and Leadership for the Twenty-First Century: Japan, America, and Britain* (Westport, Conn.: Praeger, 1991), 35.

85. Lebra, *Japanese Women*, 192–193.

86. Cyril Simmons, *Growing Up and Going to School in Japan* (Philadelphia: Open University Press, 1990), 114–118.

87. Lewis, *Educating Hearts and Minds*, 187; Stevenson and Stigler, *Learning Gap*, 69–71.

88. Robert Harvey, *The Undefeated: The Rise, Fall and Rise of Greater Japan* (London: Macmillan, 1994), 559.

89. Stevenson and Stigler, *Learning Gap*, 57.

90. Ineko Tsuchida, "Teachers' Motivational and Instructional Strategies," Ph.D. diss., University of California–Berkeley, School of Education, 1993, as cited in Lewis, *Educating Hearts and Minds*, 8.

91. Merry White, *The Japanese Overseas* (New York: Free Press, 1988), 40.

92. A Nanzan University colleague has two preteenage children who have a study desk and a bookcase. The latter acts as a room divider and a handy reference section.

93. Stevenson and Stigler, *Learning Gap*, 54–55.

94. Stevenson, "Mathematics Achievement," 88.

95. Stevenson and Stigler, *Learning Gap*, 60.

96. Ibid., 58–59; U.S. Department of Education, National Center for Education Statistics (U.S. DOE, NCES), *Pursuing Excellence*, ed. Lois Peak (Washington, D.C.: U.S. Government Printing Office, 1996), 65–66.

97. Nine percent of students watched television six or more hours each day. Ravitch and Finn, *What Do Our 17-Year-Olds Know*, 151, 154; Bennett, *Making Our Schools Work*, 18; Rohlen, *Japan's High Schools*, 275–276.

98. U.S. DOE, NCES, *Digest 1994*, 125, 137, 139, 419, 421, 424.

99. Eighty-six percent of African American parents and 80 percent of teachers agreed.

100. U.S. DOE, NCES, *Digest 1994*, 137.

101. Scott D. Thompson, "Report Card USA: How Much Do Americans Value Schooling?" *NAASP Bulletin* (October 1989): 59, 64.

102. Rohlen, *Japan's High Schools*, 276.

103. Peak, *Learning in Japan*, 129; Rohlen and LeTendre, *Teaching and Learning*, 372.

104. Peak., *Learning in Japan*, 90–94.

105. Ibid., 24; Lebra, *Japanese Patterns of Behavior*, 136.

106. Most mothers no longer prepare *bento* at the elementary school level, but I cite it as an example of cultural behavior.

107. Tobin, Wu, and Davidson, *Preschool*, 16.

108. Sakaiya Taichi, "Masters of Mass Production," *The Japan Times*, 16 June 1988.

109. Rohlen and LeTendre, *Teaching and Learning*, 371, 373.

110. Susan Ohanian, "Notes on Japan from an American Schoolteacher," *Phi Delta Kappan* 68, no. 5 (January 1987): 360–367.

111. Rohlen and LeTendre, *Teaching and Learning*, 375.

112. Peak, *Learning in Japan*, 66; Tobin, Wu, and Davidson, *Preschool*, 57–58; Lebra, *Japanese Women*, 199; Lebra, *Patterns of Behavior*, 147.

113. White, *Japanese Educational Challenge*, 97; Gary DeCoker, "Japanese Pre-schools: Academic or Nonacademic," in *Japanese Schooling*, ed. James J. Shields, Jr. (University Park: Pennsylvania State University Press, 1989), 55–58.

114. Peak, *Learning in Japan*, 62.

115. Sarane Spence Boocock, "The Japanese Preschool System," in *Windows on Japanese Education*, ed. Edward R. Beauchamp (Westport, Conn.: Greenwood Press, 1991), 103–112.

116. Peak, *Learning in Japan*, 59, 60.

117. Ibid., 61–62; Tobin, Wu, and Davidson, *Preschool*, 66–68; Boocock, "The Japanese Preschool System," 115–116.

118. Peak, *Learning in Japan*, 58–59; Lebra, *Japanese Women*, 193.

119. Peak, *Learning in Japan*, 108, 125.

120. Sixty percent of a Nanzan senior class reported that grandparents purchased their knapsacks.

CHAPTER 3

Japanese Educational Weaknesses and American Strengths

In the preceding chapters I have written at length about how Japanese education is better than American education. I must rigorously qualify that judgment in Chapters 3 and 4. A sixteen-year residence in Japan has convinced me that there is still much good in American education and much that is unsatisfactory in Japanese education. Allow me to explain my inconsistency.

First, I want to reiterate one thesis, namely, that good indigenous values, attitudes, and institutions in both the Japanese and American educational systems become harmful because they are carried to extremes. I agree with Shogo Ichikawa of the National Institute for Educational Research who commented that values in all nations' systems possess simultaneously both merit and demerit.[1] Second, isolated research only on either Japanese elementary schools or secondary schools has led to judgments that distort the totality of pre-higher education. Western treatments of Japan's early school education are almost always favorable. Conversely, their examinations of secondary schools, with the notable exception of Thomas Rohlen and Gerald LeTendre's recently edited work, *Teaching and Learning in Japan*, redound with their deficiencies.[2] However, because Japanese education is an organic whole, it is not logical to consider the two levels as if they had limited relationship with each other. Because good early education practices emphasizing order, character formation, group consciousness, school rules, and academic competence are applied more copiously and severely at succeeding grade levels, by junior high school years they end up impairing the growth of humanity and democracy in Japanese society and lessen students' confidence and creativity at the secondary level. Third, because Japanese society and the world are rapidly changing, pre-1980 educational attitudes and practices that had considerable merit have become obsolescent and obstacles to genuine reform and Japan's needs. In Chapters 3 and 4 I will highlight those harmful Japanese attitudes and practices and advocate better American ones that Japanese schools and society should adopt selectively.

JAPANESE EDUCATION IS TOO CENTRALIZED AND REGIMENTED

The 1946 United States Education Mission to Japan (USEMJ) report recommended democratizing school policy formulation, fostering academic freedom, and instituting decentralizing procedures that would make the Ministry of Education (Mombusho) teachers' servant, not master. The USEMJ advocated elected prefectural, city, town, and village boards of education and limiting the Mombusho to a professional, advisory role. To implement these recommendations the Occupation's Education Division fostered a Fundamental Law on Education (FLE) in 1947 that specifically stated education should "not be subject to improper control."[3]

Occupation reforms to decentralize Japanese education did not endure. Moreover, even after they were empowered, local educational officials and educators frustrated Education Division staff by streaming into their offices to ask what they should do.[4] Currently, most educators are still reluctant to challenge the Mombusho's leadership. The National Council on Education Reform (NCER) criticized principals for failing to take "advantage of their powers" and exercising leadership.[5] One Ministry official complained that although internationalizing education is national policy, 80 percent of local educational officials and principals have to be prodded to take appropriate measures. Teachers' passive behavior patterns lead them to accept detailed Mombusho guidance.[6]

Mombusho's powers and top-down mentality has nurtured passive teachers, administrators, and school boards. Elite bureaucrats (and most citizens) view assertive, outspoken critics as troublemakers. One Mombusho official arrogantly wrote that curriculum was "none of their [teachers'] business."[7] Even now, all new university presidents are required to make the long, expensive trip to Tokyo simply for the purpose of a ceremonial bow before the Minister of Education. Education could benefit from the deregulation of the 1980s that improved the Japanese railway and communication systems' service.[8]

Although the Mombusho no longer can simply issue imperial ordinances to decide educational affairs, it exercises a commanding role over education from six factors. First, it plays a very commanding role in financing educational affairs.[9] Second, because Mombusho exercises veto power on appointments of superintendents of education at the prefectural level and of designated cities with a population of more than a half-million—a practice that the NCER thought should be reviewed—superintendents of education and prefectural boards of education lack power. In turn, subprefectural school boards are controlled by prefectural boards, and local school boards and teachers and administrators are handcuffed by the subprefectural level and Ministry regulations.[10] A more sophisticated electorate than in 1945 warrants granting more power to elected local boards. The NCER recommended giving "concrete details of educational administration to the discretion of municipal governments, which are nearest to community people." But to give the reform meaning local levels must have greater power to levy taxes and administer their own financial condition.[11]

Third, the Ministry exercises enormous influence in establishing educational standards by demanding elaborate school surveys, reports, and excessive criteria for school buildings, class sizes, salaries, and curriculum. The establishment of a new school or university or major changes within established ones requires university administrators to submit to Mombusho, at least two years in advance, massive amounts of detailed materials regarding staff, faculty size and qualifications, supplies, and building materials and facilities.

Fourth, although educational affairs are supposed to be decided by parliamentary law, the Mombusho exerts strong influence by a generous use of "administrative guidance" and "interpretation" of Diet laws. Mombusho claims it has that authority because it executes the majority will of the National Diet, which in turn represents the majority will of the people—rationale supported by Tokyo Superior Court Justice Takatsu's decision of 1974.[12] By "administrative guidance" rather than law the Ministry commanded schools to sing the national anthem and to hoist the flag on important occasions. In 1993, teachers were shocked by a Ministry decree that forbade private companies to give mock examinations within public schools despite three decades of this practice. The Course of Studies manual coos that "each school should plan the curriculum" on the basis of local conditions and the developmental stages of students' minds and bodies, but these injunctions are mere formalities. The Ministry, with professional advice, writes the Course of Studies and curriculum and administrators; teachers may be dismissed for failing to adhere to them.[13]

Fifth, the Ministry exerts considerable power by temporary appointment of younger, capable personnel, destined for higher leadership, to prefectural and municipal educational and university administrative positions. Mombusho also achieves indirect control of educational institutions by appointing retired Mombusho officials to head important school, university, and other educational, cultural, and scientific institutes—a practice referred to as "falling from heaven."

Sixth, the Ministry of Education commands power by its direct and indirect control of in-service education.[14] Mombusho's co-optation of in-service workshops results in a prefectural selection processes that appoints submissive administrators and teachers. The Japan Teachers Union (JTU) complains further that administrators at all levels limit teachers' autonomy in conducting their own in-service programs by denying them funds, public meeting places, released time, or official recognition.[15]

Overwhelming power at the top breeds subservient Japanese educators' and students' passivity and limits local autonomy and creative responses to local needs. For the United States to borrow this system would lead to fundamental sacrifices of America's more democratic practices.[16]

TEXTBOOKS DEMONSTRATE LIMITATIONS TO EXCESSIVE CONTROLS

The preamble and articles 1, 2, and 9 of the FLE proclaim that the educational system shall aim at rearing a people "who love truth," "respect academic freedom," value "political knowledge necessary for intelligent citizenship," and "refrain from political education or other political activities for or against any specific political party." Textbook adoption procedures, however, fail to meet these ideals. They are "subject to improper control."

The CI&E's Education Division staff substituted for government-authored textbooks a free and privately authored textbook system subject only to a textbook and selection committee to guarantee professional quality. They demanded that textbooks be purged of mythology and historical content that glorified Japanese imperialism and emperors and focused narrowly on political history. Prehistory was to be supported by archaeology and Chinese records and each historical period to stress the people's economic, social, and cultural contributions.[17] Postwar history textbooks have largely followed SCAP's goals, but fidelity to SCAP objectives cannot be claimed for the textbook authorization system.[18]

The certification system severely limits the number of textbooks for each subject and grade level and maintains a degree of censorship that rejects a pluralistic society and unacceptable interpretations of poems, literature, and social and historical problems. This process violates the freedom of press and authors' academic freedom.[19] The Ministry's 1997 screening process led to the rejection of four of eighteen high school home economics textbooks because they had "not given enough attention to fostering good family life."[20] The author of a Contemporary Society textbook was ordered in 1991 to drop a passage that included the well-known historical fact that Fukuzawa Yukichi, a Meiji exponent of Western learning, had advocated Japan "disassociating itself with Asia and embracing the West." The Ministry said that expression was not typical of Fukuzawa's thought and distorted Japan's relationship with Asia during that time.[21]

Left-of-center authors complain that screened textbooks neglect treatment of minority groups, deep-seated social problems, environmental issues, Japan's aggressive post-1895 expansion into Asia and the Pacific, atrocities in East and Southeast Asia, and Occupation reforms. As a *Japan Times* subtitle indicated, "History is depicted to cast government, policies, society in favorable light."[22] The right wing counters by arguing that most history and social studies textbooks since 1945 have been written from a left-wing point of view that exaggerates the dark side of Japanese history.

Through the textbook licensing system the Ministry of Education and the right wing of the Liberal Democratic Party (LDP) have been able to eliminate or obscure facts critical of prewar Japanese foreign policy.[23] For example, they contend that the Nanjing Incident of 1937 never occurred, or they minimize it by disputing the number of victims. This tradition was continued on 16 March 1995 by Diet member Okuno Seisuke, a former justice minister, who said, "We did not fight Asian people. It is the United States and Britain that waged a war of aggression."[24] When one committee of the Prime Minister's National Council on Educational Reform wanted to recommend that the licensing system be discontinued, the LDP immediately created a study group that opposed any change because "neutrality of education" would be endangered. Although the NERC's first report recommended a free system, LDP pressure resulted in a final report that notoriously waffled by writing, "There is the opinion that efforts should be made to realize free publication and free adoption of textbooks in the long run, while there is also the opinion that we should be cautious about the abolition of textbook authorization and the shift to the free publication of textbooks."[25] Former Vice Minister of Education Hiroshi Kida rightly argues that there is no need for history textbooks deliberately to drown school children in historical guilt; nonetheless, history education has an obligation to teach truth to its youth according to their age level to enable them to better understand and prevent a repetition of the past.[26] The Ministry also has an obligation to avoid historical distortion achieved both by *omission* of facts as well as commission of error. It is in the omission of facts that the licensing system has been most culpable.[27]

By omission of supporting material, postwar social studies textbooks' treatment of the early Cold War period fail to be objective. Readers discover that the Korean War simply broke out; no assessment of responsibility is made. Textbooks gave the false impression that Eastern European countries became "socialist" spontaneously. The designation of the two sides of the Cold War as "capitalist" and "socialist" without explanation overlooks two facts: almost every country in the so-called capitalist world is now characterized by state-regulated capitalism or welfare state societies, and so-called "socialist" countries were really totalitarian communist.

Mombusho's authorization of the 1987 history textbook, *Shinpen Nihonshi* (A new edition of Japanese history), revived fears of prewar history textbook writing. A product of conservative, nationalistic scholars representing The National Congress for the Defense of Japan, this textbook features a lively style, interesting illustrations, vivid insertions separate from the running text, and an appealing emphasis on great men and women. Conversely, however, the authors tend to justify post-1868 foreign policy, extol Japanese emperors, and blur mythology and fact. Hence, the textbook has caused deep concern in Japan and abroad. Even though Mombusho insisted on many changes to remove some of the more blatant nationalism and questionable scholarship, its censorship of the political right is no more acceptable than that of the left wing. Fortunately, the textbook has captured less than 3 percent of the national market, mostly in Kyushu. However, if class discussion, debates, panel discussions, and extensive use of supplementary materials were possible in classrooms, the use of *Shinpen Nihonshi* would be welcome as a stimulus for students to engage in lively discussions of controversial issues.

American textbooks have become progressively politically correct to please domestic pressure groups, but because the views within them are those of private scholars publishing in a free market, the U.S. government is not entangled in the repeated diplomatic controversies of Japan. These books are also livelier in educational methodology and may stimulate further thought by presenting more than one interpretation of an issue. Textbook selection is left to market vagaries and the good sense of administrators and teachers. Good teachers also select a wide variety of supplementary materials to stimulate critical thinking of controversial historical issues.

The LDP and the Mombusho fear that left-wing authors and the JTU would manipulate a free textbook system to their ideological advantage. Control over textbook content stems from the myth perpetuated by the LDP and Mombusho that maintaining the present system ensures "neutrality of education." But because the LDP dominated the Japanese government until 1993 and again since 1995, the transmitting of its historical views in the nation's schools violates the FLE stipulation that schools shall "refrain from political education . . . for or against any specific political party." The censorship of history textbook content critical of Japan's aggressive post-1895 prewar foreign policies continually arouses the displeasure of neighboring East and Southeast Asian countries. Enormous government energies and money have been required by the Japanese government to defend itself from foreign criticism and from historian Ienaga Saburo's lawsuits extending over more than three decades. Sanitizing textbooks costs Japan international good will and compromises its ability to play a leadership role in East and Southeast Asia.[28]

Ironically, the view that the Japanese government should abandon the practice of screening high school textbooks gained strength from citizens' groups and normally conservative business leaders who would like to see a more diversified educational system and graduates that are more international minded, original, and individualistic. Although the LDP originally added such a provision to its draft platform for the November 1996 Lower House election, conservative LDP heavyweights removed this item on the grounds that "high school education would proceed in the wrong direction."[29]

Improved textbook procedures and somewhat greater coverage of controversial historical subjects occurred during the approximate one year that the LDP was ousted from power.[30] These few gains are now being countered by a group of conservative educators, mostly younger nonhistorians, led by Fujioka Nobukatsu, a professor of curriculum development and history education at the University of Tokyo; Kanji Nishio, a professor of German Literature; and Yoshinori Kobayashi, a cartoonist. They have formed the *Jiyushugi Shinkan Kenkyukai* (Libertarian Historical Research Society). Fujioka is a former communist who has found his new truth in nationalism. His group's goal is to write history and social studies textbooks "from the perspective of Japan and its national interests." They have become an organized political movement to bring pressure on the LDP and the Mombusho to eliminate textbook treatment that dishonors Japan. Their first major publication, Fujioka's *Kyokasho ga Oshienai Rekishi* (The history that the textbooks don't teach you) is aimed at elementary and junior high school students. The title is misleading. It does not lead into a discussion of dark aspects of modern Japanese history that have been omitted or glossed over in previously published textbooks.[31] Instead, the book provides half-truths, distorts, and whitewashes and rationalizes events not favorable to Japan. The book is a logical result of the dangerous and unacceptable belief that history education should serve a national interest rather than be written from the traditional goal of historians: objective search for truth that serves *no* national interest. "See no evil, speak no evil, hear no evil" could be Fujioka's motto. One example is the complete denial that so-called "comfort women" were forced into prostitution in wartime occupied areas by the Japanese army with the cooperation of the police and government.[32]

There is hope, however, for those who object to the present screening system. Way back in 1965, historian Saburo Ienaga sued the Mombusho for failing to pass his high school history textbook without substantial changes. Thirty-two years later Ienaga and his supporters finally have achieved a partial victory. The Third Petty Bench of the Supreme Court has ruled that the Education Ministry's deletion of a reference to the biological experiments on humans in China by the Imperial Army's infamous chemical warfare Unit 731 is unlawful. Screenings of the Nanjing Massacre of 1937 and other issues were also ruled illegal. But the Supreme Court also continued to reject Ienaga's view that textbook screening is fundamentally unconstitutional on the premise that "academic freedom does not include educational freedom in lower-level educational organs."[33]

AMERICA'S DECENTRALIZED EDUCATION'S STRENGTHS

America's greater decentralization of education allows schools to be creative and teachers and local administrators to be more flexible, innovative, and responsive to local needs. It avoids excessively standardized textbooks and courses of study and has an academic curriculum more responsive to student diversity. The American system allows local school boards much greater leeway to raise taxes, determine educational budgets, hire and fire teachers, build schools, adopt textbooks, and establish educational policy for their school districts. Mombusho and prefectures could continue to maintain high academic competence and fiscal equality through imposing high minimum standards on Japanese prefectures and local schools. Simultaneously, prefectural, metropolitan, and local school districts could adapt curriculum,

82 Japanese and American Education

courses of studies, and textbooks to their own needs. Prefectures and school districts could mandate other subjects or units within courses, even a different educational ladder system according to their needs—as encouraged by the NCER and practiced in America.[34]

Japan can learn from the effort of America's reform movements since the 1980s to encourage greater input at the local level from school administrators, teachers, and parents and to reduce the powerful role of an army of supervisory specialists at the central level. The direction in America is to reduce state regulations of the local level dealing with attendance quotas, state aid, and textbook selection. Instead, state legislatures and departments of education are encouraged to become more active in raising quality standards for such things as curriculum and courses of studies, moving federal funds to local schools, "and ensuring fiscal equality for schools."[35]

WEAKNESSES OF JAPAN'S CURRICULUM

Japanese Curriculum Neglects Individualized Education

After the Occupation ended, Mombusho revived centralized controls over the elementary and secondary curricula. The comprehensive curriculum in 90 percent of the nation's high schools is directed at the 39 percent who will go on to two-year or four-year colleges.[36] This approach should be replaced by a more comprehensive curriculum that will help noncollege-bound students achieve both academic competency and individualized education through more elective subjects at the secondary level, and greater consideration of students who cannot keep up with the academic program.

Japanese schools should serve their students more effectively by utilizing the modern technology Japan produces and imitate American medium and large schools that are using computers to achieve greater flexibility in subject and student scheduling and in curriculum planning.[37] In 1993, 74 percent of American students between grades one through six and 70.4 percent of grades seven through twelve were using computers.

Curriculum Slights Potentiality of Bright Students

The 1993–1994 secondary school curricular reforms attempt to escape from excessive emphasis upon a standardized curriculum focused almost entirely on the objective of passing entrance examinations has failed. Approximately 75 percent of secondary school students are still attending schools where even elective courses are basically similar for all. Bright students are only challenged by the competitive nature and teaching methodology of the very best private schools or cram schools.

American schools offer subject variety and student choice. Properly guided and motivated, American students in most medium and larger schools can study as much and at as fast a rate as they are capable of by being promoted beyond grade; taking accelerated courses; bussing to magnet schools for special courses; and enrolling in a college course(s) (or as full-time college students when they have outstanding abilities). In secondary schools they can take special courses such as Russian or East Asian History, Shakespeare, Great Literature, advanced composition, poetry, and advanced art, music, science, and math courses. They may elect to be challenged also by honors courses in one or all of the core courses. In them they will be expected to read widely, to write book reviews, term reports, and literary criticisms, and to undertake a difficult scientific or math project. Students are encouraged to think deeply about what has been read and to discuss and debate with their teachers and peers their understandings and interpretations.

Limitations for Handicapped Students

Japan's treatment of handicapped children is a mixed bag. In some ways it can be argued that they do a better job than American schools in mainstreaming more of the less seriously handicapped students than in America. Part of the reason is the high cost of special education. But Stevenson and Stigler argue that the reason also is that Chinese and Japanese educators "believe that the differences among children are not great enough to warrant the allocation of funds for special programs. High costs, both for the individual and for society, may result from expectations that are too low."[38]

For the more physically and mentally handicapped, American school programs and policies are superior to Japanese schools. Although progress in Japanese education has been made for handicapped students, special education is inferior to America in terms of physical facilities, equipment, staff training, and numbers of students taught in special education classes or mainstreamed in regular schools. Thirty-four percent (1.6 million) of America's disabled persons three-to twenty-one-years-old (actually too high of a percentage to allow the overwhelming majority of students to move at greater speed and content depth—another good attitude carried to excess) are being educated in regular classes.[39] Only 1 percent of Japan's total school children receive special education. Special classes are available at only 44 percent of the nation's elementary and junior high schools.[40] In fact, in 1985 only 3 percent of the total expenditures on education went to special education.[41] The Ministry of Education only began to mainstream students with less serious handicaps in elementary and junior high schools in 1990 on an experimental basis.[42] Because Ministry guidelines do not include disabled children within the authorized limit of forty students to a classroom, teachers are reluctant to accept them.

Japan's tendencies for special education are three in number. One is to treat special education children so protectively they foster dependency. Accordingly, they send the blind and deaf and the partially blind and deaf children to special education schools. A second one is to hide mentally and physically disadvantaged children because of traditional attitudes that (a) parents should restrain from pursuing their own handicapped children's gain at the expense of other nonhandicapped children, (b) the child's condition is a punishment for past transgressions, or (c) that handicapped children bring shame on parents and are an embarrassment to the surrounding society. Third, special education also has been hindered because there are few jobs for the handicapped.

Curriculum Limitations for Unitalented Students

Another casualty of the Japanese system is the student who has superior ability and interest in only one subject. Merry White describes the example of a very bright student, Yukio, with strong academic talent and interest in only mathematics.[43] There is no accelerated mathematics track for him, and he is viewed only as a mediocre student for whom hope to attend a major university "would be useless." Although the new vocational high schools, comprehensive high schools, and comprehensive programs may open the door more widely to students like Yukio, the current chances of unitalented students attending a university are severely limited because national university entrance examinations are given in five subjects, and in three subjects in most other universities. Yukio will probably enter only a low-ranking technical school and follow his father's footsteps of being a factory technician. Unitalented students end up dropping out of school or attending trade schools after graduation. Lopsided students are also at a disadvantage because Japanese industries prefer to recruit generalists who can be trained for whatever specialization companies desire. Here is another example of how the business community bends education to fit its narrow needs.

American schools are doing a better job for unitalented and gifted students because of the ability to nurture students' special skills through elective courses, magnet schools, advanced placement courses, and access of some students to college classes. By such alternatives many unitalented students can develop their specialization in college or a good technical institute. And, after they enter college and become more mature, they become more open-minded to other subjects.

Inadequacies of Curriculum for the Noncollege Bound

The merits of Japan's schools for ensuring reading, writing, and numerary competency for those not university bound are somewhat exaggerated. The number of noncollege bound graduates who can not obtain employment immediately upon graduation has been increasing every year for the past ten years because industries will not hire them without attending various kinds of special schools for one to two years to obtain the skills that companies want.[44] In 1994, the number of high school graduates who were not hired by industry.

reached a high of 400,000, and their numbers increase yearly because of the recession. The failure of the general schools and even universities to make a few courses such as English more relevant to subsequent employment makes students less attractive for industry. Japan's new vocational schools and comprehensive schools to be discussed in Chapter 7 could help graduates find employment, but the numbers of such schools are still insignificant.[45]

There are other attitude problems. In practice, Japanese society and schools slight practical subjects and anything that is not difficult. The overwhelming emphasis is on academic subject matter. The students find themselves caught in a no-win dilemma. Large industries have been prone to think only of what is good for them, and they do not particularly favor vocational education on the premise that they can teach the required technical skills; however, a large percentage of high school graduates will end up working for small industries and service industries that offer little training. Students avoid attending low-prestige vocational schools because they do not want to mortgage their future social and economic life.

Japanese schools should allow students to elect more nonacademic courses at the secondary school level and allow a greater number of vocational subjects at academic schools. The value of attending a misnamed "comprehensive" high school for its vocational program is limited if only nine to eleven school hours a week can be devoted to a nonacademic and vocational curriculum. Ironically, however, liberal Japanese and the JTU accept the view that the curriculum and the textbooks should not be significantly different for the college and noncollege bound because all students, even vocational ones, will have an opportunity to enter college. This is a delusion somewhat similar to the American dream of rising from rags to riches.

To achieve America's more individualized education, greater emphasis on individuality and democratic education will mean an increase in Japan's educational expenditures. It will also mean that Japanese schools' actual teacher–student ratios will have to be lowered and the number of counselors increased.

Three high school Japanese teacher–friends say the percentage of students who fall behind other students academically is 30 percent or more. In fact, cynics often refer to the Japanese education system as a "7, 5, 3" system— that is 70 percent can do the work in elementary school, 50 percent in junior high school, and 30 percent in senior high school.[46] Among those students who attend higher ranked schools the problem of keeping up with one's classmates is not as great. The problem occurs among the low-achieving 30 percent of elementary school students and the bottom 60 percent of secondary schools, where the lower the ranking of the school the greater the number of students who will fall behind the expectations of the mandated courses of studies. For this reason one principal of a commercial senior high school strongly recommended that steps be taken to correct reading, writing, and math skills at the elementary level before students are passed on to the next level.[47]

Limitations of Vocational Curriculum and Schools

One serious problem connected with Japanese centralized education is that it has been too explicitly geared to national economic needs. A 1966 recommendation of the Central Council for Education, Japan's highest advisory organ to Mombusho, recommended more diversified vocational education to suit students' abilities and aptitudes as well as to increase job specialization. The objective was primarily to promote government goals of high economic growth by producing junior technicians for Japan's industries, but the plan backfired. According to Takakura and Murata, the policy "lacked a definite vision for the development of industry and technology and created [a] further subdivision of vocational courses and differences in quality between the general [academic] course and the vocational course. . . . Motivation to study as well as the fundamental scholastic ability of students in the lower rank has not been adequate." Those students forced to attend vocational schools are inclined to choose apathy, resentment, violence, or dropping out of school. Between 1966 and 1992 the number of high school students enrolled in the Vocational Course decreased from approximately 1,580,000 to 1,144,180, and students in the General Course (academic course) increased from approximately 2,900,000 students to 3,859,817.[48]

Agricultural schools suffer particularly low prestige and have experienced declining enrollments over the past few years. Mito Agricultural High School in Ibaragi Prefecture, a famous dormitory school with a 100-year history and located on 125 acres, was forced to drop one department because of severely declining enrollments.

Limitations of Art and Music in Curriculum

Japanese elementary school students achieve a much higher performance than American ones in art and music, but this point needs to be qualified. In the summer of 1963, I participated in a two-month program with a group of veteran high school teachers that included two art consultants. On our daily visitations to Japanese schools from kindergarten through college, we concluded that Japanese sixth graders' art and music levels were approximately three grades superior to their American counterparts, but we were puzzled by a partial closing of the gap at the high school level. In 1997, there are still three major reasons for Japanese students excelling American students at the elementary school level: (1) art and music are offered more times a week, (2) Japanese society and schools devote greater attention to aesthetics, and (3) elementary teachers possess greater competence in art and music than their American counterparts.

Why is the gap closed at the secondary school level? Japanese students attending junior high schools before 1993 could take only seventy minutes a week each of music and fine arts in grades seven and eight, and only one class hour of each in grade nine. Because of the new high school curriculum reform, art and music courses have been further reduced. Japanese high school students can choose only one subject for one to three hours a week from among Music, Fine Art, Crafts Production, and Calligraphy (stylized writing of Chinese characters).[49] In contrast, American high school students who select art and music generally possess interest and ability. They will be able to attend those classes five times a week for each subject they elect. The Japanese curriculum should be more flexible to allow students to take more art and music. Another reason the skill gap is closed is that by the time Japanese students enter junior high school, many dislike art and music education. These subjects are considered too academic, demanding, and standardized. Students' interest is killed in art by excessively prescribed themes, colors, form, and perspective, conformity to prescribed patterns or models, and rigorous standards.

English Education

The lack of flexibility in Japanese schools and their fear of offering classes based on abilities and interests can be seen in private (as well as public schools) approach to the teaching of English. A well-developed English program from kindergarten through elementary school is often articulated. According to the Center for the Study of Book-Form Teaching Materials, 87 percent of private primary schools teach English as either a formal or extracurricular subject, and 77 percent of public primary schools and 91 percent of private primary schools believe English should begin at the elementary school level. But when students enter the first year of public junior high school, they are placed in first-year English classes with those who have studied no English to achieve group solidarity and uniformity. This practice is another example of two Japanese social attitudes carried to excess: a combination of *ashinami o soroeru* (keeping everyone in step), and *deru kugi wa utareru* (preventing anyone from standing out above others). Student skills and parental expenditures on English instruction are wasted. Those students with English skills are bored for the first two years of junior high school English classes, and many students initiated to English instruction are intimidated by those students who already possess a good foundation.

Language Laboratories and Libraries

Language laboratories and libraries are not as effectively used as in the United States. Libraries at the senior high level are primarily used as a reference room for studying entrance examination-related materials, and are generally occupied at noon and after school. Students are not ordinarily released to go to them to undertake a teacher-assigned topic nor are entire classes taken to the library for research-related tasks. Language laboratories increased greatly in Japan's high economic growth period and are of good quality, but they are infrequently used after the first year of junior high school because of the pressure of entrance examinations. The inclusion of English oral communication as a new subject in the post-1994 high school curriculum may correct this condition, but only if most universities include an oral examination in their entrance examinations.

Methodology

Under the present educational centralization Japanese secondary school teachers are severely handicapped in carrying out the goals of the Fundamental Law on Education: "cultivating a spontaneous spirit" and creating a culture "rich in individuality." Although Japanese nursery, kindergarten, and elementary teachers could provide many hints to improve the methodology of their American counterparts, the reverse is true at the secondary and college levels. American teachers try to encourage students to be creative in approaching a problem, writing an essay, sketching an object, suggesting an appropriate elective course, recommending a book, or encouraging some intellectual challenge.

Japanese secondary school teachers' goal is too narrowly focused on presenting designated textual material in as efficient a manner as possible. One Tsukuba University graduating senior said she had only encountered three secondary school teachers and two university teachers who motivated her to *want* to study. Duke thought Japanese teachers should distinguish between "instruction" and "education" and wrote, "If one were somewhat crudely to evaluate the average teacher . . . on instruction, the Japanese teacher would receive a grade of A to B; the U.S. teacher, a B to C. On education, as loosely defined above, the U.S. teacher would receive a B to C; the Japanese, a C to D."[50] This judgment on Japanese teachers is too harsh, but it has merit as a generalization because of the circumstances that force them to be much more insensitive to differing learning processes or individualized education than they would prefer.

Counseling and Specialists

American elementary and secondary schools spend too much money on supplementary professional personnel; nevertheless, Japanese schools could benefit from a greater availability of reading and writing specialists and counselors to deal with troubled individuals, dyslexia, school refusal, bullying, delinquency, and college or vocational counseling.[51] Specialists in reading, writing, and mathematics could help those students who are falling behind rather than leaving these tasks to cram schools and private tutors. To meet the different needs of a changing student population, the number of counselors was increased from 1 for every 934 pupils in 1959 to 1 for every 508 pupils in 1990.[52] That figure is inadequate. To meet the challenges the Education Ministry responded in 1995 by appointing clinical psychologists, but for only eight hours each week to three schools in each prefecture. The 1996 budget increased these specialists from 141 to 506, a start but woefully inadequate for a nation with more than 41,000 elementary and secondary schools.[53] The appointed counselors protest that eight hours a week is completely inadequate for counseling teachers and parents who do not understand children; however, they reported significant success in dealing with bullying and school-refusers. Many of Japan's gifted, slow, and troubled secondary students feel frustrated from these curriculum deficiencies. Worse, as we shall see in the next section, they complain of a school climate that excessively emphasizes rules and regulations.

SCHOOL RULES AND CONTROLLED EDUCATION

Education's goal is to preserve a balance between the needs of the individual and those of society, between the need to promote individual liberty and identity, and the need to preserve unity and social order. Indulging the former too much neglects the common good and invites anarchy. Too much emphasis on social order and uniformity, however, as in Japan, invites a subtle, oppressive conformity and collectivism. Chapter 2 discussed the positive aspects of Confucianism that engender respect for learning and the values of rank, order, and harmony. To its discredit, however, Confucianism said nothing about the innate equality of gender, of humans before the law, or about freedom or individual rights. Japanese schools, especially junior high schools and strict private and public senior high schools, impose so many rules, organizational procedures, and forms upon students that they deny students' human dignity and individuality and create passive, cautious, insecure, and conforming students. They suppress the independent spirit, individuality, assertiveness, humanity, and creativity that Japanese society needs in a rapidly changing and competitive world. I wish to strongly emphasize one caveat: *Many individual school practices, such as belonging to the same school club, are not harmful in themselves.* Indeed, as we have seen, they play a major role in shaping good student behavior, adapting students to group life, teaching class management and common sense, and helping students achieve a high academic performance. Rather, it is the *total combination of so many rigid rules, forms, and organizational procedures* that produces harmful practices in many Japanese schools.[54]

As in prewar Japan, society becomes much stricter, learning more rigorous and formal, and school rules and regulations more rigid, hierarchical, and complex after students complete elementary school. By the middle schools they constitute a rite of passage. As LeTendre says, "Up to middle school children are allowed to just 'grow.' In middle school children are trained, guided and shaped. Within middle school, children experience an academic teaching style that is far less relaxed and comforting than the one they knew in elementary school."[55] In this context *The New York Times* correspondent in Japan wrote in a lively, and generally well-informed article a slightly exaggerated view: "The tragedy of Japan's school system is that it produces cheerful and outspoken fifth graders who in junior high become surly cynics."[56]

But all the blame for secondary schools' problems mentioned above do not begin suddenly when students enter junior high school; nor is it all the fault of the entrance examination systems. Even Lewis, an ardent advocate of adopting many Japanese practices, expressed concern at peer pressures she witnessed in some classrooms, such as whether classmates had remembered textbooks, cut their fingernails, brought handkerchiefs and tissues to school, and reported delinquent class members. She also wondered whether school rules enforcing the correct way to do things such as arranging desk contents, stowing shoes, taking blackboard notes, and bringing the correct numbers of pencils, erasers, and handkerchiefs undermined "students' willingness to think and act as individuals," socialized them "to feel anxious about any difference from peers," and taught them "to look to precedent" rather than "to rely on personal judgment." She speculated significantly:

Detailed regulation of children's behavior during the elementary years may accustom children to accept, during their later development, regulation Americans would consider arbitrary. Although this method may create tractable students and employees, it may not foster thoughtful, independent behavior. Accounts of Japanese junior high school education suggest that regulation of students' behavior during this period escalates, sometimes becoming harsh, authoritarian, and arbitrary.[57]

Lewis is right to be concerned. Although most problems arising from controlled education occur at the junior high level, the uniformity imposed on students begins with early education and good school practices such as ritualism, sacrifice of self, and restraint of individual goals for achieving group consciousness and harmony; small groupings fostering responsibility, self-restrained, and self-sacrificing behavior patterns for achieving good classroom management; and self-reflection and self-discipline for achieving students' influence over their own and other students' behavior. However, these practices become progressively excessive by the upper elementary grades and junior high schools. Although I have praised nursery and elementary schools' cultivation of the Japanese virtue of *sunao* in the preceding chapter, one student wisely wrote, "However, I think always being *sunao* produces people who are very passive, always doing what they have been told, and cannot decide anything by themselves."

For another example, Nicholas Kristof has written approvingly that "teachers do not punish [elementary] students who misbehave; rather they manipulate other students to scold the culprit into feeling guilty. It is the manipulation that is a key to primary and preschool education in Japan, and the teachers are the most masterful manipulators imaginable."[58] But through this instrumental manipulation, by the time students reach secondary school they have become excessively critical of deviance from group norms, fearful of making mistakes, hesitant to act independently, and willing to accept collective group pressures that crush the individuality that the Ministry of Education wants to foster. When parents complained to Kristof that all these practices were only a formality because they had little impact on the behavior of their children at home, they were missing the point. Children can be more individualistic at home because of the traditional child-rearing practices. On the point of making mistakes I disagree with Rohlen and LeTendre that Japanese schools' learning process instills confidence.[59] Quite the contrary, the system creates considerable student insecurity, a point made over and over again by my students. Furthermore, corporal punishment also does not begin at the junior high level. Many of my students have witnessed or experienced it at the elementary school level.

One example of excessive uniformity is the current schools' opposition to diverse school supplies. One mother complained that when a second daughter entered elementary school she sent her with a knapsack and educational supplies that were in excellent condition, but had been used by an elder daughter at the same school. The male teacher objected, saying that "all the children should possess exactly the same items." Again when the younger daughter became a third grader the mother sent her to school with a good recorder (a simple type of flute) that had been used by the older sister. A different male teacher objected by saying the recorder would be different from other students and might make a different sound. The mother protested on both occasions that the schools were condoning wastefulness and imposing unnecessary uniformity on school children. Both veteran teachers silenced her by saying that she was the first parent to object to such practices—an old technique of schools to divide and rule. They made her feel foolish and uncooperative by saying "because of parents such as you, education has become more difficult."

At many schools training suits used for elementary school physical education classes must be of a different color each school year for three years, whereupon the same colors are rotated again in the same order for the next three years. Schools have adopted the attitudes that it is easier to carry on schooling and less embarrassing for children if they do not stand out from the group by different clothing and educational supplies—more uniformity.

CONTEXT FOR DIFFERING ATTITUDES
REGARDING SCHOOL RULES

Americans conceive of democracy, citizenship, and development of character as a process learned through actual experience. As *ideals*, Americans believe that students are young adults and can only acquire the democratic attitudes and maturity essential for active citizenship by increasing students' freedom, spirit of independence, and adult responsibility with the passage of each year. Teachers and administrators are expected to nurture a democratic environment by respecting students' human dignity, irrespective of age, race, sex, or religion. It is believed to be contradictory and hypocritical to surround them with regimentation and corporal punishment. Consequently, American students reflect their elders' tendency to think they are free to act as long as there are no specific rules or laws to prohibit action. They feel trusted and treated as individuals and young adults. Admittedly, viewing teenagers as young adults carries the potential for poor discipline and order, because too many students define freedom as meaning a condition without rules and punishment. Here, however, American schools face a dilemma. If they deviate from these ideals by treating students as children without rights, they seem hypocritical in students' eyes. Citizenship is killed, not nurtured.

Conversely, three things are clear about the context of Japanese school's controlled education (*kanri kyoiku*): (1) Most Japanese do not trust people to act responsibly without rules and regulations; (2) in Japanese lifestyle guidance, there is the basic view that children need to learn a correct style of living in every sense of the word, which means teachers must pay much greater attention to details regarding students' behavior and a much greater invasion of students' private life and thought than in Western society;[60] and (3) Japanese are a risk-avoiding people, increasingly so today and are uncomfortable where an absence of rules, customs, and forms invite ambiguity, diversity of opinions, and individual autonomy. They think they are only free to act *if* rules or laws *allow* them to act. The safe way is the prescribed way of custom, rule, and uniformity.

When the Allied Occupation of Japan ended, concerned conservatives argued that the reforms provided too much emphasis upon child-centered education and individuality, and that too many postwar Japanese parents lacked the confidence in child rearing to impose their authority. To fill this vacuum they argued for the revival of moral education to instill traditional values. But because postwar moral education courses have not proved very effective, school rules and regulations, forms, and group activities have taken on even greater importance as a means of shaping and controlling student behavior.[61]

Japanese reared in a Confucian tradition and a "catch up with the West" mentality have allowed the state to grant schools a wide authority over students' behavior within and outside school grounds to achieve order and to shape students' character. There is little ambiguity over schools' role and students' obligations. The Japanese say high school students are children, and schools should treat them as children with no rights. Schools are viewed as instruments for teaching character formation appropriate to public life which places priority on rank, order, and harmony. The principal of a girls' senior high school, where a sixteen-year-old died from corporal punishment administered by a teacher, kept emphasizing that he insists on a policy of "establishing school traditions through tight discipline." At the same school a survey showed that many of its teachers administered corporal punishment. Students who were tardy for class or rebellious were struck on their heads or other body parts with "clenched fists, bamboo sticks, roll call books, or the like."[62]

The total cultural matrix and fear of adverse public relations makes Japanese schools fear innovation, individual creativity, and individuality, but as a high school teacher I heard three different American principals urge teachers preparing for the new school year to "try something new this year." This American emphasis on innovation is carried to excess, but I cannot imagine Japanese principals challenging their teachers in a similar vein. The system makes principals (and teachers) a very cautious lot whose mentality toward administering a school is somewhat similar to running a factory. They and many teachers want uniformity and order to insure supplying products efficiently and qualitatively and to avoid disorder that will bring adverse public relations. Many lack trust in students, but more importantly societal pressures and good public relations make them want to escape responsibility for student accidents, harmful bullying by students, and any other problems by covering potential problems with school rules. For example, if a student gets hurt while working part time, riding a motorcycle, shopping, or while staying overnight at a friend's home, school rules against such activities release the principal and school from legal responsibility. Or if a student does not successfully pass entrance examinations, but the school has provided a strict climate that enhances their success, the parents cannot fault the school.

Another aspect that puts the Japanese educational system in context is that the pressures and rigidity of the college-bound curriculum creates student frustration and negative attitudes. One American doctoral candidate researching the bottom 20 percent of Japanese schools concludes that they manage to control the students by both academic and cultural means.

The academic method forces the students to do a fair amount of low level brain-numbing work that stifles their intellect and their spirit, but allows them to pass if they are quiet, come to class regularly, and pay attention enough to pass simple tests. The cultural method is that they are persuaded that growing up means learning to endure the unendurable and that if they work hard they may make it to college. They learn that if they do not go along, they will be kicked out. They do not understand that the whole game is rigged, that the Japanese economy needs their low-level obedient labor not in the white collar offices, but in the factories and small businesses. . . . The second not-so-cultural answer is that the enforcement of the school rules are so severe that if they do not go along, they will be kicked out. The first-year students begin with a large amount of class disruptions and general rowdiness. There are usually a large number of suspensions, (as many as three students per day, as of three years ago), which leads to a large number of expulsions (as many as 1/3 of the class at times). With the worst of the bunch out, the remaining ones lack leadership, and, finally, seem to settle down. Rather than students taking stock of their future, and getting things together, I think that the more realistic interpretation is that they have the fight kicked out of them, and they succumb to a force that they recognize as greater than themselves. Unlike dropouts in the U.S. who may become role models for other dropouts, they also know that society will look down upon those who do not graduate from high school.[63]

When I interviewed Kimura Kazumi, a retired teacher at Mitsukaido Nishi Junior High School, he thought discipline problems at that level occurred because school is compulsory, too demanding, and too controlled.[64] At a nearby junior high school on graduation day, thirteen students had engaged in a quiet protest against the school by dying their hair various colors, wearing clothing in violation of the graduation code, and stitching on the back of their gowns the words, "Mother, we are sorry to have caused you so much trouble." All of them received diplomas, but none were recommended for any high school. Only one of their mothers attended the graduation ceremony—either because they were ashamed or were working full time.

Japanese schools also exert control over the students inside and outside school boundaries because of violent university student demonstrations of the late 1960s and early 1970s that closed the doors of such universities as Tokyo University, International Christian University, and Yokohama National University, which spread downward. Just as Americans went too far in the 1960s and 1970s in emphasizing student rights, the ruling LDP and Japanese establishment came to fear nonconformity and violence. To institute crisis management, the Diet passed a University Control Act in June 1969 and revised it in the late 1970s. The government now has the right to intervene in school affairs, universities are given greater authority to suppress demonstrations and control dissidents, and many regulations require students to obtain university approval for such things as circulating fliers, holding an assembly, and giving a speech. At Tsukuba University incoming freshmen must sign an agreement that they will not participate in demonstrations. Failure to comply can lead to automatic expulsion.

At many secondary schools students occupied buildings, boycotted classes, held demonstrations, and verbally attacked teachers and administrators. Some schools met this student resistance by abolishing almost all rules, but most reacted by repression. From the late 1960s these rules and newly installed heavy steel sliding gates at school entrances create the impression that schools are containing prison inmates.[65] The NCER thought controlled education ignored children's individuality and human rights and that meeting violence with more violence was counterproductive and a serious cause for the greater bullying and school violence of the mid-1980s.[66] In general four kinds of schools carry rules to excess: many strict private girls schools, many public junior high schools, relatively new, ambitious senior high schools eager to attain prestige as an institution whose graduates attend quality Japanese universities, and the lower 40 percent of senior high schools where the pressure of entrance examinations and confidential student conduct reports has less influence on restraining student behavior.

Many of my students complain that they have become so accustomed to an environment where everything is proscribed that they lack confidence and judgment for appropriate behavior and decision making. Rules foster distrust, conformity, and an interesting paradox. At the same time as students yearn for greater freedom and choice, they gradually internalize the view that a controlling and conforming environment is "comfortable," "protective," and "easy," that is, it becomes easier to conform than to oppose or to be different from others. This contradictory thinking resulted in an interesting discussion with a 1994 Nanzan senior class that challenged my view that Japanese youth accept unconsciously these conditions more than they realize. But during a renewed discussion of this issue in the next week's class, one student who had won the Dean's prize for highest academic achievement challenged his fellow students by saying, "I think even young people in their deepest minds are uncomfortable where there is a lack of rules, customs, and regulations to govern behavior." He expanded his meaning by saying, "The invisible obligations of Japanese customs are even more important than the visible written school rules. They make even young Japanese conservative." Students laughed but felt his comments were persuasive.

About one-half of incoming Nanzan University students have attended strict junior high schools. They did not like them because of excessive rules and regimentation and corporal punishment. Many complain of their middle school teachers as "mean," too critical of their lifestyle, and "lacking common sense." One Nanzan student complained bitterly that "school rules are so strict and students so regulated that students do not know how to act independently and to know right from wrong." When strict school regulations prevail, schools and students become easier places to administer. In my view, however, the four categories of schools mentioned above are swimming against the children's physical and emotional growth stages, the needs of Japan in the twenty-first century, and the demands of a participatory democracy. Schools are treating students as sheep, when the students want to have their individuality and dignity respected. The NCER lamented that the "desolation" and "negative effects" of formal schooling were due to "the rigidity, uniformity and closedness of educational activities at school, the undue emphasis in society on the educational background of individuals, and the tendency to impose excessive controls on students."[67] One Nanzan female complained, "We could not understand why school rules were necessary, and often asked teachers about them. But they only repeated, 'Because you are still children you don't understand,' or they said angrily, 'Your duty is only to abide by school regulations.' Students hated the school rules. Some fought against teachers, but they were regarded as 'problem children.'"

Two qualifications must be made. First, many students attending prestigious private and national universities have not experienced strict regulations as secondary students. They are not familiar with teacher-administered corporal punishment, violence of students against teachers, and absurdly strict rules. Second, students are increasingly aware that many teachers are not sympathetic with some rules. One Nanzan University student wrote, "I remember that most of the teachers in charge of home rooms from elementary to high school did not enforce rules strictly. I think it is because they also considered those rules absurd. For example, I went to high school by bicycle though it was prohibited." Nonetheless, many teachers that oppose rigid school practices feel forced to forsake their individual preference for the lock-step approach they must take with other teachers.

SPECIFIC RULES AND IMPACT OF CONTROLLED
EDUCATION WITHIN SCHOOLS

The Japan Bar Association's 1985 survey of 595 junior and 293 senior high schools revealed many rigid, detailed rules covering almost every aspect of students' social and academic life off and on the campus.[68] Many schools prohibit any jewelry; junior high schools may even prohibit watches. Almost all senior high schools do not allow wearing any makeup. At stricter private schools, girls may not remain at school after 5 P.M. during most of the school year, or after 4:30 P.M. in the winter. At elementary and some private post-elementary schools the students may not ride bicycles to school. In many schools students must not leave books at school even though lockers may be available. They must carry them only in the school-designated briefcase. Some schools prohibit (rather unsuccessfully) students stopping any place on the way to and from school or carrying comic books or magazines to school. They may not be in the bathroom more than seven minutes and cannot enter as a group. One Nanzan student complained that at his sister's school the students may not wear a muffler until exactly 1 December, no matter how cold it may be. In some elementary schools in Ibaragi Prefecture the students must ride the same style and prescribed color of bicycle: Girls may ride only white bicycles; boys may ride only black ones. At other schools the prescribed color may be red. At Meisei Gakuen junior and senior high schools in western Tokyo, boys and girls may not ride bicycles from the train station to the school even though it is a fifteen to twenty-minute walk.

Rules prevail in regard to apparel. Uniforms are not bad in themselves; rather, it is the detailed rigidity regarding school uniforms and the purposes for which schools use them that are objectionable. Many schools dictate the exact length and number of pleats in girls' skirts and the style of boys' and girls' uniforms.[69] At a few schools the pockets of boys' uniforms must be sewn shut to prevent students from putting their hands in them. Uniforms are also used to prevent students bringing unfavorable publicity on the school. One Nanzan student wrote, "School rules and uniforms exist for the schools' protection, not students' human rights. These rigid attitudes inevitably suppress students' personalities."

Rules prevail in regard to other clothing. In some schools females must wear white socks no more than 5 centimeters above the ankles. Teachers measure the socks and uniforms with a ruler. One way that female students nationwide rebel against these regulations is to enter the closest restroom outside the school at the end of the school day, put on long, loose white socks that are turned down to a length a few inches below the knee, apply glue stick to their calves, and then pull the sock to that level to achieve the desired baggy effect. They are a pathetic example of youth seeking individuality, but conforming to the wear of other female students throughout the nation. One

Nanzan student complained of a strict club advisor who "always carried a bamboo sword with him to check the length of our uniforms. He marked a line on his bamboo sword at 30 centimeters from the floor. If our skirts was longer than the line, he hit us with it. Club advisors were generally stricter than homeroom teachers." Some strict, private girls' schools prohibit wearing any color of panties other than white, and at most schools girls' uniform blouses must always expose white undergarments, never bare skin. At most junior high schools, girls may not wear hair ribbons; at the senior high level they may wear only black, brown, or dark blue ones. Most junior high schools ban perfume, scented deodorant, earrings, makeup, money, and nonstandard school bags.[70]

At most schools students' hairstyles must meet precise specifications. Girls cannot perm or curl their hair or use hair mousse; it must not fall below the eyebrows or touch the shoulders unless it is tied up by a black string or ribbon. At some schools those with naturally curly or wavy hair are expected to inform the school at registration time to prevent them from being accused of getting a permanent. Males at some schools cannot part their hair.[71] Students' hair must be black. At one Okayama prefectural girls' school, a hair color check is held once a month. At the first inspection of the year, 131 of the 1,500 girls were required to have their natural hair dyed because their hair had a natural brown tint, an arbitrary rule against which one local beautician expressed much sympathy for the students.[72] Girls with naturally curly hair are under suspicion. Private girls schools may hold "wet down" inspections in the gym to determine whether girls are perming their hair. Violators have their hair cut on the spot.[73]

Until recently, in Chiba Prefecture's junior high schools and in the cities of Kobe, Fukushima, and Kagoshima, as in many other junior schools nationwide, all male students had to wear a closely cropped haircut. When the son of Aichi Education University's Professor Akio Moriyama's son contested the Okazaki City Aoi Junior High School blanket rule requiring cropped haircuts on the grounds that it violated his rights, the school was forced to back down. His hair was 6 centimeters longer than the school-mandated rule of 0.9 centimeters. The son, with strong parental backing, refused steadfastly to shave his head, and was consequently hazed by upperclassmen and sports club members. Teachers who from the beginning had characterized him as rebellious threatened him by telling him that they would have older students punish him if he did not comply with the rule. Hazing continued even after Professor Moriyama threatened a suit. Moriyama received many abusive telephone calls, some telling him to get out of town. It was only after the mass media made the boy a nationally known figure that teacher and student bullying stopped.[74] Moved into action by his own son's experience, Moriyama has become active nationwide in speaking in various communities to oppose cropped hair cuts, school rules, and teacher violence. He is both the cause and effect of a heightened citizen's consciousness over the past seven years against controlled education. At one such meeting in Ushiku City in Ibaragi Prefecture, one teacher expressed the view that large classes of forty-five to fifty-five students make it impossible for classroom teachers to deal with students as individuals.

A good critique of the extent to which rules prevail in some schools has been compiled by Takeshi Hayashi's *Fuzakeru na, kosoku!* (Stop the nonsense, school rules!). The book encouraged so many people throughout the nation to report other examples of silly rules that two sequels have been published.[75] The magazine *Sebuntin* (Seventeen) for a while carried each week an example of an absurd school rule it opposed. On a television program devoted solely to school rules, a psychologist exaggeratedly complained that the schools were worse than prisons and turned the students into robots. A 1987 national survey of 2,698 junior high school teachers showed that 86 percent of them supported strict rules. Reflecting the strong preference of Japanese for uniformity and neatness, 95 percent of them believed that disorderly attire reflected mental disorder and that nonproscribed hairstyles were related to delinquency. Two-thirds of them thought the schools should control the kinds of socks students wore and should prevent students from visiting amusement centers.[76]

SPECIFIC RULES OUTSIDE THE SCHOOL DEMONSTRATING CONTROLLED EDUCATION

Japanese school rules apply even to nonscheduled school activities beyond the schools' physical boundaries because most parents want schools to limit students' activities and to teach them the public behavior that parents should inculcate. My Nagoya University seminar class concluded that when students engage in misbehavior in Japan the tendency of observers is to comment on how schools are failing, but in America the same situation would provoke a reaction that parents are not disciplining their children. To control students' behavior outside school grounds, a number of rules and practices prevail. By national law students are forbidden to smoke and drink alcohol until they are twenty. These rules are greatly violated, but it does give support to schools. Below are examples of the authority many schools exercise outside the campus:

1. When a child commits a misdemeanor or has an accident away from school grounds, the police notify the school before they notify the parent.
2. Elementary school students are not allowed to go out of the school district or to purchase food on the way home from school. For this reason a friend's daughter refused to purchase items at a supermarket because she feared reprisals from school authorities.
3. At some junior high schools, students are required to obtain permission from the school before going on a nonschool trip involving an overnight stay or even dur-

ing school vacations and Sundays. Even if the parents are accompanying the child on a trip, permission must be obtained from the school.

4. Students at many private, and apparently some public, high schools have to carry a special student notebook that contains all the school rules and a printed form on which any deviation from the usual pattern of going to and from school must be authorized by the school and parents. If children want to see a movie they must receive written parental authorization. The destination, the name of the accompanying person, the objective, and what time the student will return home must be listed on the form.

Another interesting phenomenon is that some schools, especially newer ones, attempt to raise their prestige by adopting very strict rules, increasing their academic rigor by holding daily preschool and/or after-school classes, holding their worst students back one year (something that almost never occurs), and making sure that the students take their books home. These last three measures are not inherently bad, but schools are thinking less of the student than their own reputation. Parents and teachers also try to raise the prestige of the school and morale of the students by a system of rotating parents and teachers for greeting students on their arrival at school.

CONTROLLED EDUCATION VIA THE CONFIDENTIAL STUDENT REPORT

A powerful system for obtaining student and parent cooperation with school regulations is the much-abused confidential teacher evaluations (*naishinsho*) of students' conduct. It is transmitted at the time students seek admittance from junior to senior high school and from senior high school to colleges and universities, but it is not a serious impediment for senior high school students. The report includes not only students' grades, achievement tests, and recommendations, but also past disciplinary action and teachers' personal remarks regarding students' conduct. It gives middle school teachers too much power over the fate of students and promotes student conformity, apathy, passivity, and hypocrisy. Even though middle school students may pass entrance examinations for high school, they fear being rejected by being too vocal or unorthodox, disagreeing with teachers' views, or violating any aspect of the schools' dress code and rules.

Students believe that the *naishinsho* is unfair because it is secret, given too much weight, and holds students hostage for indiscretions of two or three years past. They complain that it discourages both student and parental opposition to arbitrary student rules and leads students to sign up for activities that will look good on the confidential evaluation. One Nanzan student wrote, "Ultimately *naishinsho* block true communications because students always have it in mind when talking to teachers." Another Nanzan student wrote that the *naishinsho* records students who quit school clubs. He noted that one-half of the baseball club at his junior high school wanted to resign, but did not because of fear of their action being recorded in the confidential report. A Yokohama National University senior reported an extreme example of the power of the confidential evaluation by a childish indiscretion. A bright junior high school classmate was not accepted by any senior high schools because she had foolishly run away to Tokyo with an older man for a week.

The confidential evaluation system also exerts a strong restraining role on parental opposition to controlled education. At the same public meeting in Ushiku City, one parent said that parents feared their negative remarks regarding school rules would be recorded in their children's evaluation.

PARENTAL SUPPORT

Other factors acting as a brake on ending controlled education are widespread support from parents and teachers for controlled education and corporal punishment, parent passivity before authority, a conservative court system that only reprimands about one-half of teachers taken to court for injuring a student, and schools playing a divide-and-rule strategy against parents.[77] Surveys show that most parents approve of the profusion of school rules and expect schools to begin character molding from preschool days. To the frustration of teachers at all levels, Japanese parents surrender much control over their children to the school, including the encouragement of physical punishment, because (a) they are reluctant to challenge teachers who use it; (b) they completely accept controlled education; (c) they cannot control their own children; and (d) they want their children's education, academic progress, and personal safety to be protected from other children. When a parent objects to the rules, some parents will call the objector's home and tell them to "get out of town." In very rare cases when a child has been killed by a teacher's corporal punishment, parents will even haze a victim's parent to the point of saying that the victim was partly to blame.

The NCER's *Second Report* repeatedly criticized the failure of homes to provide more character training and consciousness of citizenship. They asked parents to reassume the basic responsibility for moral education and instructed schools to return moral education to families.[78] One critic, Ken Kageyama at Aichi University of Education, said, "I believe that *kanri kyoiku* has come into existence because parents and citizens have completely left education to the schools."[79] The reasons for the strictness of many private girls schools is clear. Many parents want the schools to preserve the traditional image of femininity to make their daughters attractive future brides. In turn, schools need to assure parents that they provide a safe, nurturing environment.

Many newspaper articles report parents coming to the support of schools when a teacher has beaten a student severely. In fact, when the *Asahi Shimbun* and *Asahi Evening News* reported a teacher hitting a nonresisting junior high school student forty times, many parents wrote letters to the editor, objecting with such comments as, "You don't understand the miserable state of affairs in schools" and "Corporal punishment is part of education." In fact, when a senior high school girl died in the summer of 1995 from corporal punishment, 75,000 people signed a petition requesting a reduced sentence for the teacher concerned.[80] Most parents are not thinking about their *own* children being beaten. They want corporal punishment of other children to ensure "good" learning conditions for their child. Because 70 percent of Japanese teachers believed home life was largely responsible for students' problems, 30 percent of the teachers gave that as a justification for corporal punishment.[81]

Professor Moriyama complained that schools counter parents' complaints against school-controlled education by saying that parents are not raising the child properly or by reporting them to the conservative PTA as "problem parents." The PTA is prone to keep quiet issues that would bring shame on the community; hence its membership may isolate or treat coolly the complaining parents. "Other parents see this and decide to remain silent." Some parent groups or PTAs have supported a disciplined teacher for excessive use of corporal punishment, even arguing that the school needed more such teachers. Moriyama echoed a complaint of my students who do private tutoring, saying, "Some parents actually request teachers to hit their children so the child will get higher grades and can go to a better university and get a better job."[82]

SCHOOL VIOLENCE BY STUDENTS AND TEACHERS

Approximately 90 percent of Japanese school violence occurs at the junior high level for compelling psychosociological reasons. Teaching early teenagers in any country is more difficult than teaching elementary and senior high school students because of the major physical and emotional growth changes these students are going through. They are extraordinarily prone to be sensitive, critical, and moody, to cry, to feel a need to develop their identity, and to assert themselves. They do not know how to cope with their parents, teachers, or superiors. The answer of too many Japanese schools for handling this age group is to surround them with strict rules and distrust, and to look the other way and so allow upper classmates of clubs to carry out hazing or bullying of lower classmates to achieve enforcement of school rules. Most sport clubs at the secondary level require shaven haircuts for boys, and teachers are often unaware of bullying because the victims do not complain. Worse, teacher–advisors of a sports club may request nonmember "ruffians" to haze incoming junior or senior high school students to enforce discipline. One Nanzan student ruefully commented "It was the same ruffians who usually revolted against teachers." Sometimes older girls take it upon themselves to carry out a merciless hazing against younger classmates who violate rules or their interpretation of them; but in most college prep schools, this training procedure is much less cruel.[83]

Turning a blind eye to this hazing of students sometimes proves tragic. Four years ago in Chiba, students killed another student they had been bullying for months by suffocating him under wrestling mats in the gymnasium. In 1994 three students within one month committed suicide because of bullying that had been undetected. Ten students committed suicide in 1995 after one Aichi Prefecture junior high school male committed suicide.[84]

Even more striking, many younger teachers are in favor of more regulations than their elders.[85] Moriyama lamented that they are so accustomed to obeying that they apply it when they become teachers. It is probably true also that inexperienced, unconfident teachers are prone to look to rules and corporal punishment to overcome their anxiety regarding classroom control. My students think it is a cruel irony that young teachers inflict the same tortures they received as youths.

Corporal punishment is another problem of controlled education. A study by the Justice Ministry's Civil Liberties Bureau showed that two of three teachers who inflicted corporal punishment are middle school physical education teachers. This survey also supported the generalization that most cases occur at the junior high school level. Of 451 cases of teachers' corporal punishment reported between 1985 and 1989, 91 percent were male, and 65 percent were middle school teachers, 24 percent senior high school, and 13 percent elementary school teachers. Approximately one-half of the teachers were between their late twenties to early thirties. Significantly, the Justice Ministry staff admitted that most cases of corporal punishment are not reported.[86] A strong sense of shame deters schools from going public on internal troubles. A common expression in Japan is "cover up a scandal."

Another reason teachers inflict corporal punishment is that they sincerely believe in the absurd statement that "the use of the whip expresses teacher love." Professor Ken Schoolland, concluded that "about half the students [he interviewed] . . . asserted that the blows they received were for their own good."[87]

On 6 July 1990 a Kobe high school sophomore girl's head was crushed by a teacher slamming a heavy steel gate shut to prevent any tardy students from entering the school. The teacher saw himself only as enforcing school rules and had not looked up to see the potential results of his action. At that day's convoked school assembly the principal insensitively explained that the unfortunate girl's death would not have occurred had she been on time! It was her first tardiness that year. Previously, a counselor had reported to the principal on several occasions that students' skirts or books had been caught by the slamming of the gate. A police investigation determined that the death was an accident, but the teacher was dismissed, and the principal eventually resigned. The new principal announced that the gate would no longer be closed at the beginning of the school day. A national debate followed. Outraged students, parents, and professionals cited it as an example of the pathology of controlled education. In the midst of these debates it was learned that only three days earlier a roughly similar accident had occurred. On a rainy day at Shikama

High School in Himeji a senior girl wearing a hooded raincoat and riding a bicycle ran into a school gate immediately after it was closed and sustained a nasty cut on her forehead.[88]

Other cases of school-perpetrated violence can be cited. Seven teachers buried two eighth graders in sand up to their neck and left them there for about thirty minutes for blackmail and extortion of other students.[89] As a result of teacher beatings at least five students died between 1985 to 1990. One poor thirteen-year-old student, Chiyomi Watanabe, was slapped, punished, and kicked by twelve teachers in the fourth-floor conference room for riding a motorcycle for a few hours one day *during her summer vacation*. Subsequently, she was allegedly beaten every day by her homeroom teacher for the next six months. Today, she is an out-patient in a mental hospital after five hospitalizations for medical and psychological treatment. Another thirteen-year-old child, Takumi Kishi, was kicked twice in the face by her homeroom teacher, a soccer coach, for being three minutes late for lunch. The first blow killed a tooth nerve; the second one dislocated her jaw.

In an "average" junior high school in Aichi Prefecture, the *Asahi Shimbun* reported that corporal punishment was being practiced almost daily. Students who forgot their textbooks in one class were forced to bend over and grab their ankles before other students or in the corridor while the teacher hit them from the rear with a board. The school has a blacklist of second-year students who failed to pass the uniform and hair inspection. At 3:00 P.M. on 30 October 1990, the blacklisted students were called to the gym to kneel with their head to the floor and eyes closed for twenty minutes.[90] Some teachers complain that they have lost their authority because of the fear of mass media exposure for practicing corporal punishment.

There is another side to the story that makes me sympathetic to teachers, especially to female teachers. These days some junior high school students are large enough that they inflict physical damage on their teachers for the following reasons: (1) revenge against authoritarian teachers and school rules, (2) humiliation from having performed poorly in school day after day, (3) ridicule by a teacher or failure of a teacher to refrain students from making humiliating remarks, and (4) the frustration of not understanding difficult classroom content. At Nishi Middle School in Uruwa City of Saitama Prefecture, four different teachers in late October and November 1990 were assaulted by students for scolding boys for such actions as throwing an umbrella from a second-story window, smoking in the school, and misbehaving. The principal finally decided to take the cases to the school board and the police. He thought the students' principal motive was hatred of teachers.[91]

Violence perpetrated on teachers by undisciplined students is another reason for the rotating teams of parents at a few schools. Parents may patrol the hallways and sit in on classes. To prevent junior high school teachers from being hit on graduation day, when some students may vent their spleen on a teacher or teachers, parents at a few schools are expected to accompany their children to and from school. In fact, three vengeful seventeen-year-old high school students, two of whom had quit school as juniors and another who was repeating the same year, disrupted one Chiba senior high school end-of-term ceremony. They broke the pelvis of a thirty-eight-year-old male teacher by kicking him when he and ten other teachers tried to stop them from entering the gymnasium.[92]

RESULTS OF CONTROLLED EDUCATION AND EXCESSIVE EMPHASIS ON ACHIEVEMENT

One result is to increase the number of dropouts and the number of students who refuse to go to school (*toko kyohi*) more than fifty days a school year. The number of the latter between the ages of six to eighteen was 77,400 in 1995 and 81,562 in 1996. School refusers are increasing annually and now amount to 1.42 percent of the total junior high school population and 0.02 percent of elementary school students. A survey by the Ministry of Education reported that 105,414 elementary and junior high school students missed school thirty days or more for psychological reasons in 1997, an increase of 12 percent over 1996.[93] Those who had refused to attend school for fifty days or more constituted 80 percent of the total, and the number of elementary school children and junior high school children absent for the same period of time was 2.9 times and 4.4 times higher than in 1966. In 1994, 112,933 high school students dropped out of school, 27.1 percent because of "poor adaptability to school life" and 10.3 percent because of "failure in school grade." An increase of nondelinquent children, that is, of children "requiring guidance in their daily life because they are chronic truants or dropouts from school (*futoko*)" has led to an amendment to the Children Welfare Law to make all reformatory facilities open for them. Some students attending regular schools, however, fear that the new law will be used as discipline against them for nonschool attendance or problems at school. Others are happy to be in the reformatory school because they can study under less pressure from parents and school.[94]

Takahashi Shiro believes two major reasons for school refusals and dropouts are the existence of strict and detailed school rules and excessively fastidious, insensitive teachers, especially homeroom teachers. Teachers may subject the students to ridicule by criticizing them in front of classmates for being too assertive, uncooperative, and wearing improper clothing or hairstyles. Teachers' critical remarks encourage students to bully a victim. Most revealing, a Ministry of Education survey of dropouts showed that 70 percent of school dropouts were satisfied with that decision; nearly half of them planned to continue their education in other ways and to receive some form of higher education. Twenty-nine percent said they had left school because of difficulty in adjusting to school life and rules.[95]

I am not satisfied with the statistics on bullying, dropouts, school refusal, and high school graduation rates, as with many other statistics on the dark side of Japanese education. In every society there is a tendency to hide embarrassing facts; however, in Japan because of the prominent roles played by shame and the mass media to ferret out bad educational aspects, Japanese educators and schools are particularly inclined to conceal from the public school problems connected with academic pressures and controlled education. For example, almost all students are automatically promoted and graduate from high school (and college), but that occurs for a minority of students who have performed miserably from elementary school on only as a result of a desire to save students' face, favorable public relations, pressures from above, students' pregraduation contracts for employment, and a generally permissive societal attitude that a student who has spent three years in school has earned graduation. A foreign English teacher at a senior high school in Kanagawa prefecture noted that more than twenty seniors' attendance and academic records for the year did not merit graduation, but almost 100 percent of them graduated, including one female with "an extremely poor academic performance" and attendance at fewer than 60 of more than 125 English classes.[96]

Another result of controlled education is bullying. Forty percent of the children who were school refusers cited bullying or other school-related reasons as reasons for refusal. A 1996 Ministry of Education survey of 20,000 elementary and secondary students, parents, and teachers revealed that bullying students were formerly bullied themselves, and the Civil Liberties Bureau of the Justice Ministry reported that 42.2 percent of 10,884 fifth and sixth graders polled nationwide in 1998 had been bullied. Another survey, by th Management and Coordination Agency, reported that one in three elementary and junior high school students had been bullied.[97] Bullying is endemic among all age and occupational groups in Japanese society.[98] It will remain a major problem as long as Japanese society and schools fail to recognize human dignity and diversity. For example, the Tokyo Managers Union reported that 75 telephone calls of 2,300 were from teachers complaining of bullying by fellow educators.[99] Those most bullied are sometimes the students who are the most popular with students. After a two-year study, a panel report on bullying by a group of researchers cooperating with the Ministry of Education concluded that schools needed to be more flexible in allowing the bullied to absent themselves from school and to move to other schools and other classes. It recommended teachers develop students' personality by a positive manner that respects their individuality. Similarly, the Tokyo Metropolitan Institute for Educational Research and In-Service Training wrote, "Genuine human education that respects human rights does not have the place it deserves in school education."[100]

A third objection is that the present educational system is creating more docile, inward-looking, and spoiled children. One critic exaggeratedly complained that they "act like pet dogs" because they have lost their natural instincts by being "enclosed in a managed social capsule, or a situation of mutual enslavement."[101] They are inclined to avoid engagement with other people, to fear making a mistake or raising their hands in class, to not make many friends, and to be socially awkward, docile, and inward-looking. Another tendency lately is for ordinarily well-behaved students suddenly to express themselves violently from the pressures they feel from controlled education and academic demands. Lately, a related problem of serious proportions is the tendency, even among elementary school teachers, to lose control of classes.

MODERATE SUCCESS OF MINORITY MOVEMENT AGAINST CONTROLLED EDUCATION

In 1989, the Ministry of Education issued instructions to schools calling on them to relax strict and unnecessary rules.[102] A Ministry of Education survey of 1,472 schools in 1991 reported that more than 70 percent of secondary schools had reviewed their rules in the previous three years.[103] A majority had relaxed some rules such as requiring boys to crop their hair. Some had eased regulations on girls' hairstyles, and the requirement that girls wear skirts of the same length regardless of height differences. Only 3.9 percent of schools reported an increase in rules. Almost 40 percent had relaxed rules on after-school activities and dress. Nonetheless, the Ministry itself characterized the cumulative changes as "still insignificant." Accordingly, it instructed schools to press forward with an overhaul of regulations.

A weak national movement against controlled education has begun that reflects a growing sensitivity to students' rights and excessive order, uniformity, and conformity in the schools.[104] A "Goodbye to Controlled Education Conference" held in Okazaki City of Aichi Prefecture, a city and prefecture regarded as among the strictest in the nation, was attended by approximately 300 representatives of citizens' groups ranging from Hokkaido to Okinawa. In 1992 a group of citizens from nineteen prefectures met to commemorate the anniversary of the girl killed by the school gate, to oppose the "authoritarian" school system, to urge protection of children's rights, and to petition Japan's ratification of the 1989 Convention on the Rights of the Child, adopted by the United Nations General Assembly.[105]

Lawyer and citizen groups have also become more active in challenging rules that have little to do with real education and violate human rights. The Kobe Bar Association sent a letter to all public junior schools rejecting the city's claim that short haircuts reduced juvenile delinquency and fostered the practice of obeying rules. The lawyers argued that the rule violated students' constitutional rights and called for an immediate cessation of the practice. The reaction against the lack of individualized education and diversity led the Nihon Kyoiku Gakkai to feature at the 1989 meeting a symposium on the subject of "Stressing Individuality." Similarly, the Keizai Doyukai's revolutionary 1990 report said, "The idea that everybody is a precious person stemming from his uniqueness has tended to be ignored. On the contrary, Japanese have found their identity within the group and have overly valued harmony and consensus."[106] In 1986, the NCER reported a growing discrepancy between modern, urban society and home life, and schools' practices. They noted that society increasingly encourages diversification, specialization, choice, and individualization, while the schools nourish uniformity, conformity, and arbitrariness. The report lamented that schools were "creating maladjusted children."[107]

Although 46 percent of teachers in 1986 supported corporal punishment as a means of discipline, a lesser percentage would support it today. Even the conservative Tokyo District Court made the nation's first court decision upholding a student's complaint against an excessive school by declaring that a Shutoku High School principal had exceeded his discretion in expelling a junior for acquiring a motorcycle driving license. The court argued that he should have given a less stringent discipline to achieve the school's educational purpose. At the same time, however, the court reaffirmed the right of schools to restrict students' rights and freedom "even outside school" in connection with educational objectives as long as they were in line "with commonly accepted logic."[108]

Other examples support Mombusho's pessimistic reaction to schools' alleged reduction of school rules. A 1990 JTU survey of fifty-nine junior high and eighteen senior high schools showed that many of the latter had reduced rules, but 31 percent of the former had added new rules.[109] Moriyama thinks the "reported cases of corporal punishment are only the tip of the iceberg," because student beatings continue to take place in corridors or conference rooms away from the eyes of objecting teachers.[110] A Nanzan female senior said, "I think there is still much corporal punishment because I often hear stories of it from the students I have been tutoring the past three years. Schools are very skillful at keeping these things quiet."

An interesting sociological phenomenon is occurring in some older rural communities, which have become bedroom towns for commuters to large cities or those who have found employment in new industries in their area. Although student violence is attributed to the increase of these "new residents," there is another side to this issue. The friction between new and old residents is exacerbated by the organized efforts of new residents to protest schools' excessive use of rules and corporal punishment. In Ushiku City, all of these elements came to a head at a community meeting that also demonstrated the resistance of Japanese schools to citizen input. After citizens had sent letters to No. 3 Public Junior High School in Ushiku asserting that students should be able to choose their own hairstyles, the school decided in February 1991 to send questionnaires to parents to determine whether each school rule was necessary. It decided, however, not to disclose the results because "the school has no obligation to disclose the results to parents because the survey was made simply to acquaint teachers with parents' current concerns."[111] The school was forced to announce that male students would not be compelled to have a closely shaved haircut.

Mombusho learned from its 1991 survey of school rules what should be common sense. The survey showed that after 38.4 percent of the schools had drafted new, relaxed regulations after class discussions and student council meetings, students followed the new regulations more voluntarily than students "forced to follow the new rules reviewed by the teachers only."[112] Japanese schools should rewrite their rules and regulations with student help. Students would be taught a valuable lesson in democracy and obey rules they have helped make. When rewriting the rules the following simple points should be kept in mind:

1. Does the rule have any relationship to positive character formation and study habits?
2. Does the rule advance or negate human dignity?
3. Does the rule respect individuality and advance democratic principles?
4. Does the rule foster the goals of the preamble and Article 1 of the Fundamental Law of Education?

SELECTIVE BORROWING OF AMERICAN INDIVIDUALITY AND DEMOCRACY

It is not my intention to be a cultural imperialist, but rather to help Japanese society fit more closely the aspirations of Japanese youth. To meet current needs and future challenges of Japanese society, Japanese education should *selectively adopt* some strengths of American schools and society. Most Japanese misunderstand individualism; moreover, democracy has not been allowed to flower fully. When they are applied in a balanced manner they contribute to America's social, political, and educational strengths. They make Americans self-reliant, protective of the weak, and inclined to challenge social inequalities and heavy traditions that paralyze a people from reform. Americans value change, innovation, and individual choice about where they will live and what they will do (the average length of time in a first job for an American engineer is five years). This sense of control of their own destiny (often delusory) has made many Americans optimistic, assertive, strong-willed, and critical of arbitrary rules and practices.

Other important elements of American individualism that Japanese schools could teach selectively and more emphatically are the concept of human dignity and human rights. American education emphasizes civil rights in the schools. By contrast, Japanese schools slight them, and instead emphasize duties, rules, and enduring sexual, social, and traditional discriminations to achieve societal order and harmony. Maintaining silence and enduring inequality, injustice, and excessive pressure are treasured too much. These school priorities do not create the citizen that a vibrant democracy, economy, and society need.

When individualism is correctly taught in American schools it fosters equality, and voluntary services on behalf of others. (Fifty percent of American citizens perform some type of volunteer activity sometime during the year.) Many graduates of American private schools and state and private universities return acquired benefits by donations to their alma mater. Those alumni donations make it possible for most private universities to continue their existence independent of government financing and free to pursue truth. Public universities are better able to foster research. The concept of stewardship, social obligation, or *noblesse oblige* are important teachings of Judeo–Christianity and American democratic individualism, which should be nurtured in Japanese schools. Citizens' voluntary activities and donations allow some hospitals, senior citizen homes, facilities for handicapped people, and community projects to be solvent and humane.

Another positive feature of American individualism taught in the schools is to teach that yesterday's heresies may be tomorrow's truths, and that truth is not the monopoly of any collective unit, society, or government bureaucracy. Because the group, government, and prevailing mores and traditions may err, it is important for individuals to be assertive in opposing them when they believe they are wrong. Students learn that human error and prejudice are vital reasons for maintaining freedoms of speech, press, and assembly.

CONCLUSIONS ON CONTROLLED EDUCATION

Any nation's schools need to establish a climate in which it is understood that education is serious and that students are in school to learn both scholarship and responsibility as law-abiding citizens. Schools do need to establish rules to prevent disorder and student violence and to limit premature adult behavior. When rules are reasonable, students do not have the right to thumb their noses at them.

Japanese often say that they have a first-rate economy, but a third-rate political system characterized by government of the rich and powerful, by the rich and powerful, and for the rich and powerful. One reason for the latter is that the schools cultivate insecure, hierarchical, conformist attitudes that create apathy and weakness before the prevailing public sentiment and persons of greater social status, wealth, and power. In Japan children are often taught that it is stubborn, selfish, and antisocial to refuse to conform to the group. They have not learned to debate, to understand or assert their rights, to be able to disagree politely but firmly with an elder, a teacher, or even a fellow student on the merits of an issue.[113] In turn, students, elders, and superiors have not learned that a different view from their own is not an attack, but an invitation to dialogue. American children are taught at home and school to adhere to views based on reason, personal convictions, and facts because principles and "truth" are considered vital to correct injustice and undemocratic practices. Carried to an extreme this thinking becomes too combative, abrasive, uncompromising, and stubborn. Its strengths are that the individual possesses a standard from which to govern action rather than merely conforming to majority opinion, a social or political trend or fad, or an oppressive political regime or ideology. The lack of an active, assertive citizenry today is one reason for the weakness of political parties, the excessive power of an elitist bureaucracy, and increasing corruption.

Japanese-controlled education can be faulted for three overriding reasons. First, schools should not be responsible for enforcing practices that are the *responsibility of parents*. Whether a student can attend a movie, go shopping, or stay overnight at a friend's home are matters between a child and parents.[114]

Second, schools' excessive reliance on rules, force, and group punishment for the misbehavior of one student is no training for democracy or respect for human dignity. Schools must nurture initiative, independent judgment, human rights, communication, diversity, and citizenship. One way is to reduce school clubs excessive emphasis on hierarchical upper and lower classmate relations.[115] Schools are creating future citizens who cannot discuss or debate because they are not equals and are only comfortable when they are following rules, fads, and societal approved actions.[116] Japanese schools need to emphasize more strongly that students should judge the validity of a statement or action on the basis of its intrinsic merit. The practice of refraining from speaking one's own opinion must be ended in Japan's schools if students are to become active citizens and society to become more democratic. Almost all my students complain that the worst things about controlled education are that they "cannot think independently," accept uniformity and conformity, and trade responsible liberty for safety. An *Asahi Shimbun* editorial hailing a Japan Bar Association declaration on educational reforms and children's rights asserted, "Children brought up in this manner will hardly learn to make their own decisions and act on their own initiative. They are likely to become irresponsible and apathetic adults who can only follow orders from above and move in flocks like sheep. It is rather frightening to think that the next generation may be filled with these types."[117]

On these points American schools have an edge. For American students, participating in a group does not mean giving up one's individuality or assuming an inferior position before an upper classmate. As students, they learn to express their opinions freely and to be responsible for respecting the views of others. They can discuss matters more honestly and frankly because they communicate with each other in a group as equal members rather than on the basis of sex, age, or status.

Third, the confidential student report (*naishinsho*) must be made open to parents and students, and improper conduct of two or three years previously should be stricken from the record when students' behavior improves. Students and parents should have the opportunity to appeal for modification of damaging remarks. (Recording parents' criticisms of school rules should be ended forthwith.)

It must be agonizingly painful for an older generation who sacrificed so much to achieve today's prosperity for corporate Japan to realize that youth seem so ungrateful. They are inclined to criticize youth for being insensitive, too realistic, indifferent to politics, cynical, reliant on manuals or instructions for thought and action, and for avoiding close human relationships and lacking initiative, goals, and energy like the youth of the past.[118] The older generation, however, is reaping the seeds it has sown over the past forty-five years by controlled education, excessive emphasis on school achievement, and collectivistic, materialistic values that sacrifice human dignity and individuality for economic goals. A theme of a recent book compiling 339 junior high school students' letters on the problem of bullying shows that they lack faith in adults and view them as hypocritical and indifferent to the problems they face.[119]

Today's youth are changing. They want excessive educational and societal pressures diminished. They want greater freedom and a society that recognizes their dreams and dignity. They yearn for greater diversification, humanity, individuality, and democracy, rather than continued calls for sacrifice, enduring hardship, unremitting diligence, and order. For many young women, their vision of the future may be a career and a marriage based on equality, partnership, and shared domestic chores. For many young men, service to corporations that demand complete loyalty and sacrifice of personal and family goals is no longer inviting. Nor do current Japanese youth want to be exactly the same as others. As one superficial example of their desire to break out of uniformity, in the last two years so many high school graduates have begun to dye their hair to assert their individuality that they end up oddly in conforming to peers.

Others practice escapism or flights into mysticism and cults. They surfeit themselves as much as possible with what can be gained materialistically. When I asked my 1997 graduating seniors what is the purpose of life, more than 70 percent said, "It was to have fun." Life should be as enjoyable as we can make it, but one expects college graduates to have higher goals. In seeking material goods and pleasures there is the danger that today's youth may be too indifferent to social injustice and their own long range needs, but countering that coldness and lack of concern will require altered societal and educational goals and attitudes. Ikuo Amano wrote, "One of the reasons, probably the greatest reason, for the pathological phenomena occurring in the schools today, including violence and 'bullying' is the gap between the changed rules and attitudes of young people and the unchanged orientation of the older generation. The educational system and institutions, which are maintained and run by the latter, have changed little."[120] These defects of controlled education provide more examples of an obsolescent education system.

Because Japan's schools achieve a greater discipline and time on task than American schools, the academic achievement is considerably higher; however, the sacrifices are too great. American schools provide students with greater freedom and dignity, but at the loss of order, personal safety, and academic achievement. These contradictions cry out for a middle way.

There is one other objection to Japan's controlled education. Controlled education definitely undermines efforts to make Japan more international.

EDUCATIONAL AND SOCIETAL OBSTACLES TO ACHIEVING GLOBALLY MINDED JAPANESE

A major goal of the Japanese leadership since the Nakasone Yasuhiro premiership (1983–1987) is the creation of an "internationalized" Japan. Japanese tend to think that they will become automatically internationally minded by *automatic* modernization processes (i.e., by rapid technological and economic changes, increased foreign trade and travel, and advances in globe-shrinking transportation and communications systems). Instead, what will be required is a long, painful, conscious change in mental attitudes, a major challenge for Japanese schools. The late Edwin O. Reischauer, a man who loved Japan, put it strongly when he wrote, "The greatest single problem the Japanese face today is their relationship with other peoples . . . they now find themselves struggling with the largely self-created psychological problem of their own self-image and the attitude of other nations toward them. . . . Lingering feelings of separateness and uniqueness are still serious problems for the Japanese themselves. . . . To put it in dramatic terms, they find it hard to join the human race."[121] I believe that Japanese schools fail to create internationally minded people because they fail to cultivate adequately being a humanist; being curious about other nations; accepting diversity and adopting flexible attitudes; transcending narrow national concerns; and thinking globally.

CAUTIOUS INTERNATIONALISM IN EDUCATION

The Japanese government's desire to create a more international Japan is often characterized by a one-step-forward, one-step-backward approach in education. One example was the Ministry of Education's decision to require world history at the high school level and to make the subject Contemporary Society (*Gendai shakai*) only an elective from 1994. The study of world history can contribute to making Japanese more internationally minded. Unfortunately, the way world history is taught is to pour an enormous amount of factual material down students' throats so they can pass college entrance examinations. Furthermore, students sitting for almost all private and national university entrance examinations can choose Japanese history rather than world history. Many of those who elect the former will not take the study of world history seriously. Contemporary Society should be taught because it adopts a problem-solving methodology and global approach to common problems confronting the world.

The Ministry and schools have been excessively cautious in the area of extracurricular activities, such as sports, music, and art contests that provide excellent opportunities for schools to foster internationalism. Korean schools in Japan have been barred from all such contests on the basis that they are not "schools under Article I of the School Education Law." Only in 1994 were Korean high schools allowed to take part in a spring baseball tournament in one prefecture.[122] A questionnaire that I gave to three of my classes made it clear that young people are more open-minded than school and government officials. Thirty-three percent of them "strongly disagreed" and 48 percent "disagreed" with the rule that prohibits Korean junior and senior high school baseball teams from competing in Japanese regional and national tournaments. This rule remains, despite Korean schools revising their curriculum to conform to approximately 85 percent of the curriculum of Japanese schools. For the same reason graduates of North Korean high schools in Japan are also not allowed to take directly national universities' and most private and prefectural universities' entrance examinations.[123]

The following is an example of how administrative conservatism limits internationalism. Ten upper elementary Nagoya children from different schools were sent to Philadelphia in 1995 for a one-month, home-stay program with children of approximately the same age. In 1996, ten Philadelphia children came to Nagoya on the day before the first quarter of school ended for a similar experience. All the parents independently thought it would be a wonderful idea for the American students and for their classmates to attend the last day's school closing ceremony. But all these parents wishes were turned down at each school by the arguments "It would be difficult" and "There was no precedent for such an action." In other words, "No."

At the elementary school level internationalization has been severely compromised by a court ruling and Ministry of Education practices that run completely counter to this objective. The Ministry had for decades made it clear to all public elementary, junior, and senior high schools that they may not hire foreigners, including Korean residents, as full-time teachers within one school to prevent foreigners from taking part in public decision-making. It also feared that hiring foreign teachers would interfere with developing "Japanese children's identity."[124] Until an agreement between the Japanese and South Korean governments occurred in January 1991, even Koreans born in Japan and fluent in the Japanese language were prevented from taking elementary and secondary teacher certification tests—though some prefectures ignored this practice.[125] This progressive step, however, was subsequently nullified by a Ministry of Education order to prefectures to hire foreigners only as instructors, not supervisory positions.[126] If young Japanese children are not given the opportunity to be taught by foreigners from within their own society who are fluent in Japanese, it is highly unlikely they can accept more pronounced differences in those who come from abroad.

ENTRANCE EXAMINATIONS CONTENT
AND METHODOLOGY

Entrance examinations for senior high school and for university force students to be so narrowly focused that they do not have the time or the inclination to look beyond their own little worlds.[127] Social studies courses are important for fostering an international mind, but the students are less interested in their content than in memorizing answers. University students and graduates openly admit that they did not take seriously social studies courses such as *seiji-keizai* (politics and economics), *gendai shakai* (contemporary society), or *rinri* (ethics) because they were not required by the Unified Entrance Examination for National Universities or private university examinations. At the former, students only need to challenge one of five social studies courses. Furthermore, even though history is an inexact science, entrance examinations lead students to believe that there are single, definitive interpretations of historical events. The active, cheerful atmosphere of early education is replaced at the secondary school level by a methodology that impedes the creation of internationally minded students.

When I discussed an earlier draft of this chapter with Nanzan University and Nagoya University students they expressed the view that the worst thing about Japanese education was the failure of schools to foster discussion and debate among students. What a tragedy! Here we find the paradoxical condition of one of the world's most informed students being unable to enjoy lively dialogue because of the anxieties I have noted in this chapter.

FOREIGN LANGUAGE EDUCATION AS AN OBSTACLE

To create more internationally minded citizens, Japan should make English compulsory from elementary through junior high school,[128] stress oral communication by requiring a listening section in the English university entrance examination, and let English be a truly elective course at the high school level. It is not my argument that English makes one international. Although I am a strong proponent of making English a required course from elementary school through junior high school to improve the quality of English acquisition and pronunciation in Japan, I want to make it only a genuinely elective course at the high school level for those students motivated to continue their study.[129] This measure will give students the opportunity to select different languages, particularly Asian languages. Although there has been improvement since 1991, only 265 high schools were teaching an Asian language in March 1995 (though courses in Indonesian, Vietnamese, and Thai appeared for the first time in the 1995–1996 school year).[130] Similarly, although Chinese has suddenly replaced German and French at universities as the second most studied foreign language, the number of universities teaching other Asian languages is terribly low for an Asian nation interested in playing a greater role in Asia.[131] Even worse, university graduates cannot speak English despite having studied it for six to nine years. According to the Economic Planning Agency, the average Test of English as a Foreign Language (TOEFL) of Japanese applicants was only 493 out of 677 points, a score that ranked them 197th among the 214 participating countries.[132]

This sorry state of English education calls attention to another one-step-forward, one-step-back approach to internationalization that sometimes characterizes the Ministry of Education. Billions of taxpayers' yen are being spent to bring foreign English teachers to Japan for Japan English teaching programs (i.e., JET, AET), to stimulate English study, and to provide an international experience for the students, but the relatively small numbers of such teachers and the priority given by Japanese teachers and students to the passing of entrance examinations severely limits the effectiveness of the program. In too many prefectures and cities the foreign teacher can only meet students rarely, and the problem still remains: The pressure is on the responsible Japanese teachers of English to help their students get into good universities.

The results in terms of creating a more international Japan for cultural and economic activities in the English-speaking world are pitiful.[133] A panel of distinguished educators and company presidents sponsored by the English Language Education Council complained of: the lack of emphasis upon communication in English education because of the lopsided emphasis of the English entrance examinations; failure to promote people in the business and political world who are highly proficient in English and who receive MBAs in English-speaking nations (unlike other countries in the world); and Japanese prime ministers who avoid using English.[134] Since almost no university entrance examination tests students either on their listening or speaking skills or on comprehension of the English-speaking countries' cultures, Japanese teachers of English teach it as if it were a dead language or abstruse metaphysical science and use little spoken English.[135] Because they learn the foreign culture through a translation process that minimizes real understanding, most students fail to *cross over into the thinking and culture* of the people they study. By the time they graduate from high school they hate English, fear making mistakes, and panic when confronted with a foreigner.[136]

SCHOOL RULES AND EXTRACURRICULAR ACTIVITIES STRENGTHEN TRADITIONAL CULTURAL ATTITUDES OF UNIFORMITY, CONFORMITY, AND EXCLUSIVITY

Uniformity and Conformity

Traditional cultural value goals of creating order, harmony, and socialization processes foster exclusive, conformist, and inflexible behavior patterns antithetical to ethnic diversity and outside values.[137] When schools excessively emphasize group-oriented school practices and conformity and uniformity of student dress, social behavior, and thought, they frustrate the development of human dignity and greater internationalism. The NCER wrote emphatically, "Most important in the educational reform to come is to do away with the uniformity, rigidity, closedness and lack of internationalism, all of which are deep-rooted defects of the educational system, and to establish the principles of dignity of individuals, respect for the individual, freedom and self-discipline, and self-responsibility."[138]

This strong emphasis on uniformity and standardization puts enormous pressure on individuals to conform to a rigidly preconceived pattern of what is acceptable, of what is 100-percent Japanese. How can young people become international in their outlook and be tolerant of different religions, cultural behavior, and ways of thinking, when they have been subjected to a socialization process that rejects these traits?

Exclusivity

Japanese from an early age learn to distinguish the inner circle, or home, from the outer circle, or outsiders. The practical effects of this cultural attitude in Japanese society are that (a) people who are not members of the nation are excluded, and (b) people who are not members of one's homeroom, school club, faculty department, corporation, or nation are also excluded.[139] This reflects the attitude that if you are a stranger, no *giri* (obligation, courtesy) or *ninjo* (humanity, tenderness) is owed. It also results in many Japanese shunning individual identity and opinions when speaking to foreigners, practices Nobel Prize-winning novelist Oe Kenzaburo hates.[140]

Japanese schools from an early age foster exclusivity by homeroom practices, club activities, extracurricular events, and teaching methodology. The rewards of this fostering of exclusive loyalty in Japanese school clubs are that they create lifelong friendships and constant group nurturing, but they also develop persons who are not open to diversity and uncomfortable with outsiders.[141] Deep friendships are precious, but schools should play a role of weakening narrow loyalties within the curriculum and in extracurricular activities. Nanzan surveyed students agreed: 58 percent of them consider that outsider and insider thinking interferes most with Japanese becoming international. At many junior high schools all students must belong to a club. At many elementary and junior high schools even when classes are not in session students of the same grade, as a custom, generally do not enter other classrooms of their peers. Schools are building loyalty to a class, but at the expense of limiting the development of qualities that would make it easier for Japanese to meet and interact comfortably and freely with strangers from their own society, let alone with foreigners.

Many school clubs only allow (or expect) members to participate daily in one club activity for an entire year, and at the junior high, senior high, or university levels, students are normally expected to continue for three years in the same club exclusively. Some clubs are so zealous that because they meet in the morning, at lunch time, on weekends, and during vacations, they limit members' contact with other students. *As an individual group practice there is nothing wrong with such club practices*, but when these clubs' customs *are added to the practice* of the same students studying daily almost every subject in the same classroom together for a year, or with the same homeroom for three years each at both the junior and senior high levels, we can see that students' acquaintance with other students is too limited. Many high school and university students do not join any club at all because they do not want to feel confined to one club. Others who belong to a club that meets only two or three times a week would like to participate in another club, but resist doing so because their clubs either will not permit it or would criticize them for disloyalty and lack of character.[142]

What are the results for Japanese students of the exclusivity of their relationships over a twelve-year period of secondary education? One obvious result is to replicate in adult years the tribal mentality of Japanese society in which the outsider is looked upon as alien, and another is to create insecurity and tension when meeting a stranger. Time after time, in essays or in class discussions, students mention that they are shy, embarrassed, and afraid to associate with any others outside their group, not just foreigners.

A second result is to foster bullying at schools of those who look, act, and think differently, whether they are Japanese, returnees, or foreigners, including Japanese raised abroad.[143] As Yoji Morita says, bullying "reveals the dark side of Japan's social makeup that excludes anything that is foreign or from an unfamiliar culture without making any effort to understand it."[144] Many returnees have confessed to me of being bullied, but when written assignments were turned in, most nonreturnee students denied there was bullying of returnees. Returnees' written assignments, however, usually mention personal bullying or cases of other returnees being bullied. Why this discrepancy? Several students wrote, "We learn to call no attention to ourselves by any differences."

Being modern and international has meant, to most Japanese since the mid-1880s, associating Japan with the West, particularly America since 1945. In the mid-Meiji period, a famous educator and Westernizer, Fukuzawa Yukichi, proclaimed the argument that Japan should "embrace the West and disassociate itself with Asia." Changing this prejudiced view is a big challenge for Japanese education. A careful reading of the NCER report shows that it was really more interested in having Japan join the advanced countries of the West than in having them become true internationalists knowledgeable about and sensitive to non-Western peoples. This has been a mistaken view of many Japanese since the mid-Meiji period. True internationalism is hindered by a hierarchical way of thinking that leads to ranking of human beings on the basis of their race, nationality, and industrial advancement.[145] From such thinking over 50 percent of Japanese studying abroad are in the United States. There is little identification with Asian neighbors.

Although Japan's future in the twenty-first century will lie as much with Asia as with the West, Japanese have shown little respect and interest in their Asian neighbors—except recently from a profit motive. Japanese obsession with America is resented in other countries. And a poll of 200 foreign students, two-thirds of whom were from Asia, showed that a majority of them had worse feelings about Japan after they came to Japan, because they could not make friends with Japanese.[146] In fact, my students repeatedly note that Japanese associate foreigners with Westerners and think of themselves as more Western than Asian. Forty-two percent of Nanzan students said they themselves thought this way.[147] Seventy-two percent of the students surveyed agreed that "Asian students studying in Japan experience discrimination," and 75 percent agreed that Japanese "tend to have a superiority attitude toward other Asians." Only 6 percent of them selected East Asia as the area and East Asians as the peoples they "admired most." No one selected West Asia, only 2 percent selected South Asia, and 6 percent selected Southeast Asia. By contrast, 74 percent of the students looked to North America or Western Europe as the most admired regions and peoples, a point strongly supported by their travel and study abroad preferences. The most admired nations are the United States, Great Britain, Canada, Australia, and France, in that order. The least admired in descending order are China, Thailand, Korea, Mexico, Indonesia, Russia, Brazil, Israel, and Iraq. Even young Japanese wish to associate themselves most with Western countries. It is clear that Japanese education has a formidable task ahead to correct these lopsided attitudes.

FEAR OF LOSS OF NATIONAL IDENTITY

Fundamental to many Japanese interpretations of internationalism is the desire to achieve it at no sacrifice to national identity.[148] In its first report one NCER subcommittee recommended much greater internationalization of the curriculum, but another more conservative one recommended nurturing the students' Japanese identity at the compulsory elementary level, and instituting regular national flag-raising and national anthem ceremonies at all schools to keep students from becoming "rootless internationalists."[149]

A serious misconception by conservative nationalists is that Japanese should first learn about themselves, a parochial view that conservative officials, teachers, and parents have been successful in making youth believe. Japanese students repeatedly tell me how embarrassed they have been when they are unable to explain Japanese history, culture, or religion to non-Japanese. For this reason, 66 percent of the surveyed students "agreed [or] strongly agreed with the flawed view that Japanese cannot become international unless they first learn their own national identity." Two returnee Nanzan seniors, who returned to their home schools for a two-week practice teaching experience, were very disturbed by the advice they received from their supervising teachers. Both were told not to emphasize how good it was to study abroad. They were asked to say how regrettable it was to go to other countries not knowing very much of Japan itself. One said, "I was very sad. I saw the ideal and reality of Japanese education." Another one had such a strong reaction to this parochial thinking that she said, "Before I went abroad, I had expected that I would learn things which can help Japan's future be better and I had wanted to contribute my study and experiences to Japan. But now I think if this situation continues, I may come to dislike Japanese society and to lose any willingness to work for it." In fact, there is no need for nationalists to fear that returnees will lose their identity. Various studies have concluded that they have a stronger sense of Japanese identity than students who have never been abroad.[150]

Promoting national identity at the elementary level to learn what it means to be Japanese has two limitations. First, it reinforces the Japanese tendency to overemphasize uniqueness at the expense of commonality with the rest of the world.[151] Second, this goal fails to understand that the best place to create internationally oriented persons is at the elementary and junior high school levels, where minds are still open and receptive. Lewis, however, noted that the elementary school curriculum fails to introduce students to international cultural, sports, and peacekeeping organizations, cross-cultural issues, or other cultures until the sixth grade, a big mistake.[152] A whopping 92 percent of Nanzan students thought internationalism should be introduced before high school, 55 percent of them thought preschool and elementary school was the right time, and 37 percent specified the junior high level.

EDUCATION OF RETURNEES AND
CHILDREN LIVING ABROAD

The number of precollege Japanese students returning annually from study abroad has increased from approximately 2,000 in the 1960s to over 12,000 in 1994.[153] Until recently most overseas students returned to Japan as eighth or ninth graders. Most never went abroad during a time that would include high school years because of a combination of factors: until 1989 high school credits earned abroad were not recognized by the Mombusho; special arrangements to assist returnees with reentry problems were lacking in most schools; time was needed for the students to prepare for senior high and college examinations; and publicly funded readjustment (or "soft") schools aimed at assisting in such preparation did not exist. Nonetheless, the number of high school students returning over the same period has stayed at between 11 to 15 percent of the total number of returnees. Simultaneously, the number of precollege students abroad has spiraled from 11,106 students in 1967 to 49,00 in 1994.[154]

These students provide Japan with a golden opportunity to create a new internationally minded population, but currently one of the most important purposes of the eighty-two Japanese schools established abroad is to inculcate Japanese values, including conformity to the group, and to prepare students for the senior high school and university entrance examinations back home. That narrow focus discourages overseas Japanese schools from establishing a curriculum and fostering activities that open the students to the host country's culture.[155] Similarly, the objective of most schools (except for two international schools established in Tokyo, the Osaka–Kobe area, Nanzan Kokusai in Nagoya, and a school in Tsukuba Science City) is to reassimilate returnees. Of course, it is important to assimilate these students into Japanese culture, but Japan is neglecting an enormous opportunity to develop these valuable national assets, especially in those who have been abroad for three years or more. Their language skills and their knowledge of the countries in which they have lived should be nurtured for the value they will give to future

Japanese corporations, diplomacy, research, and cultural exchange. Instead, such students, upon college graduation, may be hired by large corporations only as specialists outside the policy making and fast track for company leadership. Fortunately, special quota systems at many universities now actually provide an advantage for returnees.[156]

CONCLUSION

Attitudes of internationalism can be acquired if (1) schools teach more global education, foster an expanded humanism, and develop a curriculum, extracurriculum, and staff that will encourage student diversity and flexibility; (2) parents, teachers, and political and religious leaders will teach and practice an expanded love and concern for our fellow human beings that recognize the intrinsic dignity of every individual, minority, and nationality; and (3) there is an expansion of well-formulated student and faculty exchanges.

For creating more internationally minded Japanese I strongly urge Japan to send a total of ten thousand elementary and secondary teachers abroad for a year during the next twenty years for periods of six months each to a Third World country and an advanced industrial country. The subsequent impact of these teachers on their students over a twenty-year period would be much more salutary than the existing JET program, but I must admit its success is dependent on radically altering the entrance examination system to allow these teachers to make a contribution to producing a more internationally minded Japanese.

I strongly recommend the revival of Contemporary Society as a required subject, because it takes up the study of problems from a historical, anthropological perspective, and adopts a problem-solving methodology and global approach to solving contemporary global problems.[157] Japanese students must be made aware that in the long run Japan's well-being is linked to global cooperation and prosperity.

Japan should deemphasize teaching uniqueness and national identity. When the people of any country emphasize the uniqueness of their society, history, and physical and mental differences, they foster excessive nationalism. Let us leave the study of uniqueness to scholars who are interested in promoting a true understanding of their own or other cultures, rather than to the demagogues and narrow nationalists who have a hidden agenda. What we need to do in our homes, schools, and mass media is to work harder at understanding our similarities. To interact with foreigners meaningfully and to advance their individual, corporate, and national concerns, Japanese must be free to be able to make mistakes, accept diversity, interact freely with foreigners, and be more assertive.

NOTES

1. Shogo Ishikawa, *Nihon no kyoiku, kyoiku kaikaku no riron to kozo* (Japanese education: The structure and theory of educational reform) (Tokyo: Kyoiku Kaihatsu Kenkyujo, 1991), 57–58.

2. Thomas Rohlen and Gerald LeTendre, eds., *Teaching and Learning in Japan* (Cambridge: Cambridge University Press, 1996).

3. Harry Wray, "Decentralization of Education in the Allied Occupation of Japan, 1945–1952," in *The Occupation of Japan: Educational and Social Reform*, ed. Thomas Burkman (Norfolk, Va.: Gatling Printing, 1981), 143–174; Hiroshi Kida, *Sengo kyoiku no tenkai to kadai* (Postwar educational developments and tasks) (Tokyo: Kyoiku Kaihatsu Kenkyujo, 1976), ch. 1–2.

4. Interview of Joseph C. Trainor, 9 June 1980; Interview of Mark T. Orr, 11 January 1980.

5. Japan, National Council on Educational Reform (Japan, NCER), *Second Report on Educational Reform* (Tokyo: Government of Japan, 1986), 207.

6. Shiro Takahashi and Harry Wray, *Senryoka no kyoiku kaikaku to kenetsu* (Educational reform and censorship under the allied occupation of Japan) (Tokyo: Nihon Kyoiku Shimbunsha, 1987), 107–177; Thomas Rohlen, *Japan's High Schools* (Berkeley and Los Angeles: University of California Press, 1984), 257–264.

7. Taketoshi Imamura, *Kyoiku gyosei no kiso chishiki to horitsu mondai* (Fundamental understanding of educational administration and its legal problems), rev. ed. (Tokyo: Dai Ichi Hoki Shuppansha), 52, as cited in Teruhisa Horio, *Educational Thought and Ideology*, ed. and trans. Steven Platzer (Tokyo: University of Tokyo Press, 1988), 248.

8. Estelle James and Gail Benjamin, *Public Policy and Private Education in Japan* (London: Macmillan, 1988), 97–103, 174–175.

9. Shogo Ichikawa, "Financing Japanese Education," in *Windows on Japanese Education*, ed. Edward R. Beauchamp (Westport, Conn.: Greenwood Press, 1991), 93.

10. Japan, Ministry of Education, Service, and Culture (Japan, MESC), *Education in Japan, 1989: A Graphic Presentation* (Tokyo: Gyosei, 1994), 28–29; "Boards of Education in Transition," *Asahi Evening News*, 18 January 1994, p. 9.

11. Japan, NCER, *Second Report*, 125–126, 196, 202.

12. Horio, *Educational Thought*, 201–216; Victor N. Kobayashi, "Japanese and U.S. Curriculum Compared," in *Educational Policies in Crisis*, ed. William Cummings, Shogo Ichikawa, Edward R. Beauchamp, Victor N. Kobayashi, and Morikazu Ushiogi (Westport, Conn.: Praeger, 1986), ch. 4.

13. Sho Takakura and Yokuo Murata, *Education in Japan: Teaching Courses and Subjects, 1989* (Tsukuba: University of Tsukuba Institute of Education 1989), 10.

14. Joseph C. Trainor, *Educational Reform in Occupied Japan: Trainor's Memoir* (Tokyo: Meisei University Press, 1983), 217–219; interview of Vivian Carley by D. Clayton James, 23 August 1971.

15. Harry Wray, "Significance, Changes, and Continuity in Modern Japanese Educational History," *Comparative Education Review* 35, no. 3 (1991): 452–453.

16. William Cummings, Shogo Ichikawa, Edward R. Beauchamp, Victor N. Kobayashi, and Morikazu Ushiogi, eds., *Educational Policies in Crisis* (Westport, Conn.: Praeger, 1986), 47.

17. Takahashi and Wray, *Senryoka no kyoiku*, 107–177.

18. Wray, "Significance, Change, and Continuity," 462.

19. Horio, *Educational Thought*, 151; "Nakasone Receives Final Education Reform Report," 1, and Editorial, "Education Reform," *The Daily Yomiuri*, 8 August 1987; Editorial, "The Screening of Textbooks," *The Daily Yomiuri*, 4 July 1984; "LDP Presses Firm to Revise Text," *The Daily Yomiuri*, 4 October 1988; "Textbook Writers Protest Screening," *The Daily Yomiuri*, 8 July 1990; Editorial: "Textbook Screening:

The Way Textbooks Are Screened," *The Daily Yomiuri*, 3 July 1990; Hiroshi Yamagiwa, "Textbook Screening Gets the Ministry Spin," *The Japan Times*, 27 June 1997; Shigeru Fukushima, "Textbook Screening Leads to Narrow Thinking," *Asahi Evening News*, 15 July 1996; "*Vox Populi, Vox Dei*, Education Ministry's Examination of Textbooks," *Asahi Evening News*, 7 August 1997; Kazue Suzuki, "Ministry Blasted for Its Sexist Censorship of Textbooks," *Asahi Evening News*, 6 July 1997.

20. "*Vox Populi, Vox Dei*," *Asahi*, 7 August 1997; Benjamin Duke, "The Textbook Controversy," *Japan Quarterly* 19, no. 3 (1972).

21. Tai Kawabata, "Textbook Author Will Sue Ministry," *The Japan Times*, 20 April 1993.

22. Yamagiwa, "Textbook Screening."

23. "A Matter of History," *The Japan Times*, 1 October 1986; Wray, "Significance, Changes, and Continuity," 462–464.

24. "Seoul Raps Lawmaker's War View," *Asahi Evening News*, 17 March 1995.

25. Edward Beauchamp and James M. Vardaman, eds., *Japanese Education since 1945: A Documentary Study* (Armonk, N.Y.: M. E. Sharpe, 1994), 321.

26. Hisahiko Okazaki, "Let Common Sense Prevail," *The Japan Times,* 3 December 1996; Masayoshi Suga, "Historian Struggles to Unveil Truth," *Asahi Evening News*, 30 July, 1995.

27. "A Matter of History," *The Japan Times*, 1 October 1986; Harry Wray and Shiro Takahashi, *Obei kara mita Nihon no kyoiku* (Japanese education viewed from Europe and the United States) (Tokyo: Kyodo Shuppan, 1989), 128–132; Thomas Rohlen, *Japan's High Schools* (Berkeley and Los Angeles: University of California Press, 1984), 244–250.

28. Harry Wray, "Amerika kara mita Shinjuwan" (Pearl Harbor seen from America), in *Shinjuwan moeru* (Pearl Harbor enflamed), ed. Ikuhiko Hata (Tokyo: Hara Shobo, 1991), 61–100.

29. "LDP Cancels Vow on Textbooks," *Asahi Evening News*, 27 September 1996; "LDP Presses Firm," *The Daily Yomiuri*, 4 October 1988.

30. "Survey: Text Checks Softer," *Asahi Evening News*, 11 July 1994; "Texts Acknowledge War Compensation," *Asahi Evening News*, 30 May 1996; Kimie Itakura, "Conservatives Ignite History Controversy," *Asahi Evening News*, 16 September 1997.

31. John Vachon, "Text Uses Whitewash to Turn History into Propaganda," *Asahi Evening News*, 8 December 1996; "Group Says Set Masochistic History Texts Right," *The Japan Times*, 3 December 1996; Karel van Wolferen, "On Victimhood and the Uses of History," *Asahi Evening News*, 14, 15, 16, and 17 May 1997; Kimie Itakura, "Conservatives Ignite Human History," *Asahi Evening News*, 16 September, 1997.

32. Fujioka Nobokatsu, "Sex Slave Issue Is a Scandal Invented to Bash Japan," Hayashi Hirofumi, "'Comfort Women' System Was Obviously Slavery," *Asahi Evening News*, 26 January 1997; Mayumi Maruyama, "Group Challenges Textbook Accounts of Sexual Slavery," *Asahi Evening News*, 3 December 1996.

33. Editorial, "Ienaga Textbook Lawsuits Offer Lesson in Democracy," *Asahi Evening News*, 6 September 1997; Horio, *Educational Thought*, 206.

34. Japan, NCER, *Second Report*, 197.

35. Ernest L. Boyer, *High School* (New York: Harper Colophon Books, 1983), 288, 291.

36. Ibid., 251–261; Isao Amagi, ed., *Sogo ni mita Nichibei kyoiku no kadai* (Mutually observed tasks of Japanese and American Education) (Tokyo: Dai Ichi Hoki Shuppan, 1987), 73–79, 81–82, 119–120, 214–218.

37. U.S. Department of Education, National Center for Education Statistics (U.S. DOE, NCES), *The Condition of Education 1991*, Vol. 1, *Elementary and Secondary Education* (Washington, D.C.: U.S. Government Printing Office, 1991), 185; U.S. Department of Education, National Center for Education Statistics (U.S. DOE, NCES), *Digest of Education Statistics 1994* (Washington D.C.: U.S. Government Printing Office, 1994), 434; Japan, MESC, *Education in Japan 1994*, 62.

38. Harold W. Stevenson and James Stigler, *The Learning Gap: Why Our Schools Are Failing and What We Can Learn from Japanese and Chinese Education* (New York: Summit, 1992), 111.

39. Japan, MESC, *Education in Japan 1994*, 66; Charles Sykes, *Dumbing Down Our Kids* (New York: St. Martin's Press, 1995), 183–184.

40. "Mainstreaming Disabled Children," *Asahi Evening News*, 1 November 1994.

41. Ichikawa, "Financing Japanese Education," 80; Japan, Ministry of Education, Science, and Culture (Japan, MESC), *Japanese Government Policies in Education, Science and Culture 1991* (Tokyo: Government of Japan, 1991), 83.

42. Ichikawa, "Financing Japanese Education," 80; Japan, MESC, *Japanese Government Policies*, 83.

43. Merry White, *Japanese Educational Challenge* (New York: Free Press, 1987), 155–159.

44. Michiaki Sato, "Graduates Go Back to School to Find a Job," *Asahi Evening News*, 6 April 1997.

45. Nobuo Shimahara, "Restructuring Japanese High Schools: Reforms for Diversity," *Educational Policy* 9, no. 2 (June 1995): 17, 20.

46. Benjamin Duke, *Japanese School: Lessons for Industrial America* (Westport, Conn.: Praeger, 1986), 205–207.

47. Kazunori Shibuya, "The Struggle to Prevent High School Dropouts," *Asahi Evening News*, 22 May 1997.

48. Sho Takakura and Yokuo Murata, *Education in Japan: Teaching Courses and Subjects 1989* (Tsukuba: University of Tsukuba Institute of Education, 1989), 172–174; Sho Takakura and Yokuo Murata, *Education in Japan: A Bilingual Text—Present Situation and Problems* (Tsukuba: University of Tsukuba Institute of Education, 1989), 171–172; Japan, MESC, *Education in Japan 1994*, 24–25.

49. Japan, MESC, *Education in Japan 1994*, 58–59, 62–63.

50. Duke, *Japanese School*, 200–201.

51. Japan, NCER, *Second Report*, 84, 107, 109–110.

52. U.S. DOE, NCES, *Digest 1992*, 73; Japan, MESC, *Education in Japan 1994*, 54–55; James B. Conant, *The American High School Today* (New York: McGraw-Hill, 1959), 44–46.

53. Yutaka Shiokura, "Psychologists Become Counselors to Discuss Student Problems," *Asahi Evening News*, 5–6 May 1996.

54. Another word of explanation is necessary. In the remainder of this chapter and subsequent chapters I have cited my students' personal educational experiences. The method of collecting this data was simple. Students from one Nagoya University seminar and seven Nanzan University classes over the past four years read and discussed earlier drafts of some chapters and wrote paragraphs expressing their disagreement or agreement. In addition, students in two Nanzan University British–American Studies classes and one Nagoya University Education College seminar combining senior and graduate students were given a take-home examination that required them to criticize earlier drafts of this manuscript that had already been discussed in class.

Both Nagoya University and Nanzan students of the British–American studies department rank in the upper 15 to 20 percent of Japanese university students.

55. Gerald K. LeTendre, "Shido: The Concept of Guidance," in *Teaching and Learning in Japan*, ed. Thomas Rohlen and Gerald K. LeTendre (Cambridge: Cambridge University Press), 289.

56. Nicholas D. Kristof, "Where Children Rule," *The New York Times*, 17 August 1997.

57. Catherine C. Lewis, *Educating Hearts and Minds* (Cambridge: Cambridge University Press, 1995), 142–143.

58. Kristof, "Where Children Rule."

59. Thomas Rohlen and Gerald K. LeTendre, "Conclusion," in *Teaching and Learning in Japan*, ed. Thomas Rohlen and Gerald K. LeTendre (Cambridge: Cambridge University Press), 375.

60. LeTendre, "Shido," 277.

61. Tadashi Fukutake, *Japanese Society Today* (Tokyo: University of Tokyo Press, 1974), 130.

62. Ibid.

63. Source withheld at the request of the author.

64. Interview with Kimura Kazumi, March 1991.

65. One cram school teacher stated, "Formal schools have been devastated because teachers try to control students by so many strict rules. So usually children enjoy *juku*."

66. Japan, NCER, *Second Report*, 14, 22–23.

67. Ibid., 12–14, 20–23.

68. Ken Schoolland, *Shogun's Ghost: The Dark Side of Japanese Education* (New York: Bergin & Garvey, 1990), 24–25.

69. "High School Rule Ensures No Dress Code Deviations," *The Daily Yomiuri*, 3 October 1990; Hugh Levinson, "Rigid Schools Lead Families to Emigrate," *The Japan Times*, 8 April 1997.

70. Nicholas D. Kristof, "Japanese Schools Stand Out, but Not Always for the Best," *Asahi Evening News*, 24 July 1995.

71. George Fields, "Cultural Insularity—Unofficial Part of Japanese School Curriculum," *The Japan Times*, 2 July 1987, as cited in Ken Schoolland, *Shogun's Ghost: The Dark Side of Japanese Education* (Westport, Conn.: Bergin & Garvey, 1990), 38.

72. Vernacular Views, "School Goes Way Beyond Splitting Hairs," *The Japan Times*, 28 May 1989.

73. Ken Schoolland, *Shogun's Ghost: The Dark Side of Japanese Education* (Westport, Conn.: Bergin & Garvey, 1990), 26.

74. Christian Huggett, "Okazaki Boy Struggles for Independence from School's Close-Cropped Conformity," *The Japan Times*, 27 February 1990.

75. "Young Author Jabs at Rigid School Rules," *The Japan Times Weekly*, 11 August 1987.

76. Peter McGills, "He Who Fights the School Code Loses," *Asahi Evening News*, 15 June 1988.

77. "High School Rule," *Daily Yomiuri*, 3 October 1990; Levinson, "Rigid Schools Lead Families"; Letter to the Editor, "Corporal Punishment Needed in Some Cases," *The Daily Yomiuri*, 3 April 1991.

78. Japan, NCER, *Second Report*, 21, 53, 65–72.

79. Tai Kawabata, "When 'Controlled' Education at Schools in Aichi Goes Awry," *The Japan Times,* 23 April 1986.

80. "Many Parents Say Teachers Should Use the Rod," *Asahi Evening News,* 5 March 1996; Letter, "Corporal Punishment Needed."

81. Schoolland, *Shogun's Ghost,* l03.

82. Christian Huggett, "Okazaki Boy"; Christian Huggett, "School Corporal Punishment Leaving Scars That Never Heal," *The Japan Times,* 23 April 1991.

83. LeTendre, "Shido," 278–279.

84. "Record Truants Cite Dislike of School," *The Japan Times,* 7 August 1998; Miriam Educhi, "Teacher Sanctioned Violence Pervasive," *Azahi Evening News,* 15 January 1995; "School Acquitted in Suicide of Bullied Student," *The Daily Yomiuri,* 9 August 1990; Yoko Hani, "Japan Slowly Comes to Grips with Bullying Issue," *The Japan Times,* 10 January 1996.

85. Schoolland, *Shogun's Ghost,* l04.

86. "Study: Young Gym Teachers Use Force to Punish Students," *The Daily Yomiuri,* 7 April 1991; Japan, NCER, *Second Report,* 14, 22–23.

87. Schoolland, *Shogun's Ghost,* 83. According to a Japan, National Education Research Institute survey, over 60 percent of teachers believe corporal punishment scarred the student–teacher relationship. Paradoxically, 46 percent of them believed in corporal punishment as a form of discipline. The resentment of students against this kind of controlled education is reflected in a song by Yotaka Ozaki entitled "Sotsugyo" (Graduation).

88. "Kobe School Girl Is Killed by Gate," *The Daily Yomiuri,* 7 August 1990; S. L. Bachman, "Girl's Death in Gate Fuels School Debate," *The Daily Yomiuri,* 9 August 1990.

89. "Student Buried in Sand Sues Teachers, Principal, and City," *The Japan Times,* 29 March 1991.

90. "School Corporal Punishment," *The Japan Times,* 23 April 1991.

91. "Students Assault Saitama Teachers," *The Daily Yomiuri,* 24 November 1990.

92. Ibid.; "Student Reported to Police," *The Daily Yomiuri,* 15 November 1990.

93. Mombusho shoto chuto kyoikukyoku (Ministry of education, bureau on elementary and middle grades education), *Toko kyohi (futoko) mondai ni tsuite* (On the problem of school phobia [school refusal]) (Tokyo: Mombusho, 1992), as cited in Lewis, *Educating Hearts and Minds,* 179–180. David Willis and Koji Nakamura, "Answering the Drop-Out Problem in Japan," World Conference of Comparative Education, Sydney, Australia, July 1996; "Truancy Hits All-Time High," *Asahi Evening News,* 8 August 1996; Editorial, "Revise Educational System to Ease Burden on Students," *Asahi Evening News,* 6 March 1994; "High School Dropouts Near 100,000 in Fiscal 1995," *Asahi Evening News,* 22 February 1997.

94. Etsuko Akuzawa, Manabu Hasegawa, and Yutaka Shiokura, "Reformatory Fear for School Dropouts," *Asahi Evening News,* 22 June 1997; Emiko Inagaki, "Exam Hell Explodes Bright Children," *Asahi Evening News,* 1 December 1996.

95. "Most Dropouts Are Happy They Left School, But . . ." *The Japan Times,* 24 March 1997.

96. Jamie Anderson, "Scandal of Passing Failed Students," *Asahi Evening News,* 11 May 1997.

97. "*Ijemekko no kahansu ijimerareta taiken mo,*" (A majority of bullying students were formerly bullied themselves) *Yomiuri Shimbun,* 23 May 1996; "Most Par-

ents Unaware of Bullying," *Asahi Evening News*, 23 May 1996; Kathleen Morikawa, "Opening a Pandora's Lunch Box of Bullying for Children," *Asahi Evening News*, 15 June 1996; "One in Three Students Bullied, Survey Shows," *The Japan Times*, 30 April 1998.

98. John Vachon, "Lessons in Torture," *Asahi Evening News*, 16 February 1997.

99. Isao Furumori, "Adult Student Bullies Two Sides of Same Coin," *Asahi Evening News*, 11 August 1997.

100. Isao Kanda, Tsuginobu Matoba, and Asako Miyasaka, "Two Years on: Bullying Suicide Recalled," *Asahi Evening News*, 14–15 December 1996; Editorial, "Lack of Education Freedom at Root of Bullying Problem," *Asahi Evening News*, 21 July 1996; "Bullies Target Friends, Survey Says," *Asahi Evening News*, 10 June 1996; Kunihiro Yamada, "Critical New Books on School Bullying Epidemic," *Asahi Evening News*, 8 December 1996.

101. Kyoko Fujiu, "Producing Spoiled Children Who Act like 'Pet Dogs,'" *Asahi Evening News*, 24 November 1996.

102. "School Hair, Dress Codes Seen on Rise Despite Ministry Call for Relaxation," *The Japan Times*, 5 December 1990; "School Ban on Dorms Is Upheld by Court," *The Japan Times*, 31 October 1992.

103. "Survey Shows Schools Relaxing Rules of Conduct for Students," *The Daily Yomiuri*, 13 April 1991.

104. Shinso Yaguchi, *Gakko ni okeru issei shido o kangaenaoso* (Let's reconsider the entire system of education in the schools), *Asahi Shimbun*, 9 April, 1994.

105. Atsuko Shigesawa, "Parents, Kids to Mark School-Gate Death," *The Japan Times*, 6 July 1991; Kazuya Shioda, "Draconian Discipline Rules Led to Death at School Gate," *The Daily Yomiuri*, 13 February 1993.

106. Keizai Doyukai, *Atarashii Ko no Ikusei: Sekai ni Shinrai Sareru Nihonjin o Mezashite* (Tokyo: Keizai Doyukia Hokoku, 1989), 4; an English version entitled *Fostering "New Individualism,"* was published in 1990.

107. Japan, NCER, *Second Report*, 21, 67.

108. "Ex-Student Awarded Damages over Bike Ban," *Daily Yomiuri*, 8 May 1991, 2.

109. "Survey Shows Schools Relaxing Rules of Conduct for Students," *The Daily Yomiuri*, 13 April 1991.

110. Huggett, "Corporal Punishment Leaving Scars."

111. "School Is Mum on Results of Survey," *The Japan Times*, 29 March 1991.

112. Tomoko Tsurumei, "Students Strive to Promote Human Rights," *Asahi Evening News*, 15 April 1996.

113. Ibid.

114. "Survey Shows Schools"; "Home Discipline Would Prevent School Deaths," *Asahi Evening News*, 27 July, 1995; Japan, NCER, *Second Report*, 21, 67.

115. Editorial, "Lack of Education Freedom at Root of Bullying Problem," *Asahi Evening News*, 21 July 1996; Kunihiro Yamada, "Critical New Books on School Bullying Epidemic," *Asahi Evening News*, 8 December 1996; Yoko Ito, "It Is Time for Japan to Tolerate 'Oddballs,'" *Asahi Evening News*, 12 March 1995.

116. Sadako Ogata, "First-Hand Experience Offers Hope for Solidarity," *Asahi Evening News*, 7 September 1997.

117. "Education by Force," *Asahi Evening News*, 22 October 1986.

118. Editorial, "In What Direction Are Japanese Youth Heading?" *Asahi Evening News*, 3 July 1994. According to the Japan Youth Research Institute, 23 percent of Japanese students held pessimistic views of the future compared to 3 percent of Ameri-

can and 7 percent of Taiwanese students. Fifty-two percent of Japanese students "enjoy the present without thinking of the future," compared to 22 percent of American and 13 percent of Taiwanese students.

119. John Vachon, "Lessons in Torture," *Asahi Evening News*, 16 February 1997.

120. Ikuo Amano, "The Dilemma of Japanese Education Today," in *Japanese Schooling: Patterns of Socialization, Equality, and Political Control*, ed. James J. Shields, Jr. (University Park: Pennsylvania State University Press, 1989), 122.

121. Edwin O. Reischauer, *The Japanese Today* (Tokyo: Charles E. Tuttle, 1988), 408–409.

122. Peter Milward, "Humanize Japan's Education System," *The Japan Times*, 4 November 1990; "Korean Schools Ask to Join Athletic Group," *The Japan Times*, 11 December 1990.

123. Kazunaga Fukushima, "Waiting for the Academic Doors to Open," *Asahi Evening News*, 26 February 1996; "Foreign Parents Target Schools," *Asahi Evening News*, 29 May 1995.

124. *Japan Times Weekly International Edition*, 25–31 January 1993.

125. "Foreign Teachers' Fate in Limbo," *The Japan Times,* 22 June 1991.

126. Ibid. Fourteen prefectures and seven of the eleven largest cities ignored the Mombusho ruling because they did not want to reverse their more progressive internationalization policy.

127. Fumiko Yoshigaki, "Silent Consensus for Education Change," *Asahi Evening News,* 28 March 1995.

128. "Get 'Em Young Campaign Promoted," *Asahi Evening News,* 19 June 1995.

129. Kazunaga Fukushima, "No Easy Answers for Teachers of English," *Asahi Evening News,* 29 January 1996.

130. Hiromi Kitagaki, "Japan's Educators Should Take a New Look at Asia," *Asahi Evening News,* 16 August 1996.

131. Kazunaga Fukushima, "Language Students Turn Their Backs on French, German," *Asahi Evening News,* 30 September 1996.

132. Kazunaga Fukushima, "Raising English from the Depths," *Asahi Evening News,* 8 December 1996.

133. "The Failure of English Education in Japan," *The Daily Yomiuri*, 13 September 1990.

134. Fukushima, "Raising English."

135. Laurel Dianne Kamada, "Affective Factors in English Learning in Japanese Schools," *Psychologia—An International Journal of Psychology in the Orient* 21, no. 3 (September 1989); David Wardell, "Too Much Emphasis on University Entrance Exams," *The Daily Yomiuri*, 15 November 1990; Yuriko Tamaki, "The Failure of English Education in Japan," *Daily Yomiuri*, 13 September 1990.

136. Minoru Wada, "East and West Meet in School," *Asahi Evening News,* 25 March 1996.

137. White, *The Japanese Educational Challenge*, 70–72; Editorial, "Suppressed Individuality Can Make a Good Person Do Bad," *Asahi Evening News,* 30 October 1994; "Urge to Conform Called Narcissism," *The Japan Times,* 31 March 1994; Masao Miyamoto, *Straitjacket Society* (Tokyo: Kodansha International, 1994), ch. 2, 8.

138. Japan, National Council on Education Reform (Japan, NCER), *First Report on Educational Reform* (Tokyo: Government of Japan, 1985).

139. Takie Sugiyama Lebra, *Japanese Patterns of Behavior* (Honolulu: University of Hawaii Press, 1976), ch. 2, 184.

140. Kenzaburo Oe, "The Japanese Identity," *Asahi Evening News,* 22 June 1996.

141. Japanese are more successful than Westerners at achieving superficial harmony that hides deep ideological and personal hostility; this is significant in that cooperation on group goals can then be achieved.

142. Merry White, *Japanese Educational Challenge* (New York: Free Press, 1987), 173–174; Kevin C. Kato, "Internationalized Education Fit for Individuals," *Asahi Evening News,* 6 November 1995.

143. Tai Kawashita, "Perceptions Clash in Boy's Bullying Case," *The Japan Times,* 24 May 1991; "Americans Busy Building Bridges," *The Daily Yomiuri,* 21 November 1990; Nagisa Ban, Chieko Fujiwara, and Eiichi Tsunozu, "Bullies Target Ethnic Japanese Immigrants," *Asahi Evening News,* 20 November 1990; Shinso Yaguchi, "Gakko ni okeru issei shido o kangaenaoso" (Let's reconsider the entire system of education in the schools), *Asahi Shimbun,* 9 April 1994.

144. Yoji Morita, "Blame Racism and Conformity," *Asahi Evening News,* 11 May 1997; Shigeru Fukushima, "Influx of Foreigners Changing the Face of Japanese Classrooms," *Asahi Evening News,* 25 March 1996.

145. Editorial, "Japan's Acceptance of Other Asian Countries Is Essential," *Asahi Evening News,* 19 September 1994.

146. Izumi Miki, "Foreign Students in Japan: Change of Attitudes on Both Sides Is Needed," *The Japan Times,* 30 June 1988; Kyoichi Miyagawa, "Most Foreign Students Want to Have More Interaction with the Japanese," *The Japan Times,* 2 April 1989; Masago Minami, "Being Asian Makes It Worse," *The Daily Yomiuri,* 27 November 1987.

147. The questionnaire I administered gave students the opportunity to react in varying degrees of agreement or disagreement to twenty-five comments surveying their attitudes. To prevent bias, the questionnaire was administered on the first day of the school year to two sophomore classes, one comprised of Japanese Language majors and the other one made up of British–American Studies majors, and to one senior class of the same majors.

148. Toru Yano, "Our Internationalization or Yours," *The Japan Times,* 28 September 1989.

149. Schoolland, *Shogun's Ghost,* 174.

150. Roger Goodman, *Japan's "International Youth": The Emergence of a New Class of School Children* (Oxford: Oxford University Press, 1990), 164–169.

151. Reischauer, *Japanese Today,* 395–397; Kenzaburo Oe, *Asahi Evening News,* 22 June 1996; Edwin P. Hoyt, "Democratic Rhetoric Hides Rampant Racism," *The Daily Yomiuri,* 3 April 1991.

152. Lewis, *Educating Hearts and Minds,* 172–175.

153. Sho Taka Kura and Yukuo Murata, *Education in Japan: A Billingual Text—Present System and Tasks/Curriculum and Instruction* (Tokyo: Gakken, 1998), 109–111; Merry White, *The Japanese Overseas* (New York: Free Press, 1988), 26, 54; Goodman, *Japan's "International Youth,"* 149–151; Mombusho kyoiku kaikaku jitchi honbuhen, *Kokusai rikai to kyoryoku no shinten* (The development of international cooperation and understanding) (Tokyo: Gyosei, 1988).

154. The respective percentages for elementary, junior high, and senior high students was 39.9, 40.3, and 19.89. White, *Japanese Overseas,* 54, 197; Sho Takakura and Yokuo Murata, *Education in Japan: A Billingual Text—Present System and Tasks/Curriculum and Instruction* (Tokyo: Gakken, 1998), 109.

155. White, *Japanese Overseas*, 197; Goodman, *Japan's "International Youth,"* 28–29; "Keio University Makes Start of High School in New York," *The Japan Times*, 26 October 1990.

156. Goodman, *Japan's "International Youth,"* 182–189, 212; Editorial, "For Less Conformity in Education," *The Japan Times*, 31 January 1993.

157. Otsu Kazuko, "Shakaika ni okeru gurobaru kyoiku no 4 tsu no apurochi" (Four possible approaches to global education in social studies), *Kyoikugaku kenkyu* 61, no. 3 (September 1994): 279–286.

CHAPTER 4

The Distorting Influence of School Ranking,
Entrance Examinations,
and Supplementary Institutional Educational Systems
on Individuals and Schools

Japan's educational policy deliberately limits college entry, especially the number accepted to national universities. The number of students taking the 1996 National Center Test for University Admission totaled 574,000, but the number accepted was approximately 131,000; that is, only about ten out of every forty-four students were admitted.[1] This selection method is less costly for the public sector and private universities than the American system of opening the doors to most students who want to go to college and failing those who do not perform satisfactorily. However, it contributes to huge costs for the parents of students wanting to attend college in three ways: (1) by sending them to cram schools (after the regular school day ends); (2) by sending them to expensive private secondary schools to heighten their chances of entering a prestigious university; and (3) by sending them to private tutors and college preparatory schools after graduation until they can pass entrance examinations.

SOCIETAL OBSESSION

Entrance examination systems are the central focus of Japanese education. The cultural attitudes behind them are Japan's number-one enemy in terms of reform and true education. Benjamin Duke refers to them as a "mania" and Thomas Rohlen as a "national obsession."[2] The enormous emphasis on them is illustrated by private companies gathering past university entrance examinations from more than three hundred universities and publishing them in thick volumes for anxious students at a handsome profit.[3]

Because of entrance examinations' harmful influences, reforms of a tinkering nature are attempted periodically; however, often they create an even worse affect on secondary schools. Although former Prime Minister Nakasone Yasuhiro headed one of the strongest postwar governments, he failed in his bid to deemphasize entrance examinations and school ranking. Nakasone made their reform the rationale for establishing the blue ribbon NCER directly under the jurisdiction of the prime minister's office. He hoped the NCER would be as important in radically reforming the educational system as the Japanese Committee on Educational Reform had been under similar institutional arrangements during the Allied Occupation.[4] Nakasone managed to privatize the railroad and public communication system, but he could not reform education.

SECRECY AND SURVEILLANCE

Entrance examinations are prepared in the strictest secrecy and held in the tightest security because of the close connection between passing the high school examination and quality post–high school employment or between entering a good university and the quality of graduates' future employment. Graduates of the "best" universities are on the fast track to becoming top-level bureaucrats and executives of major corporations. The stakes are so high to enter universities that annually at least one shameful examination scandal occurs. Top-secret activities associated with all four stages of planning, preparing, administering, and grading the entrance examinations for "examination war," truly resemble a war that boggles the mind. It is standard procedure at university faculty meetings for all distributed materials dealing with the forthcoming entrance examinations, the names of members who will serve on various examination committees, and even notifications of meetings to committee members overseeing a particular subject area to be secret. During the actual administration and grading of a university entrance examination, gates and buildings are locked or guarded to prevent possible bribery of instructors, theft, or tampering with examinations. Examinees are assigned only examination sheet numbers to prevent favoritism. They sit at assigned desks with a card and attached photograph for identification. If the examination is a national one, graded by the Education Ministry's National Center for the University Entrance Examination, the answer sheets are delivered by truck under strict surveillance.[5]

RELUCTANCE TO REFORM
FUNDAMENTALLY THE SYSTEM

One reason the Japanese fail to reform the entrance examination systems is that Japan successfully modernized in part by establishing a fair and meritocratic entrance examination system that recruited the best talent regardless of geographical location or social origin for its industries and bureaucracy. Japan has not been able to find an attractive substitute selection and sorting system.[6] A second reason is related to the national character. Japanese tend to be conservative, deliberate, and fearful of failure and criticism. When Japanese fear taking an action or do not want to try something new, they can be counted on to invoke the words "there is no precedent" (*zenrei ga nai*). Characteristically, Japanese do not act until they have thought, researched, and achieved time-consuming consensus on all policies, especially those affecting sensitive human relations. Rohlen remarked aptly, "Without exams . . . school systems and individual teachers would be more innovative and more independent of the Ministry of Education, and education itself would become more colorful and chaotic. I doubt that most Japanese would find such a development comfortable."[7]

A third factor that makes Japanese reluctant to reform fundamentally is that entrance examinations are believed to be important to character formation. They assume that children cannot achieve maturity unless the growth process from childhood to adulthood is challenging spiritually and emotionally. As Rohlen and LeTendre put it, the stages of development from early schooling centering on curiosity, spontaneity, energy, and collective activity move progressively at the secondary level to emphasizing concentrated effort, individual work, suffering, attainment, and self-discipline to achieve individual perfection.[8] From this point of view, rote memory, drill, repetitive imitations of forms and processes, and textbook and teacher-centered learning activities are believed to develop character and higher cognitive thinking.

A fourth closely related reason for failing to reform the system is a crisis mentality. Although Japan has become an affluent society and a powerful force in the international economy, modern Japanese education and society have been shaped by the fear that potential disaster looms just around the corner. This thinking derives from three factors in Japanese geography and modern history. From primitive times to World War II Japan has been a poor, overwhelmingly agrarian society. Farmers have been grimly aware of the capacity of frequent natural disasters to destroy the narrow margin between economic survival and catastrophe. National anxiety increased with Japan's efforts to become a modern nation under the slogan "rich country (read: industrialization) and strong military," because it lacked nearly every natural resource. Japan became dependent on other nations' raw materials.[9] In the last thirty years Japanese have become extremely dependent on other nations' foodstuffs. Given its present huge trade surplus, Westerners may view this crisis mentality with some skepticism. To many Japanese over forty years old, however, there is no other way for Japan to compete with the West (and now other developing Asian nations) than to continue existing educational policies and practices. In short, Japan's geography and success breeds conservatism. Most Japanese fear radical reform will jeopardize Japan's future.[10] Finally, more affluent parents and bureaucratic self-interest perpetuated higher-ranked schools' and universities' prestige.

OCCUPATION'S INABILITY TO CORRECT
ENTRANCE EXAMINATIONS

During the Occupation of Japan, the CIE's Education Division tried to eliminate school ranking and the severe competition of entrance examinations by transplanting indigenous American values, practices, and institutions. That meant permitting students to attend schools only in their own geographically proximate school districts, free tuition through the compulsory education stage, and a comprehensive curriculum to maximize equal opportunity and satisfaction of individual needs, interests, and abilities. The Education Division staff assumed that by expanding equal educational opportunity in Japan they could eliminate the school ranking and the excessive competition that had characterized prewar secondary and university entrance examinations. Accordingly, in 1947 they extended compulsory education for three years and introduced coeducation and a single track, 6–3–3–4 educational ladder system. The Americans failed to realize, however, that

1. American-induced reforms coupled with economic affluence would increase student competition by making high school and university education available to many more aspirants.
2. No penalties would be imposed on students attending high schools or universities outside their district or prefecture.
3. The profusion of new secondary schools and universities, parental ambitions, and indigenous values preferring a vertical (hierarchical) society would lead to an even more elaborate ranking of secondary schools and universities.[11]
4. Business and government leaders would prefer an intensely competitive meritocratic system.

The difference between a student's school record and the difficulty of a given school's entrance examination is referred to as the deviation value (*hensachi*). A student's high deviation score reflects a strong possibility for passing the entrance examination of a good senior high school or university. From the late 1960s mock examinations administered by commercial educational companies cram schools (*juku*) and college preparatory schools (*yobiko*) have served two purposes: They tell students the extent to which they have mastered subject matter in every subject they might be challenged on in entrance examinations; and they project the level of a school or university that a student may enter successfully by providing a match up of students' test score with a given high school's or university's deviation score. Students attempt to raise their deviation scores to get into the highest ranking school possible by private study of entrance examination reference works in schools or public libraries, by purchasing them at bookstores, and by either hiring a home tutor or attending a cram school at the end of the school day. When they fail university examinations, they may attend a *yobiko* as a so-called *ronin* until they pass the entrance examination at the university of their choice.[12]

Students can learn the deviation score of every secondary school and university (as well as departments within universities) on the basis of detailed information published by highly competitive private educational testing companies, usually synonymous with their *juku* or *yobiko*. Before the Mombusho forbade them from administering mock tests within junior high schools in 1993, they often were not given by the schools themselves. The Ministry banned mock tests because it believed education was distorted by junior high schools using them as the only measure for entry to high school. Its ban, however, is contradictory because it is in part due to entrance examination policy that this pressure on students and schools has been perpetrated. To cope with this condition schools are engaging in various subterfuges.

In general, stratagems that one could predict are occurring.[13] Students themselves contract with private companies for periodic mock testing. Companies are also allegedly supplying students' scores to senior high schools or, unofficially, selling tests to schools that now are administered and graded by teachers. Private companies and universities also hold tests at selected sites. In this manner approximately 46,000 students, a little more than one-half of all junior high school third-year students in Saitama prefecture, are taking examinations administered by the same firm that used to give examinations within the schools. Finally, some schools are combining their efforts to design interschool tests or to give tests developed by the association of school principals. Mombusho treated a symptom, not the disease.

THE BASIC MEANING OF EDUCATION IS DISTORTED

In this chapter I want to examine more specifically how entrance examinations grievously distort Japan's education system. But first it is necessary to raise two fundamental questions: What is the meaning of education? And, what are its purposes? If education means simply the accumulation of factual matter or serving a nation's industrial needs, Japan's modern educational system is one of the best in the world. If education means developing critical thinking, enjoying quality leisure time, coping with diversity, nurturing internationally minded persons, meeting students' individual interests, arousing curiosity and imagination for further study, and fostering civic consciousness, Japan possesses one of the world's worst educational systems.

The word "education" means to lead the mind outward. Education should help children to master the basics, to be creative, to enrich future adults' leisure, to develop critical judgments, to foster individuality and human dignity, to make them informed of their human rights, and to take an interest in community, national, and international problems. On all these aspects Japanese schools are failing because children are pushed along in a giant exercise in memorizing as much subject matter as possible for the purpose of passing examinations.[14] The result is to create a student population that is absolutely spongelike in absorbing masses of factual data. One student who had studied in an American secondary school for four years observed,

Throughout my four years of college life at Nanzan, I learned that most Japanese students are not good at answering "What do you think?" and "Why do you think?" questions. Japanese education tends to teach in "manual" ways, not in "imaginative" ways. Students are taught how to "memorize" for their entrance examinations. Japanese teachers are limited from using a more intellectually stimulating and creative methodology in dealing with students individually. It is not the teachers' fault; it is the system of Japanese education that is to be blamed. Students who were taught in manual ways become teachers, and they follow what they were taught as youngsters.

Japan's highest rewards go to those students who limit distractions and narrow their focus on mastering details pertinent to entrance examinations, especially at Japan's five top-ranked universities: Tokyo University, Kyoto University, Hitotsubashi University, Keio University, and Waseda University. The all-around, Renaissance man or versatile student who excels in various areas or sports in Western society are anomalies in Japanese schools. (If students want to be outstanding athletes, they will attend those few private and public high schools that have developed a reputation for winning teams and compete in only one sport.) The time required daily by sports means that ambitious students hopeful of gaining entrance to high ranked high schools and universities will be severely penalized.[15] Similarly, clubs requiring too much daily effort may cause students to forsake them. In fact, schools usually require students to withdraw from club activities in the second and third quarters of ninth and twelfth grades. A Nanzan senior female gloomily wrote, "I remember that I used to think 'When I enter senior high school, I can relax and enjoy more.' In senior high school I thought 'When I enter the university, I can enjoy my life at last.' And then when I entered the university, I learned of the difficulty of women getting a job after graduation. Japanese students tend to think that their happiness is so much in the future that we cannot enjoy our lives right now."

Japanese university students and graduates joke about how they devour huge quantities of facts, regurgitate them for examinations, and proceed to forget quickly much of what they have learned.[16] When I polled each of my 1994, 1995, 1996, and 1997 Nanzan University classes of approximately forty English majors on whether they thought they could still pass the university's freshmen English entrance examination without any preparation, they unanimously agreed that they could not. What a travesty!

In the social sciences and humanities, the meaning of education is particularly distorted. In Japanese history education, circumstances compel students to believe that the textbook version is the only correct interpretation of a historical event. Teachers may hold differing opinions from textbooks; however, for them to discuss frequently these shortcomings penalizes students needing to master only factual knowledge for entrance examinations.[17] One Nanzan senior commented ruefully

Because I attended a "high level school," almost all teachers taught us just what we needed for the entrance examination, but I remember one outstanding teacher of Japanese history. Actually he was hated by most of the students and other teachers, because he often taught us things irrelevant to the entrance exams. He used many materials without using textbooks. But looking back, he was the most impressive teacher I had. He just doesn't fit the education system.

Several Nanzan students who studied under the same teacher have made the same remark over the past five years.

WAYS IN WHICH ENTRANCE EXAMINATIONS DISTORT EDUCATION

Entrance examinations reinforce excessive conformity, passivity, standardization, anxiety, group consciousness, and controlled education. One Japanese study showed that 76 percent of junior high school students worry about study and school advancement, 45 percent higher than any other category.[18] One Nanzan University senior lamented, "In elementary school we had many occasions to give our opinions, however, after we entered junior high school, we did not get such opportunities because all the studies are for high school entrance examinations, and all the studies in high school are for university entrance examinations. One who is considered 'intelligent' is one who can get good grades, not those who have their own opinions."

Beginning in middle school education becomes teacher and textbook centered. Lectures replace the multitask classroom organization and small group activity of elementary school years. There is almost no discussion and no time for students' opinions, digression, or group problem solving (with the exception of math and science). Rebecca Irwin Fukuzawa's research showed that in only 1 out of 103 class observations did a teacher take the time to break the students into small groups to discuss the relevance of a reading to a contemporary problem. She also discovered that teachers of academic subjects based at least 60 percent of the semester grade on examination scores that tested memorization of lecture and textbook material. Verbal ability, class participation, or ability to write well played no significant role in affecting grades. Attitude played only about a 10 percent role in grading.[19]

My analysis of the impact of entrance examination over the past ten years has led me to appreciate deeply Rohlen's judgment that "the ambition to succeed in education is the ultimate source of discipline. Without the entrance exam competition, neither textbooks nor curricular requirements would be sufficient to keep instruction as strictly focused on the narrow path of encyclopedic learning as it now is."[20] Entrance examinations are a powerful "club" over the heads of students, forcing their compliance. But they are not as effective with all students, especially at the junior high school level where one study showed 95.7 percent of school violence occurs.[21]

Excessive emphasis on passing entrance examinations plays a contributing role in killing most students' interest in studying and scholarship after entering a university, especially for those outside the science, engineering, and medical areas. Students exhausted by the dehumanizing methodology lose motivation and curiosity. A survey by the National Federation of University Cooperative Associations of Japan revealed that the average time a university student devoted to book reading was forty-five minutes a day; 2 percent of freshmen reported they were not reading any books at all. Many do not read their textbooks, but only cram over lecture notes. At the very moment of their highest level of intellectual potential, most college students are disgusted with study and only look forward to four years of enjoying themselves before entering the demanding life of a white collar worker. Some Japanese, including faculty members, contemptuously refer to the universities as "large playgrounds" or "leisure lands." But many contribute to poor study habits by adopting an indulgent attitude toward the students' mediocre performance.

One harmful impact of the entrance examinations is at the teacher level. Many Japanese teachers resent the constant pressure to do better than other schools, the distortion of real education by the cramming system, and the lack of autonomy they have to teach to individual differences and to local needs. One innovative Japanese history teacher in a middle level Yokohama high school, where less than one-fourth of the students will go on to college, told me of his great pleasure in teaching in a school where he could develop class materials and lectures appropriate to the geographic area and students' interests.

Secondary school teachers in most schools, however, feel compelled to teach in the most efficient manner content from published volumes of past examinations in their daily lessons. They feel forced to devote their energies during the school day, before and after the regular school day, and during school vacations, to ninth and twelfth graders so that they will pass the examinations for the next school level. A Nanzan student complained, "At my high school teachers made a desperate attempt to help their students enter a high ranking university. If the number of successful candidates in those universities' entrance examinations was less than that of the average years, they were given less respect. Teachers sometimes resigned from the responsibility of taking charge of the special classes for college-bound students."

Entrance examinations have a harmful impact on real learning in high school courses that are not relevant to those university entrance examinations for which students will not sit. Students taking the Unified Entrance Examination for National Universities must take examinations in English, Japanese, social studies, natural science, and mathematics. They need to be tested on only one of the five courses offered in the social studies category, usually only two subjects (and sometimes only one) of the four within the natural science category, and none in the art, music, and health categories.[22] Many of my undergraduate and graduate students admit to having worked on other subjects or to have listened inattentively during lectures that had no relationship to the entrance examinations. Students have learned "to work the system," and it is demoralizing for teachers.

To take another case, students selecting either a "science" or "literary" specialization in preparing for the college entrance examinations are inclined in their junior and senior year to slight those subjects that have no relationship to the type of entrance examination they select. Because literary students who plan to take examinations exclusively at private universities sit for only three examination subjects, social science (usually either Japanese History or World History), English, and Japanese language, they do not take seriously high school subjects unrelated to the subjects they will be tested on in the entrance examination. For example, because Japanese History is considered easier than World History, students overwhelmingly choose it in their entrance examinations. One *juku* teacher told me that only forty of the four-hundred students at her combined *juku* and *yobiko* took World History. Similarly science students taking private university entrance examinations will study seriously only English, Japanese, math, and either physics or chemistry within the science category. As an admission of this student tendency and the need to show greater diversification of the curriculum in 1992–1994 curricular reforms, the National Center for University Entrance Examinations in 1997 increased the number of subjects from five subjects and eighteen subcategories to six and thirty-four.[23] What we see here is an effort now to backtrack on a reform of a few years ago to reduce the number of subjects. The struggle between designers of tests and students to outmaneuver one another continues annually.

One strategy capable of exerting greater effort from some students in the nonentrance examination courses (besides their own desire to excel and the hated confidential record), is vying for recommended status. "Recommended status" applies to those students who obtain entry to private Japanese universities on the basis of their total academic performance and good conduct. Since 1995, Mombusho has forbidden universities to allow recommended status to students to exceed 30 percent. They must study every subject seriously until the end of the first semester of the senior year (a point Shogo Ichikawa had in mind when he argued that the negative impact of the entrance examinations is less than is stereotyped because some students can enter a university without taking them).[24] One Nanzan university senior coed wrote, "Nearly half of us wanted to be recommended students for some universities, so we joined classes and we studied hard." A decision in the 1980s to allow private universities two other options has had a harmful impact on true education. One option grants universities freedom to enroll students through a "self-recommendation" process of selection. Students only need to make a presentation of their specific talent. A second option allows private universities to reduce the existing number of examinations for which students must sit from three to two, or even one. These "reforms" reflected the growing concern of private universities facing potential bankruptcy to compete for a declining student enrollment. By 1993, 42.7 percent of private colleges had introduced one- or two-subject entrance exams.[25] The impact was felt immediately in high schools. Literary students planning to sit for only one of the three subjects of Japanese, English, and social studies were slighting other subjects. Science students could decide to choose between either physics or chemistry. Students might then be admitted into a Japanese literature program or history department, or engineering or science program, without having sat for any of these examinations. Regrettably, universities have found that students who had passed the "self-recommendation" examinations and the one- or two-subject entrance examinations were not qualified in the basics. For the first time in modern Japanese history universities have found it necessary to offer remedial courses, something that had not been in the Japanese experience. To remedy the damage from these "reforms" some universities and junior colleges have returned to the old three-subject examination. Still, 30 percent are continuing with them.

The success of prestigious private six-year schools in helping students enter good universities has resulted in two phenomena for advancing students into their own university: (1) many students are passing up public high schools in favor of good private six-year ones; and (2) many universities, from prestigious ones such as Keio University to lower ranking ones, have developed their own "escalator system" of not only junior and senior high schools, but also kindergartens and elementary schools. Although the ratio differs from school to school, the parent university may automatically accept as many as the top 50 or 60 percent of the students from their own feeder system; however, Keio University and Chuo University accept over 95 percent of their own high schools' graduates. But "escalator" seniors with low deviation scores are not able to enter scores for preferred departments. Instead, they are admitted into whatever department matches their deviation score and grade point average. This practice leads to low academic motivation for students assigned to a department discipline in which they are not really interested. Escalator students could take entrance examinations at other universities, but they seldom do for two reasons. First, their original motivation for entering the escalator system is because they wanted to enter the parent university. If students are attending a famous escalator system, such as Keio University, the social and economic value of Keio's name outweighs students' academic preference. Second, because entrance into the parent university is relatively automatic, students will not have spent their secondary school years cramming for university examinations.

Undesirable results of the entrance examinations are lower writing, creative, and cognitive abilities in students, for all subjects except mathematics and science. In fact, I have been left incredulous by four- or five-line answers in their own language to essay questions for which students in the United States would write two or more pages. Typical examples have occurred at Yokohama National University and Nanzan University when I have proctored other professors' examinations. Usually, for a fifty-minute examination, only four or five of fifty students may write answers that continue for three or four more lines on the back page of one answer sheet. Most answers to examination questions were only three to five lines. Good American eighth-grade students may write longer, better essay examinations than many Japanese college students.

Western professors teaching Japanese college students must make a big adjustment in their expectations of students' performances in English essay examinations, even in take-home essay examinations. Nine years ago I was confronted with the problem of what to do with a class in modern Japanese diplomatic history at a national university that I taught in English as a visiting professor. By normal standards I would have failed 75 percent of the students taking the final examination. Students had been given an advance list of ten complex questions from which I would select three. Yet, most answers were completed in only five or six lines! These short answers reflect the lack of seriousness that some university students adopt toward study because most know they will be passed. They also reflect their lack of familiarity with essay questions requiring students to explain the "why" of a problem; the belief by students that teachers may only want short answers; or the fear that a longer answer will carry the danger of conflicting with what a teacher believes. To correct this writing deficiency some universities now are requiring more short essay examinations. Taking their cue, *juku* and *yobiko* are now teaching how to write short essay answers.

Several close Japanese secondary school teacher–friends fluent in English complain that they cannot teach English conversation because their students' ability to pass entrance examinations would be handicapped and their prestige and that of their schools would suffer in comparison with other teachers and schools. English teachers' dissatisfaction was well documented by a comprehensive, four-volume General Survey of English Teaching in Japan, which showed well over 50 percent of teachers believed that "the current status of English language teaching in Japan is not good."[26] This condition prompted Tetsuo Tamara, the director of Shibuya Kyoiku Gakuen junior and senior high schools, to propose in vain to the Central Council on Education that the English exam be revised to evaluate examinees' proficiency to communicate in English. Tamura said, "The real purpose of my proposal was to make the point that entrance exams as they are now test neither the students' academic ability up to senior high school level nor their aptitude for university. They test their ability to regurgitate what they have been told. They are obedience tests."[27]

While I was at Yokohama National University, I served on the committee for the English section of the entrance examination. When I suggested on a couple of occasions that my current college junior students would not know the vocabulary of entrance examination questions we were going to adopt, other faculty readily agreed; but they did not accept that as a valid reason for making the examination easier. Why? There was a clear recognition by them that seniors taking the examination would know more English than they had as college juniors, even though they would have taken English three more years at the university level.

A national TV program a few years ago revealed the amazing oddity that three native English speakers who were teaching in Japan could not pass the Tokyo University English entrance examination. The interviewed teachers laughingly complained that the English was often archaic and abstruse, and the examination allowed only one answer, whereas for a native speaker two or more were possible.[28] Even though entrance examination vocabulary may be beyond that of some sophomores in American colleges, most students who can pass them cannot create an intelligent English sentence. Recently, the Central Council of Education admitted that entrance examinations have such a disastrous affect on acquiring competence in English oral communication that it took the radical step of recommending to the Ministry of Education that English be considered only as an option rather than as a required college entrance examination subject.[29] Instead of fundamentally reforming the entrance examinations and putting greater stress on oral English communication from elementary school, the Council is committing a major blow against English education. If this "reform" occurs, English education will experience the same effects that other subjects experience when they are not related to the entrance examination. This is "throwing out the baby with the bath water."[30]

As a result of entrance examination pressures, by the time students enter the upper elementary school grades and secondary school, textbooks tend to be too standardized, orthodox, dull, and difficult because they must cover *all* items required by the Ministry's standardized courses of study. The NCER's final report complained, "Today's textbooks . . . [place emphasis] on transmitting knowledge, and little attention is paid to developing in students thinking power or creativity, or to enhancing the willingness to learn. Textbooks have not always succeeded in [being] neutral and impartial. . . . The existing textbook authorization system is not adequately open, and the screening is apt to enter into too much detail."[31]

Even Mombusho-approved, easier supplementary textbooks are beyond the intellectual reach of poorer students. One former teacher at Tokyo Metropolitan Nerima High School, a lower ranking school where no more than nine or ten of forty students in each class will attend a university, told me the bottom half of social studies classes found them too difficult. A senior high school teacher in Yokohama working simultaneously at both a high ranking and a low ranking high school complained that the easier supplementary textbooks of the latter are still too difficult because they are geared to university entrance examinations and students feel frustrated, rebellious, and disposed to talk and ignore her lectures. Recently a principal of Yotsuya Commercial Senior High School in Tokyo complained that the high rate of dropouts was directly related to a condition where their skills do "not even match that of fifth grade elementary school students in terms of reading comprehension, composition, and . . . arithmetic."[32] He maintained that the cause was inherent in the excessive amount of material students were required to master and the practice of pushing students on to higher grade levels before they had mastered the basics.

A final criticism of the entrance examinations is the distorting impact they have on family living. Mothers are judged too much by the educational success of their children rather than their intrinsic merit. The keen competition to get into the most prestigious six-year private schools and escalator university systems places pressures on mothers, even of fourth-, fifth-, and sixth-grade pupils, to get their children into higher ranked six-year schools, senior high schools, and universities by various motivational techniques, private tutors, and cram schools. Some mothers become so competitive that they deny to other mothers how long their children study and conceal the name of their children's cram school, for fear their offspring may lose an advantage over another mother's son.

According to the Labor Ministry, the pressure to get into good high schools and universities results in nearly 500,000 fathers leaving their families behind (especially those living in the large cities) when they are transferred or go abroad for a work assignment. Japanese families fear that children's future success will be permanently handicapped if the children move to a foreign country or Japanese community with a lower ranking school system. This phenomenon could not exist in Japan if schools were forced to accept all students of parents living in the district.

In fact, however, each prefecture enjoys autonomy over high school entrance requirements, and schools' ranking from one residential area to another may very remarkably. There is no automatic reciprocity for acceptance among schools in different prefectures, as is the case among American states. Hence, high school students will not be accepted by a public high school in another prefecture if the school in their new residential area has a higher reputation than the school they have been attending. Here we see a clear manifestation of Japanese society to be exclusive and rank oriented. The major concern of the family is their children's future in passing the college entrance examination; the school's concern is maintaining its reputation. One of my Nagoya friends, a devoted family man, complains of neurosis after having been transferred to Tokyo three years ago. The fear of harming his two children's university entrance examination prospects prevented him from moving the whole family to Tokyo.

Most parents all over the world consider living abroad for a couple years or more to be a desirable cultural experience and intellectual stimulus for their children. Because of the intense importance of entrance examinations, however, many families will not accompany their husbands–fathers on overseas assignments for fear that the children's future success in getting into an appropriate school at each level may be jeopardized. In the event that the student's father is transferred abroad, the Ministry of Education has recently reformed the method of handling returnee students by requesting schools to recognize thirty credits for one to three years of education abroad and allowing those who have spent three years or more to take special entrance examinations at designated universities. But the reform seems tightfisted. The graduate of an overseas high school who has spent less than three years abroad may be required to attend two more years.

JAPANESE SCHOOL RANKING AND THE NEED FOR CHANGED ATTITUDES

Japanese entrance examinations ultimately reflect hierarchical sociocultural values and attitudes implemented to an extreme, which means school ranking. Japanese rank everything, from banks, electrical companies, and automobile companies, to all levels of schools and people. Language levels are finely attuned to correspond to social rank, age, and sex.[33] This pronounced custom to rank persons by schools and universities attended is a limitation of Japanese democracy and humanity.[34] One scholar of the entrance examination system and cram schools wrote categorically, "The fundamental nature of the college entrance examination will not change so long as the hierarchical structure of universities and students' striving for a high-ranked university persist."[35] Because the system has provided the nation with its best and brightest, the elite wish to preserve the system, and because it seems fair, the Japanese people accept it as an inevitable result of necessary competition.

Overall, the emphasis on gaining entrance into the right schools at every level possesses more negative than positive features. Ranking pressure increases the complexity, competitiveness, and pervasive impact of the entrance examinations. Vested interests, parental fears and ambitions, and an indigenous preference for a hierarchical society have sabotaged all efforts at fundamental reform of school ranking and entrance examination systems.

How did the ranking system become so intense? In Tokyo, by the late 1960s, the competition among the very highest rated public schools unintentionally became even more severe and tension ridden. Two formerly famous schools, Toyama High School in Shinjuku Ward and Hibiya High School in Chiyoda Ward, were competing intensely for the reputation of sending the most students to Tokyo University. At that time, bright students from other wards and even other cities could attend both schools. Not only were the entrance examinations at both schools very difficult, but also when graduating seniors failed Tokyo University's entrance examination, both schools held special classes to help them pass the next year's entrance examination. My friend Ichiro Tanaka had taught at both high schools and related:

I remember roughly that one year in the 1960s approximately 120 Toyama students passed the Tokyo University entrance examinations thereby surpassing Hibiya in the number of successful students. The next year, however, Hibiya surpassed Toyama. Teachers at both schools, including myself, worked hard with their senior classes in compensatory classes for unsuccessful graduates (*ronin*) of the past two years to surpass each other. These compensatory classes seem to have had a long history. Teachers from both schools even gathered on the morning of Tokyo University's announcement of successful candidates to learn whether they had excelled one another. The war between the two schools intensified and other higher ranking schools copied their practices. Many of the teachers had to support the system, but in our hearts we thought this was a sad education system that should be revised. Many parents also objected at the extreme pressure on their children.[36]

Around 1969, the Tokyo Metropolitan Education Office decided that compensatory lectures would be prohibited, clusters of wards were designated for the entire city, and students from other cities and wards could not attend schools outside their cluster. For example, only students from Minato Ward and Chiyoda Ward could attend Hibiya High School, and only students from Shinjuku and Setagaya Wards could attend Toyama High School. All other public schools within each cluster were ranked according to their prestige. In some other cities variations of this procedure were tried.

Professor Tanaka continued his observation: "This cluster system looked good on paper, but it severely weakened the reputation of Toyama and Hibiya High Schools and raised enormously the prestige of some six year private secondary school students. Now famous private schools such as Nada and Gyosei are competing as feverishly for the best students and the prestige of their graduates entering Tokyo University as Toyama and Hibiya Public High Schools were previously."[37] In 1998 only two students from Hibiya High School and sixteen students from Toyama High School entered Tokyo University. Those parents who want their children to enter Tokyo University today must dig deep into their pockets to send their children to more competitive and expensive private schools.

This well-intentioned reform had unfortunate ramifications from which Tokyo suffered until recently. To simplify the matter, let us say that in one designated cluster of two or three Tokyo wards there were fifteen high schools ranked in order of prestige and difficulty to enter. Students elected to take the entrance examinations for schools in their own wards or at schools in other wards that were a member of the cluster and at the level their teachers thought they could successfully pass based on mock examination scores. The system forced many students to travel long distances across wards to attend the best school of their choice. A second, more devastating result for the public school system and equal educational opportunity was that students and parents who could afford it selected (and now on a national level are selecting) private schools that have enhanced their reputation for graduates entering high ranked universities.

A third tragedy was that students who failed the examination at the school of their choice (for various reasons other than ability, such as sickness, or family problems) found that they had to enter a school ranked two, three, or four levels below the school at which their deviation score seemed to qualify them, because enrollment capacities had been filled. In the new lower ranked schools they were surrounded by peers of lesser ability and competitive zeal and teachers and textbooks of lower expectations. Consequently, students adopted various expedients. Some attended *juku* after school for the next three years to compensate for their new handicap. Others attended *juku* for awhile, but gradually gave up because their new learning environment reduced their competitive enthusiasm. Many gave up attending a university. Still others dropped out of school. Finally, a very few of those dropouts attended a full-time *juku* to take university entrance examinations. A friend who had taught at Nerima High School, a lower ranked school in Nerima Ward, told me that every year in his combined classes there were six to ten students who adopted these alternatives because they had been misplaced victims. Although he dislikes *juku*, he advised these students to attend them or to hire a home tutor to compensate for their new disadvantages. When one considers the number of schools in Tokyo where one can expect a similar phenomenon to have occurred over a twenty-five-year period, we can see why the Tokyo Metropolitan School Board finally decided two years ago that this error-prone and unjust system had to be scuttled. Thousands of students have been victims.[38]

To eliminate intensive competition to get into good senior high schools, the NCER recommended a continuous six-year public secondary school rather than the present 3–3 system, a recommendation the Central Council on Education and Education Ministry revived in 1997, along with fifty-nine other recommendations for Prime Minister Hashimoto Ryutaro's Cabinet to enact.[39] There are powerful arguments for adopting such a proposal. The pressure on the junior high school student to pass examinations in order to get into ranked senior high schools could be delayed until high school, and hopefully only during the last one-and-a-half years of that level. A continuous, six-year secondary school program would allow more emphasis on gaining credits rather than grades and allow greater curriculum flexibility. Students could choose vocational courses and challenging electives geared in a broader sense to their interests, abilities, and needs, and study.

Critics of the proposal to establish a six-year secondary school, however, maintain that the excessive pressure on junior high school students and the distortion of education will still continue. Pressure simply will be pushed downward to elementary school students. That means there will be more ambitious parents who will intensify their pressure on upper elementary school children to study with private tutors and *juku* because their chances will be improved for getting admitted into the most successful six-year private schools, a practice already very well entrenched among ambitious parents. Because the elementary schools have been highly regarded as nurturing institutions stressing character formation and possessing a more casual academic atmosphere and fewer rules and regulations, a transfer of harmful junior high school practices to the elementary school will occur. Furthermore, over the past twenty-five years many famous private schools, such as Nada, have adopted the very same 6–6 system for a different purpose, namely as a strategy to increase their students' ability to pass university entrance examinations. They cover most of the required six-year courses of studies and curriculum within four-and-a-half or five years, and use the remaining time to review and go beyond those requirements. (These generalizations are not valid for the more rural islands of Shikoku, Kyushu, and Hokkaido, where public schools generally continue to be more prestigious than private schools.) If the Hashimoto Cabinet adopts the 6–6 system proposal, one corrective would be to make all public secondary schools six years in duration.

These problems have created a political battleground and a series of painful dilemmas over the direction of Japanese education. On the one hand, idealists are eager to preserve the merits of the present neighborhood, egalitarian 6–3 public school system and to prevent undue pressure on elementary school children. On the other hand, the more affluent, the more socially ambitious parents, and the large number of less affluent parents who fear their children will suffer a permanent handicap in the competition with their peers anguish over painful and costly alternatives. Some will elect at great cost to send their children to private schools at the seventh grade—and more at the tenth grade. Others will calculate that it may be cheaper to send their children to a public secondary school, and choose to supplement that course with a private tutor or *juku*. This condition favors the affluent and severely challenges the cherished Japanese view that they are a classless society. I would like now to take up more specifically the impact of school ranking on schools, students, and society.

IMPACT ON KINDERGARTENS

Employment benefits and social prestige from entering a good university have even affected Japanese kindergartens.[40] Although foreign researchers have correctly tried to explode the myth that most Japanese preschools are academically oriented, the pressure on parents and preschools to teach reading, writing, and arithmetic cannot be denied, especially in very prestigious urban kindergartens.[41] Such pressure comes mainly from upper class, urban families, but also exists in all social classes, even in relatively rural areas. One former elementary teacher and vice principal who served three years in a rural area as a kindergarten principal after retirement, told me that one of the biggest reasons he was glad to leave the job was because of the constant pressure he encountered from parents who wanted a more academic curriculum.

A few highly selective private academic kindergartens within escalator systems, such as Sacred Heart, Keio, Gakushuin, Seijo Gakuen, and Aoyama Gakuin, that are eager to maintain their prestige, administer syllabary tests and various skill and intelligence tests not only to the children applying for admittance, but also to their mothers! The pressure of overzealous mothers on kindergartens to teach numbers, Chinese characters, and reading and writing has resulted in an increasing number of kindergartens unwillingly teaching them. Competition for pupils forces them to acquiesce to parental pressure.[42]

NEGATIVE IMPACT ON ELEMENTARY SCHOOLS

The effect of school ranking and entrance examinations is being widely felt in today's elementary schools, especially those in larger cities. In order to keep up with the academic demands of the course of studies, and the cancellation of school two Saturdays a month, many elementary schools are holding compensatory classes for an additional week during the summer holidays. More and more fourth, fifth, and sixth graders at the conclusion of the school day are attending or studying with private tutors for two to three hours a day, three to six times a week, a subject to be discussed more fully in Chapter 7.

NEGATIVE IMPACT OF RANKING ON SECONDARY SCHOOLS

Richard Lynn, looking at the Japanese school ranking system from the standpoint of motivation, incentive, and achievement, was moved to write, "In Japan it is not a mere handful of schools that are hierarchically ranked for academic excellence, but all schools. The effect of this is that all Japanese 14-year-olds are provided with the incentive to attempt to obtain entry to as good a school as possible. . . . Hence it is quite possible for a Japanese teenager to fail to get into any senior high school."[43] I disagree. First, in practice, any Japanese student wanting to get into high school can manage to do so, although it may be a very lower ranking school. Second, the placement of students in ranked schools at age fifteen (or twelve for those who elect more challenging private schools) is too undemocratic, premature, and demoralizing.

In the previous chapter we noted the dropouts and school refusers at elementary and secondary school has increased to approximately 112,000 and 81,000, respectively. Some drop out because they are unable to keep up with the curriculum; others reject the entire examination and school ranking system. Some never return to school; others participate in home-study programs; still others choose from among more than 270 small "alternative schools" programs characterized by encouragement of innovation, greater freedom, friendliness, and limited pressure.[44] A growing number do not attend school but elect to study on their own, at a cram school, or with a tutor, and then take a national examination for entry into a university. Today such students number 25,000.

TOO MUCH PRESSURE AND SELF-INTEREST

Affluent and well-educated parents are eager to increase the social prestige and earning power of their own children, and elite career bureaucrats are eager to perpetuate a system in which they have developed a narrow, vested self-interest in perpetuating, in order to derive maximum benefits from the system. Their attitude is that the system should not be reformed at the expense of abandoning their ambitious personal interests for their own children and national interests for Japan.[45] Higher-ranked schools and universities also zealously endeavor to preserve their status over lower-ranking ones, even at the expense of other institutions.[46] As a result of these pressures, schools at every level are holding special classes during the summer. Almost 70 percent of high schools are increasing the number of class hours a week beyond the required thirty-two hours and requiring students to take eighty-six or more credits, thereby exceeding the minimum of eighty credits required by the Education Ministry.[47] Many secondary schools try to maintain their ranking by recommending a high school or university with as high a rank as possible to enhance their reputation, a practice that angers students.[48]

PREMATURE AND UNDEMOCRATIC RANKING'S HARMFUL EFFECTS

School ranking is undemocratic and prone to error. It overlooks scientific data that amply demonstrates that some students mature later than others in growth, abilities, and interests. Placement in a poor or middle level academic high school arbitrarily penalizes severely "late bloomers." It is undemocratic because those parents in urban areas of Honshu who can afford to send their children to good private high schools enjoy an advantage over poorer students of the same ability in getting admitted to a good university. It continues to deny equal educational opportunity, because those who fail to gain entry into the best public high schools are dealt a severe handicap for the competition three years later to enter a good university.[49] A Churchill, an Einstein, or an Edison would not have emerged in the current Japanese educational system.

I told a friend, Ken Arasaki, a bicultural neurologist, that, as a late bloomer, I would never have made it to college in this system. He countered by saying that the Japanese socialization process would have made me more realistic about studying and attending good schools from an early age. His judgment is probably valid for many students; nonetheless, the line ending educational opportunity is drawn so early that many students who are short-sighted, "late-blooming," or come from an educationally disadvantaged home suffer a permanent handicap because there is almost no "second chance."[50] Unless high school graduates continue to take annual university entrance examinations until they pass them, elect to go abroad, or enter one of the foreign universities now located in Japan, no second chance exists. By closing the doors on students arbitrarily, society is penalizing them prematurely.

Because approximately 95 percent of all Japanese students will go on to high school, the secondary school ranking and sorting system is demoralizing. Students are already labeled in their early teens by the rank of the school they attend. The junior high school student who scores poorly in high school admission criteria and is placed in a typical vocational school will suffer a handicap in terms of future employment, social prestige, and marriage. The present system requires many young secondary students in all of Japan's larger cities to travel one hour or more to attend a public school to which they have been assigned on the basis of test scores. Some Tokyo students will travel one-and-a-half-hours to attend a private school. A passenger of a Tokyo train at 6:30 A.M. will discover that approximately one-fifth of the passengers are young students commuting long distances to school.

Ranking causes students who attend less famous high schools and universities to hide their high school or university's identity. An extreme example of the pressure to get into a good high school can be found in the city of Iwaki in northeastern Japan. Students attending the best junior and senior high school there must attend classes for three hours every Sunday morning. So famous is the high school that gaining admittance and graduating from it is valued by local people more highly than graduating from famous Japanese universities. For a female student from another city school, marrying a graduate of the high school is considered a prize catch.

The American high school and university system is more democratic, egalitarian, humane, and fair. Since public schools are forced to accept all students regardless of race, sex, religion, or ability in their district, students at most schools do not need to feel inferior. Americans have the following options: (1) to enter automatically comprehensive public high schools in their school districts; (2) to enter a junior or community college to raise their academic grades and then transfer to a more famous four-year college; (3) to take courses part-time at a four-year college until they qualify academically for full-time entrance; and (4) to enter college in their twenties, thirties, or later. The exercise of the last three options means that they are also able to find new and better employment after a delayed college graduation because they are evaluated on their college performance and character rather than what university they attended or at what age they graduated. The Japanese situation reflects excessively rigid attitudes and premature judgments.

TOO MUCH EMPHASIS ON GETTING INTO "GOOD" UNIVERSITIES

Graduation from good secondary institutions not only maximizes students' chances of gaining successful entry into universities, but also fulfills the ultimate goal of obtaining better jobs after graduation. In 1987, of Japan's 5,453 high schools, only three supplied approximately 10 percent of the successful entrants to Tokyo University.[51] Graduation from a top-ranking institution such as Tokyo University guarantees that students will not only be hired by a prestigious company or government agency, but also that they will be promoted to the top positions. Yet, the University of Tokyo only graduates every year slightly over one-half percent of all Japan's university, college, and junior college graduates.[52] Graduates of the "best" universities rise to the highest positions because "the education credential, not the individual talent, determines initial employment with the more prestigious companies and remains a major consideration in any advancement."[53]

Conversely, graduation only from high school, from a third-rate university, or an American university either in Japan or in the United States means that the Japanese student will either be hired by a company lacking prestige or will have little chance of ever proceeding beyond the middle level of a company or government bureaucracy. Another Nanzan graduate vividly demonstrated the handicap as follows:

I have a good friend who graduated from the University of Washington this spring and majored in computers. He wanted to work for such companies as NEC, Panasonic, Hitatchi, and Toyota but he got the "brush-off" from every company at which he interviewed because he had not attended a Japanese university. He finally obtained a job at a Toyota dealership in Kobe selling cars. He told me that being a different individual in Japan is not liked and considered as a delinquent or an "enemy of society." I learned during job interviews that it was considered important to have an education in a Japanese university simply to know the hierarchical system of Japanese society.

This is often called learning common sense. It means adapting to hierarchical values and losing the ability to engage in a dialogue over differing views. It also means that because such persons have not imbibed a uniform set of national values, they are a threat to the pervasive system of social control. As Mamoru Tsukada says, they have not been legitimated.[54] Many top companies only interview graduates from a select group of universities on these underlying assumptions plus another one that those who pass entrance examinations are endowed with the character that companies demand.[55]

When the results of Nanzan University's entrance examinations are posted each spring, one can witness a variety of aspirants' emotions. On one occasion I used the opportunity to talk to three students who had passed the examinations and their three teachers. The leader said his school was called B., S., and T. Gakuin, or "Blood, Sweat, and Tears School." One girl had taken ten entrance examinations that spring, four of them for different colleges and departments within Nanzan University. Another student had taken entrance examinations at eight universities and had taken two Nanzan University college exams. When I asked the first girl why she had exerted such effort and financial expense (¥30,000 or approximately $275 an examination) to enter Nanzan, she was nonplussed to answer a question that seemed so obvious. Her teacher responded, "It was her dream. She has attended my *juku* for six years, almost always four times a week, and from two to four hours to realize that dream."

Examples Highlighting Ranking Attitudes and Practices

In 1966, doctoral research in Japan found me living next door to a Japanese family. The oldest son, Kunitake, upon graduation from high school, had decided (mistakenly) that his prospects for employment in Japan's prestigious Foreign Ministry or some major company's fast track would be enhanced by graduation from an American university. Accordingly, he graduated from a small, but good private liberal arts college, Bucknell University. After graduating, he decided to further improve his English and widen his experiences by taking employment in New York City for approximately six months.

By the time Kunitake returned to Japan in the mid-1960s he and his family had concluded that graduation from an American university doomed him to a midlevel career. Consequently, he decided to remedy this condition by entering graduate school in the International Relations Division of Waseda University, a famous private university. After successfully passing the graduate school examination and studying for one year, Kunitake concluded that he still was mistaken. Thereupon, he took a special examination along with eighty other students for entrance to the Tokyo University economics department as a junior. He and one other student passed the examination. Two years later, when it came time to obtain employment, one of the less tradition-bound and leading new electronics industries in Japan and abroad, Sony Corporation, was so interested in him that they allegedly gave him a special examination differing from other applicants. Kunitake became the private secretary to the chairman and president of the corporation. Later he was sent to Harvard University for an MBA, and for a few years he was second in command of a large joint venture insurance company established by Sony with Prudential Insurance Company. At forty-five, he became President of Sony Engineering and Manufacturing of America. Recently, he has returned to take a top executive position in Sony's home office.

Obviously, Ando Kunitake is bright and possesses outstanding managerial ability. And clearly too, his graduation from an American university and his competence in English were reasons the parent company hired him. Nonetheless, even Sony would not have hired him nor given him leadership roles over the years had he not graduated from Tokyo University. Incredibly, this able young man spent three years of his life to rectify the mistake he had made in choosing an American university and a famous Japanese graduate school.

General Examples of the Impact of Ranking

Another phenomena is the practice of students entering a lesser ranking private or prefectural university and transferring one, two, or even three years later to a more prestigious national university. Although Yokohama National University's College of Economics ranks within the top ten economic departments, every year three to six students transfer from freshmen, sophomore, and junior class to Hitotsubashi University or Tokyo University. Students from other lesser ranked universities transfer into Yokohama National University's College of Economics. Two years ago a Nanzan senior transferred to a famous Japanese university with freshman status because she had passed its examination! For some high school students the goal of getting into Tokyo University is both cynical and altruistic. They want to make a contribution to society, but know that their opinions and their books will gain far more authority if they have graduated from Tokyo University.

Other Distortions of Education through Ranking

The very best Japanese high schools achieve their rank because they can boast of getting a high proportion of their students into the best colleges and universities. Not only does each school feel its prestige depends on the success of its students in the entrance examinations, but the teachers of individual departments also feel the same pressure. From a Western point of view, however, some of the most famous Japanese secondary school and *juku* teachers might not be considered good; they may only be bright, very competent technicians skilled in analyzing previous university entrance examinations and stuffing students with appropriate factual data for passing entrance examinations at the best universities.

Rohlen characterized the relationship of the students and teachers at the best schools as inclined to be more impersonal, businesslike, distant, and discipline prone. In contrast, the relationship between students and teachers at the poorest schools, especially night schools, are close, candid, personal, and humane. This teacher–student relationship reflects both the absence of pressure and the sympathy teachers feel for their charges.[56] David Slater, a Ph.D. candidate at Chicago University, spent three years researching two low ranking Tokyo schools, one of which is a night school. He found that the students in the night school are personally much more interesting, likable, and active than the students he has observed at Japan's better schools and universities.[57]

What is clear is that the student–teacher relationship at the low ranking night schools is not one dominated by teachers. Instead several teachers have told me that they have to teach the students more as equals, to reduce emphasis on academic perfection, rigor, and drill, and to instruct students through more discussion. At older famous public schools the teachers may not push the students; instead, students know they must study. Some new public high schools in Japan's expanding suburbs, however, that are anxious to achieve public acclaim as a high ranking school, such as Togo, Honda Higashi, Gojo, and Shinkawa High Schools in Aichi Prefecture, deliberately practice very strict school rules. A severe, almost authoritarian relationship between teachers and students prevails. There, students are more frequently admonished for not studying, and they are compelled to attend supplementary lectures one hour before the beginning of the regular class day. Such is the price of achieving "success." But the most excessive result of the entrance examinations and ranking syndrome can be found in what Tsukada refers to as Japan's "institutionalized supplementary educational system."[58]

JAPAN'S INSTITUTIONALIZED SUPPLEMENTARY EDUCATIONAL SYSTEM

A supplementary system of home tutoring, *juku*, and *yobiko* further distorts education because they emphasize memorization of subject matter and commercialized profit-making practices; demonstrate socioeconomic pressure rather than enthusiasm for learning; constitutes a powerful lobby with a vested interest against educational reform; force the sacrifice of the needs of mothers, children, and family life to Japan's economic needs; pose a serious threat to equal educational opportunity; and undermine public schools, good study habits, and respect for education by the practices of the *juku*, the parents, and the public schools themselves. The supplementary educational system can be seen as a natural consequence of good attitudes and practices carried to unfortunate extremes.

Nature and Pervasiveness of *Juku* and *Yobiko*

Almost two decades ago, a well-meaning American Commissioner of Education, Terrel Bell, hosting a Japanese–American Educational Conference, unwittingly praised the *juku*. The Japanese delegation was embarrassed and the Minister of Education replied that he would really prefer to abolish them. In fact, *juku* are extralegal, and are not included in Mombusho's official descriptions of the school system, despite the fact that they have in reality become an integral part of the education of most Japanese students today. Many Japanese consider them a national tragedy. I agree wholeheartedly.

A well-balanced treatment of Japanese education by the U.S. Department of Education defined *juku* not simply as "cramming schools" but also as "private, profit-making tutorial, enrichment, remedial, and preparatory schools."[59] Though the term "enrichment" (or nonacademic) is appropriate for calligraphy, abacus calculation, swimming, music, art, and sports *juku* at the elementary school level, the descriptions of them as remedial and college preparatory "cramming schools" are much more appropriate for the academic *juku*. Parents anxious to help their children keep up with the pace of a difficult curriculum send their children to remedial cram schools. Other parents eager to obtain an advantage for their children over other students in gaining admission into higher ranked secondary schools and universities and into the power structure send their children to *juku* for accelerated learning and superior techniques for passing entrance examinations.[60]

In 1977, a Ministry of Education survey showed there were approximately 22,000 *juku* attended by approximately one million students, one-third of them junior high school students and almost one-fourth of them fourth, fifth, and sixth graders. Since then the percentage has increased dramatically. Now *juku* number over 47,500, and 70 percent of them have been founded since the late 1970s.[61] In 1997, there are approximately 150 cram schools for pre-schools in Tokyo alone, and one of them, *Shingakai*, enrolls 8,000 in Tokyo and Saitama and Kanagawa prefectures. In 1993, 24 percent of elementary school children and 60 percent of junior high school students nationwide were attending *juku* (not counting private tutors).[62] They are attended by at least 3 million students. In metropolitan Tokyo, Yokohama, Osaka, Nagoya, and Kyoto, approximately 75 percent of fifth and sixth graders and junior high school students attend them.

Yobiko focus primarily on *ronin*, students who have graduated from high school but have not successfully passed a university entrance examination of their choice. *Ronin* attend a *yobiko* full time for the exclusive purpose of passing the next year's entrance examinations. *Yobiko* compile their own mock examinations and charge a simple fee for students who wish to avail themselves only of this service. Like the large chain *juku*, they possess sophisticated educational technology, testing and audio–visual materials, data-bank materials on past university examinations, graded textbooks, classes tracked according to ability, and courses aimed not only at subjects but also specifically geared to the most famous universities in each region.[63] (For example, in the Nagoya area, some *juku* and *yobiko* offer courses aimed specifically at either Nagoya University or Nanzan University.)

In fact, the distinction between *yobiko* and *juku* is sometimes artificial, since some eleventh and twelfth graders attend *yobiko* after school, on weekends, during school vacations, or only for a special lecture series. Furthermore, sometimes famous *yobiko* are combined with *juku*. During the summer, New Year's, and spring vacations, and even on New Year's Day, the most famous *juku* and *yobiko* add additional teachers and run classes all day and evenings. Some of them also hold special lectures, trimester courses, or one to four week summer sessions all day and all evening five to seven days a week in cool, mountain resort towns. Many capable, young university students earn a considerable amount of money teaching at *juku* or tutoring. The more highly ranked their university the more payment they command. One twenty-nine-year-old "seventh" year student at Yokohama National University supports a wife and young child while managing a small *juku*. Annually, a total of between 260,000 to 400,000 *ronin* plan a second try at the university of their choice. Of these students, 40 to 50 percent are studying at the three largest national chains: Yoyogi Seminar Preparatory School (73,000), Kawaijuku (37,000) and Shundai Yobigakko (30,000).[64] The majority of *yobiko* are attended by 100 to 500 students.[65]

Another type of *yobiko* specializes in helping *ronin* enter dental and medical schools. The number of students is usually less than one hundred, and tuition ranges from approximately $14,000 to $33,000, three to ten times more than the cost of other *yobiko*.[66] Approximately 50 percent of Japan's 440,000 yearly applicants for universities are *ronin*, but their number increases to approximately 57 percent and 65 percent of all applicants for the famous seven former imperial universities and highest major private universities, respectively.[67] Today almost as many females as males attend *juku*, but five times more males attend *yobiko* than females.[68] The percentage of students from metropolitan areas is higher than rural ones, and higher for Honshu than other islands.

The absurd competition and the extent to which *yobiko* and *juku* have spread is indicated by the current practices of these institutions. The most famous are trying to ensure their prestige by six strategies. First, *yobiko* give tuition-free grants to a few outstanding high school graduates who may fail or have already failed to enter a highly ranked university on their first attempt, but who they believe will be able to enter Japan's top four or five universities, or the best university in their region, as a result of studying at their *yobiko* for one year. When that occurs, they can boast of their reputation in public advertising.[69] Second, *juku* and *yobiko* also hold their own entrance examinations so that they can select only the best students. Once they have the best students, they try to ensure their success by placing all the students in tracked classes according to the students' scores on mock examinations. After the results of the summer mock tests are known, students are again retracked into classes on the basis of those scores, sometimes even on the basis of weekly or monthly scores. Textbooks for each subject are assigned according to tracked classes. The practices of posting the names of their students who have successfully entered famous senior high schools and universities and rearranging students seats after weekly tests are now extending to *juku* for elementary pupils.[70]

Third, highly competent or popular public and private school teachers are lured to *juku* by salaries more than double or triple their regular income. Some outstanding *juku* and *yobiko* teachers travel weekly via the Bullet Train for lectures at two or three different sites as much as 300 to 500 kilometers apart. Their fame helps *juku* attract more students than their competitors. Fourth, smaller *juku* are combining with larger ones to provide more sophisticated technology. Fifth, the big three *yobiko* are strengthening their TV lessons by hooking up with communications satellites and developing software programs for home, a point to be discussed later.[71] Sixth, even *juku* for elementary school students publicize their success rate in getting graduates into good private junior high schools. At Nichinoken *juku*'s Shibuya school, a long list of 199 students who sat for entrance exams is displayed. It boasted that 184 passed, or a 92.5 success rate.[72] These strategies achieve good public relations and economic survival in a diminishing seller's market.

Cram school teachers must be resourceful, energetic, and dynamic in return for their good salaries. They must command an expert's knowledge of entrance examinations and convince students that they are the gurus who hold the entrance key to the universities of the students choice.[73] The work is fatiguing and demanding. Accordingly, cram schools often release teachers at age fifty or earlier because their energy and effectiveness have diminished. There is nothing of the heralded benevolent paternalism and lifetime seniority system here.

Attending *Juku* Demonstrates Socioeconomic Pressures

Lynn wrote rosily,

We have suggestive evidence that Japanese children are strongly motivated for academic work. During the teenage years approximately half of Japanese children attend the supplementary coaching schools known as the *juku* during the evenings, at weekends and during the school holidays. It is an interesting question why similar extramural coaching schools have not been established in Britain, the United States and Continental Europe. The answer to this must surely be that neither parents nor their children are sufficiently motivated to make use of such schools.[74]

What are the facts behind Japanese students "voluntarily" attending *juku* and senior high school? The alleged "failure" of American and European countries to adopt *juku* should be seen as common sense. Parents in those countries do not want their children from the fourth or fifth grade studying at *juku* on weekends, school vacations, or after the regular school day has ended.

Furthermore, the extent to which Japanese are committed to real learning needs severe qualification. The general lack of interest in study once students have entered a university is one contradiction of this commonly exaggerated view. We have also seen that a large proportion of Japanese are going to senior high school and college for reasons of social prestige, better income, and to be a part of the ruling elite. Students who do not graduate from high school suffer a greater social and economic handicap than in the United States and Great Britain. Parents send their children to *juku* less from love of education than from the enormous pressure they feel to guarantee their future and keep up with the Suzukis.

Cram Schools Are Big, Powerful, and Have a Vested Interest against Reform

Juku and *yobiko* have become big, powerful businesses.[75] One of the larger, more attractive eight-story buildings in downtown Yokohama is owned by Kawaijuku, famous for its teaching equipment. At its Nagoya headquarters the same *juku* has three relatively new, high-rise buildings on very expensive land near the Nagoya train station and another very large building near the Chikusa district. Yoyogi Seminar Preparatory School is located in Tokyo and is famous for its teaching methods. It has approximately 700 branches. In 1990, before the cheaper dollar exchange rate, it was estimated that there

were over 100,000 *juku* and that annually they netted more than 800 billion
yen, or approximately $9 billion.[76] One *juku*, with seventy-eight schools na-
tionwide and a total enrollment of 35,000 children in grades three to six, had
an income in 1996 of 10.5 billion yen, and tuition per pupil for those four
years was 2 million yen ($17,000).[77] In fact, so profitable and so competitive
is the market for a dwindling student population since 1992 that the big *juku*
and *yobiko* are extending themselves into even medium-sized cities and driving out of business or absorbing local *juku*.[78] Tsukada showed that the arrival
of a large chain in Hiroshima resulted in a drastic decline in enrollment of
three other local *juku*.[79]

A good friend, Reiko Yamamoto, who has run an English *juku* part time for
over twenty-five years said philosophically, "Students are less interested in a
comprehensive approach to English. I can't provide them with any of the
sophisticated computer information and mock testing that will tell them where
their deficiencies are."

Recently, Reiko told me that her grandson is attending a chain *juku* as an
eighth-grade student. She was impressed at the level of technical sophistication. One lesson presented twenty rules for conjugating different irregular
verbs. The grandson had memorized the rules, but to her surprise he had no
idea of how to apply them.

The decreasing student market is intensifying cut-throat competition and is
now pushing attendance at *juku* to even the first four grades of elementary
school.[80] The number of eighteen-year-olds (and students taking university
entrance exams) has begun to decline from a peak in 1992 of 2.5 million. The
projected number of eighteen-year-olds by 2000 is 1.51 million and by 2110,
1.21 million, and the number of high school graduates cramming for university entrance examinations is expected to decline by 160,000 in 2000.[81] By
2010, the number of students seeking admission to schools is expected to be
equal that of the number of openings.[82] Kawaijuku pessimistically expects
the number of college and university openings by 2009 for the first time to be
greater than the number of students who will be challenging two year colleges' and four universities' entrance examinations. Consequently, chain *juku*
and *yobiko* are becoming more economical, renting classrooms as offices,
designing recently completed buildings to be converted to hotels, and focusing on elementary and secondary schools and homes. One correspondence
school or *juku*, *Kodomo* (Children) Challenge, claims 7 million preschoolers
between one and six years are enrolled in its popular nationwide correspondence courses that includes workbooks to teach *katakana* (syllabary writing
system) and mathematics.[83] Nichinoken *juku* is extending its correspondence
school program from the second and fifth grades to the first grade. Sapix *juku*
began its operations in 1989 with an enrollment of 500 fourth to sixth graders, but will have increased its enrollment to 4,500 by enrolling third graders
in 1992, second graders in 1993, and opening two new schools in 1997. *Juku*
are developing as rapidly as possible and are introducing new technology,

TV lessons, and software programs that can be beamed into nationwide class-rooms through communications satellite linkups. For example, Yoyogi Yobiko is transmitting lessons in thirty courses to its branches and to 185 high schools. It also has three satellites and plans a fourth one for students at home. Nagase (also known as Toshin High School) hopes to increase the transmission of lectures by popular teachers from 600 franchised schools to 1,280 by 1999 and to begin test broadcasting for in-home teaching by April 1996.[84]

For those who think declining college student numbers means the end of the cram schools, they are mistaken. The big will get bigger, and most of the smaller will die. It can be predicted that once the chain cram schools capture the nationwide high school telecommunications market, they will develop lessons for junior high and elementary schools. They will also succeed in reducing the costs of in-home lessons to the extent that they can be used for a mass market. Instead of opposing their entry into the schools, teachers and administrators seem to be eagerly welcoming them.[85] It can be surmised that most hard-pressed teachers are strongly encouraging students to take these TV lessons because of their quality and relief from teaching the same classes. The only way that Mombusho can stop this trend is to prohibit schools from using them. But even as powerful as Mombusho is, it may find such an action too drastic for the economic consequences it would bear. Even in that case, the *juku* and *yobiko* probably will survive via the development of the in-home market.

A few *juku* and *yobiko* have become almost shamelessly bold and aggressive. One brazenly claimed that because regular schools were providing a poorer form of education than the *juku* the latter should be accredited as official educational institutions. One *juku* has purchased an American university. Some skilled teachers from private schools supplement their income by "moonlighting" at *juku*, but Mombusho has prohibited public school teachers' from employment at a cram school.[86]

Indeed, the *juku*, *yobiko*, and those private businesses profiting from the sale of educational equipment and materials may justifiably be viewed as powerful lobbies with a vested interest in preventing real reform of the entrance examination systems.[87] A successful reform would drive thousands of businesses into bankruptcy and lead to unemployment or reduced incomes for well over 100,000 full-time teachers, office personnel, and university students.

Bad Impact on Families and Equal Educational Opportunity

Mothers as Victims and Victimizers. Society puts pressure on mothers because there is really no second chance in the Japanese educational system. According to Ichikawa Juri, a counselor at Waseda University, anxious mothers, especially college graduates, forced to give up their careers take out their frustration by concentrating on educating their children, and generally feel lonely and isolated because local communities provide less support, and husbands are too busy.[88] Entrance examinations become a social enemy. Mothers and children become linked in an alliance which forces the former to use snacks, material gifts, and sacrificial service as bribery so the child will concentrate his or her energies excessively on study. What begins as admirable maternal affection and nurturing can end up having a less benevolent aspect to it.[89] In this context, George de Vos has shown that Ruth Benedict's view, in *The Chrysanthemum and the Sword*, that Japan is a shame culture, not a guilt culture, has to be qualified. He demonstrated that Japanese mothers manage to produce achievement-oriented children by creating a sense of guilt in them. Their mothers' sacrifices make children feel they must perform.[90] Well-meaning mothers are socialized by the establishment and national ethic to believe that their personal merit is measured by the academic success of their children. They are the ones who make the decision to pare the budget to make it possible for a child to attend an expensive kindergarten, private school, or *juku*; who elect not to move to another region or to go abroad for fear of entering a poorer academic environment; who decide that their children must return home with them from abroad while father remains; or who decide to send children back to Japan to live with a relative from the fear that failure to attend a Japanese high school will penalize their academic success.[91] They are Japan's self-sacrificing warriors cooperating with the nation's drive to achieve wealth.

Impact on Families and Equal Educational Opportunity. The supplementary education system limits equal educational opportunity because it penalizes the poor, rural, and less affluent families.[92] Two interesting ironies, however, have occurred. First, because of parental insecurity, an increasing number of mothers feel forced to work part time to pay for classes, and many Japanese are concerned about the damage done to the family unit because mothers are working part time to make attendance possible for their children.

The second irony is that attending *juku* no longer confers an advantage on those attending them. Thirty years ago, when not many Japanese were attending *juku*, those children who did so gained an advantage in the race to get into a good secondary school or university. Today no great advantage accrues to attending *juku* because the number of students attending them or receiving home tutoring has become common practice. What we are seeing is that mothers and children now must make greater financial and family sacrifices simply to help their children keep up with other children. If it were not so pathetic, the situation would provoke laughter, but the more appropriate reaction is pity for parents and children. They are on a treadmill of insecurity and ambition from which they cannot get off until children enter a university. *Juku*, *yobiko*, and private tutors force parents to surrender large chunks of money. Cram schools to help preschool children pass private schools' elementary school examinations cost 50,000 to 70,000 yen ($40 to $60) a month and correspondence courses for one- to four-year-olds cost 1,500 yen a month.[93] A 1987 survey by the Tokai Bank focusing on metropolitan families showed that they spent approximately 24,000 yen ($210) monthly per student. That figure today will pay for only one course offered twice a week!

For example, one family has only a middle class income, but they bought into a plan which costs 383,370 yen (approximately $3,150) for two-hour lessons three times a week during the school year and lessons during the spring, summer, and winter vacations—almost a month's pay for lower income families. (Such year-round plans are now becoming common.) Below is an itemization of the expenses for an ordinary *juku*, perhaps 15 to 20 percent cheaper than more famous ones:

February 18 to March 26; for two-hour lessons three times a week	¥37,980
Spring term vacation	24,720
Second term, April 6–July 29	101,280
Summer vacation period (10 days)	32,440
Third term, September 8–December 22	101,180
Winter vacation period	21,630
One year: mock examinations	12,360
Textbooks	3,620
Air conditioning and heating	10,080
Total	¥383,370

Because in two years a younger daughter will become an eighth grader, the father and mother have reluctantly decided that the mother must commence working part time. This is an example of a Japanese family that had elected not to disrupt their family life during a child's elementary and first year of junior high school years by sending him to a *juku*. But now they must spend a large amount of money to send their children to *juku* for at least two years to help them get into a good public senior high school rather than an expensive private high school. Furthermore, they will probably feel the necessity to send their two children to a *juku* again in the last year or year-and-a-half of senior high school to improve their chances of entering a good university.[94]

I was astonished in June 1995 to learn from an informal poll of ten classrooms of approximately forty-five students each, that roughly 50 percent of Nanzan Girls Junior High School students and almost 80 percent of Nanzan Girls Senior High School students are attending *juku* at least two or three times a week to study English, Japanese, and (less frequently) mathematics. (The much lower number attending a *juku* for mathematics illustrates again that these students have no intention of taking entrance examinations requiring a mathematics test.) Not only is the tuition there already much higher than lower income families can afford, but also Nanzan has a strong reputation for a difficult curriculum and successful placement of their students in highly ranked universities.

The prevalence of *juku* and their advanced technology produces an adverse affect also on rural children. One of my junior high school teacher–friends from a rural area in Shikoku complained that Mombusho's sudden banning of mock exams by private companies in public junior high schools had two bad effects. First, it increased parents' and students' dependence on *juku* for their sophisticated computer information. Second, it produced a stunning handicap because "rural and poor children cannot afford to attend them in terms of both distance and money. Teachers in small, rural junior high schools are handicapped when comparing their students' ability to get into high schools or universities."[95] In some rural schools the disadvantage is offset to some extent for graduates who fail to pass entrance examinations on the first attempt by schools offering them supplementary lectures.

Enrichment *juku* also undermine schools and limit their capacity to achieve equal opportunity for all children in a nonacademic way. Literally thousands of them exist throughout the country, especially in metropolitan preschools and the elementary schools, for teaching sports, gymnastics, ballet, art, English conversation, motor skills, calligraphy, abacus calculation, and music, especially the piano.[96] Thirty percent of children three and younger are enrolled in enrichment lessons. Hideyo Emori regrets that children of parents who can afford academic and nonacademic *juku* have distinct physical and psychological advantages over others because they can swim faster, play musical instruments with greater skill, and draw and paint more effectively. Young students in the elementary and junior high schools who cannot afford such (or do not want to attend them) *and* possess lesser skills and consequently become demoralized and fall further behind in both physical and mental skills.

Abnormal Childhood. More abused by the tragedy of *juku* are the children. A child should have time for play, but in most neighborhoods of larger cities today one sees few children playing outside after school. At the upper levels of elementary school, most children's friends become clearly divided into those who do or do not attend *juku*. On the streets of Tokyo, Yokohama, and other metropolitan areas you can see junior high school students, especially boys, at 10:00 and 11:00 P.M. returning from three or four hours of supplementary lessons.

The Ministry of Education's decision to abolish school on all Saturdays by 2003 is premised on the argument that it will put schools on the same work schedule as Japan's larger industries, give students more time with their parents, and allow children to spend more time simply playing. Reflecting an age and a society where many parents believe that all play must be school organized and supervised, opponents fear that students will not be supervised if there is no school on Saturday. One survey showed that "a third of the parents in a sample of 2,116 pupils replied that they could not use this time for family activities because they were working. A total of 42 percent answered 'undecided' when asked whether they approved of the plan."[97] Other opponents of a five-day week fear that it will only lead to students attending a *juku* on Saturday mornings. The first crude statistics indicate that at least 30 percent of urban students are indeed attending *juku* on their free Saturdays.

Impact on Children's Health

One examination *juku* by-product concerns children's health. According to the Ministry of Education, 10 percent of elementary school children are overweight. For the first time in Japanese history children are obese from bad eating habits and lack of sufficient exercise that examination demands and *juku* life impose. (The number of children who break their bones on Japan's ski slopes and in certain sports has increased because they have less protective muscle and weaker bones.) Obesity also stems from snacks children are eating before, during, and after the *juku* classes. Another reason is that more children are eating junk food rather than normal family meals because evening meals with parents are decreasing.[98]

In a 1993 study, over half of the parents lamented that their children suffered health problems, irritability, lack of free time, and limited time to experience actual life. A major problem is lack of sleep.[99] Fifth and sixth graders attending *juku* sleep at least thirty minutes less. One father complained, "Since my daughter started sixth grade she gets two hours less sleep a night. Maybe that's why she catches cold so easily."[100] Another problem is eyesight. One reporter noted that at one *juku* class lasting only seventy-five minutes, three of the pupils were wearing spectacles, but at the next three-hour lesson for forty-three fifth graders, seventeen pupils wore spectacles.[101] One boy while living abroad for two years was pushed by his mother into taking a Japanese correspondence course and private tutoring. On his return to Japan, the obsessive mother realized he would not be able to pass entrance examinations for a private junior high school. Accordingly, she enrolled him for a year in a *juku*, but was told it would take two years to accomplish that objective. Although the boy's grades rose, he had to be removed from the *juku* because "his eyesight was deteriorating, his eating and sleeping habits losing balance."[102] Another twelve-year-old girl pushed by her father into studying practice exercise books since she was two, forced into a *juku* costing 36,000 yen a month at eight, and then forced to go over her exercise books at night, for two hours before *juku* on Saturday, and for one hour after the usual *juku* test on Sunday. Finally she could not stand the strain, and now refuses to attend school.[103]

Toshiyuki Shiomi of the faculty of education at Tokyo University maintains that some preschoolers develop psychosomatic symptoms, including tics and crying at night. He said, "When children, who have been repressed, reach puberty and encounter various obstacles, they are unable to solve problems themselves. They tend to become violent or come down with 'apathetic students syndrome.'"[104] Such children are contributing to teachers' loss of classroom control even at the elementary level. One *juku* teacher told me that her students are not childlike, lack varied interests, and respond primarily to extrinsic motivations.

An American who had taught one year in a combined *juku* and *yobiko* was very concerned about the impact on her students. Her institution, through an arrangement with the University of California–Berkeley, was trying a one-year integrated class on English for *ronin* aiming to enter Tokyo University and who were living in the cram school dormitory. Her task was to stress a comprehensive mastery of English reading, writing, speaking, and listening through discussions and written assignment, stressing thought rather than memorization. But this emphasis proved so threatening and traumatic to *ronin* that within four months, 70 percent of the students had dropped out of class. At the same institution four students had nervous breakdowns. She found many students paranoid and under severe stress, yet the school had no arrangements for counselors or recreational activities.

Undermining of the Public School System

Undermining by Juku. *Juku, yobiko*, entrance examinations, and school ranking are a cancer insidiously destroying the health of Japan's public school system. Ever so gradually *juku* are subtly supplanting public schools as the place where "real" education takes place. One Nanzan University senior wrote, "Teachers know that students go to *juku* so they only teach what is in the textbook and nothing more. Students have a lot of homework from *juku*, making it hard to do homework from school. They are more interested in *juku* classes. Some high school seniors often attend *juku* or *yobiko* during the school day, so much that they skip high school classes to attend them."

Undermining by Parents. I sometimes engage young students in conversations that turn out to be revealing about their experiences. The first conversation with a fourth grader and her mother took place in a Yokohama bus:

Q. How often do you attend *juku* a week and for how many hours?

A. Three times a week, three hours each day.

Mother (With exaggerated pride) But next year you will go four times a week!

A. Yes, that's right. I will attend one four times a week.

Q. What time do you attend the *juku*?

A. 5:30.

Q. What time do you get home from school?

A. About 4 P.M., except on club-activity day. Then I get home about 5 P.M.

Q. What time must you leave the house to get to the *juku*, and do you eat prior to leaving the house?

A. I must leave by five. Usually mother fixes a snack for me, but at the *juku* I have a break for eating mothers' prepared lunch.

Q. What time do you get home and do you eat again?

A. I get home about 9 P.M. Mother has a snack ready for me.

Q. Do you have homework from school?

A. Sometimes I do, so I must prepare that before going to bed.

Q. What time do you go to bed?

A. Sometimes 11 o'clock, sometimes later.

Q. Do you like the *juku*?

A. Yes, it's fun. All my friends are there. We can play together. If you don't attend a *juku*, there aren't any friends to play with after school.

Q. Is the lesson more interesting than at school?

A. Yes, the teachers are younger and we can joke and talk with them. We can also act more freely in the classroom.

Q. Why are you attending one and why will you go more times next year?

A. (The child looked puzzled and could produce no answer. She looked to her mother for help.) Mama, why am I going to a *juku*?

Mother. (With slight embarrassment, but sensing a good opportunity to stress to the child the significance of a previous decision) You know, don't you! Remember, you are planning to go to that good private secondary school two years from now.

A. (With pride) Oh yes, I forgot.

Another conversation of five years ago was with a fifth-grade student, Naoto Ito, a son of a well-to-do dentist living in Yokohama. The story demonstrates how a bright child understands the impact of *juku*, and how his affluent parents advanced his and an elder brother's future prospects by electing private school education rather than public schooling. He told me, "I am taking a break from attending *juku* this year because studying all the time is a grind. But I must attend one next year." "Why?" I asked. "Because I was in the top of my class in mathematics. Now, that I am not attending a *juku* I am falling behind in my class ranking."

Naoto and his parents wanted him to attend the same academically prestigious six year private school—Gyosei International, 2½ hours away in Chiba Prefecture—as his brother, Hiroto. Accordingly, for two years Naoto attended a *juku* two nights a week and was tutored at home twice more a week by the same Yokohama National University student who had helped his older brother pass Gyosei International's difficult high school entrance examination. This strategy proved successful, as Naoto passed Gyosei International Junior High School's entrance examination. After a rather ceremonial high school entrance examination and good grades, he has become a high school tenth grader. His chances of getting into a top-ranked university from Gyosei International are now excellent. His older brother is now a second-year student in Kanagawa Dental University, after being recommended for entrance by his high school, taking a short essay examination, and presenting a confidential report that proved satisfactory to the university. (Incidentally, this Catholic boarding school's rules are strict. It enforces study hours from 7:00 to 10:00 P.M. every night. Students study twenty days successively, inclusive of weekends, and then take a week break—when they may return to their homes or remain at the dormitory.)

Undermining by Public School Teachers. In 1977 Lynne Riggs predicted that *juku*'s competitive practices would force public schools to innovate.[105] It has not happened. (There is a lesson here for those American advocates of choice as a panacea for our educational ills.) Although most public school teachers consider *juku* a harmful influence, they themselves are undermining the public school system by advising their students to attend *juku* to keep up with their classes or to obtain accelerated study. Because of the *juku* some teachers are indirectly undermining the public and private school system by adopting a salary worker's eight-to-five attitude. Even some conservative public school, upper level elementary and secondary teachers are reducing homework, pushing students less, and handing over real study to the *juku*.

CONCLUSION

The present Japanese educational system has become obsolete and lacks humanity. Japanese society has changed so much that the thinking, administration, and methodology of the pre-1980s is no longer appropriate in meeting Japan's needs. Young people are increasingly alienated by the establishment's ranking of institutions and human beings. Hata Masaharu's research on Fukuoka Prefecture fifth and sixth graders in 1992 and 1995 showed that "30 percent felt stress one way or another and that those under heavy stress had a strong urge to obstruct lessons or vandalize school equipment." He also found that children with good scholastic records were more stressed than underachievers.[106] Even corporations no longer think that such an educational system provides them with the talent, individuality, and creativity needed to compete internationally.

Entrance examinations and school ranking should be radically reformed because they are dehumanizing and demeaning. They deny full human dignity to the losers who are branded for the rest of their life. The winners' dignity and individuality have also been denied because they have sacrificed their energies, interests, and youth to a narrow curriculum and the all-consuming goal of getting into the best schools and universities to achieve social status and economic and political power.[107] The system is fault-prone and discriminatory because it determines children's future prematurely. Students who are sorted out into lower ranked schools experience lower teacher expectations and a less challenging peer environment. Teachers are forced to become efficient, narrow technicians to help students master textbook content. The joy of making students think, discuss, and debate material and to explore occasionally subjects that will challenge them and open them to a wider world is limited. The public school system is undermined by parents and students who bypass it at the secondary school level to maximize the chances of their children entering good universities and future prestigious employment, a condition made even worse by the ubiquitous presence of private tutors and *juku*.

Clearly indigenous attitudes favoring a meritocracy and hierarchy have been carried to an extreme. One Japanese sociologist recognized the extreme difficulty of reforming the present educational system by writing of these attitudes as follows:

To make the fundamental changes in the college entrance examination system, three parties (parents, teachers, and students) should make fundamental changes in their view of the university ranking custom. They all may agree in public about the need for such changes, but it is likely that parents and teachers will continue trying to send their own children to better schools and students and also are likely to continue competing for better schools. It is hard to change values that have been institutionalized historically and socially, but we must start it now by ourselves; otherwise, no change will occur.[108]

If, however, Japan really wants to recognize the individuality and humanity of all children and to foster creativity, flexibility, and critical judgment for a changing society, some sacrifice of grouping, hierarchical values, and self-interest must be made.

One way to start is to establish comprehensive secondary schools at the secondary level that students must attend in their neighborhood, or for students to attend private schools. In them students should be allowed to exercise greater choice of subjects not only in the academic track, but also in vocational subjects. For example, every graduating student should know how to type and use the computer and Internet. Universities must accept students on the basis of grades, recommendations, aptitude tests, and a balance of differing interests, abilities, geographical location, and ethnicity. An increase in the number of recommended students that high schools may nominate to universities is desirable. An entrance examination system that tests students for their general knowledge across several subjects within a discipline will reduce the student tendency to ignore or slight those subjects that have limited relevance to university entrance examinations. Universities should be more responsible and less profit oriented. They should prohibit students from sitting for examinations for more than two departments to limit a condition where students select universities not departments. This condition will encourage students to cultivate true interests at the secondary and university level. "Escalator" systems must reduce the overwhelming preference they give to their own students for entrance into high school and university. To do so means they must think of long-range benefits for students and society, not self-interested ones. One way to do that is to require students to declare a major subject area interest in their sophomore or junior year in high school and to prevent them from entering other departments not directly related to it. Businesses must institute practices which hire persons on their total performance at school rather than the ranking of schools.

By gradual evolution, the *juku* and public schools are developing an informal division of responsibilities. The *juku* assume the task of preparing students for the entrance examinations; the regular schools continue the role begun in the elementary school of forming character, fostering group consciousness, and providing a high level of egalitarian education. Some Nanzan,

Yokohama, and Tskuba University students told me they concentrated on the school as a place to enjoy friendships and club activities.

For three reasons I view *juku* as a grievous cancer progressively undermining public schools and lower ranked private schools. First, a school and its faculty are dependent on respect; however, most teachers, parent, and students maintain that schools and teachers are less respected by today's parents and students because they credit *juku, yobiko,* or tutors with their success. As the prestige of *juku* rises, the reputation and importance of public schools and lower-ranking private schools decline. Less respect for teachers, especially home room teachers, also occurs because *juku* now play the principal role of advising students on university placement and preparing students for entrance examinations. Poor teaching at the schools and better teaching at the *juku* also undermine the public school system and the role of teachers in providing whole-person education. Many of my students completely agreed with the sentiments expressed by one student who wrote, "It may be public school teachers' fault that students and their parents do not respect them because many do not try to make students understand. Teachers in *juku* try hard to make students understand because they are easily fired if they are not good teachers." One Nanzan University graduate put her finger on several reasons for *juku* popularity, one of which supports my criticism of controlled education:

When I did part-time work at a *juku* helping to put grade information into computers I noticed that students talk much more with the teacher, even in the middle of classes. Why? First, school teachers are expected not only to take care of students study, but also to supervise their daily activities and personal items including hairstyle, clothes, and relationships between boy friends and girl friends. Therefore, students feel uneasy and find it difficult to talk with them. Second, because *juku* teachers do not grade students, the latter feel less pressure. Public school teachers have lost students' respect and intimacy and public schools have become more irrelevant.

Without a sense of pride and a commitment to mission, a school lacks an ethos; without an ethos it dies. In Japan, *juku* are gradually destroying teachers' and schools' self-respect, pride, and purpose.

Second, the impression abroad, even in Japan, of all students willingly going to receive accelerated education or studying on their own four to six hours a day is a misconception of the study habits of a large number of secondary school students of middle and lower ranked schools. Instead, a growing number of them do not study much during their secondary school days. Many students do little homework. When I ask them how they plan to pass university entrance examinations, they reply that they will attend a *yobiko* after graduation. The tendency of more and more students to escape the horrors of the examination hell in favor of enjoying high school days is increasing. Japanese teachers, parents, and the establishment regret this tendency very much; some refer to it as an American sickness. But it is less an American sickness than complacency resulting from modernization, economic affluence, a desire for greater freedom and individuality, and a reaction against Japan's hot-house educational system.

This newer phenomenon also affects parents financially because ultimately they pay for the lackadaisical attitude of their children. One assistant principal told me of his deep disappointment at his son's failure to gain entrance into Waseda University because he had failed to study seriously. "Now, we are paying dearly this year to the *yobiko*." More younger parents are supportive of this attitude. Naturally, teachers and the establishment are becoming alarmed because more students are studying less.

Finally, the *juku* are deeply significant in reinforcing the negative, dehumanizing, and distorting results of the entrance examinations on students' study habits.[109] Students associate education and learning with being a passive recipient of already processed information through a high class teacher–technician rather than active inquiry on their own.[110] This kind of education will not produce the innovative, creative students that the NCER advocated for Japan to meet its future challenges. One Nanzan student referred to the counseling she received from her teacher. She said, "Before I attended a *juku* I had always tried to understand my subjects. But my *juku* teacher warned me: 'You can study like that after you enter a university. Memorize things without any question.'" The Japanese emphasis on effort and perseverance praised in Chapters 2 and 3 has been allowed to become distorted and excessive. Here again we see the marriage of personal ambition and traditional "spiritual attitudes," which makes students victims.[111]

The student who studies independently and actively is becoming a vanishing breed. One Nanzan returnee student wisely put her finger on the fear-driven concerns that *juku* and *yobiko* market to explain their success: "Cram schools are taking advantage of the pressure and insecurity of students and parents by brain-washing them to believe that the only way to pass entrance examinations is to enroll in their programs. Japanese society will decline if the present situation continues."

Some parents justify attendance by asserting that "children really enjoy themselves more at *juku* than at regular schools."[112] Many of my students also agreed that *juku* attract students because they provide what public schools lack: teachers with humor and enthusiasm, freedom from scolding, limited rules, absence of corporal punishment, and students acting and asking questions freely. Profit-motivated *juku* know child psychology well enough to make the lessons as pleasant as possible. For many youth it is a time to be with classmates in a more voluntary, relaxed, and academically stimulating environment. Well-organized lessons and visual aids and friendly, young teachers, who enjoy high salaries or part-time wages, and teach with enthusiasm and humor make learning more efficient and pleasant. Significantly, this praise of *juku* calls attention to the shortcomings of present Japanese education.

In the *juku* what we see is a case of the cart coming before the horse. If there were no *juku*, children could play together daily. If there were no *juku*, regular classroom teachers would be required to teach more energetically. If there were no *juku*, compilers of university entrance examinations would not have to make the tests harder every year, and teachers and schools would not have to perpetrate on students a dehumanizing methodology and the grind of constant mock examination testing.

Japanese attitudes and values in the educational area have become confused. If adults cannot make a critical assessment of the many casualties of this system, we cannot expect children to be able to do so. Students do not seriously lead an attack against the system because they are kept so busy studying for the entrance examinations that they do not have time to focus on the larger questions of life and to understand that the entire system itself is at fault. Tsukada is correct when he says students also accept both entrance examinations and the *juku* because they come to believe that their success or lack of it has been *legitimatized* by a scientific selection and sorting system that objectively assigns rank and status in Japanese society.[113] It is made legitimate because of students' repeated experience with socialization and mind-numbing tests in *juku* and school. Students think they are playing on a fair and transparent field. They do not imagine that the objectives and the rules of the educational game could be different. And adults and scholars who want to perpetuate the myth that Japan is one big middle class are closing their eyes to the evidence that the *juku*, *yobiko*, entrance examinations, and school and university ranking systems are undermining education. This condition for students resembles a giant airplane without a pilot or navigator carrying its passengers to potential danger.

Parents and grandparents who should know better have let this system distort education and social life. Students attending *juku* and *yobiko* reflect the excessive values placed by bureaucrats and other adults on credentials, status, and a national ethic of social control. Gradually students themselves show greater respect for their peers who have graduated from more prestigious high schools.[114] A society that puts so much emphasis on credentials and status symbols ends up weakening the meaning of true education and the dignity and diversity of individuals. The present education system cripples the ability of society and individuals to make critical judgments and to challenge existing mores, attitudes, and practices.[115] To build a more diversified, humane, and democratic society not only the *juku* and *yobiko* must go, but also the feudal and obsolescent attitudes and practices that sustain the entrance examination system.

NOTES

1. In 1996, 547,000 students took the National Center Test for University Admission, but only 131,000 students will be accepted by the 269 public and private universities requiring the test. "Record Turnout for Test," *Asahi Evening News*, 14 January 1996.

2. Benjamin Duke, *The Japanese School: Lessons for Industrial America* (Westport, Conn.: Praeger, 1986), 67; Thomas Rohlen, *Japan's High Schools* (Berkeley and Los Angeles: University of California Press, 1984), 77.

3. Nobuharu Niitsu, "Reference Book Nutrition," *Asahi Evening News*, 18 March 1996.

4. Leonard James Schoppa, *Education Reform in Japan* (London: Routledge, 1991), ch. 8; Harry Wray, "CIE, Mombusho, and Kyoiku Sasshin Jinkai," (The Connection between the CIE, Ministry of Education, and Educational Reform Committee), in *Tenno ga Baiburu o Yonda hi* (The day the emperor read the Bible), ed. Ray Moore (Tokyo: Kodansha, 1982), 59–113.

5. Entrance examinations at private and public senior high school levels only differ by being smaller in scale.

6. Robert L. Cutts, *An Empire of Schools: Japan's Universities and the Molding of a National Power Elite* (Armonk, N.Y.: M. E. Sharpe, 1997), 13–17.

7. Rohlen, *Japan's High Schools*, 317–318.

8. Thomas P. Rohlen and Gerald K. LeTendre, "Introduction: Japanese Theories of Learning," in *Teaching and Learning in Japan*, ed. Thomas P. Rohlen and Gerald K. LeTendre (Cambridge: Cambridge University Press, 1996), 8–10.

9. James B. Crowley, *Japan's Quest for Autonomy: National Security and Foreign Policy, 1930–1938* (Princeton, N.J.: Princeton University Press, 1966).

10. Students disagree. One wrote, "On the contrary, our present uniform education will weaken national power. It is important to study willingly instead of being forced to study."

11. Herbert Passin, *Society and Education in Japan* (New York: Teachers College Press, Columbia University, 1966), 109; Japan, Ministry of Education, Science, and Culture (Japan, MESC), *Education in Japan 1994: A Graphic Presentation* (Tokyo: Gyosei, 1994), 23.

12. John Singleton, *Nichu: A Japanese School; Case Studies in Education and Culture* (New York: Holt, Rinehart, and Winston, 1967), 36–40.

13. Kiyomitsu Komoriya, "Junior High Testing System Won't Die," *Asahi Evening News*, 29 November 1994.

14. Rohlen, *Japan's High Schools*, 100.

15. Merry White, *The Japanese Educational Challenge* (New York: Free Press, 1989), 159–160.

16. "Asahi Shimbun," 28 January 1982, cited in Benjamin Duke, *The Japanese School: Lessons for Industrial America* (Westport, Conn.: Praeger, 1986), 202–203.

17. One Nanzan University senior wrote, "I enjoyed studying more in elementary school because I had more chances to express my own way of thinking." For a contrary situation see Rohlen, *Japan's High Schools*, 20.

18. Somucho, Seishonen Taisaku honbu, *Seishonen hakusho* (White paper on cildren and youth) (Tokyo: Okurasho Instsukyoku, 1991), as cited in Cahterine C. Lewis, *Educating Hearts and Minds* (Cambridge: Cambridge University Press, 1995), 188.

19. Rebecca Irwin Fukuzawa, "The Path to Adulthood," in *Teaching and Learning in Japan*, ed. Thomas P. Rohlen and Gerald K. LeTendre (Cambridge: Cambridge University Press, 1996), 299–301. Editorial, "Japan's Education System Desperately Needs Overhaul," *Asahi Shimbun*, 1 October 1997. A Ministry study showed that for junior high social studies, "The ability to think from various angles and to express one's own ideas is weak."

20. Rohlen, *Japan's High Schools*, 266 (emphasis mine).

21. Editorial, "8 nen buri Kasosen Konai BoryojkuManbiki Ohabagen," (Pickpocketing and school violence decreased greatly for first time in eight years), *Asahi Shimbun*,

29 December 1984; 1,123 teachers suffered personal violence at the hands of students, compared to 39 attacks on senior high school teachers; M. S. Reeves, "Schooling in Japan: The Paradox in the Pattern," *Education Week*, 27 February 1985, 24.

22. One Nanzan student wrote, "In Japan, it is not important that students have artistic or musical ability. Only students who are good at the main subjects for an entrance examination are respected. Moreover, students cannot study their favorite works, but only their teacher's favorite ones to get good grades for entering high school."

23. "New Entrance Exams Fail Test," *The Daily Yomiuri*, 3 February 1997.

24. Shogo Ichikawa, *Nihon no kyoiku; Kyoiku kaikau no riron to kozo* (Japanese education: The theory and structure of educational reform) (Tokyo: Shopan Hakko, 1991), 77–80.

25. Tatsuro Hoshina, "Admitting Ignorant Students," *Asahi Evening News*, 23 February 1997.

26. Ikuo Koike, "Survey Shows English-Teaching Faults," *Asahi Evening News*, 4 March 1996; Ikuo Koike, "Japan Needs a New Culture," *Asahi Evening News*, 29 January 1996.

27. Hoshina, "Admitting Ignorant Students."

28. Hideharu Tajima, "Entrance-Exam English," *Asahi Evening News*, 16 January 1996.

29. "English for Exams Examined," *Asahi Evening News*, 25 May 1997.

30. Carol Rinnert, "Importance of Classroom English," *Asahi Evening News*, 10 October 1995.

31. Cited in *Japanese Education since 1945: A Documentary Study*, ed. Edward R. Beauchamp and James M. Vardaman (Armonk, N.Y.: M. E. Sharpe, 1994), 315.

32. Shibuya Kazunori, "The Struggle to Prevent High School Dropouts," *Asahi Evening News,* 22 May 1997.

33. Chie Nakane, *Japanese Society* (Berkeley and Los Angeles: University of California Press, 1972), 25–40.

34. One Nanzan female wrote: "The Japanese attitude toward hierarchic organizations was one of the aspects of my 'reverse culture-shock.' This attitude, combined with the obsessive nature toward uniformity and form prevents major change in education."

35. Mamoru Tsukada, *Yobiko Life: A Study of the Legitimation Process of Social Stratification in Japan* (Berkeley and Los Angeles: Institute of East Asian Studies, University of California, 1991), 108.

36. Telephone conversation and correspondence, 27 July 1988, from Ichiro Tanaka, professor at Kawamura University, Chiba Prefecture. Cited with permission.

37. Ibid. Hirofumi Yokoyama, "Tokyo to Alter High School Entrance," 10 November 1993.

38. A Nanzan senior complained, "The ranking system lessens students' interest in study because those who are placed in a lower ranking school in their early teens develop an inferiority complex. They may have abilities, that have not yet developed. It is like tramping down flowers which are blooming. It is too inhumane."

39. Japan, National Council on Educational Reform (Japan, NCER), *First Report on Educational Reform* (Tokyo: Government of Japan, 1985); Editorial, *Asahi Evening News*, 6 June 1997.

40. Recently a Japanese man was sued because he deceived a family into believing that he could get their three-year-old into Keio University's kindergarten at age five—for a sum of a million yen.

41. One kindergarten test showed a partial side view of the left-hand side of a bus. Kindergarten aspirants were required to identify which way the bus was proceeding.

42. Joseph J. Tobin, David Y. W. Wu, and Dana H. Davidson, *Preschool in Three Cultures: Japan, China, and the United States* (New Haven: Yale University Press, 1989), 53–57; Lois Peak, *Learning to Go to School in Japan* (Berkeley and Los Angeles: University of California Press, 1991), 65–68; Savane Spence Boocock, "The Japanese Preschool System," in *Windows on Japanese Education*, ed. Edward R. Beauchamp (New York: Greenwood Press, 1991), 121–122.

43. Richard Lynn, *Educational Achievement in Japan* (Armonk, N.Y.: M. E. Sharpe, 1988), 29.

44. Mariko Akinato, "Alternative Schools Listed," *Asahi Evening News*, 1 April 1996; Mayumi Vjroka, "Home Schooling Best Solution for Some," *Asahi Evening News*, 22 December 1996.

45. Robert L. Cutts, *An Empire of Schools: Japan's Universities and the Molding of a National Power Elite* (Armonk, N.Y.: M. E. Sharpe, 1997), 1, 239–240.

46. Rohlen, *Japan's High Schools*, 203–204.

47. "Schools Failing to Cut Classes," *Asahi Evening News*, 25 June 1994.

48. A Nanzan student objected, "I sometimes heard public school teachers tell us to study hard and pass the entrance exams for the school's name. Students resist this thought."

49. One Nanzan student wrote, "At lower ranked schools regular exams are easier and teachers tell students the content of the examination prior to giving it. My private student wants to go to a university, but his textbook is so easy that he will probably have to become a *ronin*."

50. Carol Linda Susan Yamada, "Family Culture and Educational Attainment in Japan," Ph.D. diss., University of Tsukuba, 1988.

51. Karel von Wolferen, *The Enigma of Japanese Power* (New York: Vintage Books, 1990), 85.

52. Cutts, *Empire of Schools*, 4–5.

53. Ibid., 258–260.

54. Tsukada, *Yobiko Life*, 103–107.

55. Thomas P. Rohlen, "The *Juku* Phenomenon: An Exploratory Essay," *Journal of Japanese Studies* 6, no. 2 (1980): 219; U.S. Department of Education, *Japanese Education Today* (Washington, D.C.: U.S. Government Printing Office, 1987), 45.

56. Rohlen, "The *Juku* Phenomenon," 20–21, 33.

57. Conversation with David Slater.

58. Mamoru Tsukada, "Institutionalized Supplementary Education in Japan," *Comparative Education* 24, no. 3 (1988): 285–303.

59. U.S. Department of Education, *Japanese Education Today*, 11.

60. Tsukada, "Institutionalized Supplementary Education," 287.

61. Mombusho, Daijin Kanu Chosa Tokeika, *Zenkoku gakushu juku toi no jittai* (A fact-finding survey on the question of nationwide attendance) (Tokyo: Mombusho, 1977).

62. In 1973 the figures were 12 percent and 38 percent. Takuro Noguchi, "Are Exam Crammers a Necessary Evil?" *Asahi Evening News*, 23 February 1997.

63. Robert L. August, "*Yobiko*: Prep Schools for College Entrance in Japan," in *Educational Productivity in Japan*, ed. R. Leestma and H. J. Walberg, 274.

64. U.S. Department of Education, *Japanese Education Today*, 11.

65. August, *"Yobiko,"* 276.

66. Tsukada, *Yobiko Life*, 13.

67. Approximately 10 percent of them attended high schools where at least 50 percent of graduates attend college. "Toshihiko Wada" (Academic Ability of and the Actual Situation of Entrance Examinations), *Daigaku Shingaku Kenkyu* (*Research on Students' Advance to Universities*) 6, no. 2: 20–23; August, *"Yobiko,"* 278.

68. Tsukada, "Institutionalized Supplementary Education," 288–289. One foreign teacher at a famous *juku* said her classes for *ronin* were comprised of 90 to 98 percent males.

69. The daughter of a friend failed to pass Tokyo University's entrance examination on her first attempt, but a famous *yobiko*, correctly calculating that she would pass on a second attempt, offered her attendance at no expense. Takuro Noguchi, "Japanese Children Jinxed by *Juku*," *Asahi Evening News*, 16 February 1997.

70. Ibid.

71. Masashi Nakamura, "Crunch Time Has Come for the Culture of the Crammers," *Asahi Evening News*, 6 November 1995.

72. Takuro Noguchi, "Japanese Children Jinxed."

73. Tsukada, *Yobiko Life*, 27–33.

74. Lynn, *Educational Achievement in Japan*, 47–48 (emphasis mine).

75. Rohlen, "The *Juku* Phenomenon," 214.

76. U.S. Department of Education, *Japanese Education Today*, 12.

77. Noguchi, "Are Exam Crammers a Necessary Evil?"

78. A friend in Kumamoto City feared losing her job because *juku* chains were coming.

79. Tsukada, "Institutionalized Supplementary Education," 288.

80. Nakamura, "Crunch Time Has Come."

81. Rohlen, "The *Juku* Phenomenon," 213.

82. Nakamura, "Crunch Time Has Come."

83. Sayuri Saito, "Cramming Youngsters." *The Daily Yomiuri*, 3 February 1997.

84. Nakamura, "Crunch Time Has Come."

85. Ibid.

86. Public elementary and junior high school teachers decreased from 6 percent to 1 percent. U.S. Department of Education, *Japanese Education Today*, 13.

87. Tsukada, "Institutionalized Supplementary Education," 301; "The Development of Japanese Educational Policy 1945–1985," in *Windows on Japanese Education*, ed. Edward R. Beauchamp (Westport, Conn.: Greenwood Press, 1991), 39–40.

88. "Anxieties about Preschool Education," *The Daily Yomiuri*, 3 February 1997.

89. Christie Kiefer, "The Psychological Interdependence of Family, School, and Bureaucracy in Japan," in *Japanese Culture and Behavior*, ed. Takie S. Lebra and William Lebra (Honolulu: University of Hawaii Press, 1974), 353–355; Peter Milward, "Education Mothers," *Asahi Evening News*, 8 February 1996.

90. George A. DeVos, "Achievement Orientation, Social Self-Identity, and Japanese Economic Growth," *Asian Survey* 5, no. 12: 575–589.

91. Merry White, *The Japanese Overseas* (New York: Free Press, 1988), 36–37, 58–59; Roger Goodman, *Japan's "International Youth"* (Oxford: Oxford University Press, 1990), 186–189, ch. 7.

92. Rohlen, "The *Juku* Phenomenon," 237–241. A doctoral dissertation suggests that family cultural aspirations rather than money are decisive in deciding whether

parents will dig deeply enough into the family budget to provide students with the money to attend *juku* or hire tutors. Carol Linda Susan Yamada, "Family Culture and Educational Attainment in Japan," Ph.D. diss., University of Tsukuba, 1988.

93. Sayuri Saito, "Cramming Youngsters," *The Daily Yomiuri*, 3 February 1997.

94. M. Ejima, "Problems of Educating for a Caring Community in Contemporary Japan," *New Era in Education* 69, no. 2 (1988): 55–56; U.S. Department of Education, *Japanese Education Today*, 14.

95. Letter from Tokui Sadao.

96. Lois Peak, "Formal Pre-Elementary Education in Japan," in *Japanese Educational Productivity*, ed. R. Leestma and H. J. Walberg (Ann Arbor: University of Michigan Press, 1992), 40, 46, 58.

97. Kawamura Gakuen Women's Survey as reported in *Asahi Access* 3, no. 48 (14 December 1992) as cited in Byron Marshall, *Learning to Be Modern: Japanese Political Discourse on Education* (Boulder, Colo.: Westview Press, 1994), 251.

98. Shigeru Nakanishi, "New Lifestyle Threatens Japan's Children," *The Daily Yomiuri,* 9 January 1996.

99. Noguchi, "Are Exam Crammers a Necessary Evil?"; Kaoru Ahonabayashi, "Teachers Sound Alarm on Children's Lack of Sleep," *Asahi Evening News*, 16 November 1997; *Chugakusei no juku kayoi: Seikatsu sara ni yorugata e* (Middle school students attending *juku*: Life style becomes nocturnal), *Asahi Shimbun*, 28 April 1996.

100. Noguchi, "Are Exam Crammers a Necessary Evil?"

101. Noguchi, "Japanese Children Jinxed by *Juku*."

102. Ibid.

103. "Banishing the Curse of Crammers," *Asahi Evening News*, 20 July 1997.

104. Saito, "Cramming Youngsters."

105. Lynne Riggs, "The Idioms of Contemporary Japan: Ranjuku Jidai," *The Japan Interpreter* 11, no. 4 (1977): 541–549.

106. Emiko Inagaki, "Exam Hell Explodes Bright Children," *Asahi Evening News*, 1 October 1996.

107. Tsukada amply documents the misery of Yobiko life: "It was such a hardship, however, that I would not ever have wanted to go through it again." Tsukada, *Yobiko Life*, 113.

108. Ibid., 108.

109. Ibid., 94–99, 113–114.

110. Tokui Sadao, a friend who taught in a Shikoku junior high school, thought his son succeeded in entering Tokyo University because he had developed strong personal study habits at home by *not* attending a *juku*.

111. Tsukada, *Yobiko Life,* 114.

112. Most Nanzan and Nagoya University students object to *juku* in principle, but found them to be enjoyable. One student wrote, "I liked going to the *juku*. It was fun. I even went there when I had a fever and absented myself from the regular school." Over 77 percent of third-year junior high school students and 83.9 percent of sixth-grade elementary school students say they enjoy attending cram schools according to the National Coordinating Council of Parents–Teachers Associations. "Most Cram School Students Like Attending, Survey Finds," *The Japan Times*, 25 April 1998.

113. Tsukada, *Yobiko Life*, 103–107.

114. Tsukada, "Institutionalized Supplementary Education," 297–299.

115. Rohlen, "The *Juku* Phenomenon," 241.

CHAPTER 5

Societal Attitudes Debilitating
American Education and
the Compelling Need for Educational Reform

In the postwar period, Japan has succeeded in producing disciplined students with academic competence. This policy nurtured able and disciplined human resources for Japanese factories, farms, and government bureaucracies. Conversely, the failure of American schools to require many youth over the past four decades to master self and subject matter has contributed to the detriment of individuals, society, and the nation.

But is it fair to compare Japanese and American education? Can two educational systems with such strikingly different values and traditions as the following borrow from each other?

Japan	United States
Duties, form, and order	Inalienable rights, liberty
Respect for learning	Antiintellectualism
Effort and perseverance over ability	Aptitude and IQ valued
Group identity and uniformity	Individualism
Hierarchical and homogeneous	Egalitarian and heterogeneous
Centralization and bureaucracy	Decentralization, antibureaucratic
Conformist and passive citizenry	Active, vocal citizenry
Situational moral values	Absolute moral values
Loyalty and harmony	Truth, justice, and freedom
Deference to and trust of officials	Distrust of officials and antipathy to orders and regulations

Notwithstanding these differences, three reasons make educational comparisons valid, and selective borrowing feasible. First, both nations possess a single-track, 6–3–3–4 educational ladder system. Second, both provide equal educational opportunity, at least through junior high school.[1] Third, both school systems reflect democratic, capitalistic, social welfare societies.

EDUCATION REFLECTS SOCIETAL ATTITUDES, THE MAJOR OBSTACLE TO REFORM

In this chapter, I maintain that the deteriorating quality of American schools and society and their ability to overcome this condition are handicapped by the following attitudes:

1. A false sense of superiority
2. Complacency and parental apathy
3. A lack of consensus on educational goals and values
4. Antiintellectualism
5. Confused national and educational priorities
6. Apathy to social injustice and disorder
7. A myth of unlimited natural and fiscal resources
8. Failure to accept responsibility for our individual and collective actions
9. A loss of role models

False Sense of Superiority

Deep in the American psyche is the assumption that their way of life is unique and superior. They hear repeatedly that the United States is the greatest country in the world. Because America emerged from two world wars as the greatest military and economic power in the world, victory was interpreted further as a triumph of American science, technology, and values. It seems the more the United States declines in power and quality of life the more compulsive becomes the need to prove America is number one. Americans need to recognize that their achievements are less the result of superior human qualities than the result of enormous resources and wise democratic institutions established more than two centuries ago.

American education and society have been shaped by a predominantly white, Anglo–Saxon, Protestant, ethnocentric view that a *unique* people were sifted from Europe and given a historical destiny to lead other peoples to a freer and higher civilization. The absolute Christian values of Puritan ancestors have contributed to a tendency to think categorically in black and white terms. Because Americans often righteously presume their behavior in foreign policy is based on moral principles, compromise becomes difficult.

American education perpetuates these attitudes. When children enter elementary school they are led through a celebration of American values and achievements. Christopher Columbus's virtues are extolled, while his ruthless actions against Native Americans are passed over. America's blatant seizure of Mexican territory is justified as Manifest Destiny. If high school students are not taught by good history teachers, they will never be lead to any critical evaluation of the American experience, unless they attend a university. This educational environment limits objective self-examination and makes borrowing better attitudes and practices from abroad for improving American schools hard.

Complacency, Mediocrity, and Parental Apathy

Complacent thinking throughout the land is now seen by scholars as a major reason that the educational reform movement of the early 1980s has not found fertile soil.[2] One North Carolina County Superintendent of Education told me, "Our biggest problem is there is little awareness among students and their parents that we live in a much more keenly competitive and complicated world that requires greater discipline and higher educational achievement." John Gardner warned over three decades ago that "a rejection of all standards and tolerance of mediocrity and shabbiness in every aspect of our national life" threatened America's future well-being.[3] His prophecy was echoed by *A Nation at Risk* in 1983 when its authors wrote "the educational foundations of our society are presently being eroded by a rising tide of mediocrity."[4]

Complacency is engendered by misleading school statistics. One study commissioned by the US Office of Education stated, "Clearly it is the exception rather than the rule for a state to report that its students, particularly its elementary school students are performing below the national average. . . . A substantial majority of districts reports that their students are performing above average (i.e., more than 50% of the students are reported to be above the national median)."[5] The 1995 Gallop Poll on public attitudes toward education revealed that on a scale of one to four, four equaling an "A," the public gave schools a national rating of 1.97, but their own local schools a 2.47 rating. If they had no children in school, the respective ratings were 1.98 and 2.43.[6] If people nationwide think their own schools are not so bad, no wonder communities are silent on the need for nationwide reform.

Teachers' and administrators' attitudes reflect these detrimental attitudes. A Harris poll of late 1989 revealed that 92 percent of teachers thought their present school was giving its students a good or excellent education. Incredibly, among teachers in inner-city and heavily minority-populated schools, "fewer than one in five evaluated the quality of education as less than good."[7] When asked to rate their own schools in another survey 90 percent of the superintendents and 88 percent of the principals gave their own schools A or B grades. Although school boards were slightly less generous in awarding accolades to schools, 79 percent gave their own schools A or B grades. Finn thought the reasons for these discrepancies with actual deteriorating standards is "the system's preference for public relations."[8]

American students agree that our schools are too lax. A Gallup poll of 1979 showed that 58 percent of American teenagers thought they had not been asked to study sufficiently in the elementary schools; 45 percent felt similarly about high schools.[9] Of two thousand high-achieving students listed in *Who's Who among American High School Students*, a striking 82 percent thought that the reason some students graduate from high schools without basic skills is that they were allowed to select easy courses. Most public school seniors interviewed wished they had studied more.[10] These responses demonstrate students' deep-down realization that they need the guidelines and expectations that schools and parents have lacked the courage and wisdom to provide.

Too many American parents are so wrapped up in their own personal lives that they do not concern themselves adequately with their children's educational well-being. In 1987 and 1991 an overwhelming majority of teachers cited lack of parental support as the most serious problem in their schools.[11] They complained that parents show limited interest in their children's education and fail to discipline them, feed them nutritionally, limit their part-time work, monitor their television programs, or supervise their evening activities.

Lack of Consensus over Educational Goals and Values

Over Educational Goals. Several years ago James Doi, professor emeritus of the University of Washington's College of Education, said, "We no longer have any consensus in America about values and educational objectives. We did when we occupied Japan." Our schools, communities, and political system are divided by controversies over separation of church and state, individual rights versus societal order, absolutist arguments from the right and left, and what values should be taught in a multicultural society. For at least the past seven decades Progressive Education's philosophy and methodology in various forms has dominated the thinking of most professional educators. They hold romantic, sentimental ideas of children and education. Education for them is to be child-centered and to help students understand their feelings, enjoy learning, deal with immediate problems of living in a complex society, and develop self-esteem and self-identity. They value relevant life-adjustment courses. Progressive education is continually revived in new forms and slightly altered pedagogy, such as Life Adjustment Education, Mastery Learning, or Outcome Based Education.[12]

Traditional educators dissatisfied with America's declining educational standards have countered with the arguments that schools are to help students achieve basic skills and physical, spiritual, and intellectual discipline, that is, achieving reading, writing, and mathematics competence and critical judgment and self-discipline by rigor, high standards, and effort. They emphasize the need for drill, memorization, and acquiring the fundamentals by focusing on the basics of education. Traditionalists contend that professional educator's faddish curricular and subject matter are responsible for the low academic standards in America today. They argue that self-esteem follows from achievement rather than the other way around. This loss of consensus handicaps our schools in forming character and achieving higher academic standards.

Lack of Consensus on Values. The late 1960s and first half of the 1970s was an exciting time of bringing to an end an unjust Vietnam War and a period of challenging authority and searching for personal and ethnic freedom. Old values were attacked and experimentation in alternative lifestyles occurred. Destroying proved easier than building. Parental loss of confidence in rearing children, a breakdown in authority, and a romantic worship of youth's innocence and wisdom flourished. Secondary schools' and universities' academic and ethical standards declined. More and more parents, teachers, and administrators challenged by the question "Whose values?," ended up adopting safer, neutral, and noncontroversial stances. Many discriminatory societal and school practices needed to be challenged, but the attack on existing cultural traditions and the emphasis on minority ethnocentrism by multiculturalists and the politically correct now pervades society.[13] In the process unity and a lack of consensus over essential common ethical and academic standards are lost.[14] A society that allows its values to be scorned cannot survive because values are the glue of a society. Good, old ones must be supported; new, better ones need to be forged and agreed upon.

On Multiculturalism. Today, demographic changes and a strong civil rights movement have produced a more pluralistic society and more militant minorities committed to achieving equality and social justice. But unfortunately schools have become afraid to stress common and unifying values for fear of offending every pressure group, because each religious, racial, and ethnic group wants to stress that its values are different.[15] By the year 2000 the minority population in the United States will reach at least 35 percent, the Hispanic population in the United States will become the fifth largest in the world, the Asian population is expected to reach approximately 12 million, and most Americans will be descendants of non-Europeans. Already the combined African American and Hispanic school population is 76 percent in Los Angeles, 80 percent in St. Louis, 84 percent in Chicago, and 92 percent in Atlanta.[16]

Educating such a large, heterogeneous population is not a new phenomenon. In 1909 almost 58 percent of the pupils attending schools in the larger cities were either foreign-born or the children of immigrants. But today, among the relatively larger minority population, a large percentage are oppressed by prejudice, job and wage discrimination, and culturally underprivileged home conditions that produce low educational expectations and despair among their children. These conditions have transformed urban schools. Gerald Grant researched a New York State urban public school (given the fictitious name of

Hamilton High) that had been predominantly college-preparatory oriented in 1954. Thirty years later however population migrations and racial integration had changed the student-body population from 95 percent non-Hispanic white and 5 percent African American to 51 percent white, 36 percent African American, 10 percent Asian, and 3 percent Hispanic. The African American population in the late 1960s and 1970s largely resisted the existing school lifestyle. The sudden desegregation of the school made African American students realize how far behind the whites they were in academic achievement. Their daily humiliation because of lower reading, writing, numerary, and general academic skills created resentment and reinforced their disadvantaged historic American experience. It also meant a loss of face for white teachers who did not know how to teach them. This formerly distinguished high school has lost its academic orientation, achievement ethos, and close, harmonious relations among students, faculty, and the community.[17]

Faculty advocates of "political correctness" and some teachers of ethnic studies attack traditional American values as subjective, white, or class dominated. Their graduates have gone into our elementary and secondary schools to undermine student respect for traditional and unifying values. Arthur Schlesinger, Jr., wrote

The militants of ethnicity now contend that a main objective of public education should be the protection, strengthening, celebration, and perpetuation of ethnic origins and identities. Separatism, however, nourishes prejudices, magnifies differences, and stirs antagonisms. The consequent increase in ethnic and racial conflict lies behind the hullabaloo over "multiculturalism" and "political correctness," over the iniquities of the "Eurocentric" curriculum, and over the notion that history and literature should be taught not as intellectual disciplines but as therapies whose function is to raise minority self-esteem.[18]

On Individualism. Achieving consensus on educational goals is also difficult because of an excessive emphasis on individualism. Americans think positively of individualism, but it has grown into an excessive search for identity and self-esteem without considering the consequences. Individuals want to make themselves the norm for all behavior and the object of educational largesse. Excessive individualism reflects an exaggerated distortion of Henry David Thoreau's famous saying that "Every man marches to a different drummer." As James Q. Wilson has written, "We have tried to free ourselves from public opinion and private prudery" and no one should be told what to do, nor is anyone better than anybody else. He called this liberating and leveling.[19] Two attitudes flourish: "Who cares (what others think!)"; and "I will not interfere in your affairs and I do not expect you to interfere with mine." These attitudes foster adversarial, shrill, combative relationships at the expense of cooperation, civility, and community. Americans have become a people too quick to object to the rules and common values that unite them in a social contract.

Antiintellectualism: A Negative Attitude
Affecting American Education

Another attitude in serious need of correction is antiintellectualism. The prejudice against eggheads, "book larnin'," and academia in America has a long history. American antiintellectualism is grounded in frontier life, where the ability to survive depended less on books and ideas than on the capacity to create practical solutions to everyday problems. It also results from two other attitudes. First, early American settlers associated education negatively with European and early American aristocracy. The Jacksonian Democratic Movement (1824–1840) emphasized the common man and egalitarianism so strongly that adherents believed public officials did not need higher education. Second, twentieth century progressive educators taught that learning about how to live was more important than amassing knowledge.

Many of America's folk heroes expressed antiintellectual sentiments. Thomas Alva Edison quit school after the third grade and ridiculed the educational world. Henry Ford said, "History is bunk." John Wayne's movies portrayed him as a man of few words, much action, and with a limited interest in books or theory. More recently, Arnold Schwartzenegger, and Sylvester Stallone are examples of macho brawn over brains.

A strong stereotype exists that persons of advanced formal learning lack common sense: "He may be bright, but he doesn't know enough to come in out of the rain." Einstein's greatness is qualified by disparaging his lack of common sense. Young Lincoln's farmer-neighbors criticized him as lazy because he read whenever he could.[20] Many negative terms exist for bright and studious students such as "bookworm," "egghead," "Einstein," and "nerd."

Two negative results of antiintellectualism are prominent. One is the strong tendency of many high school students, even college students, to avoid sophisticated courses, demanding teachers, and companions concerned with intellectual matters. A second one is that many bright secondary level students avoid appearing too intelligent and too ambitious in the selection of academic subjects. Most students lack the strength to resist this powerful peer pressure unless they are placed in mutually supportive honors classes or attend very good schools.[21] African American male students, especially from the inner-city schools who do well in school, are intimidated by peer accusation that they are "acting white, laughed at, looked down upon, ridiculed and embarrassed for doing well."[22]

The much greater recognition that society gives secondary school athletes and athletics compared to high academic achievers reflects antiintellectualism. Graham cited H. G. Bissinger's *Friday Night Lights: A Town, a Team, and a Dream* as an example of how one community—Odessa, Texas—reflects a widespread distortion of education by an excessive emphasis on athletics at the expense of learning and players' health.[23] Abraham J. Tannenbaum's survey of 615 school juniors in a New York City high school showed that athletes were valued over nonathletes. Being studious was almost as bad a trait as being a nonathlete. Brilliant, studious nonathletes ranked last in prestige.[24] Many youth, especially African American athletes, minimize academic achievement because they feel that through sports they will become famous and rich. Harry Edwards, has calculated, however, that only about 4,000 "gladiators" out of a male population of more than 100 million has a chance to make the grade in professional sports, and even an exceptionally talented athlete has only a one-in-200,000 chance.

Lack of National Priorities

America's focus on national economic and military power reflects a society with confused priorities. The focus should be to educate *all* our children well, develop foreign markets, retrain blue collar and white collar employees on a massive scale, advance civil rights, and overcome crippling racial injustice. Nonetheless, despite the end of the Cold War, the national budget in 1991 allocated the Department of Education only $85 million for educational research, but awarded the Department of Defense $36 billion out of a total budget of just under $300 billion.[25] America's excessive emphasis on national security during the 1980s indirectly helped to destroy the Soviet Union, but simultaneously supply-side economics increased the wealth of the top 5 percent by 34 percent at the expense of the poorest 20 percent and important environmental and social programs.[26] The burden on the poor and lower middle class increased while taxes on the richest 1 percent were lowered by 25 percent, and the richest 10 percent by 9 percent.

Middle class frustration with corruption in welfare programs and the decline in economic status is appropriate, but misdirected. The 1994 Congress Republican leadership's "contract with America" is an example of confused priorities. Although the contract turned out to be "politics as usual," it advocated higher defense spending, tax cuts of $200 billion for the more affluent over the next five years, and slashing of badly needed social welfare budgets. To compensate for a loss in a targeted capital gains tax cut, they planned to cut support for school lunch programs ($7 billion), aid to handicapped children, foster care and adoption ($4 billion over five years), drug abuse programs, summer jobs for poor youth, fuel oil to the poor, assistance to homeless veterans, and a national service corps.[27] America, however, already ranks near the bottom of advanced countries in providing universal health care, subsidized child care, and extensive leaves from work for families with children under age three.[28]

Children are our most priceless heritage. A good social environment and education are vital to their health and the humanity and orderliness of our society. Yet, today over 33 million children (23% of all children) are living below the Census Bureau's criteria for poverty (about $14,000 for a family of four); one-third of our children will live in poverty before they reach sixteen.[29] In 1992 almost one-half of African American children fell into the poverty bracket. More than two-thirds of school age children return to a home where they will not be greeted by a parent because the single parent or both the father and mother are working—an increasing trend also in Japan.[30]

Among the six national educational goals to be achieved by 2000 is making our children ready for school at grade one.[31] In reality, however, in 1993 only 71.9 percent of first graders had ever entered an early childhood program before kindergarten and only 34 percent of three- to four-year-olds were enrolled in prekindergarten education programs—28 percent less for low income than high income families, and 8 percent lower than in 1973.[32]

Programs to reduce poverty and raise minority performance do work. Graham cited a Perry Preschool Head Start Project in Ypsilanti, Michigan, where an experiment was conducted by placing an experimental group in a high-quality preschool program and a control group that received no preschool education. At age nineteen more of the experimental group had graduated, attended college, and were gainfully employed. They were less likely to have been placed in special education classes, to have been arrested, to have borne a child, or to have received welfare assistance. The research concluded that there had been net savings of $28,000 for each $5,000 spent on a child.[33] Furthermore, although President Johnson's war on poverty has often been ridiculed, the number of Americans living in poverty in 1973 had been reduced from 33.2 million (17% of the population) to 23 million (11%).[34]

Another confused national priority exists in the area of attitudes toward financing and administering education. Practices of the present obsolete decentralized system deny equal educational opportunity to children in many of the nation's 15,000 local school districts and states by the great disparity in funding schools. Traditionally, schools relied for 90 percent of their revenue on taxes assessed on the value of local community property; however, the increased flight from rural areas and the larger cities to the suburbs and sunbelt states by affluent whites (and even minorities) and by "clean" industries means that depressed and reduced property values in many inner-cities and rural areas can no longer effectively support equal educational opportunity and uniform, high academic standards.

Today, children of the wealthy have double or more dollars invested in their schooling as the children of the poor. Shocking disparities occur of more than 300 percent in local support of schools within states.[35] In Massachusetts the poorest school districts invested $1,500 yearly per child, but the richest districts spent from $6,000 to $15,000.[36] One affluent Massachusetts suburban community, Newton, paid teacher salaries averaging $44,308, but a poorer community, Chelsea, only paid its teachers $26,089.[37] According to the National Center for Education Statistics, the wealthiest districts in terms of household income provide at least 16 percent more revenue per student than the poorest districts. School districts with less than 5 percent of children living in poverty provide 20 percent more revenue per student than those school districts with more than 25 percent living in poverty.[38]

The title of Jonathan Kozol's book, *Savage Inequalities*, poignantly describes the extremes in fiscal support of schools. He contrasts schools such as Winnetka's New Trier High School in the suburbs of Chicago, where there are seven gymnasiums for dancing instruction, wrestling, basketball, fencing, and an Olympic-size pool, with schools in East St. Louis, where approximately one-fifth of the students have textbooks, buildings are in disrepair, and toilets do not work. The annual expenditure per student at Rye High School in New York is $12,570, but at Carl Schulz High School in Chicago the annual expenditure per student is $5,276. Kozol noted that in Texas, "Even after 23 years of court disputes and numerous state formula revisions per pupil spending ranges from $2,000 in the poorest districts to some $19,000 in the richest."[39] (Texas is one of ten states that provide no financial assistance for school construction to local districts.) The richest districts could draw on property worth $14 million for each student, but the poorest ones only $20,000.

To avoid racial integration, overcrowded, debt-ridden, and deteriorating neighborhood schools, and educational inequality, some parents illegally enroll their children in affluent public school districts. Some districts are spending hundreds of thousands of dollars a year to educate students who should be attending neighborhood schools. For example 8,000 to 10,000 students in New Jersey are illegally enrolled in suburban districts to escape poorer educational conditions in Newark, Camden, Paterson, and other urban areas. States have responded by making fraudulent student registration punishable by thirty days in jail and a $500 fine.[40]

The difference between the best and poorest school districts is further accentuated by the tendency of wealthy corporations or individuals to donate to the former. *The Wall Street Journal* reported an example in Atlanta, Georgia, where an affluent suburban school district possessed three times the funds for classroom computer software as an inner-city school. Suburban school children probably already had computers at home.

These "savage inequalities" have spawned state supreme court cases in states such as Texas, New Jersey, and Kentucky, where courts have ruled that such disparities are unconstitutional.[41] State governments, however, are crippled by foot dragging, "anti-tax vigilantes," political gerrymandering, lawsuit challenges, bigots, and self-interested affluent suburbanites reluctant to support greater fiscal equity for rural and inner-city poor.[42]

To achieve equal educational opportunity, states over the past three decades have tried to offset local community taxpayer revolts against increased property taxes by financing schools through state income taxes.[43] But many southern and Rocky Mountain states have been reluctant or unable to provide adequate financial support to overcome local school districts educational inequality.[44] Egregious disparities of over 200 percent in state support of schools across states occur, even when adjustments are made for differences in cost of living. Four states can be cited. For the school year 1994–1995, Mississippi and Alabama spent only $4,080 and $4,405 per pupil, respectively, compared to New Jersey's $9,774 and New York's $9,623. In 1995–1996, Mississippi spent an average of $28,482 and Alabama an average of $32,206 for teacher salaries, but New Jersey spent $49,277 and New York $49,488.[45] The relationship between poor state financial support and poor performance on the SAT scores is telling. In 1995 North Carolina spent the least per student, $743, and ranked forty-eighth among the fifty states on the annual nationwide SAT report.[46] One critic wrote, "Higher-quality, better-paid teachers are more likely to be found in the wealthier school districts of the country, with the students who are deemed easiest to educate. This situation is comparable to paying a doctor less for treating the sick and more to care for the healthy."[47]

Why have Americans been reluctant to correct a system of financing and administering education? Colonial and frontier experiences and geographical isolation led early Americans to place higher priorities on freedom and self-reliance than order and uniform standards. Subsequently, immigrants sought refuge from despotic governments and went in search of the "American Dream." Americans concluded that "the government that governs least governs best." A 1980 Gallup Poll showed that 68 percent of Americans still believe the local level is where decisions should be made about what should be taught. Only 9 percent chose the federal level, a marked contrast with most nations, especially East and Southeast Asian nations where national governments have achieved high standards by taking a commanding role in curriculum development, financing, and transmitting indigenous values. Based on their historical experience, the "founding fathers" of the U.S. Constitution delegated responsibility for education to individual states. In turn, each state (with the exception of Hawaii) established only minimum standards and surrendered to local schools control over textbook selection, curriculum, and school financing.[48] The federal government has been restricted to subsidizing scholarly research, testing, science and vocational education equipment, school-lunch programs, foreign-language equipment, and special educational programs (i.e., Education for All Handicapped Act of 1975). The National Assessment for Educational Progress is still prevented by state and local education officials from testing that compares states, districts, or schools. Vested interests of professional educational associations and politicians lacking vision limit greater national action.[49]

These facts notwithstanding, changed attitudes toward federal involvement in education are occurring gradually. One Gallup poll in 1988 showed that 73 percent favored the idea of a national high school graduation examination. Another poll in 1989 showed that 70, 69, and 72 percent, respectively, favor requiring schools "to conform to national achievement standards and goals," "to use a standardized national curriculum," and "to use standardized national testing programs to measure the academic achievement of students."[50] In principle, approximately 90 percent of the American people are accepting a greater federal government role in education such as national goals for 2000, a nationally recommended James Madison core curriculum, and national assessment pilot programs in 1990 for eighth-grade math and in 1992 for fourth graders. Yet, strong anti-Washington feeling results in an "odd dance of trying to establish guides that would lift national achievement without ceding an iota of local control."[51] Stevenson and Stigler wrote, "[America] will continue to suffer the consequences of mediocre schools until Americans are clearer about what we really want from our public schools. At present, widescale confusion exists about nearly all aspects of education, including its function in a democracy, its financial support, and the control of educational policy. . . . The United States needs a national educational policy."[52]

Neglect of Social Justice and Social Order

To give young people a belief that education is important and that it will give them a greater stake in society, America desperately needs to correct fundamental social and economic injustices and drug problems. It is time for plain and honest talk. America is still a racist society. Until democratic goals of equality, liberty, and justice for *all* are achieved Americans cannot correct their educational problems. The time to do it is now.[53]

In the past three decades our nation's social health has deteriorated and our culture has become increasingly macho and violent. The Annie E. Casey Foundation annual study of 1994 showed that there are 3.9 million American children living in "severely distressed neighborhoods characterized by a poverty rate above 28 percent; more than 40 percent female-headed households; a high school dropout rate over 23 percent; more than 47 percent of males 'unattached to the labor force,' and more than 17 percent of the families on welfare." Drug consumption is destroying an entire society.[54] Youthful gangs and sick adults terrorize peaceful citizens and policemen in such cities as Los Angeles, Denver, Omaha, Louisville, Norfolk, and Dallas. Americans should strive to be the best educated, safest, and healthiest nation, not one of the most violent and drug prone.

Limited Interest in Education from Adversity. One major current problem is deciding what can be done to create a greater interest in education on the part of minority children and low-income groups in general. According to the Casey Foundation report, one-fourth of all children under six live in poverty, and 25 percent of black children live in severely distressed neighborhoods compared with 10 percent for Hispanic Americans and less than 1 percent of whites. Unemployment, underemployment, poverty, poor home conditions, racism, and low educational expectations by parents, school administrators, teachers, and counselors deny these children educational incentives.

I want to indicate the depth of racism and unmet social needs. The unemployment rate for African American college graduates in 1991 for ages 20 to 24 was almost double that of whites with the same qualifications (12.2%, compared to 6.5%). The unemployment rate for African Americans aged 16 to 19 with four years of high school and aged 20 to 24 with one to three years of college was 33.5 percent and 15.9 percent, respectively; their white counterparts' rate was 13.3 and 6.8 percent, respectively.[55] Employment rates for recent high school graduates (aged 16 to 24) not enrolled in college in 1993 for whites was 71.9 percent, but only 42.2 percent and 43.4 percent for their black and Hispanic cohorts respectively.[56] African Americans with high school diplomas and full-time employment earned $5.89 an hour in 1986; their white counterparts earned $7.11.[57] When poor blacks and Hispanics experience these conditions, educational achievement loses meaning; they lose hope.

Problem of Increasing Economic Inequality. A second problem is that of a shrinking middle class and a gap between the rich and the poor, which is greater than at any time since record keeping began forty-five years ago. America's middle class shrank from 75 percent in 1976 to only 60 percent by 1991. Incomes of the richest 1 percent grew more than 87 percent from 1980, but the incomes of the poorest dropped over 5 percent. The combined incomes of the richest 2.5 million Americans is almost the same as that of the 100 million with the lowest incomes.[58] In 1994, the Census Bureau used the word "astounding" to report that the percentage of those working full time but earning less than the poverty level for a family of four has risen by 50 percent in the past thirteen years.[59]

Problem of Increasing Single-Parent Homes. A third social problem affecting education is the rapid increase in single-parent homes. Such families are often not equipped by their educational background and income to give children the quality time, care, and money to provide a good academic environment. Yet, education is essential for escaping the vicious cycle of poverty and illiteracy. In 1989, 21 percent of America's 63 million children lived with only one parent; 55 percent of all children under eighteen with poverty status were being raised in a single-parent, female household.[60] Approximately 80 percent of poor African American and 40 percent of Hispanic American children live in female-headed families.[61] These conditions do not give much hope of achieving social justice for their children. Most will never know a world of books, music, art, and satisfying leisure time activities. Many are doomed to drugs, early pregnancies, alcoholism, crime, and dehumanizing poverty.

Instead of dealing adequately with social justice, the mistaken American answer to violent crimes from 1993 to 1995 was to build more expensive prisons and hand out tougher sentences. Yet, a Rand Corporation study showed that harsher measures had failed in reducing violent crime and had only slight effects on property crime and root causes of increasing violence and drug addiction. Young African Americans who engage in drug dealing and pimping are not stupid. They do not see inviting alternatives. (Actually, because only 3 million of 34 million serious crimes in this country are detected, young people believe they will not be caught.) Maxine Waters from Washington, D.C.'s House of Representatives stated it aptly, "If we don't take some direct action, if we don't admit it's going to cost us some money and be willing to spend it, there will not be enough jails and prisons. . . . I don't want to go around trying to frighten anybody, but this madness won't be contained to ghettos and barrios forever."[62]

A potentially bleak future looms ahead because by 2000, discontented minorities in many of our major metropolitan areas will achieve majority status. The polarization of society is demonstrated by the approximate three-quarters of African Americans who thought O. J. Simpson was innocent and three-quarters of whites who thought he was guilty. In doing his research on a new book on racism, Pulitzer Prize–winning journalist David K. Shipler found that nearly every black male he interviewed had a tale of being hassled by the police.[63] The National Opinion Research Center showed that 52 percent of Americans regard blacks as less intelligent, less hard-working (66.2%), and more desirous of living on welfare (72.7%). Shipler reported that one white couple discovered that they were routinely alerted by teachers when their two white children's performance declined, but never when their half-black child slipped.[64] At the time of the Persian Gulf War, African Americans constituted only 12 percent of our population, but constituted 22 percent of our armed forces and only 7 percent of all commissioned officers.[65] I would not die in battle for a society that failed to provide me with adequate social justice.

Almost three decades ago the Otto Kerner Commission raised the specter of two nations within one, if the dominant white class did not end racial discrimination. Nonetheless, segregation in both the north and south and urban and rural areas (in such different places as West Hartford, Connecticut, and Summerton, South Carolina) continues. At Clarendon, one school district in Summerton, the local population is 75 percent African American, but the student population is 98 percent African American.[66] In 1997, at Walterborough, South Carolina, none of the schools can be said to be integrated. At the local hospital African American college graduates find themselves working under white high school graduate supervisors; only one department head was an African American. We are sitting on a time bomb.

Americans face the real possibility of future nationwide racial wars that will ravage the society. One warning was the South Central Los Angeles riot of 1992. Paradoxically, it provided a positive example of the impact of enlightened business practices. Although hundreds of businesses were looted and torched by angry, resentful African Americans, not one McDonald's restaurant was touched. Why? There, McDonalds' are owned by African American entrepreneurs, who hire African American managers, who hire African American employees.[67] McDonald's various subsidies to high school employees for study also provide examples of what should be done on a national basis.

Our Natural, Fiscal, and Human Resources Are Unlimited

Americans believe that their natural and human resources are unlimited. This attitude has translated itself into a profligate waste of our precious resources. Everyone wants others to practice conservation, but does not want to reduce their own consumption or be affected adversely by environmental controls. Ralph Waldo Emerson wrote, "Things are in the saddle and they ride mankind." At the turn of this century Americans seem to be happily ridden by wants.[68] As individuals, businesses, and governments, Americans spent 102 percent of what they made during the latter half of the 1980s. America needs a higher savings rate and reduced spending and consumption, and needs to pay higher taxes, such as the gasoline tax, to preserve our natural resources (two and three times less than other industrial societies), but everyone wants someone else to pay the necessary taxes. If every new tax suggested for the rich were enacted, the exponential effect would destroy their incentive to produce and to invest.[69]

Americans also think that there is no need for national alarm about the declining quality of human resources and work force. They think that the skills and abilities that we need should properly be left to laissez-faire natural market forces. The myth exists that like will find like, capital will find labor, labor will find its market. This hands-off attitude was partly responsible for the lowered productivity and competitiveness of American companies until 1992.

American's Failure to Accept Responsibility and to Make Tough Decisions

Recently, a young American who moved to Australia nine years ago told me what bothered him most on returning to the United States was that "it is as if people want to jump off a fifty-story buildings and sue the owner of the building for being the cause of an accident. Last year when I was home I read in a newspaper of a man who rescued a baby from the back seat of a car on fire. By the time he rescued the mother who was in the front seat, she was badly burned. She sued him in court for failing to rescue her first. She won the lawsuit." Presidents and Congress blame each other for the budget deficit and the declining fortunes of the United States. Labor unions and management accuse each other for reduced profits and productivity. Pregnant women who smoke and drink and men who have smoked all their lives want to sue tobacco companies for birth deformities and cancer. Insured clients collude with doctors and automobile repair shops to gouge insurance companies. A surfeit of lawyers feed on excessive individualism and personal irresponsibility. Youth observe and duplicate adult irresponsibility. They engage in premarital sex without practicing self-restraint or taking proper measures to avoid pregnancy, venereal disease, or AIDS. In Washington, D.C., 68.3 percent of minority births are illegitimate, in Baltimore 80 percent, and nationwide approximately 35 percent. Children born out of wedlock has increased by more than 200 percent from 1970 to 1991.[70]

What is the relationship between this massive irresponsibility and education? Schools are severely hampered in teaching ideals, character, and good ethical values when all around them school children see adult venality, partisanship, hypocrisy, rampant self-interest, lack of self-discipline, and prejudice. Let me provide five examples of irresponsibility that impacts on American schools ability to achieve higher educational standards and to form good character.

Mass Media and Personal Irresponsibility. Irresponsibility reigns in the mass media. The American Psychological Institute concluded that a child witnesses 8,000 murders and more than 100,000 acts of violence on TV before finishing elementary school.[71] Parents blame television producers and sponsors for increasing violence and sexually explicit programs, but fail to monitor the TV set. Preschool children watch approximately thirty hours of TV a week despite the belief of educators and child psychologists that more than ten hours a week is harmful to children's attention span, language and communications skills, and creative abilities.

Gun Control Irresponsibility. The National Rifle Association (NRA) spends incredible amounts of money lobbying state legislators and Congress to defeat gun control legislation. Protection of individual gun holders has taken precedence over protection of the community and schools. Viewed from abroad the failure of Americans to carry out effective gun control, in spite of 38,317 murders, suicides, and accidents from guns in 1991 alone, seems like national insanity. Currently, more Americans, who themselves truly want gun control, are feeling compelled to purchase them out of self-defense.

These adult activities and the pathology of the world outside the classrooms affects our schools. According to the 1992 Youth Risk Behavior Survey, 24 percent of male youths between twelve and twenty-one had carried a weapon at least one day in the last month; of them 60 percent said they often carried a knife, and 25 percent a gun. Consequently, homicide is the second leading cause of death for fifteen- to twenty-four-year-olds. Between 1985 and 1991, the arrest rate for violent crime by youths aged ten to seventeen rose 50 percent. These conditions caused Los Angeles to prohibit guns from being brought to school, the possession of firearms within 300 meters of a school, and the permission of unscheduled gun checks in the schools. These solutions, however, only treat symptoms. The cure for the problem is strict legislation limiting gun sales and making dealers, manufacturers, and importers of handguns and assault weapons legally responsible for damage perpetrated by gun toters.[72] Despite 13,220 murders by handguns in the United States, more than 36 times the numbers of such murders in Sweden, 128 times more than in Canada, and 60 times more than in Japan, the NRA continues stubbornly not to hear, speak, nor see any evil regarding guns.[73] Defenders of the status quo point to Thomas Jefferson's and the Founding Fathers' insistence on the constitutional right to bear arms. But Jefferson said that it is as foolish for a society to abide by obsolete laws as it is to expect a man of twenty-five to wear the clothes of his boyhood.

Need for Greater African American Responsibility. African Americans have long struggled against prejudice and economic discrimination, but they must also practice the greater self-discipline, family values, and personal responsibility that they called for in the "March on Washington" of 1995. A society that pays increasingly high taxes to support welfare programs for teenagers with children (though the largest percentage are white) does not feel moved to help African Americans. In the long run, it is only through enlightened popular opposition against permissive social and educational practices, active support of social and economic reforms, and the development of academic competence that the "underprivileged" can truly escape poverty and functional literacy. African Americans must back gun control because guns are the leading cause of deaths for African American males in their twenties.[74] African Americans should take some heart from what Asian minorities modestly have accomplished by hard work and study. Although Asian Americans are still unjustly discriminated against in salary and managerial positions, they are conspicuous by their academic achievement awards and moderately improving conditions.[75]

Parental Irresponsibility. A national law requiring fathers who escape child support by moving across state lines is urgently needed. Fathers who fail to provide child support to their wives sacrifice the quality of their children's education and add enormous burdens to overextended single mothers.

Educational Irresponsibility. Administrators, teachers, and educational associations reflect national tendencies. Graham has charged bluntly that educational change has been slow because "educators' operations do not inspire confidence in their efficiency or effectiveness, in particular, there are too many middle management administrators; and, present teacher-associations' attitudes and practices protect the job security of experienced teachers at the expense of the job insecurity of newly hired ones."[76]

Lack of Positive Role Models

In a 1992 speech, Leo Buscaglia, the author of many books dealing with love, told a group of teachers, "We do not learn anything except through models, but everywhere we look there is negativism." I agree completely. Our students have a need to look up to models of scholarship, community service, and social justice. The mass media, however, seem more interested in destroying reputations.

In a democracy, freedom of the press must prevail and the public has a right to know, but the mass media, biographers, and pulp magazines compete excessively for profits by focusing on those who flaunt accepted mores. They undermine the reputations of many in the public limelight, from movie stars and athletes to statesmen and minority leaders. The message to students is that nothing is sacred and that everyone is corrupt and self-interested. Unfortunately, American political leaders make the mass media's dirty work easier. Recent elections have reached a new low in character assassination. Youth are alienated from public service by the mudslinging of the 1996 elections at all levels.

On television and in the mass media the models one sees are not good teachers, diligent students, sacrificing nurses, dedicated community leaders, and conscientious parents whose actions in everyday life make their communities better. Parents and teachers are portrayed as bungling, ineffective, and incompetent. These attitudes are in need of correction if Americans are to build a safer, more civil society, foster better character, and raise low educational standards.

THE COMPELLING NEED FOR AMERICAN EDUCATIONAL REFORM

In the spring of 1990, I was honored by being asked to give a final lecture to faculty and graduate students at Tsukuba University. During the discussion period Professor Miwa Tatsuro, a mathematics educator, made the observation that no substantial progress had been made in American educational standards, especially in mathematics education, despite ten years of so-called educational reform. The Scholastic Achievement Test (SAT) Board's annual announcements of verbal and mathematics scores validates his judgment. Since 1976 the mean scores of whites have fallen eight points in the verbal section and have risen only two points on the mathematics section.[77] In 1993, the average SAT score for the verbal and mathematics sections was 424 and 468 respectively, but thirty years earlier it was 466 and 492 respectively.[78] And the reaction? It is business as usual. In South Carolina, where the decline was the greatest of all states, the Assistant Superintendent of Education stated that her "gut feeling" was that the scores were not too meaningful.

More nonsense and gobbledygook! Suppose you were a stockholder of a company that had experienced a significant decline in profits and productivity between 1963 and 1979. Suppose further that, after numerous studies of the causes, the adoption of a series of minor reforms, and the pouring of considerable money back into the company for "improvements," the company president announced that profits and productivity were still 15 percent lower than 1960. Then suppose the same president told you that his "gut feeling" was that the statistics were not really meaningful. Would you not think that something was fundamentally wrong and that you needed a new president?

The Need for Reform—Prophetic Voices and Disturbing Statistics before 1984

In 1983, President Reagan's National Commission on Excellence in Education wrote *A Nation at Risk: The Imperative for Education Reform*, and Ernest Boyer, a former U.S. Commissioner of Education, wrote *High School:*

A Report on Secondary Education in America. The former made the dramatic judgment that "if an unfriendly foreign power had attempted to impose on America the mediocre educational performance that exists today, we might well have viewed it as an act of war." The Commission discovered that nearly 40 percent of seventeen-year-olds could not draw inferences from written materials; a mere one-fifth could write a persuasive essay; only one-third could solve a multistep problem; and over 50 percent of gifted students were not performing at school at a level commensurate with their tested ability.[79] Boyer could write, "There remains, however, a large, even alarming gap between school achievement and the task to be accomplished . . . and quality education in the 1980s and beyond means preparing all students for the transformed world the coming generation will inherit."[80]

Former Secretary of Education William Bennett's report to President Reagan reported that the 1982 International Association for the Evaluation of Educational Achievement (IEA) found American seventeen-year-olds in the lowest fourth of all nations studied; and in an advanced algebra test American students placed fourteenth of fifteen nations.[81] In the same IEA test of eighth-grade students in mathematics for eighteen countries, the United States was eleventh with a score of 45.3 percent; Japan ranked first with a score of 62.1 percent.[82]

In science the comparative results with Japan and other countries were equally bad. In a study by Comber and Keeves of eighteen countries in 1973 discovered that Japanese ten-year-olds had the highest average scores of all nations for biology, physics, chemistry, and earth sciences.

The National Report Card on Our Schools after 1983

New, qualitative studies have continued to demonstrate the inadequacies of the present educational system. They highlight the point that never in the history of American education has a high level of achievement for *all* children been a seriously pursued objective for our schools.[83] In 1992, Chester E. Finn, Jr., former Assistant Secretary of Education, and in 1995 Charles J. Sykes, both angrily attacked the educational establishment for its resistance to meaningful educational reform.[84] They asserted that no real reform will occur without a revolution at the grassroots level and altered attitudes by professional educators and teachers' associations. Harold W. Stevenson and James W. Stigler's research over the last seventeen years has demonstrated why Japanese, Taiwanese, and Chinese elementary schools are doing a better job of educating their students.[85] The combined effect of all the post-1983 research is to call attention to the lack of purpose, ethos, priority, and leadership in too many schools. For example, data from the 1991 International Assessment of Educational Progress (IAEP) in twenty countries showed that in almost every area the average score of American students is last or nearly last. *The Condition of Education 1995* grimly reported that "mediocre scores of American students in international assessments pose challenges for the future."[86]

As a result of concern growing from the pre-1984 studies, it was decided that Americans needed more detailed national assessments of our students' skills in every subject. The rationale ran thus: If proof could be given to the American public that our students were not mastering the basic skills, then more money, better programs, altered structures, and more public support could be marshaled to overcome educational deficiencies. Accordingly, in 1984 the National Assessment of Educational Progress (NAEP) began testing students in reading, writing, mathematics, geography, history, literature, science, and, computer competence. The tests give special attention to problem solving and critical thinking and measure the literacy of young adults aged twenty-one to twenty-five. Unfortunately, the NAEP and other test results demonstrate clearly that the quality of national life and individual lives are still at risk.[87]

Geography. The 1988 NAEP geography test given to twelfth graders showed that almost three out of ten students surveyed did not know that the Mississippi River flows into the Gulf of Mexico, only 37 percent could locate Southeast Asia on a world map, and only 64 percent of the students had taken any geography course work in grades nine to twelve.[88] Less than two-thirds of the high school students demonstrated familiarity with the concept of longitude and latitude. One-fourth of them did not know that the United States was an exporter of grain.[89] In an international test in 1988 administered in nine countries for geographic knowledge, respondents were to identify sixteen countries or bodies of water on a world map. Americans in the eighteen to twenty-four age bracket scored last.[90] Incredibly, one Washington, D.C., fifth- and sixth-grade school teacher reported that many of her students cannot locate the nation's capital on a map of the United States.[91] As early as in 1957, I was shocked when 90 percent of my students in one middle-achieving eleventh-grade U.S. History class did not know that New England was located in the northern part of America and could not find South Carolina on a U.S. map. When I directed them to look at the southern portion of the map for its location, they responded, "But how do you know which portion of the map is south?"

Writing and Reading. The gloomy 1988 and 1992 NAEP assessment of students' writing and reading skills was that the level of performance for students in grades four, eight, and eleven have not shown any statistically significant improvement between 1984 and 1992 for all groups. For example, the average reading proficiency score for seventeen-year-olds increased only from 288.8 to 289.7 in 1992.[92] This score means that readers have only the ability "to search for specific information, interrelate ideas, and make generalizations," but do not "understand complicated information" (level 300 to 349) nor "learn from specialized reading materials" (level 350 and above).[93] The National Center for Educational Statistics stated in its 1988 report that "more than half of the nation's seventeen-year-olds appear to be inadequately prepared either to perform competently jobs that require technical skills, or to benefit substantially from specialized on-the-job training."

Stevenson and Stigler's international team chose Japanese students from Sendai, Japan; Chinese students from Taipei, Republic of China (Taiwan); and American students from Minneapolis for comparative studies of first and fifth graders' mathematical and reading achievement, an excellent total sample of 324 classrooms. They concluded that 31 percent of American fifth graders were only reading at a third-grade level, compared to 12 percent of Chinese and 21 percent of Japanese children.[94]

The NAEP's assessment of writing skills was "quite simply, bad." It judged that fewer than one-fourth of students possessed writing ability adequate for college work. In 1992, only 2 percent of eleventh graders could provide "effective, coherent responses."[95] Albert Shanker, President of the American Federation of Teachers, reported that only 15 percent of high school students can write a simple letter and that fewer than one-fourth of all high school students could perform at an "adequate" level considered essential for college work. The Adult Performance Level calculated that 22 percent of Americans cannot address a letter properly, and 20 percent cannot write a check that will be processed by their bank.[96] Only 2 percent of high school juniors are able to meet national goals for writing.[97] These assessments explain two points: the reason college remedial English classes have proliferated, and the embarrassing paradox that currently 50 percent of American high school graduates are entering college!

Perhaps most distressing is what has happened in California in reading skills and educational support as a result of funding cuts and a reading curriculum that abandoned the use of phonics, spelling, and vocabulary development. The state ranked forty-third nationally in 1995 in education spending, and fourth graders' reading skills are ranked at the bottom, along with Louisiana. Sixty percent of fourth graders are below the minimum reading level, and white, nonimmigrants finished in the lower fifth of the fifty states.[98]

Mathematics. In mathematics only 59 percent of seventeen-year-olds could satisfactorily handle "moderately complex procedures and reasoning," and only 7 percent of them could do "multistep problem solving and algebra."[99] In a test conducted by the *Dallas Times Herald* for twelve-year-olds of eight countries, American students finished last, with an average score of 25.3 percent. The Japanese score was 50.2 percent. Although very few of the math test questions were included in American elementary schools' curriculum, the Japanese officials said that all but three of the test questions were covered in their elementary public school curriculum. Stevenson and Stigler's math results showed that of one-hundred fifth graders who achieved the highest scores, only one was an American student, but eighty-eight were from Japan. Significantly, they concluded that these different results did not reflect deficiencies in innate intellectual or mathematical ability.[100]

In 1988, when the International Assessment of Educational Progress tested thirteen-year-olds from twelve countries and provinces in mathematics for numbers and operations, relations and functions, geometry, measurement, data organization, and logic and problem solving, Americans finished last in every area except logic and problem solving, where their score was 15 points below the United Kingdom. The United States finished twelfth in the category of "able to draw conclusions on the basis of available data (integrates)."[101] Japanese students finished first.[102] In 1991, the United States finished last, 48 scale points below South Korean counterparts, "suggesting that U.S. students at age 13 may be performing at levels similar to Korean 9-year-olds."[103] Again in 1992 the mathematics assessment of fourth, eighth, and twelfth graders noted that a "substantial percentage of students, sometimes as many as one-fifth, simply left their papers blank." In the TIMSS conducted in 1995, of half a million students from forty-one countries for eighth graders, the international average was 513, and the U.S. core was 500, significantly below the international average, 143 points below the leader, Singapore, and 105 points below Japan. The U.S. Department of Education put it this way: "In mathematics, the scores of our very best U.S. eighth graders, who perform at the 95th percentile for our nation, are not significantly different than the scores of average eighth graders in Singapore, who perform at their nation's 50th percentile. In comparison to Japan, the scores of our best students, who are at the 95th percentile for our nation, are significantly below the scores of the top quarter of Japanese students, who perform at their nation's 75th percentile."[104] Finally, an American Federation of Teachers report showed that ninth-grade Japanese and French and tenth-grade German entrance examinations stressed geometry, measurement, and algebra, but the American eighth-grade curriculum was dominated by arithmetic.[105]

Science. On the 1988 IAEP test for science, more than half of the American thirteen-year-olds could not answer whether plants leaned toward or away from light.[106] In 1988, science test scores for tests conducted by the International Association for the Evaluation of Educational Achievement for ten- and fourteen-year-olds in seventeen countries, U.S. students averaged test scores of 13.2 and 16.5, but the Japanese students' corresponding scores were 15.4 and 20.2.[107] Among thirteen countries the United States finished last in biology, next to last in chemistry, and ninth on the physics test. In the physics test those American seniors with one year of instruction managed to answer only 34 percent of the twenty-six questions correctly. In the TIMSS for science only, 13 percent of U.S. students were included in the top 10 percent of international students, and the national performance was seventeenth, slightly above the international average, 63 points below Singapore, and 31 points below Japan. (The difference in science performance between eighth graders in the United States and Singapore is almost three times the difference between American seventh and eighth graders. Between the same cohorts for Japan and the United States, the difference was almost one-and-a-half times.)[108]

History and Literature Assessments. The best confirmation that American students are being fed an inadequate intellectual diet in history and literature is found in the writings of Diane Ravitch and Chester E. Finn, Jr. On the basis of their analysis of the NAEP history and literature assessments given to 7,812 seventeen-year-olds, who were representative of race, sex, geographic regions, and number of students attending public and private schools (NAEP standard procedures), they concluded the following:

The assessment consisted of 262 cognitive or "knowledge" questions, 141 of them in history, 121 in literature. . . . The questions were not difficult . . . over clusters in the history section, thirteen in literature . . . [and] most of the information assessed by these 262 questions represent knowledge that most literate people ought to possess. . . . Even with this lenient standard . . . the students' overall performance is unsatisfactory. . . . Barely a tenth of the questions reveal A or B level knowledge on the part of American eleventh grade students. . . . Sixty of 141 questions were passed while eighty-one were failed, i.e., they were answered correctly by fewer than three-fifths of the students.[109]

In the history assessment the average student could achieve only a 54.5 percent score on the 141 questions. Yet, 78.4 percent of the students (juniors) were taking U.S. History at the time of the assessment and almost another 20 percent had taken U.S. History as freshmen or sophomores.

I taught U.S., World, and East Asian History in high school for eight years and learned that many American students do not like history because unqualified teachers only emphasize memorizing dates, names, and events. They fail to make history meaningful by developing the human dimension and the interrelationship and significance of events. Even though memorizing chronology should not be the main goal, a general knowledge of the chronology of American history is indispensable for understanding interrelationships among major events and for comprehending the sequence of the nation's development. But American students averaged a score of only 51 percent on historical chronology. An appalling 31.9 percent did not know that Columbus had reached the New World before 1750, and only 32.2 percent of the students could place the Civil War in the proper half-century. Even in the twentieth century, a mere 43 percent could place World War I between 1900 and 1950; only 28 percent of the students knew that the Great Depression occurred within the first half of the twentieth century.

One-third of the students did not know that the Declaration of Independence proclaimed the American colonies' decision to sever their connection with England. On fundamental questions regarding the U.S. Constitution, only 54.4 percent of the questions were answered correctly. Ravitch and Finn cynically thought that a prize should go to the 30.1 percent of seventeen-year-olds who believed that "one consequence of the Spanish–American War (1898) was the destruction of the Spanish Armada (1588)." African American youth should be especially sensitive to civil rights, but they could answer only 54.9 percent of the questions relating to this category.[110]

According to a survey of America's Talking/Gallup Poll, 60 percent of Americans cannot name the president who ordered the nuclear bomb attack on Japan, 35 percent of them did not know it was dropped on Hiroshima, and 4 percent thought it had been dropped on some other country. An election night poll revealed the prejudice that Americans have against foreign aid and welfare by showing that almost one-half of voters believed that one or the other were the largest items in the federal budget; they are two of the smallest ones.[111]

The NAEP's literature assessment was even more discouraging. Only an average of 51.8 percent of the students could supply correct answers to the various literature categories. Just 17 percent of the students could link Dostoevsky to either *Crime and Punishment* or *The Brothers Karamazov*. Over 80 percent of the students could not identify Dante, Chaucer, Whitman, Cather, Ibsen, Hardy, Joyce, and Conrad.[112] Fifty years ago these authors were studied in good schools. Ravitch and Finn concluded from their historical and literature analysis as follows:

> We do not assert that American 17-year-olds are stupid. . . . We merely conclude that [this generation] is ignorant of important things that it should know, and that it and generations to follow are at risk of being gravely handicapped by that ignorance upon entry into adulthood, citizenship, and parenthood . . . and if you conclude, as we do on the basis of this assessment, that today's youngsters have not learned nearly enough of such things, then you must hold the adults ultimately responsible.[113]

Civics. In a 1988 NAEP Civics Assessment of 11,000 students from 1,000 public and private schools of grades four, eight, and twelve, just 6 percent had a proficiency level of "Understands a Variety of Political Institutions and Processes."[114] The average civics proficiency of male and female seventeen-year-olds in 1988 declined significantly from earlier assessments in 1976 and 1982. Only 7 percent of eighth graders and 19 percent of twelfth graders could write "well-developed responses to a question on the president's responsibilities." These poor results occurred despite 89 percent of the former having studied American government or civics since the fifth grade, and 93 percent of the latter having taken a course in one or the other. These facts clearly demonstrate that more than the subject being offered in the curricululm, there is a clear need to make the content more rigorous.

SUMMARY OF THE NATION'S REPORT CARD

What, then, has been accomplished after approximately fifteen years of educational reform? American schools have managed only very slight gains in different regions, in some schools, and in some areas of education, such as teacher qualification and salaries, lowered dropout rates among African Americans, and an improved teacher–student ratio (from 29–1 to 21–1), the lowest in the world. States and school districts have achieved some structural or quantitative changes, such as increasing the number of years that high school students are required to take a common core of basic academic subjects in order to graduate, decreasing the high school dropout rate, and moderately increasing teaching salaries. Nonetheless, measures to raise the quality of subject matter and character formation of high school graduates and competence of teachers have failed.[115]

LOW EXPECTATIONS BY PARENTS, STUDENTS, TEACHERS, AND UNIVERSITIES

On a visit to the Netherlands, John Gardner and his wife asked their hostess why children in that country showed such an extraordinary high incidence of language skills. "We expect it of children," the woman said simply, "We think it important."[116] A major reason for American schools' low academic standards and poor discipline is that society, parents, universities, and students do not possess high expectations. Expect much; reap much. Japanese expect much and they get much. Americans expect much of their undergraduate and graduate programs and get much. The Japanese expect little from them and they get little. There is a moral here for those open to its message. It is a truism, but it is so ignored in our society that it needs to be shouted at every American parent until their ears ring. *Children are motivated to read, to be curious, and to be interested in school and the issues of a larger world by parents who read to them, who talk with them, who discuss as much as possible at appropriate children's age levels political, moral, scientific, and community issues, and who introduce them to plays, concerts, libraries, museums, and lectures.* If American fathers put one-fourth of the energy and expectations they devote to nurturing their children's athletic skills into their children's education, the nation would reap rich educational dividends. Child rearing is a full-time job equally as important as parents realizing their potentiality.

The authors of *The Shopping Mall High School* noted that most students liked their large public school because they could "do your own thing," and it was "friendly," "tolerant," and "relaxed." One student explained, "We're Americans. Why argue? Let's all have fun."[117] Students liked the school because:

"Nobody's going to push you." "They'll help you if you want help. If you don't they'll leave you alone and let you fail." . . . For themselves they chose courses that were easy, met at convenient times, and enrolled their friends. They did homework as long as it was not too much. . . . They never complained when little was expected of them. "Why should we? We just want to get out." They thought their teachers . . . were as much "goof-offs" as the students, as much anxious for the end of school so they too could begin their second jobs.

They are right about low teacher expectations. Dr. Antoine Garibaldi, Vice President of Academic Affairs at Xavier University, showed that six of every ten teachers—black and white—of African American students did not believe their male students would go to college.[118]

University entrance requirements reflect America's low expectations and wasteful practices. A mistaken attitude by state university boards of regents is that it is a fundamental right in a democratic society for state tax-paying residents to enter public universities despite inferior high school grades. This attitude confuses democracy with acceptance of mediocrity. American high school teachers know that increasing or decreasing university admission prerequisites has an immediate impact on high schools. (Of course, the increased availability of junior and community colleges qualify this generalization.) Although currently the most competitive universities admit only about 10 percent of applicants, 35 percent of universities still have open admission policies. Less selective universities may require no foreign language, only one year of math, and a grade point average 30 or 40 percent less than that required for the most competitive universities.[119]

Correspondence between universities lower entrance requirements and high schools lower graduation requirements can be seen by examining foreign language requirements. In 1915, when most universities required entering freshmen to have studied a foreign language for at least two years, 36 percent of all high school students studied at least one foreign language.[120] Today, not one of the fifty states requires foreign language study of all high school students. But because some states now require high school students who elect an honors program or college preparatory track to take one or two years of a foreign language, the number of students electing two years of foreign languages increased only from 12.1 to 22.3 percent between 1982 and 1987.[121]

Even though students may rank only in the bottom one-third of their high school class, they are still eligible to enter many post-secondary institutions. Those graduating at the very bottom of their high school classes will be able to enter most junior and community colleges. Once students are admitted to four-year universities, many find graduation difficult and unimportant. Only 32 percent of college basketball players and 42 percent of football players from Division 1-A colleges graduate within five years, and some have been discovered later to possess only lower junior high level academic skills.[122] Placing such institutions on probation and requiring them to reform within two years or lose their university accreditation would send a strong message to secondary schools that athletes also must study.

When the NCAA enacted Proposition 48 in 1986 to prohibit colleges from giving financial aid to athletes lacking a 2.0 grade point average in a high school core curriculum and a combined score of at least 700 on the Scholastic Assessment Test (about 200 points below the national average for college-bound seniors), many coaches opposed it as discriminating against African American students. The NCAA thought that (a) a strong message should be sent to high schools to force higher standards for athletes; and (b) more black athletes might be admitted to professional programs where they are critically needed and future employment prospects would be good. Opposition required the NCAA to amend Proposition 48. The revised rule allows universities to give need-based, nonathletic aid to freshmen athletes who fail to meet all its standards. Commercialized sports won another victory; academic integrity and African Americans' long-range interests suffered.

In 1995, the NCAA presented Proposition 16, a proposal to require freshmen athletes to present a 2.5 average and more math and English courses on their high school transcripts. But again opponents argued that it would greatly reduce African American enrollments. Because only 15,000 African American students out of a total of 1.3 million in college are athletes, the argument is hollow. Furthermore, Proposition 48 had resulted in a 6 percent increase of black collegiate athletes–graduates. The reason: They were better qualified academically. The moral for "every high school coach and every sports-struck kid . . . no grades, no ball game."[123]

The proliferation of remedial courses at American universities sends a bad message to America's schools. Japanese college-bound high school graduates must remedy their deficiencies prior to entering university at their own effort and expense. The availability of university remedial courses creates the attitude among college-bound high school students that they do not have to achieve competence levels in reading and mathematics. In the immediate enthusiasm of the post-1983 reform movement, many American colleges and universities announced that within five years they would abolish the remedial courses.[124] In fact, in 1996, 80 percent of public four-year higher educational institutions and 95.5 of public two-year colleges offered remedial instruction or tutoring, and a quarter of college entrants need tutoring or remedial courses in math and one in eight in English.[125] Offering remedial courses to incoming freshmen is incredibly wasteful, reflects a tendency to "pass the buck" upward for overcoming academic deficiencies, and demonstrates higher education's fear of declining enrollments.

Finally, American universities and federal and state governments are contributing to the unmotivated study of many non-Asian minority students by their compulsory admission quota system. Minority students must be helped for a certain period to overcome educational handicaps of poverty, low incomes, and discriminatory employment practices, but the quota system should be phased out within six years for all but new immigrants to make minority students more realistic about the need to master subject matter. Duke reported that in one large metropolitan high school, the school had dropped a special course to prepare students for the SAT test because non-Asian minority students realized that they would be approached by recruiting representatives from universities all over the nation, eager to fill their quotas.[126] Many of these minority students are forced to drop out because of unacceptable grades and poor study habits. These wasteful practices produce huge economic costs, but universities have met federal government quota requirements.

NATIONAL GOALS

That the reform was not substantial was attested to by the response to two major educational events in 1989 and 1991. In the first instance, President Bush and the nation's governors held an Education Summit devoted solely to educational issues, the second such meeting of the twentieth century. They called for achieving six national goals:

1. By the year 2000, all children in America will start schools ready to learn.
2. By the year 2000, we will increase the percentage of students graduating from high school to at least 90 percent.
3. By the year 2000, American students will leave grades four, eight, and twelve having demonstrated competence over challenging subject matter, including English, mathematics, science, history, and geography.
4. By the year 2000, U.S. students will be first in the world in science and mathematics achievement.
5. By the year 2000, every adult American will be literate and possess the knowledge and skills necessary to compete in a global economy and exercise the rights and responsibilities of citizenship.
6. By the year 2000, every school in America will be free of drugs and violence and will offer a disciplined environment conducive to learning.[127]

The second major occasion took place in 1991, when President Bush devoted an entire speech to Congress on a national program for education and spoke vaguely of the need for changed attitudes.

The six national goals, like the war on drugs, are a cruel joke. They create the impression of a crusade to lead our children to a Promised Land, but they suffer from the failure to spell out how they are going to be achieved.[128] How can children be ready for first grade if children living in poverty cannot attend preschools, and if the national government and states deny adequate funding for preschool education? In fact, the Carnegie Corporation reported that four of five programs, both public and private, flunk quality standards, and that 71 percent of the 13 million three- to five-year-olds enrolled in preschools come from upper income families.[129] How can mathematics students become the best in the world without some drastic changes in the present mathematics curriculum, teacher methodology, and students' and parents' attitudes toward mathematics?[130]

ASSESSMENT AND CHOICE

Some scholars and politicians have promoted the view that American schools can raise their educational standards by two new panaceas: choice and assessment.[131] What they mean by "choice" is providing parents with tuition-free vouchers to send their children from poor public schools to good public or private ones. Lynne Cheney, former Chairman of the National Endowment for the Humanities, expressed choice advocates' goal by commenting that "unsuccessful schools that no one wants to attend will either reform themselves or be forced to close."[132] The concept sounds good, but it overlooks at least three practical obstacles. First, where differences exist between one region of the country and another, among regions within one state, or between inner city and suburban schools, students' geographic immobility and fiscal constraints will prevent the great majority of disadvantaged students from taking advantage of choice. Second, excellent schools would attract far more students than they could possibly physically handle. Third, choice will severely damage the public school system and benefit the affluent at the expense of the poor. As one North Carolina County Superintendent of Education told me, "Choice is a political agenda and dangerous for a democratic society. The rich will get richer schools and the poor get poorer ones."

Of course, assessment has an obvious appeal as a means to raise educational standards because schools need to be checked for their performance. But assessment is primarily a valuable tool for measuring large units, such as one state's or one metropolitan area's educational performance against another. But when looked at carefully, assessment breaks down as a magic solution. Schools and students located where parents and peers are well educated will do well on some kinds of testing regardless of what the school has done for them. Schools where students come from very poor environments will not be accurately assessed because children's knowledge will reflect students' economic and cultural background more than what they have learned at school.[133]

Another major limitation to the arguments of advocates of choice and assessment is that the recommendations call for no attitudinal changes, the area most critical for improving American schools' performance in character education and academic standards. What is taught, how it is taught, and what attitudes need to be corrected are much more fundamental concerns.

DROPOUT PROBLEM, STUDENT ACHIEVEMENT, AND LABOR OUTCOMES

A major problem of American education is high dropout rates. Only 65 percent of African Americans and 55 percent of Hispanic Americans graduate directly from a three- or four-year senior high school. Their academic performance is so unsatisfactory that 40 percent of them are classified as functionally illiterate. At New York City's Park Side West High School the dropout rate was so great that in 1986 graduating seniors comprised only 7 percent of that school's total enrollment. In 1991 the percentage of all dropouts from central cities was 45.4, from suburbs 34.9, and from nonmetropolitan areas 19.7. More to the point, all these dropout statistics do not reveal the human costs incurred.

American educators have tried to limit the number of students who drop out of school. It is a cruel irony, however, that in spite of their very diversified, less demanding curriculum to appeal to individual student's needs, interests, and abilities, they have not been able to retain them. Ironically, the dropout percentage is much lower in the Japanese schools where the curriculum is rigorous and narrowly academic. The American high school graduation rate has improved since 1965, but only to an unacceptable 75 percent. If, however, we calculate the American high school completion rate in a manner to include those who have graduated at age twenty-nine by either receiving a diploma or taking the GED (General Educational Development) examination, the high school completion rates in 1996 by race and ethnicity for all students are 87.4 percent of whites, 86.5 percent of blacks, 57 percent of Hispanics, and 80 percent of other races. This American dropout rate is misleading because it is calculated at age twenty-nine, and it is unclear how much improved graduation statistics were made by sacrificing academic standards. Because the graduation rates for African Americans is significantly greater than twenty years ago, Linda Darling-Hammond of Columbia University's Teachers' College said, "The 25- to 29-year-old African Americans were the first kids to have an opportunity to go to schools that were as well resourced and funded as white schools. This just goes to show you if you offer kids decent schools, they achieve."[134]

Two questions: Does the American 25 percent dropout rate also represent student dissatisfaction from not being challenged to a higher performance and, thereby, not attaining the inner pleasure of achievement? What percent of them drop out because they take the easy way out? For such students, attending high school is not a privilege but a duty they have fulfilled by age sixteen, or in a smaller number of states by seventeen. They drop out for a combination of reasons such as laziness, indifference, antiintellectualism, pregnancy, despair, and excessive optimism. Students in this latter category believe that an adequate living can be made without a high school education or that they will have a second chance later to rectify their mistakes. In this connection, one of the most disturbing pieces of information gleaned from government-sponsored research is that "the majority of students who dropped out over the last year [1991] were white, were under 20 years old, and lived in middle or high income families and in suburban or nonmetropolitan areas."[135]

Dropouts constitute an American educational and social tragedy because they acquire severe handicaps.[136] On a purely monetary scale alone their future is bleak because they will repeat the vicious cycle of poverty and apathy toward education often bequeathed them by their parents.[137] It is estimated that high school dropouts will earn an annual income of only $12,000, high school graduates $24,000, and college graduates a salary of $44,000.[138] Their unemployment rate between 1979 and 1990 has averaged about 30 percent.[139] In 1993, 25 percent of dropouts sixteen years old and older were unemployed, twice that of high school graduates of the same age.[140] Worse for the dropouts are the severe psychological and social toll on human beings who are being denied their dignity and social justice.

AMERICA'S UNACCEPTABLE LITERACY RATE

Put bluntly, at least 23 million Americans are only functionally literate: 56 percent of Hispanic Americans, 44 percent of African Americans, and 16 percent of white adults. Forty-seven percent of all African Americans and 29 percent of all Hispanic Americans aged twenty-one to twenty-five read below the eighth-grade level.[141] The U.S. Department of Education discovered that 90 million adults perform at a low level of literacy. The Secretary of Education was shocked enough to write, "It paints a picture of a society in which the vast majority of Americans do not know that they do not have the skills they need to earn a living in our increasingly technological society and international marketplace."[142] Of 8 million unemployed adults, four to six million lack the skills to be retrained for high-tech jobs. By the tenth grade, one-fourth or more of the students in regular classes may have a reading level more than four grades below their classmates. New York City's third graders lag 3.4 percent lower on reading tests than for New York State as a whole; the difference is over 10 percent by the time students are in high school.[143]

BUSINESS DISSATISFACTION WITH AND CONTRIBUTION TO POOR EDUCATIONAL SKILLS

American businesses are not happy with schools' failure to achieve greater competencies in the basic skills. A 15 July 1990 United Press release showed that three-fourths of company executives were unsatisfied with high school graduates' skills and concluded that math competencies were poorer than five years before. Research shows that one of every eight employees can read at no higher than a fourth-grade level, and one in five reads at an eighth-grade level or less. The president of the Aetna Institute for Corporate Education has reported that only one applicant for employment in five or six has 80 to 90 percent of the necessary skills. The Motorola Company had to reject one-half of 3,000 applicants because they could not qualify for the required fifth-grade math and seventh-grade reading competency levels. John Bishop of the Center for Advanced Human Resource Studies at Cornell University, using a growth accounting method, concluded that (a) the decline in productivity growth from the late 1960s and achievement scores occurred concurrently; (b) the decline in the General Intellectual Achievement accounted for 20 percent of America's productivity decline in the 1980s and 40 percent of the 1990s decline; (c) students graduating in 1989 were more than one grade level below that of two decades earlier; and (d) that the impact of low educational test scores on productivity compared to other nations will cost America $175 billion by the end of this century.[144]

American industry, however, must accept much blame for the sad state of the schools today. One study showed that employers granted only a 1 to 5 percent wage increase per standard deviation improvement in test scores or grade point average.[145] Although Japanese businesses show a strong interest in high school job applicants' transcripts, American employers' indifference to character formation and academic achievement is shown by only 14 to 15 percent of employers bothering to ask for high school grade transcripts and by failing to reward high school graduates for schooling subsequent to their employment.[146] A survey of the National Federation of Independent Business membership showed that employers ranked "reading, writing, math, and reasoning ability" only fifth among six abilities they thought were important when hiring. The message to high school students not intending to go to college is clear: "Who cares what you did in the past?"

CONCLUSION AND PRESCRIPTIONS

Americans are paying an enormous economic, political, and social price for their failure to demand more from schools. Although advances in technology make a higher level of educational competence more compelling, the serious impact that low academic competencies have on industry is becoming increasingly clear. Foreign businesses will not find the skills in this country they need for efficient factory and business operations, and American corporations will continue to go abroad, where more educated and disciplined work forces exist. American businesses should do more to reward good study habits and academic achievement. The mass media should give greater publicity and scholarships to students of high academic and aesthetic achievement, character, and civic participation.

Instead of Americans concerning themselves primarily with correcting the problem of low academic standards and poor attitudes at the secondary level, schools need to undertake annual competency skill tests from the lowest grades through high school to ensure that a higher performance in basic skills is achieved at each school level. Some American philanthropies such as the Lilly Foundation have recognized these needs and are donating resources and money to correct existing conditions. Their efforts are as important for the publicity they give to academic excellence as the actual assistance. But money will only help so much. Altered attitudes and greater effort are more important.

America needs to introduce its most educationally deprived students to a wider world view and greater occupational opportunity. Without education, there is no hope or dream. Without education the world is narrow; with it a whole world of opportunity opens up.

One of the most outstanding examples of what can be accomplished is the Eugene Lang story. Lang, now a seventy-nine-year-old African American millionaire, returned to his old Harlem elementary school in 1981 to give a speech to sixty-one graduating sixth graders. Halfway through his speech Lang was so moved by the pathetic future facing these poor, intellectually undernourished children that he promised to send every one of them to college if they would finish high school. Because Lang knew that in normal circumstances as many as 50 percent might not graduate, over the next six years he personally took these children to such places as universities, hospitals, operas, lawyers' offices, the stock market, business offices, symphonies, and art and science museums. In the process he opened up a whole new world of exciting careers and opportunities that students in the ghetto world did not know existed. Some students returned to Jamaica, but of the fifty-four who participated in the program, forty-five finished high school and thirty-seven are completing or have completed university degrees. Lang challenged them to new horizons and showed the possibilities that exist for those who pursue an education seriously. He subsequently organized the I Have a Dream Foundation, which has introduced more than 16,000 other children to 170 programs in sixty-three cities. America needs hundreds of thousands of Eugene Langs who will help children from intellectually impoverished homes, ghettos, poor rural areas, and broken homes to open new vistas and demonstrate that someone cares for them. But what Lang said is true for all children: If America's educational standards are to be raised, "you've got to start from the beginning and you've got to support them to the end."[147]

It is time that Americans become better role models and take a greater sense of responsibility. It is time to shake off the excesses of the late 1960s and 1970s and dedicate themselves to better behavior than greed, power, irresponsibility, and moral passivity. Americans cannot correct their school problems until adults become more responsible.

Negative and excessive educational attitudes must be changed. If Americans use their precious financial resources more wisely, they can develop from the savings good head-start programs, competence testing every two or three years, a ten-month school year, and an additional month from the elementary level through high school to help students who fail to achieve adequate competence levels. Second, Americans tend to believe that they may err on the side of generosity with their children. To make college-bound students more realistic, they should suffer the consequences of failing to study. Some parents and many teachers tell students that if they do not study harder, they may fail college. Instead, they should be able to tell them that they will not be able to enter universities at all. Moreover, for the noncollege bound they should be able to tell their children that their employment and future earning power will be determined by their study habits and academic performance.

Third, Americans think they can continue to practice racial discrimination without paying any penalty in the quality of our national life. Denying equal opportunity and complete acceptance in American communities means that both the victimizer and the victim suffer spiritually. If hope for America's minorities is denied, dreams are dashed, and frustration, apathy, disillusionment, and violence take seed.

Americans need more active federal and state governments in education. Although the federal government cannot ensure equality of fiscal support for our schools, it can finance meaningful national testing that compares communities and states, and can also establish minimum standards for curriculum. The federal educational research budget has been cut by almost 80 percent in real dollars since 1972.[148] New legislation allows the federal government to subsidize and to highlight good schools. We already know what makes effective schools.[149] But instead recent political trends point to gutting federal programs and placing more financial responsibilities on inadequate state budgets.

More federal assistance to financially strapped state and metropolitan governments is necessary to finance education. At the state level there is a need to learn from the Japanese example. With federal assistance, states need (a) to equalize educational financial assistance to local public school districts; and (b) to achieve higher minimum standards for courses of study, textbooks, curriculum requirements, and student academic achievement.

Americans should consider making compulsory education end at the completion of the tenth grade. American public comprehensive senior high schools are legally required to accept all students in their neighborhood district, because compulsory education extends to age sixteen or seventeen, depending on the state. Most American students will be half-way into their junior year by the time they reach the end of the compulsory education age. This condition creates a significant, negative psychological attitude that education is a duty and a favor that students are extending to the school. By my proposal students who attend school beyond that point would realize they are enjoying a privilege. They would exert greater effort and behave better. For those Americans who worry that the result would produce greater liabilities for those ending their education, three points can be made. First, a teacher morale problem is that many resent "keeping kids off the street" and being wardens for sixteen- or seventeen-year-old juvenile delinquents who are very disruptive in the classrooms. Second, most students, as in Japan, would elect to attend high school for reasons of social prestige and economic benefits. As dropouts mature many will return to high school or take the high school equivalency examination. Dropping out would be less of a stigma. Third, a diploma would not be one's birthright, but rather something to achieve. Ending compulsory high school education would make students more realistic about schools as a place to learn and help them to become good citizens and develop their character and personality.

From the savings made by ending compulsory education at the tenth grade, Americans can create noncompulsory two-year, multitrack, diversified voluntary schools at public expense to meet students' differing needs, interests, and abilities. All students not experiencing a learning disability at the tenth grade, however, would be expected to master minimum competency levels in math, reading, and writing before they are allowed to end their first ten years of schooling. Students wishing to learn the more specialized technical, clerical, and labor skills needed for today's age could attend schools that develop those needs. Those students who want to go to a university could elect a more intensive college preparatory program in the multitrack program that would follow the tenth grade. As a matter of practicality, smaller communities will have to share a division of labor and services. This proposal could take some of the pressure off students who do not want to go to college and give greater dignity to those who would prefer to contribute to society in other ways.

Adopting higher teacher salaries, a ten-month school year, and an eleven-month period of teacher employment are important reforms, but the real change must take place in the attitudes within and around the schools. For example, parents who oppose homework need to realize that their children will develop stronger character and greater competence for work and for citizenship by greater effort. Without attitudinal changes, all the other educational reforms of the 1980s will bear only a mediocre harvest.

I strongly recommend that Americans undertake a year-long, nationwide discussion in every community for the purpose of arriving at a consensus of what old and new cultural and civic values and attitudes should be taught to all children. Americans need such a consensus to achieve goals, prevent disunity, and avoid a continued decline in the quality of American life.

NOTES

1. Japan, Ministry of Education, Science, and Culture (Japan, MESC), *Education in Japan 1994* (Tokyo: Gyosei, 1994), 19–21.

2. Chester E. Finn, Jr., *We Must Take Charge* (New York: Free Press, 1991), ch. 6.

3. John Gardner, *Excellence* (New York: Norton, 1987), 29.

4. The National Commission on Excellence in Education, *A Nation at Risk: The Imperative for Educational Reform* (Washington, D.C.: U.S. Government Printing Office, 1983), 5.

5. Robert L. Linn, M. Elizabeth Graue, and Nancy M. Sanders, "Comparing State and District Test Results to National Norms: Interpretations of Scoring Above the National Average" (Boulder, Colo.: Center for Research on Evaluation Standards, and Student Testing, University of Colorado, October 1989), 28, as cited in Chester E. Finn, Jr., *We Must Take Charge* (New York: Free Press, 1991), 101.

6. U.S. Department of Education, National Center for Education Statistics (U.S. DOE, NCES), *Digest of Education Statistics 1996* (Washington, D.C.: U.S. Government Printing Office, 1996), 29.

7. Finn, *We Must Take Charge*, 97.

8. Ibid., 98–104.

9. George H. Gallup, "The Annual Gallup Poll of the Public's Attitudes toward the Public Schools," *Phi Delta Kappan* 61 (September 1979): 33–45.

10. *Education Week* 3, 16 November 1983; Arthur G. Powell, Eleanor Farrar, and Daniel K. Cohen, *The Shopping Mall High School* (Boston: Houghton Mifflin, 1985), 191.

11. U.S. DOE, NCES, *Digest 1994*, 32. In 1987, 90 percent of teachers cited lack of parental support as a problem in their school, and 51 percent of the regional winners of the Teacher of the Year awards complained that "parental apathy was the biggest problem they faced." Patricia Alberg Graham, *S.O.S.: Sustain Our Schools* (New York: Hilland and Wang, 1992), 52.

12. Charles Sykes, *Dumbing Down Our Kids* (New York: St. Martin's Press, 1995), ch. 18.

13. Arthur M. Schlesinger, Jr., *The Disuniting of America* (New York: W. W. Norton & Company, 1992), 12–20, ch. 4.

14. George Will, "New U.S. History Standards Earn a Pass," *The Japan Times*, 8 April 1996; "Students in U.S. Need to Be Taught History," *Asahi Evening News*, 11 May 1997.

15. Alan Bloom, *The Closing of the American Mind* (New York: Simon & Schuster, 1987), 27.

16. Mark Hanson, "School-Based Management and Educational Reform in the United States and Spain," *Comparative Education Review* 34, no. 4 (November 1990): 526–529.

17. Gerald Grant, *The World of Hamilton High* (Cambridge: Harvard University Press, 1988), 1–95.

18. Schlesinger, *Disuniting of America*, 17.

19. James Q. Wilson, "A Shameless Attack on Morals," *The Japan Times*, 25 June 1995.

20. Graham, *S.O.S.*, 41–43.

21. Ann Greenwood, Coordinator of Admissions at prestigious Thomas Jefferson High School for Science and Technology in Fairfax, Virginia, remarked that bright students "are not afraid to be diligent or to act intelligently, because they are surrounded only by bright students."

22. "Programs Seek to Boost College Enrollment of Black Men," *The Washington Post*, 21 March 1994.

23. H. G. Bissinger, *Friday Night Lights: A Town, a Team, and a Dream* (New York: Addison-Wesley, 1990), cited in Graham, *S.O.S.*, 50–51.

24. Sage Sitzer, *Sociology of American Sport* (Dubuque, Iowa: William C. Brown, 1980).

25. U.S. Office of Management and Budget, *Budget of the United States Government, Fiscal Year 1992* (Washington D.C.: U.S. Government Printing Office, 1991).

26. "In 1981, American men and women spent over $12.8 billion on beauty aids—hair preparations, cosmetics, and the like. We spent more than $3.9 billion in 1981 to feed our dogs and cats. And in fiscal year 1982 the nation's defense budget was $214.1 billion. By comparison, Americans in 1981 spent $116.3 billion to educate more than 40 million children in 80,000 public elementary and secondary schools." Ernest L. Boyer, *High School* (New York: Harper Colophon Books, 1983), 296.

27. Bob Herbert, "In America, Inflicting Pain on Children," *Asahi Evening News*, 3 March 1995.

28. Susan Chira, "Dark Future for Children in the U.S.," *Asahi Evening News*, 19 April 1994.

29. Graham, *S.O.S.*, 92; William Bennett, *American Education: Making It Work* (Washington, D.C.: U.S. Government Printing Office, 1988), 32.

30. U.S. Department of Education, National Center for Education Statistics (U.S. DOE, NCES), *The Condition of Education, 1995* (Washington, D.C.: U.S. Government Printing Office, 1995), xi, 28–29.

31. Over 90 percent of French, Italian, and Belgian children are enrolled in preschool programs. Lois Peak, "Formal Pre-Elementary Education in Japan," in *Japanese Educational Productivity*, ed. R. Leestma and H. J. Walberg (Ann Arbor: University of Michigan, 1992), 36–37; Sarane Spence Boocock, "The Japanese Preschool System," in *Windows on Japanese Education*, ed. Edward R. Beauchamp (Westport, Conn.: Greenwood Press, 1991), 99–100.

32. U.S. DOE, NCES, *Condition 1995*, 30; U.S. DOE, NCES, *Condition 1991*, 104–110; Boocock, "Japanese Preschool System," 98.

33. Graham, *S.O.S.*, 85.

34. Bob Herbert, "Policies That Deepen Poverty," *Asahi Evening News*, 8 January 1995.

35. Theodore Sizer, *Horace's Compromise* (Boston: Houghton Mifflin, 1983), 16; U.S. DOE, NCES, *Condition 1990*, 168.

36. Jonathan Kozol, *Illiterate America* (New York: New American Library, 1985), 23–34, 65–67, 73; Dwight Allen, *Schools for a New Century* (Westport, Conn.: Praeger, 1992), 50, 154–155.

37. Graham, *S.O.S.,* 75.

38. U.S. DOE, NCES, *Condition 1995*, 150-151.

39. In Glen Rose, Texas, the school district spends $9,326 per pupil, three times more than poor school districts of the Rio Grande Valley. Jonathan Kozol, *Savage Inequalities* (New York: Crown, 1991), 46–65, 124–125, 133, 223, 225.

40. "Illegal Enrollment Crackdown," *Asahi Evening News*, 12 February 1997.

41. Wealthier Kentucky schools were given $4,200 per pupil, but poorer school districts received only $1,700. Ibid., 166–172, 223, 228; Allen, *Schools for a New Century*, 50.

42. Kozol, *Savage Inequalities*, 228–229.

43. U.S. DOE, NCES, *Digest 1989*, 148; U.S. DOE, NCES, *Condition 1990*, 168; U.S. DOE, NCES, *Digest 1994*, 153; Japanese Study Group, "Educational Reform in the United States," *A Report of the Japan–United States Cooperative Study on Education* (January 1987): 34.

44. U.S. DOE, NCES, *Digest 1989*, 148; U.S. DOE, NCES, *Condition 1990*, 168; U.S. DOE, NCES, *Digest 1994*, 153.

45. U.S. DOE, NCES, *Digest 1997*, 85, 170.

46. Editorial, *The Herald-Sun*, Durham, N.C., 25 August 1995.

47. Allen, *Schools for a New Century*, 50.

48. Decisions over textbook selection rest at the state level in twenty-two states.

49. Finn, *We Must Take Charge*, 173–178, ch. 5; Sykes, *Dumbing Down*, ch. 17.

50. Finn, *We Must Take Charge*, 67–68.

51. Peter Applebome, "One Size Doesn't Fit," *The New York Times Weekly Review*, 13 December 1996.

52. Harold Stevenson and James Stigler, *The Learning Gap: Why Our Schools Are Failing and What We Can Learn from Japanese and Chinese Education* (New York: Summit, 1992), 202; Allen, *Schools for a New Century*, 43–46.

53. Graham, *S.O.S.*, 36.

54. Correspondence with Dr. Jack Nicholson, 6 February 1991.

55. U.S. DOE, NCES, *Digest 1991*, 77–79; U.S. DOE, NCES, *Digest 1992*, 389; Graham, *S.O.S.*, 69.

56. U.S. DOE, NCES, *Condition 1995*, 88–89.

57. "Hispanics Made Little Progress in Decade," *The Japan Times*, 12 April 1991; U.S. DOE, NCES, *Digest 1991*, 377; U.S. DOE, NCES, *Condition 1991*, 180.

58. Richard Morin, "Middle Class Squeezed by Both Ends," *The Daily Yomiuri*, 4 December 1991; "Overspending Is the American Way, Recent Study Finds," *The Japan Times*, 17 March 1992; David S. Broder, "Some Costs of a Do-Nothing Social Policy," *The Japan Times*, 30 May 1991.

59. Jason DeParle, "More Americans Fall into Poverty Pit," *Asahi Evening News*, 16 April 1994; "U.S. Study Warns of Job Underclass," *Asahi Evening News*, 4 June 1994.

60. U.S. DOE, NCES, *Digest 1991*, 27.

61. In 1990, 12.8 percent of babies were born to mothers under twenty, and in York, Pennsylvania, it is estimated that teenagers accounted for 21.3 percent of all births in 1991. "County Sets Date to Curb Teen Sex," *The Japan Times*, 24 March 1993.

62. Sean Jensen, "Forum Aims Big Guns at Youth Violence," *Black Issues in Higher Education*, 12 August 1993, 11.

63. David K. Shipler, "Why Black Men Identify with O.J.," *Asahi Evening News*, 15 February 1997.

64. David K. Shipler, "Deadliest Racism Is Hidden," *Asahi Evening News*, 20 October 1997.

65. Richard L. Fernandez, "U.S. Recruits Drawn from Varied Backgrounds," *The Daily Yomiuri*, 21 December 1990.

66. At Clarendon Hall, a private school founded in 1965 where the tuition is $1,620 a year, no African American has ever applied. Christina Connor, "Racial Divide Still Deep after 40 Years," *Asahi Evening News*, 24 May 1994, p. 9; "Integration Shatters Suburban Serenity," *Asahi Evening News*, 28 February 1995; Brent Staples, "Apartheid on Campus, Continued," *The New York Times Weekly Review*, 4 July 1993.

67. Twenty-five percent of McDonald's executives, 70 percent of management, and almost half of corporate department heads are minorities and women.

68. Marilyn Geewax, "Boomers Complain, but Work Long Hours for 'Stuff,'" *Asahi Evening News*, 17 July 1995.

69. "Overspending the American Way," *The Japan Times*, 17 March 1992; Steven A. Holmes, "Census Shows Americans Living Longer," *Asahi Evening News*, 20 November 1994.

70. Ibid.

71. Leha Williams, "Americans Asked to Turn off TVs for One Week," *Asahi Evening News*, 4 March 1995.

72. Carolyn Scorneck, "U.S. Agency Tries to Trace Guns in Schools," *Asahi Evening News*, 16 November 1993; "Justices Study Gun Ban in School Zones," *Asahi Evening News*, 3 May 1994; "U.S. Murders up 3%," *Asahi Evening News*, 4–5 May 1994; "Chicago's Mayor Wants to Impose Tax on Firearms," *The Japan Times*, 25 February 1993.

73. Guns kill fourteen children and teenagers every day. Bernard Levin, "A Gun in Every Hand—An American Nightmare," *Asahi Evening News*, 25 July 1994.

74. The Sentencing Project, a Washington law-based research group, reported in 1990 that nearly one in four African Americans between age twenty and twenty-nine were in prison, on probation, or on parole on any given day.

75. At Berkeley, 25 percent of the students were Asian in 1987, but only one out of 102 top level administrators was Asian; less than 0.5 percent of the 29,000 officers and directors of the nation's thousand largest companies are minorities. Ronald Takaki, *Strangers from a Different Shore: A History of Asian Americans* (Boston: Little, Brown, 1989), 473–484.

76. Graham, *S.O.S.*, 9–12.

77. U.S. DOE, NCES, *Condition 1995*, 68–69.

78. Holmes, "Census Shows Americans Living Longer."

79. U.S. National Commission on Excellence in Education (U.S. NCEE), *A Nation at Risk: The Imperative for Educational Reform* (Washington, D.C.: U.S. Government Printing Office, 1983), 5, 8–9.

80. Boyer, *High School*, 6.

81. Bennett, *Making It Work*, 12; U.S. DOE, NCES, *Condition 1991, Elementary and Secondary Education*, Vol. 1, 24–36.

82. On the same IEA test for geometry, twelfth-grade Americans finished fifteenth, but the Japanese were first. U.S. DOE, NCES, *Digest 1989*, 389–390; U.S. DOE,

NCES, *Digest 1991*, 398–399; National Research Council, *Everybody Counts: A Report to the Nation on the Future of Mathematics Education* (Washington, D.C.: National Academy Press, 1989).

83. Graham, *S.O.S.*, 16.

84. Finn, *We Must Take Charge*; ch. 12; Sykes, *Dumbing Down*, 210–240.

85. Stevenson and Stigler, *Learning Gap*, ch. 2, 4, 5.

86. U.S. DOE, NCES, *Condition 1995*, 3.

87. U.S. DOE, NCES, *Condition 1991*, 24–36; *America's Challenge: Accelerating Academic Achievement, a summary of Findings from 20 years of NAEP* (Princeton, N.J.: Educational Testing Service, 1990).

88. Educational Testing Service, *The Geography Learning of High-School Seniors* (Princeton, N.J.: National Assessment of Educational Progress, 1990), 13.

89. U.S. DOE, NCES, *Condition 1991*, 8, 34–35.

90. U.S. DOE, NCES, *Digest 1989*, 391.

91. Karen Diegmueller, "Experts Decry Poor Grasp of Geography among Children, Adults," *Education Week*, 8 June 1994.

92. U.S. DOE, NCES, *Digest 1994*, 113.

93. U.S. DOE, NCES, *Condition 1995*, 54; U.S. DOE, NCES, *Digest 1994*, 2.

94. Stevenson and Stigler, *Learning Gap*, 34, 48, 50.

95. U.S. DOE, NCES, *Condition 1995*, 56–57.

96. Kozol, *Illiterate America*, 9.

97. Catherine S. Manegold, "Students Make Strides but Fall Far Short of Goals," *The New York Times*, 18 January 1994.

98. "Betrayal in California," *The New York Times*, 10 February 1997; Sykes, *Dumbing Down*, 102.

99. National Assessment of Educational Progress, *The Mathematics Report Card: Are We Measuring Up?* (Washington, D.C.: U.S. Government Printing Office, 1988), as cited in U.S. Department of Education, National Center for Education Statistics (U.S. DOE, NCES), *The Condition of Education, 1995* (Washington, D.C.: U.S. Government Printing Office, 1995), 30–31; U.S. DOE, NCES, *Condition 1995*, 58.

100. Stevenson and Stigler, *Learning Gap*, 34–35, 48, 50.

101. U.S. DOE, NCES, *Digest 1989*, 388. In the same category, nine-year-old American students finished ninth of ten countries surveyed. U.S. DOE, NCES, *Digest 1991*, 412, 417; U.S. DOE, NCES, *Digest 1989*, 388–390; U.S. DOE, NCES, *Condition 1991*, 8.

102. U.S. DOE, NCES, *Digest 1991*, 400.

103. U.S. DOE, NCES, *Condition 1995*, 64–65.

104. U.S. Department of Education, National Center for Education Statistics (U.S. DOE, NCES), *Pursuing Excellence*, by Lois Peak (Washington, D.C.: U.S. Government Printing Office, 1996), 97–98.

105. "U.S. Students Have Easier Math Courses," *Asahi Evening News*, 25 May 1997.

106. Lynne V. Cheney, *Tyrannical Machines* (Washington D.C.: National Endowment for the Humanities, 1990), 2.

107. U.S. DOE, NCES, *Digest 1989*, 390–391.

108. U.S. DOE, NCES, *Pursuing Excellence*, 21–25.

109. Dianne Ravitch and Chester E. Finn, *What Do Our 17-Year-Olds Know?* (New York: Harper & Row, 1987), 43–49.

110. Ibid., 63, 72; U.S. DOE, NCES, *Digest 1989*, 114.

111. Bob Herbert, "A Nation of Nitwits," *Asahi Evening News*, 12 March 1995.

112. Ravitch and Finn, *What Do Our 17-Year-Olds Know?*, 85, 87, 99.

113. Ibid., 201–204.

114. Educational Testing Service, *The Civics Report Card* (Washington, D.C.: U.S. Department of Education, 1990), 7, 9, 13.

115. Bennett, *Making It Work*, 1–2.

116. Gardner, *Excellence*, 149–150.

117. Powell, Farrar, and Cohen, *Shopping Mall High School*, 190–191.

118. Mary-Christine Phillip, "Trying to Save a Generation at Risk," *Black Issues in Higher Education*, 12 August 1993, 7.

119. Japanese Study Group, "Educational Reforms in the United States," *Japan–United States Cooperative Study on Education*, January 1987, 49–50, 52–54.

120. James Bryant Conant, *The American High School Today* (New York: McGraw-Hill, 1959), 69–70.

121. U.S. DOE, NCES, *Digest 1992*, 131, 133, 143–147. Asian students averaged 2.17 Carnegie credits of foreign language compared to a national average of 1.46 in 1987.

122. "Study: Most Cagers Don't Finish College," *The Daily Yomiuri*, 29 March 1991.

123. "No Grades, No Ball Game," *Asahi Evening News*, 5 November 1994.

124. U.S. NCEE, *A Nation at Risk*, 9.

125. U.S. DOE, NCES, *Digest 1997*, 323; "When Everyone Gets an A, Grades Are Meaningless," *USA Today*, 25 March 1997.

126. Benjamin Duke, *The Japanese School* (Westport, Conn.: Praeger, 1986), 176–177.

127. *Educating America: State Strategies for Achieving the National Education Goals* (Washington, D.C.: U.S. National Governors' Association, 1990).

128. Lowell C. Rose, "After the Goals—What?" *News, Notes, and Quotes: Phi Delta Kappa* 36, no. 4 (Summer 1992): 1.

129. Beth Ashley, "Many Pre-Schools Failing to Help Kids, Says Report," *USA Today*, 16 September 1996.

130. Bernard J. Fleury, *Reform of Schooling* (New York: University Press of America, 1995), 68.

131. I am referring here to such conservatives as Bennett, Finn, and Cheney. That thinking is also represented by John E. Chubb and Terry M. Moe, *Politics, Markets, and America's Schools* (Washington, D.C.: The Brookings Institution, 1990).

132. Cheney, *Tyrannical Machines*, 21–24.

133. Graham, *S.O.S.*, 76–77.

134. U.S. Department of Education, National Center for Education Statistics (U.S. DOE, NCES), *The Condition of Education, 1995* (Washington, D.C.: U.S. Government Printing Office, 1995); U.S. Department of Education, National Center for Education Statistics (U.S. DOE, NCES), *Dropout Rates in the United States: 1991* (Washington, D.C.: U.S. Government Printing Office, 1992), 39, 41; U.S. DOE, NCES, *Condition 1995*, 244.

135. U.S. DOE, NCES, *Dropout Rates*, vi; Tamara Henry, "Educational Racial Gap Narrows," *USA Today*, 7 September 1996.

136. Fifty percent of the household heads classified below the poverty line are not able to read an eighth-grade book. Bennett, *Making It Work*, 16, 20.

137. U.S. DOE, NCES, *Digest 1990*, 364; U.S. DOE, NCES, *Digest 1992*, 394; U.S. DOE, NCES, *Digest 1992*, 391–392.

138. U.S. DOE, NCES, *Condition 1990*, 158–159, 166–167, 364; U.S. DOE, NCES, *Digest 1992*, 391–392, 394.

139. U.S. DOE, NCES, *Digest 1994*, 397; U.S. DOE, NCES, *Condition 1995*, 94.

140. Graham, *S.O.S.*, 136; Kozol, *Illiterate America*, 8–13; Michael Rhea, "Half of U.S. Can't Read Bus Schedule," *Asahi Evening News*, 4 January 1994.

141. Graham, *S.O.S.*, 136.

142. Seymour Itzkoff, *The Decline of Intelligence in America* (Westport, Conn.: Praeger, 1994), 62–63.

143. "Illiteracy Still Dogs New York Schools," *Asahi Evening News*, 19 January 1997.

144. John H. Bishop, "Is the Test Score Decline Responsible for the Productivity Growth Decline?" *American Economic Review* 79 (March 1989), as cited in Charles Sykes, *Dumbing Down Our Kids* (New York: St. Martin's Press, 1995), 23; John Bishop, "Incentives for Learning: Why American High School Students Compare so Poorly to Their Counterparts Overseas," Unpublished paper for the U.S. Department of Labor, Commission on Workforce Quality and Labor Market Efficiency, February 1989, 2, as cited in Scott D. Thomson, "Report Card USA: How Much Do Americans Value Schooling," *National Association of Secondary School Principals Bulletin* (October 1989): 53.

145. Thompson, "Report Card USA," 55.

146. Correspondence with Dr. Jack Nicholson, 6 February 1991.

147. "Millionaire Renews Promise of Education," *Asahi Evening News*, 25 May 1997.

148. Graham, *S.O.S.*, 90–91.

149. Finn, *We Must Take Charge*, 23–25, 49, 108, 289.

CHAPTER 6

Teaching Morale, Policy Input,
Remuneration, Competence, and Professional
Education in Japan and the United States

Good schools depend on enthusiastic, competent, and diligent teachers. Japanese schools achieve a higher academic performance and more effective character formation for learning because society expects more of them, respects them, and rewards them better than American society. Different Japanese attitudes toward teachers produces higher morale, job satisfaction, and diligence.

The following issues are items that affect the ability of teachers and schools in any nation to accomplish their mission:

1. morale and administrative support
2. input on policy, curriculum, and daily activities
3. remuneration
4. competence
5. professional education
6. certification

Japan is handling these items better than the United States.

Based on the belief that teachers were essential to democratize Japan's wartime instructors, Occupation forces made reeducating them its highest priority.[1] For the same reasons, in the past fifteen years in both Japan and the United States, a number of books and blue ribbon committee reports have dealt with common teaching problems: teacher entry and competence, teacher training, preservice and inservice education, recruitment of competent applicants from outside teaching, teacher status, and classroom management. Despite some similarities, there are different national concerns. Japan is primarily concerned about teacher in-service education and certification standards, while the United States is chiefly concerned about retaining veteran teachers, improved teacher preparation, effective classroom management, and teacher morale and salaries.[2] Americans can learn a great deal from Japan in all these areas.

ISSUES PERTAINING TO TEACHER RETENTION

Teacher Morale

One way to demonstrate low job satisfaction of American teachers is to look at teacher retention. Although former Assistant Secretary of Education, Chester Finn, is correct in maintaining that the actual percentage who leave teaching is not as high as commonly thought, the numbers leaving it or considering leaving it have a profound impact on education.[3] In 1987, 52 percent of teachers polled said they were seriously considering leaving teaching to go into another occupation; another 22 percent said they were "likely to leave the teaching profession to go into some other occupation within the next five years."[4] Nine years later 37.4 percent of teachers indicated that the "chances were about even," "probably would not," or "certainly would not" be willing to teach again.[5] In fact, one of five full-time teachers leave the teaching profession; nearly half of all beginning teachers leave within five years.[6] Almost two-thirds of superintendents of the nation's largest one-hundred school districts have held their position for less than five years.[7] Moreover, although American schools badly need to attract minority teachers, even among satisfied minority teachers more than 20 percent say they are likely to abandon teaching. Among newly hired minority teachers 55 percent said they were likely to quit teaching.[8]

Of what significance are these statistics? What would be the results in other professions if 52 percent were dissatisfied, almost 50 percent of beginners left a profession within five years, and 31 percent would "probably" or "certainly would not" choose the same career again? It would provoke a national soul-searching for the causes and effects of this career exodus. Would we be as willing to submit ourselves to surgeons, tax advisors, or attorneys if those professions had such employment dissatisfaction and turnover? I doubt it. But Americans yawn and take teachers' dissatisfaction and classroom desertion for granted.

Teacher morale is intangible, but vitally important. People outside of the teaching profession fail to recognize the extent to which teachers are psychologically affected by the social and cultural climate. When teachers are part of a professional staff where they are mutually supportive, rewarded financially, respected, supported administratively to make their teaching load more endurable, and where they consider themselves engaged in a cooperative relationship with their community, they feel motivated to devote 100 percent of their energies.[9] Research shows that at such schools educational achievement improves; conversely, a poor educational environment nurtures poor teacher attitudes and morale.[10] Japanese teachers' morale is better than their American counterparts because Japan achieves these conditions better than in America. As a result Japan can recruit and retain teachers who are generally more qualified, diligent, and dedicated.

I will discuss five reasons why Japanese teachers possess higher morale than their American counterparts: (1) greater administrative support for their classroom role and daily work load; (2) a physical arrangement of teachers at schools that facilitates greater teacher collegiality coordination; (3) broader curriculum objectives to help teachers deal in a multidimensional relationship with children; (4) teacher participation in school policy making and practices; and (5) greater financial remuneration.

Greater Administrative Support for Teachers

In the United States, teaching is one of the most frustrating and lonely vocations because teachers receive limited support and recognition. Administrative evaluation is rare and bureaucratic.[11] When I taught high school, I learned that if teachers push students to achieve, they will require book reports, term papers, frequent quizzes, experiments and laboratory reports, monthly essays, examinations, and will advise students informally and formally. In my first two years of teaching most evenings and weekends were spent preparing for classes and grading papers because I taught all six periods of a six-period school day, was freshmen football, basketball, and baseball coach from 3:30 to 6 P.M., and was the international relations club advisor. Essay examinations every three or four weeks required twenty hours to grade them.

English-teaching colleagues told me that to develop students' competent written prose they ideally should assign them one theme a week. The general public has little awareness of how long it takes to grade 150 compositions, but we can assume fifteen to twenty hours a week on top of preparing and teaching five or six classes a day. Similarly, many elementary teachers must prepare for five to seven different subjects and schedule frequent meetings with parents.[12]

Two things happen to American teachers' ideals. First, they must cut back writing assignments and essay examinations to cope with job and personal needs. Second, they come to resent a society and school system that gives them limited respect, time for class preparations, and salary. As a result of limited salary many teachers are forced to work part-time jobs or over the summer.

When the general public compares American educational standards unfavorably with Japan, they conveniently overlook five administrative practices that make secondary classroom teachers' load lighter than American teachers. American secondary teachers usually teach twenty-five classes a week, but Japanese high school teachers teach only fifteen hours. Tokyo metropolitan high school teachers, all national elementary and secondary teachers attached to a national university, and some private elementary and secondary school teachers enjoy one free day a week.[13] At the elementary and junior high levels Japanese teachers ordinarily teach 25 to 27 class periods, but because these periods are only 45 to 50 minutes per week, the schools are able to comply with the legal requirement of no more than 22 hours.[14] Beijing elementary school teachers teach only three hours a day, or four hours if they are homeroom teachers. Japanese junior high school teachers are usually on the firing line 20 to 22 hours.[15] At the elementary level, however, whether Japanese teachers teach fewer hours is controversial.[16]

After I left my first two high school teaching jobs I enjoyed a teaching schedule at a larger school that taught me the value of East Asian teaching practices. True, I taught five class hours a day, twenty-five class hours a week. But, significantly, the number of classroom hours seemed less because the school offered students a seven-period day. This schedule allowed teachers two free periods for class preparation, grading, counseling, and conferring with other teachers. Community and parental support was good. Teacher morale and the quality of instruction were excellent.

A second Japanese administrative arrangement is to create larger classes, but to keep the total ratio of students to teachers at a level higher than in the United States.[17] In 1990, Mombusho reduced the legally permitted class size for public schools from 45 to 40 students at the elementary and junior high levels and 45 students at the senior high school level.[18] The average Japanese elementary school student–teacher ratio in private schools is approximately 45 to 1, but classes in private secondary schools of fifty students are not uncommon. Officially, the public school teacher ratio is approximately 29 to 1, but that ratio is misleading because Japanese schools have fewer professional specialists and Japanese secondary teachers teach fewer, though larger classes.[19]

Although larger classes deemphasize teachers' attention to individuals, several comparative international surveys indicate that there is little relationship between class size and educational achievement, research that undermines the argument of American educators and the Clinton administration that lower class size results in better student performance.[20] There are two ironies here. Despite larger Japanese class sizes, the Japanese educational achievement is higher than in the United States. More important than class size for effective learning are students' and teachers' attitudes and the amount of time that teachers achieve interaction with the entire class, a topic of the next chapter.[21] Ideally, school boards of medium to large secondary schools can give teachers a five-period teaching schedule and apply other savings made by recommendations I have made to keep class sizes down. But, in such a case, if small classes are only a convenience for teachers rather than a real benefit for students, classes of 30 to 35 may be allowed.

A third Japanese administrative procedure allows high school teachers to teach only one-half day daily for one week during the three times of the year when term examinations are held for all subjects. Because students must leave the school at noon, teachers are completely free to grade their examinations during the afternoon. Furthermore, their grading burden is lighter because objective exams take less time to grade; moreover, they may be examinations prepared by private companies. Fourth, although elementary school teachers are required to make home visits once or twice a year to discuss a student's academic performance and behavior and to observe home conditions, administrators schedule five-and-a-half days of release time for this purpose. A fifth Japanese administrative practice that helps reduce teacher burnout is the practice of rotating teachers' grade levels annually or biennially at the elementary school level and subjects and grade levels in secondary schools. By this practice teachers have a broader knowledge of the schools' and their discipline's larger objectives.

Structural Constraints Affecting Teacher Morale and Efficiency

In most American schools teaching is lonely because teachers are largely confined to their own classrooms throughout the working day. Shimahara and Sakai observed of one teacher that her "individualist view of (elementary) classroom management required her to develop her own coping strategies, and classroom management remained Ellen's personal struggle for most of the year."[22] In Japanese elementary schools the desks in a common teachers' room are arranged so that teachers for each grade adjoin one another. At the secondary level desks are arranged according to grade level, homeroom, and subject area. These crowded physical arrangements reflect the strong custom of working in groups. Teachers need privacy less and tolerate distracting noise better. Three researchers dealing with time and student anonymity concluded that

Few things contribute to student anonymity more than the isolation of their teachers from one another. Teachers in such circumstances might even have the time and the obligation to talk to each other about education itself, and perhaps to watch each other teach. A sense of collegiality, built around instruction, is indispensable for the creation of common educational purpose. Teachers need time for it, especially when fragmenting forces, such as departmental specialization, discourage it.[23]

Brief, daily teacher meetings before classes begin and coordinated planning for subjects, grade levels, and extracurricular activities are normal procedures. When problems of delinquency, curriculum, or extracurricular activities occur, teachers meet in their respective groupings and grade levels to arrive at appropriate solutions and follow them up with discussions involving all teachers and administrators. Although I have never witnessed such interaction and question how often they occur, Stevenson and Stigler learned that at some schools teachers from other schools gather to hold "teaching fairs" at which teachers critique each other's performance.[24]

To maintain uniformity there is much teacher peer pressure for all teachers of the same subjects or grade levels to eliminate discrepancies in grading practices and to cover textbook material at approximately the same speed (a good practice carried to extremes). This practice (referred to as *ashinami o soroeru*—acting in concert with others) also establishes unified practices regarding observance of school rules and discipline.[25]

Limited Teacher Input on Policy Formation

American schools' physical arrangements, policy constraints, and pedagogical practices nurture undesirable teacher practices that form excessive attitudes of individualism and personal autonomy. Instead of becoming cooperative, teachers' come to view schooling in a narrow, territorial fashion.

These conditions ultimately nurture a condition in which only the school board and administrators make educational policies. A British study of fifty elementary schools, however, concluded that teacher involvement in curriculum making and school policy was one of twelve key factors for achieving total school effectiveness for students' cognitive and noncognitive development.[26] Unfortunately, however, only a minority of American teachers are dissatisfied with their weak policy role. That minority wants to be involved in major policy issues because they believe teachers are more knowledgeable than state and local school boards and school administrators in understanding directly the impact on children's character, but they are relatively powerless. Other than having a common interest in achieving good teaching salaries, the majority of teachers have become primarily concerned with their own classrooms, subject matter, and teaching competence. They do not obtain the satisfaction that comes from a team effort in helping shape school or school district policy.

School boards and superintendents of education in larger school districts are no longer close to schools, children, or complex school problems. Administrators are separated from the classrooms, subject to pressure groups and disgruntled taxpayers, and sometimes recommend new policies and curriculum fads to school boards that sound good and serve public relations objectives, but are not always educationally sound. They sometimes provide misleading statistics about their school's educational achievement. School boards and administrators should welcome teachers' input and perspective. The quality of children's education should be a common goal striven for equally by administrators, school boards, teachers, and parents.

It would be foolish to say that Japanese teachers exercise an influential role in making national or prefectural educational policy; in fact, I have criticized the Ministry of Education for its overwhelming domination. Nevertheless, Japanese teachers play a stronger role in the overall educational policies and practices of local schools than American teachers because of their responsibility to the total school program. They feel more like a team working together to achieve common objectives than American teachers do. With input comes loyalty and camaraderie. Another area having a marked impact on teacher morale is teachers' salaries.

Impact of Remuneration on Morale, Recruitment, and Retention

Teachers' Salaries in the United States. Teachers' remuneration is only one issue affecting morale, quality education, and attracting and retaining good teachers. In fact, one statistical analysis of thirteen economically advanced nations showed no positive relationship between teachers' remuneration and educational achievement.[27] Worse yet for advocates of higher salaries this research showed that academic achievement was higher in countries where teacher remuneration was poorer. But let us not jump to the ludicrous conclusion that poor salaries are preferable! This data should only encourage teachers' associations and unions to direct greater attention to educational policy, attitudes, and content.

Teachers do have a legitimate right to be dissatisfied with current salaries. Americans talk about how they value education, but most American teachers know that it is often lip service. Because America fails to pay higher salaries and give teachers greater respect, schools and communities (1) cannot attract the top 30 percent of each year's graduating classes at the high school and college levels into the teaching field; (2) cannot overcome teachers' disenchantment and mediocre teaching performance; and (3) find many teachers from the mid-1970s engaged in union activity and an adversarial relationship with administrators and the public. Forty-one percent of public school students are "not at all interested" in a career in education.[28]

Although between 1980 and 1994 the average teacher's salary increased (after adjustment for inflation) by 21 percent to $36,495, salaries had slipped so badly in the 1970s that the net gain in real wages between 1981 and 1993 was minimal: $1,717. In 1987, salaries for elementary and secondary teachers one year after college graduation were $15,800. These salaries were $10,800 under those of engineers, $6,800 less than health profession employees, $6,700 under those of employees in physical sciences, mathematics, and computer science, and $5,300 under those of business and management employees.[29] Are our children's minds and attitudes that much less important than our bridges, dams, and businesses? The average annual earnings for all bachelor degree recipients in 1992 was $38,530, but even though prose literacy scores for teachers was similar to their cohorts, the average annual earnings for teachers was substantially lower at $25,983, or $12,517 less.[30] Today, judging only from salaries, teachers are ranked below realtors and funeral directors in prestige.

Comparative societal earnings and respect are points neglected by Finn and the American public, but have not been overlooked by the Japanese. Teachers compare themselves with other occupations' salaries. When their income status is low compared to those of other groups with similar or lower educational credentials, they feel contempt for the public's values. It comes out in the classroom in diminished teacher performance and cynicism.

When the Illinois University system suffered from runaway inflation from 1973 to 1981, university administrations introduced austerity budgets, a moratorium was placed on new programs, and remuneration for attending professional conferences and funding for research projects was severely reduced. Salaries in real wages plummeted at least 25 percent. Professional jealousies surfaced, teachers' unions were born, and the campus atmosphere became dark, petty, and cynical. Teachers found it necessary to take extra part-time jobs such as painting houses, driving taxis, clerking in grocery and clothing stores, and engaging in construction work. The negative impact on teacher morale and faculty–administration relationships was so great that a teacher union was formed, and a legalistic contractual and adversarial relationship between faculty and administration occurred—a nationwide characteristic.[31]

Similar developments occurred at elementary and secondary education levels throughout the nation with unfortunate implications for teachers' relations with the general public. The Holmes Group Report noted that over the past 25 years the direction of educational reform has moved from practicing educators to inexperienced policy makers because the public is "distrustful of the expertise of teachers and principals" and perceive teachers as *primarily* interested in improving salaries.[32]

Japanese teachers are incredulous of two American conditions. First, American teachers' salaries are not adjusted automatically to keep in line with an increased cost of living. Second, American senior teachers reach the top of their salary schedules after fifteen to seventeen years of service. At that point, they are paid only twice that of beginning salaries, or only $11,292 more than new teachers.[33]

For these concrete reasons the most academically qualified American teachers leave the profession; the less academically qualified tend to remain. Linda Darling-Hammond's research revealed that 67 percent of those American teachers who placed in the top decile of the national teachers' examination left the profession within seven years. Simultaneously, only 33 percent of those in the bottom 10 percent left within the same time interval.[34] Other researchers wrote forlornly, "Thus, if these teachers continue to leave, our schools may become a refuge for the least able and the most 'stuck.'"[35]

Salaries in Japan and Other Industrialized Nations. Other advanced industrial nations pay their teachers better than Americans. In 1984, a National Association of American School Principals report showed average salaries of Canadian and Western German secondary school teachers respectively were 35 percent and 9 percent higher than American counterparts. In relationship to the per-capita gross domestic product produced by all Americans, West Germans, and South Koreans, West German society rewarded its teachers 25 percent more and South Korean society almost "two and a half times more" than American society. The same report gave Americans "Cs" for how much they value schooling in two other categories: "achievement incentives by employers" and "socioeconomic status of teachers." South Korea received a "B" and an "A" for the same two categories, while Germany scored a "B" for both.[36]

Japanese teachers' salaries for the first fifteen years of teaching are not more attractive than American ones in terms of buying power, but they compare favorably with other professions. Shogo Ichikawa estimated that when 1983 salaries were adjusted for purchasing power (expensive housing and groceries consume a larger percentage of Japanese salaries), a beginning Japanese teacher was paid only 76 percent what an American counterpart would receive, and average salaries were even slightly poorer.[37] But these considerations are misleading. What is really important to human beings in terms of their occupations are three issues: (1) How does my salary at all age levels compare with those of my peers in other occupations? (2) What will my salary be in the last two-thirds of my career when my children are attending college and getting married? and (3) What will be the retirement benefits at the end of my career compared to other occupations? Relatively low salaries in any country can be endured if our peers in educational qualifications, age, and work experience are paid more or less the same amount.

Japanese Salaries and Fringe Benefits Relative to Other Occupations. Japanese society has concluded that, if it fails to reward teachers on a competitive basis with other professions, good teachers cannot be attracted or retained. Americans should emulate seven aspects of teaching salaries in Japan. First, in 1984 Japanese teachers' beginning salaries were 12 percent higher than those of beginning engineers with a bachelor's degree and 15 percent higher than the starting salary of a white collar employee with an equivalent degree in a private company.[38] Second, the ratio of the average teacher salary to average wages in manufacturing is 1 to 6 in Japan, as compared with 1 to 2 in the United States. In 1983, Japan also paid its teachers an average salary 2.4 times more than the nation's per capita income compared to 1.7 times more in the United States.[39] Third, at age fifty-three, teachers' salaries are higher than those of engineers, white collar workers, and pharmacists.[40] For these reasons, unlike in the United States, there is actually a surplus of qualified mathematics and science teachers. Fourth, Japanese salaries are paid on a twelve-month basis. Professor Seishiro Sugihara, comparing the U.S. practice of nine (or ten) months salaries, wrote, "There is a clear educational meaning behind this. During the summer vacation, teachers feel a strong subconscious responsibility for their pupils."[41]

Fifth, in 1974 the Japanese Diet passed the Human Resource Procurement Act, under which all elementary and secondary teachers are paid at least 10 percent more than civil-service workers with corresponding length of service.[42] Sixth, teachers in poorer, rural areas of Japan do not have to compare their salaries or working conditions negatively with those of teachers from richer, urban regions, because the central government allows tax credits to local governments, establishes uniform nationwide criteria for teacher salary schedules,[43] and provides discounted special housing. Seventh, teachers are also protected by medical insurance and by survivor annuities. In addition, allowances for dependents, cost-of-living, head teachers, and commuting costs amount to about one-fourth of the base salary. Three bonuses during the year totaling about one-fourth of a teacher's fixed salary also reward Japanese teachers. And if there remains any doubt about whether better salaries attract a larger pool of applicants, we should note that since the 1974 legislation, the number of applicants taking the prefectural and metropolitan examinations has doubled, from 128,000 to 245,000.[44]

Senior Teacher Salaries. Japanese senior teacher salaries are better than those of American teachers. This is a period of life when large expenditures are required for children attending college, getting married, and purchasing a home. Although American teachers' salaries level off after fifteen years of service, Japanese salaries keep rising. After twenty years of service their salaries are "substantially higher than those of their American counterparts." In fact, since Japanese teacher salaries increase yearly for thirty-nine years, they are 2.8 times higher than those of beginning teachers. If they become administrators, their salaries are three times higher.[45] Ichikawa estimated that at the retirement age of sixty, Japanese teachers' salaries were 40 percent higher than salaries in the United States.[46] Japanese also show their appreciation for teacher loyalty and dedication at the end of their careers.

Retirement Benefits. Japanese teacher retirement and pension benefits at the end of career are superior to those in the United States and compare favorably with those in other Japanese occupations.[47] First, at the retirement age of sixty, teachers receive a lump sum equivalent to more than two years' salary.[48] Second, they receive an annual pension amounting to approximately 40 percent of their last year's salary for those who retire with twenty years of service, 55 percent for those with thirty years of service, 62.5 percent for those with thirty-five years of service, and 70 percent for those who retire after forty years of service.[49] In the event of death, a spouse receives one-half of the yearly pension.[50]

All these benefits are directly related to Japanese schools' greater ability to retain good teachers. In 1992, 45 percent of Japanese teachers had taught more than fifteen years; 34 percent had taught twenty or more years. In 1981, only 22 percent of American teachers had taught full time over twenty years.[51]

The benefits of greater monetary attractiveness of teaching in Japan needs to be qualified. Many Japanese youths, often with maternal encouragement, admit that they are choosing teaching because it is safe and steady—a legacy of the prewar period when many farmers' second sons chose teaching. (Japan's current recession has led to a huge surge in the number of university students who decide to obtain a teacher certificate as an additional means to hedge on future employment possibilities.) More Americans go into teaching because they want to be teachers. Prior to beginning teaching, 83 percent of American teacher candidates in one survey strongly believed that "they can really make a difference in the lives of their pupils."[52] Four out of five American school teachers stated that "the desire to work with young people" was the most important reason for going into teaching. Other factors, in descending order, were "value or significance of education in society," "interest in subject matter field," "job security," and, "a long summer vacation." In sixth place came salary.[53]

Teacher Competence

Superior American Internship and Qualification by Degrees Held. Japanese teachers are paid better because they are better qualified. Such a sweeping statement will raise the hair on the back of American teachers' necks. Beginning Japanese teachers, however, are certainly not better qualified in terms of student teaching experience. Prospective secondary and elementary school teachers are only required to spend two weeks (two credits) and four weeks respectively in practice teaching. Even graduates of education colleges at national universities spend only eight weeks in practice teaching. By contrast, many American teacher education programs offer one or two weeks of student teaching during the junior year and a semester of practice teaching in the senior year.[54] Moreover, in some American graduate programs teacher candidates in the first semester observe classes for four to eight weeks, students teach the same class or classes for six weeks, and practice-teach one class intensively for a semester.

Why is the length of student teaching for Japanese so short? Leonard Shoppa thought the reason was to prevent placing too great a burden on the schools, since only 40,000 of 180,000 graduating seniors who do practice teaching will be hired.[55] The more important reason at the secondary level is because inexperienced practice teachers are believed to lower schools' abilities to help students pass university entrance examinations.

American teachers are also better qualified than Japanese teachers in terms of holding a bachelor's degree or advanced degrees. In fact, a survey of fourteen economically advanced countries in 1973 showed that American teachers ranked first in length of university education required for both elementary and secondary teachers. In 1986, 99.7 percent of them had a bachelor's degree, and 50.7 percent held either a master's or specialist degree.[56] Although an equal percentage of Japanese and American classroom teachers, 0.7 percent, possess a doctorate, only 3 percent of Japanese teachers possess a master's degree, and approximately 70 percent of them teach at the high school level. When Cummings wrote in 1980 that "nearly 100 percent of Japan's teachers have the proper qualifications for the subject areas and levels they teach," his statement was misleading because many Japanese elementary and junior high school teachers of that date only attended junior college.[57] In the last ten years, however, 90 percent of *new* Japanese teachers are graduates of a four-year university, hence 77 percent of all elementary school teachers currently are graduates of four-year universities.[58]

There are four explanations for the lower level of Japanese teacher credentials. First, at the elementary and lower secondary level, teachers can receive a second class certificate by graduating only from a junior college (i.e., by taking only sixty-two credits). Such Japanese teachers are becoming a vanishing breed. In 1985, only 5.9 percent of new elementary school teaching positions were filled by junior college graduates. (Most choose preschool education.) A second explanation is that teacher demand increased rapidly because abrupt Occupation reforms increased educational opportunity and Japan's amazing economic development made high school attendance affordable for 89 percent of middle school graduates by 1970. By 2000, at least 95 percent of elementary and close to 100 percent of secondary school teachers will hold a bachelor's degree. Teachers holding master's degrees also will increase dramatically, because certification requirements have been raised, advanced degrees carry prestige, and the number of institutions providing master's degree programs for full-time teachers has increased from three to forty-three.[59]

Third, the U.S. emphasis has been on developing teacher competence *prior* to entry in the field. In fact, Japanese and American solutions for improving teacher quality are studies in contrasts. In the United States, because of the opposition of teacher unions and associations to teacher competency tests after entry into the profession, American reforms have been directed primarily at offering higher salaries for those who will take graduate courses after entering teaching. Since the Japanese already generally attract bright teacher candidates, their focus is upon improving teacher competence after they enter teaching. Fourth, higher credentials in the United States increase status and professional mobility. In Japanese education, however, as in most sectors, credentials beyond college graduation have not been very important for appointment, prestige, promotion, salary, or going into administration.[60]

Better Japanese Teacher Selection, Assignment, and Preteaching Training. More bachelor's and master's degrees and longer internships do not automatically mean better teachers and better schools. American teachers are not more competent than Japanese teachers in other ways. Stevenson and Stigler concluded, "When we compare the ways that teachers are trained and the nature of the teaching profession in American and Asian societies, it quickly becomes clear that despite being faced with an incredibly arduous and demanding task, American teachers are inadequately trained. Furthermore, they often lack the support and cooperation of parents and society, the social status and financial compensation commensurate with the importance of their job, and perhaps, above all, opportunities for personal development."[61]

In what ways are Japanese teachers better qualified? A greater percentage of them are teaching subjects in which they majored. Although there has been improvement, a deeply disturbing practice in American schools is that of assigning teachers to teach subject matter areas in which they did not major or minor. Research shows that only 72 percent of social studies teachers, 66.6 percent of science teachers, and 66.4 percent of English teachers majored or were certified to teach at the secondary level in their primary assignment.[62] The percentages were slightly lower for the elementary level. Only slightly more than one-half (59.7%) of all math teachers had majored and were certified in that subject. If we include teachers who have either majored or minored in their main assignment field, 76.8 percent of teachers fit that category, but for mathematics and science the percentage is only 68.7.[63]

Japanese teachers are more competent because they are drawn from the top 30 percent of high school graduates. Only that level of students can pass the difficult university entrance examinations. In contrast with these entry standards, American university education departments have accepted too many students who are academically in the bottom half of their high school and university classes. The authors of *A Nation at Risk* complained that "too many teachers are being drawn from the bottom quarter of graduating high school and college students."[64] Although many college graduates with teachers credentials do not go into teaching, a later study of 1993 showed that 48 percent of newly qualified but not yet employed teachers had grade point averages exceeding 3.25, compared with 42 percent of other bachelor degree recipients.[65]

Before Japanese prospective teachers enter higher education they have already absorbed more subject matter in all subjects at the elementary and secondary school levels than American students. At the university level they take more subject matter courses and fewer professional education courses. Japanese elementary school teachers' well-grounded knowledge in *all* subjects is a major reason for the greater academic achievement of their students and a reason they do not need to hire so many specialists.

Japanese teachers are also more academically competent because of the rigorous teacher-selection process administered by prefectural and metropolitan boards of education prior to entering the profession. Only one of four applicants for public school teaching will pass these difficult written examinations, skill tests, and interviews; approximately 40 percent only pass them on their second or third attempt.[66] Because Japanese teachers will be hired into a system of lifetime employment, and dismissal is exceedingly rare, prefectural and metropolitan boards use strict interviews to screen teacher candidates who have passed the written, physical fitness, and skill tests.

Teacher applicants at all prefectures but two must be under thirty. The age qualification reflects both the desire of Japanese employers to hire applicants at a young age when they can be molded into their image, and also the view that older teachers are less likely to be able to endure the long hours and six-to seven-day weeks teachers are expected to work in extracurricular activities in the first ten to fifteen years.

Teacher qualification tests are difficult.[67] Written examinations test examinees rigorously over two areas: (1) the specialized fields in which applicants wish to teach, and (2) fields within professional education: theory, methodology, school law, educational psychology, principles, testing, and measurements. Because elementary teachers are usually required to teach all subjects, they must also pass skill tests in art, music, and physical education. All applicants for secondary education must also pass difficult written tests, plus English conversation. Lower secondary education candidates must pass a physical fitness test. It should be noted, however, that a frequent educators' complaint is that caring, enthusiastic candidates are passed over in favor of bookish, bright, and less well-rounded individuals with limited understanding of slow learners.

Japanese are more competent to teach because the availability of a national curriculum, courses of study, and teachers' manuals enables teachers to become expert technicians at imparting narrowly proscribed material directed at an entire class. Japanese teachers do not need to "create their own curriculum" or to use panel discussions, debates, class discussion, and individualized projects to develop students' self-identity, self-esteem, and differing needs and interest. Instead, they learn at the elementary school level to fine-tune the given subject matter to the whole class by efficient, coherent lessons that are presented in a thoughtful, relaxed, and nonauthoritarian manner.[68] Stevenson and Stigler thought Americans and American colleges of education assume that teaching is an art that cannot be taught; accordingly, teacher candidates "emerge from colleges of education with little training in how to design and teach effective lessons."[69] Instead, too often teacher education offerings consist of courses on theory and learning that have limited application to actual classroom teaching. The same authors thought such a teacher education background results in a "sink-or-swim" model for beginning teachers, but beginning Japanese teachers face a worse situation because their practice teaching experience is so brief.

Also, Japanese gain an edge in competence over American teachers after they begin teaching because they are given much more formal and informal guidance by vice principals, head teachers, and experienced teachers over a longer period of time. In some schools, head teachers organize very practical sessions with younger teachers to discuss teaching techniques, advise on lesson planning, and suggest how to ask interesting questions and motivate students. In theory they enjoy the same egalitarian status as all other teachers, but, in fact, beginning teachers are considered to be apprentices to older teachers and administrators. Culturally, it is expected that they will turn to their role-model seniors for informal advice in the first five years of teaching. This informal "culture of teaching" helps them hone their skills in designing and teaching prescribed materials.[70] Through coordination and consultation with other teachers of the same grade level and subject area, beginning teachers acquire much useful information.

American teachers, however, are looked upon as autonomous beings who from the start either have or do not have the ability. They are expected to be their own curriculum and to improve themselves by individual effort and expense through educational workshops or college courses at night or during the summer vacation. Although senior teachers may offer "recipes" for classroom management and for various activities, they restrain themselves from telling their juniors what and how to teach. The implicit assumption after only a year on the job is that the beginning teacher has "now earned his or her dues"; thereafter, limited coordination and consultation takes place.[71]

Certification, Professional Education Courses, and Teacher Competence

Both Americans and Japanese are concerned about improving the quality of teachers. That objective necessarily involves examining how they are trained before and after they become teachers. Current criticisms of American teachers' professional education and certification standards are still as valid as they were over three decades ago when historian Arthur Bestor and Harvard President James B. Conant severely criticized professional education courses as "fraud[ulent]" and "bankrupt."[72] Dwight Allen argues that the lack of national standards for teacher certification results in a "giant charade" of ambiguity and low standards because each school district is "captive to a state certification system that is ambiguous at best."[73]

For purposes of certification, America's prospective teachers are required to take too many professional education courses. The authors of *A Nation at Risk* complained, "The teacher preparation curriculum is weighted heavily with courses in 'educational methods' at the expense of courses in subjects to be taught. A survey of 1,350 institutions training teachers indicated that 41 percent of elementary school teacher candidates' time is spent in education courses, which reduces the amount of time available for subject matter courses."[74] Lynne V. Cheney noted that a survey of seventeen southern universities showed the odd inconsistency that teaching majors took fewer courses in their subject major than arts and science students majoring in the same subjects.[75]

Too often professional education courses are redundant, easy, and irrelevant to actual classroom conditions. Sykes wrote cynically, "The schools of education have become priesthoods of good intentions and well-meaningness, where would-be teachers are taught how to cope with low self-esteem, dysfunctional families, and learning disorders: teachers as therapist, social worker, and Big Sister. The idea of education as the passing on of knowledge is a strangely alien nation to these idealists."[76] For that reason bright, prospective teaching majors sometimes switch majors in disillusionment.

As teacher candidates, we were required to memorize the progressive educators' sacred "Seven Cardinal Principles of Education," but who can remember a single one today? Textbooks told us of the twelve ways of teaching a unit or ten ways of leading a discussion. Most of the professional education courses are concerned with therapeutic practices and sentimentality about developing the self-esteem and individuality of each child. In addition,

Shimahara and Sakai noted limited contact and guidance by American professional educators during student-teaching experience.[77]

More education courses and more advanced degrees in professional education, even in one's subject matter, do not guarantee good teachers.[78] They only help people who have the potential to become good teachers become better ones. In one study, the correlation between the length of teachers' college education and the achievement of ten-year-olds in science was zero, while the same correlation for thirteen-year-olds in mathematics was not considered statistically significant.[79] Professional educators have misled the public into confusing quantification of education courses and advanced degrees with quality.[80] More objective professional educators candidly admitted that "teacher education has not been organized to encourage the application of principles to practical experience in classrooms; nor to provide the systematic trial teaching followed by critique that is necessary to improve skills; nor to convey the value commitments inherent in the work of teaching."[81] The sad fact is that advanced degrees or graduate credits primarily reflect teachers' desire to improve their salary or to be "promoted" to an administrative position.

In the United States, increasing the number of professional education courses is difficult because most arts and science academicians serving on the all university curriculum course committee do not view professional education as an adequate social science discipline. Most Japanese teachers also are not happy with professional education courses and prefer more courses in their specialized field.[82] Teachers of professional education are used sparingly at in-service workshops.

Powerful Japanese forces are trying to require more professional education. Over the past four decades, the Ministry of Education, the Central Council on Education (the Ministry's advisory body), the Teacher Education Council, and the National Council on Educational Reform have complained of the inadequacy and number of required professional education courses for Japanese teacher candidates, especially for internships.[83] By the early 1990s, those forces had succeeded in getting the number of education credits increased slightly from fourteen to nineteen credits at the secondary school level and from thirty-two to thirty-five at the elementary level. The Ministry of Education's discontent led to its controversial creation of three new undergraduate universities of education and a graduate university of education in the late 1970s over the strong opposition of the JTU, the Japan Pedagogical Association, the Association of National Universities, and private colleges and universities.

In Japan there are three types of regular teacher certificates: advanced, first class, and second class. Certification for elementary school entitles a teacher to teach all subjects, but secondary school teachers are qualified by one academic discipline. Advanced certificates require a master's degree or twenty-four graduate level credits in a subject area or professional education. First class certificates require a bachelor's degree at all levels.[84]

To obtain first class secondary school certificates, Japanese candidates are required at all universities to take a minimum of 124 credits in three areas: 19 hours of professional education, 40 credits in their teaching subject, and 48 to 52 credits in general education courses. The latter requirement includes at least 12 credits each in the humanities, social sciences, and natural sciences; 8 to 12 credits in foreign languages; and 4 credits in physical education. As a result of Japan's open certification system, approximately 85 percent of Japan's universities and junior colleges offer teaching certificates. One-third of the Japanese teacher openings at the elementary level, two-thirds at the lower secondary level, and nearly nine-tenths of the teacher openings at the upper secondary level are filled with teachers who are *not* graduates of colleges of education. This means that the overwhelming majority of secondary school teachers have taken only a minimum number of 19 credits in professional education courses, at least 11 to 17 credits less than American education majors.[85] In fact, many teacher candidates meet minimum professional education qualifications by obtaining as many of these credits as possible through the easier route of taking intensive two-week courses or night courses. To obtain a second class certificate Japanese kindergarten, elementary, and junior high school teacher candidates are only required to complete junior college and to take 23, 27, and 15 credits of professional education courses, respectively.[86]

National universities' colleges of education, however, require secondary school teacher candidates to take more than the required 19 credits of professional education, more than the minimum number of courses ranging from 124 to 159 credits for a teaching certificate, and many more subject matter courses than American university graduates. Shimahara showed that they average between 160 to 180 credits, but sometimes take as many as 200 credits (my experience also at Tsukuba University).[87] They take far more credits than required because they want to improve their chances of employment by being certified in more than one teaching major, or by having a more attractive transcript. Freshmen and sophomores are so busy taking approximately 22 to 25 courses each semester (each course meets 75 minutes) and intensive courses during the spring and summer breaks that they have little time to reflect on what they are learning. The work is not rigorous, however, because 25 courses often means passively sitting in five 75-minute classes a day Monday through Friday from nine to five, or taking 23 classes Monday through Friday and two classes on Saturday morning.

Secondary teachers' science education requirements for the two nations do not differ greatly. Compared to the 40 credits in science that Japanese science teachers are required to take, New York State teacher candidates must take 36 credits, though the level of academic rigor expected at a Japanese university will be less. Japanese science majors must take courses in four science areas: physics and physics laboratory, chemistry and chemistry laboratory, biology and biology laboratory, and earth science and earth science laboratory, whereas their New York counterparts' course work is narrower. The latter must take 15 credits in the science subject they plan to teach and college level study in at least two sciences.[88] Accordingly, the primary difference is that Japanese science teaching candidates have greater leeway within the required 124 credits to take more subjects in their major and allied fields.

RECOMMENDATIONS TO IMPROVE AMERICAN TEACHER EDUCATION AND COMPETENCE

Japanese teachers envy the practice of American school boards subsidizing teachers' tuition cost for taking university courses after entry into the field and for increasing teachers' salaries and status by receiving advanced degrees, but school boards should evaluate a teacher's request for financial support on the merits of the applicant's proven skill and future leadership potentiality. The primary solution to America's school crisis is not in granting more graduate courses. A poor classroom teacher lacking dedication, real interest in students, teaching, and enthusiasm for cooperative collegial teamwork should not be rewarded for taking graduate courses, nor should a bright, ambitious, but boring teacher lacking imagination be rewarded for becoming more boring.

Also, superior teachers must be rewarded more generously by school boards for their classroom competence and contribution to the school's total curriculum and subject matter areas. They can be given increased responsibilities in their subject matter discipline, leadership in training new teachers, financial support for graduate work, and improved salary for their contribution to educational policy and practices.

In fact, if teachers are put on a ten-month school year and an eleven-month teaching year, school boards and universities will need to become more flexible and imaginative. They will have to devise scheduling arrangements to allow deserving teachers to use the eleventh month for such purposes as in-service education, teaching of gifted students or poor students failing to achieve grade-level competence, and contributing to curriculum and subject matter development. Here is an area where some savings can be made in one area, and good teaching can be rewarded in another.

Third, to keep educational theory and methodology grounded in practice, no teacher should be allowed to teach professional education courses at the university level unless they have taught at the elementary or secondary level for at least two years. They should be teachers noted for their skill and dedication to high academic standards. The current practice of hiring professional educators who go straight from graduation into doctoral programs without teaching a day in classrooms is unacceptable.

Fourth, education department faculty should be required during their sabbaticals to return to the classroom at least half-time and spend the rest of the time researching actual problems classroom teachers and administrators face.

A side benefit would be to break down the artificial psychological barrier between university faculty and elementary and secondary faculty. On the basis of her own secondary school teaching and Harvard professional experience, Patricia Graham made the sensible recommendation that schools of education should be required to use more faculty for actual undergraduate teacher education rather than "higher-status pursuits such as applied psychology or policy studies."[89] I disagree, however, with her view that a desirable trend in colleges of education is the replacement of ex-teachers with professional researchers. If she means ex-teachers who are not interested in research and who regale their classes with war stories and romantic notions of children, I completely agree. Is it not possible, however, to hire former teachers with firsthand experience of actual teaching conditions and with real interest in research? The Holmes Group made the sensible observation that Professional Development Schools should reward nontertiary and tertiary teachers who cooperate in common educational research.[90] Dwight Allen recommends that the "majority of faculty members at institutions with teacher education programs should be designated as teaching faculty, without research obligations."[91]

Fifth, a larger percentage of college of education resources should be focused on the average or "unspecial" student, instead of the lopsided emphasis on the gifted, the handicapped, and the dysfunctional students. College of education's resources are going for research related to only 15 percent of elementary and secondary school students.[92]

Sixth, prospective teacher candidates need to get some classroom teaching experience earlier than their senior year of college to gain a greater understanding of what is actually involved in teaching. By a more judicious awareness of deficiencies teachers will select professional education and teaching major courses.

Seventh, states must adopt flexible alternative certification policies. People of competence and dedication without general education degrees must be brought into the profession on probation as teachers and administrators, that is, by alternate certification. They can add the necessary professional courses later as individual state certification agencies mandate. Many states' certification requirements, however, do not allow highly qualified persons to be teachers or administrators because they lack prescribed education courses (a reflection from 1950 of the dominance professional educators had gained in state accrediting agencies).[93] It is absurd that people with good undergraduate academic records and master's and Ph.D. degrees cannot teach in elementary or secondary schools in most states unless they have taken approximately a year of mind-numbing teacher education courses. Yet students who have taken only a bachelor's degree in teacher education with a middling grade point average in a mediocre college may teach in their home states, and may be able to teach in many other states for at least a two-year period. Individual state requirements of "appropriate" education courses contribute to the severe shortage of mathematics and science teachers.

Some states, such as New Jersey, have opened their doors by "alternative certification" to over 1500 teachers and administrators who have taken professional education courses. Studies have shown three benefits: (1) an increase in minority teachers, to double that of the national average; (2) higher scores on the National Teacher Examination for all alternative teacher candidates than teacher-education graduates; and (3) a higher percentage of those who come late into the field remain in teaching.[94]

Guest teachers and administrators should also be allowed to be brought in from the private or public sector for the purpose of teaching and administering for one to three years. Extreme care should be exercised, however, in hiring administrators with no previous teaching or educational administrative experience. An outstanding business or government administrator will not automatically be a good school administrator.

Eighth, to ensure an adequate number of minority teachers and well-qualified beginning teachers to replace the approximately 50 percent of current teachers who will retire or leave the profession by the year 2000, America needs to mount large-scale scholarship programs for teacher candidates entering universities. In return, recipients must be required to remain in teaching for five years or repay an appropriate percentage if they elect an early departure from teaching. Graham recommends a national government program to finance model one-year teacher education programs for 500 minority teachers and 1,000 teacher candidates irrespective of ethnic origin, subject to the requirement that they must remain in teaching for three years or pay back their benefactors over a period of five years.[95] A more effective state and federal long-range approach would provide four-year scholarships and require a five-year service term. For example, North Carolina annually gives four hundred of its best high school graduates four-year scholarships if they will choose a teaching major.

Ninth, American educators need to undertake the creation of scientifically valid, nonethnically biased teacher competency tests for those entering or already in the field. Since 1983, forty-six states have passed laws establishing teacher competency requirements for those who want to teach. But because these are minimum competency tests, in practice mere graduation from a university with an education major that certifies a certain number of education courses almost automatically permits one to teach. Unlike in Japan, most American teachers are not rigorously tested or interviewed by state or metropolitan boards of education, but are instead hired only by applying at individual school districts.

Most American states still have no statewide examinations for screening teachers *already* in the field. Arkansas, Georgia, and Texas have adopted such tests. In 1985, about 10 percent of the public school teachers in Arkansas failed either the reading, writing, or arithmetic parts of the competency examination. In one predominantly African American county, 34.5 percent of the teachers failed the competency examination—a statistic that supports the frequent claims that children in predominantly African American schools are still receiving a poorer quality of education than students in predominantly white districts. Texas tests made such a mockery of testing competence that one fourth-grade Texas teacher remarked "a lot of my students could have answered those questions."[96] So politically explosive was this teacher competency test issue that it played a prominent role in the 1986 defeat of a Texas governor who advocated it. The controversy surfaced again over the Texas Master Teacher Examination of 1990. The powerful Texas Education Association led an unsuccessful costly and vigorous campaign against this reform.

American teachers have been their own worst enemy in failing to police their profession. They want to equate themselves with the medical and legal profession, but fail to give substance to that comparison by establishing rigorous qualifying examinations and internal policing standards and practices. For teacher associations and unions, job security and teacher immunity seem to be more important priorities than maintaining high standards. Students need good models of cooperation and maturity rather than incessant self-interested behavior and confrontational teacher–school board relations. When combined with the low academic ability of people entering the teaching field, reluctance of teachers to put in a longer school year, and the attrition of good teachers, it is easy to see why the general public is less supportive of teachers than in Japan.[97]

Last, arts and science faculty must work more closely with colleges of education to develop new courses or tailor old courses that have greater applicability to actual classroom teaching conditions. Too often the former are so smug, they refuse to recognize college of education colleagues as legitimately academic.[98]

TEACHER COMPETENCE AND IN-SERVICE EDUCATION

Teachers in both Japan and the United States need more quality in-service education, but Americans can learn much from Japan's superior practices. (Ironically, in-service workshops were introduced to Japan during the Allied Occupation of Japan.)[99] The Ministry of Education has put more effort into in-service education because of strong opposition to changing present teacher entry certification standards. It wants to overcome them by committing teachers to a "mission." Teachers are expected to play a holistic role. But critics of the in-service and internship programs allege that the Ministry and conservatives real objective is to create compliant teachers who support the Ministry of Education's conservative ideology and dominance.[100]

In-service education workshops are carried out through prefectural and metropolitan centers of education. These workshops of one to five days are held throughout the year for teachers at various stages of their careers in such areas as subject matter, classroom realities, and character formation. Sixth-year teachers participate in three-day workshops at educational centers. Workshops are held for four to eight days a year for administrators, particularly first-year administrators, and chairpersons groomed for vice principal and principal roles. The Hiroshima Municipal Center also offers annually six months of released time for six teachers and three months of released time programs to twenty-two additional teachers.[101]

At the national level, the National Education Center at Tsukuba offers eleven one-month in-service workshops a year each for approximately three hundred teachers and administrators. Eight of these workshops are for potential administrators and actual administrators, and the three others are for English teachers and counselors. Provinces also provide Science Education Centers for the purposes of strengthening veteran teachers in their subject areas; developing science education research on topics such as teaching materials, teaching techniques, and education aids; organizing lecture series; and bringing science to children.[102]

A second Japanese educational reform of potential merit is the internship for first-year teachers. It was instituted in 1989 after almost thirty years of opposition from the JTU. The legislation's objective is also to create teachers with a "mission." This NCER recommended reform requires new teachers carrying a full load of classes to (a) participate in a program of at least sixty days of in-school training under a veteran teacher's tutelage, and (b) spend thirty days off-campus training through lectures, visiting other schools, and participating in overnight training camps.[103]

Internships have the potential for giving beginning teachers much assistance in coping with their new profession. The one-year internship requires a three-day in-service education session at the provincial and metropolitan education centers, a three-day retreat, a fourteen-day in-school workshop under the supervision of veteran teachers and one-year supervision by a senior teacher. At schools where senior teachers direct two or more teachers, they are given released time from all teaching duties, but when only one new teacher has been hired, a substitute veteran teacher (sometimes retired) is hired for supervisory purposes.[104] Interns are to lead demonstration classes over subject areas before their colleagues, followed by feedback and personal guidance. At the Hiroshima Municipal Center first year teachers also are integrated with other teachers in city-wide study-group meetings to discuss various educational matters, including methodology and curriculum.[105]

Three points need to be stressed about Japan's in-service education. First, here is another example of where Japanese society puts its money where its mouth is. In 1989, the Japanese government appropriated nearly $200 million for 14,505 beginning teachers' internships.[106] Second, in-service programs are mostly led by experienced teachers and administrators because novitiates want practical advice from their colleagues on how to cope with various school problems.

Third, preliminary research by Shimahara and Sakai, however, indicates that the internship program is not proceeding as the Ministry of Education and the NCER had hoped because of the "culture of teaching."[107] According to them, teachers learn how to teach from an informal "culture of teaching" involving much interaction between inexperienced and veteran teachers more than from supervisory teachers. (This occurs in part because supervisory teachers provide limited direct guidance.) If that is so, the physical arrangements of common teachers' rooms provide Japanese teachers an advantage.

TEACHING, ADMINISTRATION, SPORTS, AND COACHES

Because American school administrators receive significantly higher salaries than classroom teachers, many of the latter enter school administration. Unfortunately, many mediocre teachers also leave the classrooms to become administrators or counselors. The loss of good classroom teachers to administration, counseling, and other occupations is a tragedy. The exit from the classrooms of poor teachers into administrative positions is a greater tragedy. A third tragedy is the disproportionate number of ex-coaches in administrative positions.

Of course, there are many coaches who are good, dedicated teachers and administrators as interested in academics and character formation as in sports, but generally, their scholarship is likely to be subordinated to public relations with the community. Such administrators undermine teachers' morale. The normal pattern is for coaches' competency in basic skills to be average and their interest in scholarship less than subject matter teachers. Their close community ties, social skills, and semiadministrative experience in administering large athletic programs, however, become important factors in being appointed to administrative posts.

In Japan, educational priorities come before athletics. At most schools sports play second fiddle to academic pressures and a balanced extracurricular program for both sexes. Few teachers are hired because of athletic ability; many have not played sports in college. Japanese school sports place greater emphasis on character formation and less on winning than American sports.

(There is an important exception to the above generalization. It sometimes happens that prefectural and metropolitan offices of education and private schools choose beginning teachers with completely undistinguished academic records because they had been captains of a club. This often causes considerable surprise among the university faculty where such students have majored.)

During a speech to a Japanese audience I touched briefly on the subject of why many American students dislike history. I pointed out that history teachers are sometimes poorly qualified for two reasons: (1) they may have been originally hired to teach another subject in which they majored; and (2) they may have been hired primarily for their coaching skills. I explained that the attitude of too many boards of education and school administrators is "Anyone can teach history"—or for that matter social studies, English, and sciences. I wanted to point out that coaches without majors in history (or other

academic subjects) often teach academic subjects rather than physical education; consequently, they may not be well-qualified or zealous teachers. In the
subsequent question-and-answer period, the listening audience could not
fathom this condition because their public school teachers are hired and assigned at the prefectural and metropolitan level on the basis of passing difficult examinations. Recently, in some American school districts, however,
coaches are only allowed to teach physical education. This ruling is unjust to
some outstanding coach-teachers, but on the whole the ruling will benefit the
nation's schools.

TEACHER RESPECT AND DILIGENCE

Teachers do not manage to live on the basis of respect, but it is important.
A 1975 survey of Japanese public opinion showed that principals and teachers ranked ninth and eighteenth, respectively, in prestige. Elementary teachers ranked higher than civil and mechanical engineers, white collar employees
in large firms, and municipal department heads.[108] The designation *sensei*
(teacher) inherently connotes respect for those who have wisdom to guide
because they have experience, that is, literally were "born earlier." More telling was the name for a normal school in the prewar period—*shihan gakko*,
literally a place where one gains the virtue of a master.

Generally speaking, Japanese teachers are respected more than American
teachers because they are considered competent and dedicated; they work a
long school year; they play an important role in inculcating cultural values;
they skillfully transmit academic content; and they command professional
salaries. Foreign researchers have noted that even at the preschool level teaching is relatively prestigious for young women, and that the salary is roughly
equivalent to that of other college-educated women (in sharp contrast to the
United States, where more and more potential female teachers are being attracted to professions previously closed to them). An education major is the
third most popular course of study at the Japanese junior college level.[109]

Extensive research by Shimahara demonstrates that teaching has become
even more attractive and competitive for young Japanese over the past decade. Annually, 32 percent of Japan's approximate 180,000 college graduates
earn a teacher's certificate. Annually more than 200,000 applicants (including previously unsuccessful examinees) compete for fewer than 40,000 available positions in the public school system.[110]

Japanese teachers are respected more than American teachers because on
the whole they work harder at transmitting academic knowledge and perform
important cultural expectations, a difficult statement to make because of the
many very good American elementary and secondary teachers I knew. Because of Japanese teachers' responsibilities as advisors to sports clubs and
other clubs many Japanese teachers in the first ten years work too much—
Saturdays and Sundays, averaging sixty to seventy hours a week. For week-

end overtime, Japanese teachers are only compensated for a maximum of four hours at the rate of 500 yen per hour (about $4.50)—not even enough to pay for most teachers' commuting costs. Even preschool teachers work an eight- or nine-hour day. Many teachers are required to supervise club activities and to accompany students on various school excursions, such as ski trips. Sometimes an additional burden is placed on the teachers by scheduling school visitations on Sundays to involve fathers. Although many teachers complain of "burnout" from their heavy teaching burden, they are culturally bound to accept it.[111]

Foreign scholars are in agreement that Japanese teachers are "positive, supportive, and industrious."[112] Duke reported on a Tokyo survey showing that 30 percent of nonadministrative elementary and junior high teachers in the thirty-five to forty-four age bracket daily returned home from work about 8 P.M.[113] A later JTU survey of 1993 showed that one in two teachers work on Sundays, sleep less than other workers, spend only 13 minutes for meals at schools (females 8 minutes) and work 9 hours and 28 minutes a day.[114] One junior high school teacher responsible for having to write school reports for students applying to senior high schools complained that at that point he worked 160 hours of overtime that month and could only sleep four hours a night. Stevenson and Stigler found that "[Elementary school] teachers in Sendai, Beijing, and Taipei spent an average of 9.5, 9.7, and 9.1 hours at school per day, respectively compared to 7.3 hours for the American teachers" in Chicago and Minneapolis. When surveyed on how important they considered homework on a nine point scale (nine being important and one unimportant), Taiwanese teachers scored the category 7.3, Japanese teachers 5.8, and American teachers 4.4.[115] Lynn thought that there were four reasons why Japanese teachers worked harder than American and English public school teachers: strong competition to maintain their schools' reputation; teachers' desire for self-esteem; competition of public high schools with private schools; and the voluntary nature of Japanese education after fifteen, when compulsory education ends, as compared to ages of sixteen for Great Britain and sixteen or seventeen in the United States.[116]

There are important cultural reasons why Japanese teachers work diligently. Teachers are under the pressure of modeling morality, perfection, suffering, scholarship, and diligence.[117] Indeed, this strong cultural demand of teaching is a compelling reason why many young graduates do not find teaching attractive enough to sacrifice their own personal and family lives. A word of qualification, however, is in order. It is unkind to say so, but one result of the excessive cultural expectations under which teachers work is that too many become rigid, narrow, and lacking in humor. One professor-friend who often lectures to teacher groups considers their lack of humor to be one of the worst features of Japanese education, a prewar legacy.[118]

Despite the fact that Japanese teachers push their students in mathematics, their students generally have a high regard for them. The Husen international study of achievement in mathematics for twelve economically advanced nations showed that Japanese eighteen-year-olds rated math teachers only slightly lower than Israeli students, and thirteen-year-olds respected their math teachers more than their counterparts from any other nation. The latter responded, "My mathematics teacher required me not only to master the steps in solving problems, but also to understand the reasoning involved."[119]

The other side of the coin is that Japanese society's predominant dependence on its teachers results in subjecting them to constant criticism. For example, the NCER criticized them as lacking "ability to guide," "flexible understanding and adaptability," and "insight into what children are thinking." The Central Council of Education urged them to a higher "sense of mission" and motivation.[120] When bullying and classroom violence make national headlines, teachers and schools are strongly criticized. These societal pressures and work load often lead to fatigue, depression, and, occasionally, suicide.[121]

A qualification to the above description of Japan's hardworking teachers must be made. Most female teachers will return home by 6 P.M.; married women with children by 5:30 because the traditional attitude prevails that their place is at home. Furthermore, some male teachers do not return until 7 or 8 P.M. only because they (a) are active JTU representatives who make certain that nothing is carried out without their input, (b) do not want to go home, and (c) are busy visiting or playing games like mahjong or *go*.

TEACHERS' UNIONS AND TEACHER ATTITUDES

The presence and power of teachers' unions in postwar Japan constitutes a radical break with the prewar period when teachers unions were not permitted, and the Mombusho subsidized and controlled prewar teachers' associations. During the Occupation of Japan, however, the Labor Division of the Economic and Scientific Section of SCAP (to the displeasure of the Education Division of the CI&E) legitimized and encouraged teachers' unions to improve teachers' economic welfare and political power. Both Divisions wanted to give teachers a voice in the political process and to make school administration and policy formulation more democratic.[122] The JTU disappointed the Education Division because its domination by left-wing Marxists led to a primary concern with economic and ideological issues and political power. However, JTU membership has steadily declined in the last decade to 39 percent of all teachers because (a) of its radical political orientation; (b) of greatly improved teacher salaries and fringe benefits in the 1970s under the conservative Liberal Democratic Party's rule; and (c) of a more politically apathetic younger teacher generation. Until recently an intense adversarial relationship has characterized the relationship of the JTU with local administrators and the Ministry of Education.[123] By relying on the JTU, teachers *collectively* are no longer meek, compliant, and automatic instruments of government will.

On the one hand, the JTU constitutes the only powerful countervailing force to the Ministry's overcentralization, standardization, and excessive educational emphasis on producing students for narrow national economic goals. In schools where the JTU is strong it maintains an element of democracy in making school policies and in keeping the elementary and junior high schools egalitarian. On the other hand, the JTU refuses to accept a role of leadership for the principal and vice principal. Its members were committed to class struggle and confrontation politics to overthrow capitalism. One young Japanese teacher in a Tokyo school where 98 percent of the teachers are JTU members told me the principal and vice principal are almost completely ignored by the JTU leadership.[124] Because he believed that the school administrators should lead, he often consulted with the principal or vice principal. JTU colleagues told him, "You don't understand the way things are done, do you?" Opponents of the JTU make the following generalization: In schools where it is strong, the academic level, the teacher–principal relationship, and teacher–community relationship are all poorer than in schools where the union is weak. JTU activists are often seen as *sarari man* (salaried wage earner) teachers, that is teachers with a minimum commitment to professionalism, to students, to extracurricular activities, and to the rah-rah-100-percent enthusiastic *Nekketsu Sensei* image described by Bruce Feiler.[125]

In fact, there is a marked discrepancy between the views of Japanese teachers and administrators over who should make policy and decisions. Nearly six of ten teachers think that school staff meetings should be the final decision-making body, a significant change in postwar teachers' thinking regarding their role. The Ministry of Education and nine out of ten principals, however, view the staff meeting only as a deliberative body lacking responsibility for policies and decision making.[126]

The JTU is the enemy of ambitious parents and students because its egalitarian orientation scorns education geared to entrance examinations. Parents wanting their children to get into good high schools and universities are unhappy that they have to choose among (a) allowing their children's future university and employment prospects to be compromised by attending public schools where the JTU is strong, (b) sending their children to *juku* to compensate for the allegedly poorer quality of teaching in the public schools, or, in Honshu's larger cities, or (c) sending them to expensive, private schools with reputations of their graduates entering Japan's higher ranked universities.

By what criteria are JTU-dominated schools poorer? The same question is being asked in Nagano Prefecture's public schools, where the JTU is strong. Nagano has enjoyed a reputation since early Meiji days of being a prefecture actively concerned about education. Yet recent statistics on the much lower number of Nagano high school students passing university entrance examinations has caused a loss of prestige and much consternation. Although Nagano is now being looked upon as a failure, were it judged on the basis of producing a more well-rounded person and a more egalitarian educational system, it may be looked upon as a success.

America's teacher unions have also exerted both negative and positive influences on schools. One ex-high school teacher-friend, now a professor of education, commented bitterly upon reading an earlier draft of this manuscript

Frankly, the union movement has been a disaster. Public educators spent decades in the 30s and 40s and 50s trying to decide whether they were a profession or not. Finally when push-came-to-shove, and often with prodding of unenlightened school boards and coach-administrators, we decided to be coal miners and auto workers and install in toto their union design. Collegiality was lost.

TEACHER–PUPIL CONSPIRACY TO AVOID EFFORT

Despite strong criticism of education standards over the last decade, too many American teachers still do not want to challenge students to a higher performance. (No such climate exists in Japan, where students and teachers feel the pressure of entrance examinations.) Such teachers have negotiated "treaties" with students at all levels, what Theodore Sizer refers to as a "conspiracy of the least." These treaties are tacit agreements between teachers and students that encourage the latter to perform at whatever level they want as long as they do not cause problems for the teachers. Sizer wrote that this conspiracy reduces "the efforts of both students and teachers to an irreducible and pathetic minimum."[127] Some teachers are content to show many films, limit severely class preparation, provide daily in-class time for students to do homework, use workbooks frequently in class, allow students to distract them from teaching subject matter, and adopt the attitude that grades, competition, tracking, and too much emphasis upon learning academic content is detrimental to children.

Rosy student report cards, especially for students who are not doing well at the elementary school level, mislead children and parents. Teachers overly concerned about children's self-esteem reward mediocrity. Finn reported that, of 150 student reports of one elementary school, almost none were negative; instead, they were full of positive feedback, gushy with affection, or "peppered with exclamation points and decorated with little 'smiley' faces."[128]

CONCLUSION

The British study noted in previous chapters concluded that among twelve factors characteristic of effective elementary schools were such items as purposeful leadership of the staff by the head teacher, intellectually challenging teaching, maximum communication between teachers and pupils, and involvement of teachers in curriculum planning, decisions on spending, and school policy.[129] American teachers can reverse present low educational achievement; however, changed teacher and societal attitudes are indispensable.

It must be emphasized that America absolutely shall not succeed in getting good teachers by the present low social and financial rewards. These conditions lead better high school seniors to avoid a teaching major and our most qualified teachers to leave the field. America can learn from the Japanese example of providing a salary 10 percent higher than that of civil service workers with the same years of service. But teachers must show their sincerity and commitment by accepting a ten-month school year and an eleven-month teaching year.

American federal, state, and private scholarship funding agencies should require teacher candidates on scholarship after graduation to spend four years teaching in rural and inner-city areas as a means of ensuring a supply of young, academically well-qualified teachers. Schools need to be able to hire competent teachers at the outset, to assign young teachers to a superior, veteran teacher for assistance and supervision for at least one year, and to institute a system of warnings, penalties, suspension, and fines for older teachers who are failing to meet the above guidelines or who need to maintain greater time on task.

Present American teaching salaries must be raised, but they must be contingent on a longer school and teaching year. Lack of adequate competence and limited efforts by *some* teachers must not be used as an excuse for accepting poor financial rewards for *all* American teachers. Two measures must be adopted to break out of this moot argument. First, teachers must be placed on a twelve-month contract premised on a ten-month school year and an additional month's work for teacher planning, production of teaching materials, and teaching gifted and slow learners. *Teachers must comprehend that they will never win from the American public adequate salaries unless they work a longer school year.* They cannot win support from the public by the arguments that teaching stress is so great that the long summer vacation is justified, or that their average number of forty-nine working hours per week spent on all teaching duties is greater during their nine-month school year than other occupations.[130] Other people who work long hours under stressful conditions and who log in eight or more hours of work a day, twelve months a year, simply will not buy that argument. Furthermore, if the American educational performance were high in international comparisons despite our shorter school year, the American public might be more sympathetic to conceding higher salaries.

As a second measure, the public must be willing to err temporarily on the side of generosity by rewarding *all* teachers with better salaries. Good salaries will attract more competent teachers, and, equally important, greater remuneration will justify establishing higher teacher qualifications. Improved annual salaries must be made contingent on teachers accepting:

1. The ten-month teaching school year and eleven-month teaching year.
2. Higher standards for those coming into the profession.
3. Scientifically valid, nonethnically biased competency tests for those already in the profession to weed out the incompetent.
4. Removal of teachers whose performance is mediocre and whose influence on children's character is negative.

Communities and school boards have the leverage to make improved salaries contingent on teacher acceptance of a longer teaching year and more rigorous competency standards. A teacher housecleaning can be accomplished more easily now at the time of entry because the federal government projects a demand for new teachers to reach a high of 243,000 in 2000.[131]

America is engaged in a profligate waste of precious human resources. Inability to retain teachers or to recruit top graduates are major reasons schools cannot shape youth's character and hone their academic skills adequately. Because teachers and administrators leave the profession or lose vision and energy, they do not transmit sufficient academic knowledge and cannot create school environments that nurture more disciplined children.

Administrators, school boards, state legislatures, and Congress all need to be honest with education and educators by improving the conditions that affect teacher morale and attitudes. Teachers should help themselves and our schools by playing a more active and constructive role in shaping educational policy and practice in every school district.

NOTES

1. Robert King Hall, _Education for Japan_ (New Haven: Yale University Press, 1949), 429–450; Joseph C. Trainor, _Education Reform in Occupied Japan: Trainor's Memoir_ (Tokyo: Meisei University Press, 1983), 203–208.

2. The Holmes Group, _Tomorrow's Schools_ (East Lansing, Mich.: The Holmes Group, 1990), 38, 58–59.

3. C. Emily Feistritzer, _Teacher Crisis: Myth or Reality?_ (Washington, D.C.: U.S. National Center for Education Information, 1986), 65–66; Mary Rollefson, U.S. Department of Education, "Teacher Turnovers: Patterns of Entry to and Exit from Teaching," Paper presented to 1990 Annual Meeting of the American Educational Research Association, Boston, Mass., 18 April 1990, as cited in Chester E. Finn, Jr., _We Must Take Charge_ (New York: Free Press, 1991), 79; U.S. Department of Education, National Center for Education Statistics (U.S. DOE, NCES), _Digest of Education Statistics 1992_ (Washington, D.C.: U.S. Government Printing Office, 1992), 78, 80.

4. Finn, _We Must Take Charge_, 78, 80.

5. U.S. DOE, NCES, _Digest 1997_, 79.

6. U.S. Department of Education, National Center for Educational Statistics (U.S. DOE, NCES), _The Condition of Education 1995_ (Washington, D.C.: U.S. Government Printing Office, 1995), 165; Patricia Alberg Graham, _S.O.S.: Sustain Our Schools_ (New York: Hill and Wang, 1992), 38. In California 65 percent of beginning teachers drop out in the first two years. Denis P. Doyle, Bruce S. Cooper, and Roberta Trachtman, _Taking Charge: State Action on School Reform in the 1980s_ (Indianapolis: Hudson Institute, 1991), 13.

7. A North Carolina commission concluded that the failure of the state "to attract and retain minority and Caucasian teachers threaten[ed] the existence of the public system." Editorial, "A Desperate Plea," _The News & Observer_, 22 September 1995.

8. Doyle, Cooper, aned Trachtman, _Taking Charge_, 8–9.

9. Nobuo K. Shimahara and Akira Sakai, _Learning to Teach in Two Cultures: Japan and the United States_ (New York: Garland, 1985), 49–52.

10. J. H., Parkerson, D. P. Schiller, R. G. Lomax, and H. J. Walberg, "Exploring Causal Models of Educational Achievement," *Journal of Educational Psychology* 76: 638–646.

11. Graham, *S.O.S.*, 9.

12. Peter Mortimore, Pamela Sammons, Louise Stoll, David Lewis, and Russel Ecob, *School Matters* (Berkeley and Los Angeles: University of California Press, 1988), 59.

13. U.S. Department of Education (U.S. DOE), *Japanese Education Today* (Washington, D.C.: U.S. Government Printing Office, 1987), 4, 25, 34, 42.

14. Harold W. Stevenson and James Stigler, *The Learning Gap: Why Our Schools Are Failing and What We Can Learn from Japanese and Chinese Education* (New York: Summit, 1992), 164; correspondence from Harold W. Stevenson, 24 March 1996.

15. Japan, Ministry of Education, Science, and Culture (Japan, MESC), *Outline of Education in Japan 1989* (Tokyo: Government of Japan, 1989), 43. The average number of teaching hours per week for public elementary, junior high, and senior high school teachers in 1986 was 18.8, 14.9, and 14.4 percent respectively, a 40 percent reduction in teaching load from 1965.

16. Japanese third- and fourth-grade teachers teach all subjects; fifth- and sixth-grade teachers teach all subjects but two for a total of twenty-seven, forty-five-minute periods per week. Catherine C. Lewis, *Educating Hearts and Minds* (Cambridge: Cambridge University Press, 1995), 66, 68. Stevenson and Stigler estimated that Japanese elementary school teachers are "in charge of classes only 60 percent of the time they are at school." *Learning Gap*, 164.

17. Stevenson and Stigler, *Learning Gap*, 164.

18. "Too Many Students Per Teacher," *The Daily Yomiuri*, 27 March 1992.

19. Japan, Ministry of Education, Science, and Culture (Japan, MESC), *Education in Japan 1989: A Graphic Presentation* (Tokyo: Government of Japan, 1989), 56; Japan, Ministry of Education, Science, and Culture (Japan, MESC), *Statistical Abstract of Education, Science, and Culture* (Tokyo: Japan, Ministry of Education, Science, and Culture Research and Statistics Planning Division, 1992); Lewis, *Educating Hearts and Minds*, 15.

20. Richard Lynn, *Educational Achievement in Japan* (Armonk: N.Y.: M. E. Sharpe, 1988), 110–130; 163; Mortimore et al., *School Matters*, 228, 254, 281; Allan Odden, "Class Size and Student Achievement: Research Based Policy Alternatives," *Education Evaluation and Policy Analysis* 12, no. 2 (Summer 1990): 213–227.

21. Stevenson and Stigler, *Learning Gap*, 144–146; Nobuo Shimahara and Akika Sakai, *Learning to Teach in Two Cultures: Japan and the United States* (New York: Garland, 1985), 69–70, 84, 139; Mortimore et al., *School Matters*, 226–227, 242.

22. Shimahara and Sakai, *Learning to Teach,* 109.

23. Arthur G. Powell, Eleanor Farrar, and David K. Cohen, *The Shopping Mall High School* (Boston: Houghton Mifflin, 1985), 319–320.

24. Stevenson and Stigler, *Learning Gap,* 160.

25. Shimahara and Sakai, *Learning to Teach*, 223.

26. Mortimore et al., *School Matters*, 250–251, 225, 233–234.

27. H. H. Passow, H. J. Noah, M. A. Eckstein, and J. R. Mallea, *The National Case Study: An Empirical Comparative Study of Twenty-One Educational Systems* (Stockholm: Almquist and Wilsell, 1976), as cited in Richard Lynn, *Educational Achievement in Japan* (Armonk: N.Y.: M. E. Sharpe, 1988), 106–108.

28. U.S. DOE, NCES, *Digest 1997* (Washington, D.C.: U.S. Government Printing Office, 1997), 83.

29. U.S. DOE, NCES, *Condition 1995*, 158–159. U.S. DOE, NCES, *Digest 1992*, 83, 398. Beginning teacher salaries increased 17 percent between 1980 and 1994.

30. U.S. DOE, NCES, *Condition 1995*, 160–161.

31. Dwight W. Allen, *Schools for a New Century* (Westport, Conn.: Praeger, 1992), 97.

32. Holmes Group, *Tomorrow's Schools*, 62–63 (emphasis mine).

33. U.S. DOE, NCES, *Digest 1992*, 81; Sugihara Seishiro, "Educational Expenditure in Japan and the United States," *East West Education* 11 (Spring 1990), 49.

34. Linda Darling-Hammond, Report to the National Commission on Excellence in Education, 1983.

35. Doyle, Cooper, and Trachtman, *Taking Charge*, 8, fn. 6, 7.

36. Scott D. Thompson, "Report Card USA: How Much Do Americans Value Schooling?" *National Association of American Secondary School Principals Bulletin* (October 1989), 58.

37. Shogo Ichikawa, "Financing Japanese Education," in *Windows on Japanese Education*, ed. Edward Beauchamp (Westport, Conn.: Greenwood Press, 1991), 86.

38. Ibid.

39. Japanese teachers' average salary is equal to professionals with comparable education and tenure, but American teachers' salaries are only 70 percent of other professions. Stephen M. Barrow, "International Comparison of Teachers Salaries," cited in Cummings, "Japan's Science and Engineering Pipelines," in *Windows on Japanese Education*, ed. Edward Beauchamp (Westport, Conn.: Greenwood Press, 1991), 207.

40. U.S. DOE, *Japanese Education Today*, 19.

41. Seishiro Sugihara, "Educational Expenditure in Japan and the United States," *East West Education* 11 (Spring 1990): 49.

42. Ibid., 50; Nobuo Shimahara, "Teacher Education in Japan," in *Windows on Japanese Education*, ed. Edward Beauchamp (Westport, Conn.: Greenwood Press, 1991), 267.

43. Ichikawa, "Financing Japanese Education," 86–87.

44. Shimahara, "Teacher Education in Japan," 269; Nobuo Shimahara, "Teacher Education Reform in Japan: Issues of Ideology and Control," in *Teacher Education in Industrialized Nations: Issues in Changing Social Contexts*, ed. Nobuo K. Shimahara and Ivan Holowinsky (New York: Garland, 1995), 32.

45. U.S. DOE, *Japanese Education Today*, 19–20; Sugihara, "Educational Expenditure," 49; U.S. DOE, NCES, *Digest 1992*, 81.

46. Ichikawa, "Financing Japanese Education," 86; Sugihara, *Educational Expenditure*, 49.

47. U.S. DOE, *Japanese Education Today*, 19.

48. This meant a teacher at a national school received a lump sum of approximately $120,000 and a principal $128,000. Sugihara, *Educational Expenditure*, 45, 48.

49. Ichikawa, "Financing Japanese Education," 86; U.S. DOE, *Japanese Education Today*, 20.

50. A teacher-friend receives a pension of 260,000 yen ($2,600) a month after taxes.

51. U.S. DOE, NCES, *Digest 1992*, 77–78; U.S. DOE, NCES, *Digest 1991*, 72, 77, 85. Slightly more than 62.4 percent of Japanese teachers have taught more than ten years. Japan, Ministry of Education, Science, and Culture (Japan, MESC), *Education in Japan 1994: A Graphic Presentation*, rev. ed. (Tokyo: Gyosei, 1994), 83. Only 44.5 percent of American teachers had taught ten to twenty years. U.S. DOE, *Japanese Education Today*, 15.

52. Ibid., 82.

53. C. Emily Feistritzer, *Profile of Teachers in the U.S., 1990*, 48, as cited in Chester E. Finn, Jr., *We Must Take Charge* (New York: Free Press, 1991), 79.

54. Shimahara and Sakai, *Learning to Teach*, 20–21.

55. Leonard Schoppa, "Education Reform in Japan: Goals and Results of the Recent Reform Campaign," in *Windows on Japanese Education*, ed. Edward Beauchamp (Westport, Conn.: Greenwood Press, 1991), 74, fn. 30.

56. U.S. DOE, NCES, *Digest 1992*, 77–78. Only 0.6 percent of elementary school teachers, 1.8 of junior high school teachers, and 6.5 percent of high school teachers have taken graduate work. Jaoan, MESC, *Education in Japan 1994*, 82–83.

57. William K. Cummings, "Japan's Science and Engineering Pipeline," in *Windows on Japanese Education*, ed. Edward Beauchamp (Westport, Conn.: Greenwood Press, 1991), 181.

58. Japan, MESC, *Education in Japan 1994*, 82–83; Shimahara, "Teacher Education in Japan," in *Windows on Japanese Education*, ed. Edward Beauchamp (Westport, Conn.: Greenwood Press, 1991), 269.

59. Shimahara and Holowinsky, *Teacher Education*, 36.

60. Shimahara and Sakai, *Learning to Teach*, 231.

61. Stevenson and Stigler, *Learning Gap*, 157.

62. *Education Week*, 17 April 1991. U.S. National Commission on Excellence in Education (U.S. NCEE), *A Nation at Risk* (Washington, D.C.: U.S. Government Printing Office, 1983), 23.

63. U.S. DOE, NCES, *Condition 1995*, 162–163.

64. U.S. NCEE, *A Nation at Risk*, 22; Lynne V. Cheney, *Tyrannical Machines* (Washington, D.C.: U.S. National Endowment for the Humanities, 1990), 6–8.

65. U.S. National Center for Education Statistics (U.S. NCES), *America's Teachers: Profile of a Profession* (Washington, D.C.: U.S. Department of Education, 1993), 62.

66. U.S. DOE, *Japanese Education Today*, 17; Shimahara, "Teacher Education," 259–260.

67. Shimahara, "Teacher Education," 264, 270.

68. Shimahara and Sakai, *Learning to Teach*, 176–177, 131–132, 152, 206.

69. Stevenson and Stigler, *Learning Gap*, 157–160, 173; Shimahara and Sakai, *Learning to Teach*, 155, 158.

70. Shimahara and Sakai, *Learning to Teach*, 151–155, 158.

71. Ibid., 46–47, 149, 157.

72. Cheney, *Tyrannical Machines*, 5.

73. Dwight Allen, *Schools for a New Century* (Westport, Conn.: Praeger, 1992), 70.

74. U.S. NCEE, *A Nation at Risk*, 22.

75. Eva C. Galambos, Lynn M. Cornett, and Hugh D. Spitler, *An Analysis of Transcripts of Teachers and Arts and Sciences Graduates* (Atlanta, Ga.: Southern Regional Education Board, 1985), 79, cited in Lynne V. Cheney, *Tyrannical Machines* (Washington, D.C.: U.S. National Endowment for the Humanities, 1990), 7.

76. Charles J. Sykes, *Dumbing Down Our Kids* (New York: St. Martin's Press, 1995), 88.

77. Shimahara and Sakai, *Learning to Teach*, 147, 237–238.

78. In 1986, 53.1 percent of American teachers had taken college credits during the previous three years. U.S. DOE, NCES, *Digest 1992*, 78.

79. L. C. Comber and J. Keeves, *Science Achievement in Nineteen Countries* (New York: John Wiley, 1973), as cited in Lynne V. Cheney, *Tyrannical Machines* (Washington, D.C.: U.S. National Endowment for the Humanities, 1990), 111–112.

80. Finn, *We Must Take Charge*, 22–28, 64–65, 199–202, 268–270.

81. Holmes Group, *Tomorrow's Schools*, 47–48.

82. Finn, *We Must Take Charge*, 265, 237–238; Shimahara, "Teacher Education," 264–265.

83. Shimahara and Sakai, *Learning to Teach*, 266–268.

84. Japan, MESC, *Education in Japan 1994*, 84–85.

85. Shimahara and Sakai, *Learning to Teach*, 268; U.S. DOE, *Japanese Education Today*, 16.

86. Shimahara, "Teacher Education," 266.

87. Ibid., 265.

88. Willard J. Jacobson et al., "Science Education in Japan," in *Japanese Educational Productivity*, ed. R. Leestma and H. J. Walberg (Ann Arbor: University of Michigan Press, 1992), 157.

89. Graham, *S.O.S.*, 26, 31.

90. Holmes Group, *Tomorrow's Schools*, 66.

91. Allen, *Schools for a New Century*, 138.

92. Finn, *We Must Take Charge*, 222–230; Sykes, *Dumbing Down*, 85–87.

93. Diane Ravitch, *The Troubled Crusade: American Education 1945–1980* (New York: Basic Books, 1983), 51–67.

94. Cheney, *Tyrannical Machines*, 10; Finn, *We Must Take Charge*, 195–196.

95. By 2000, 30 to 40 percent of school children will be from minority groups, yet minority teachers are less than ten percent. Graham, *S.O.S.*, 102–103.

96. William Bennett, *American Education: Making It Work* (Washington, D.C.: U.S. Government Printing Office, 1988), 42; Finn, *We Must Take Charge*, 43–45.

97. Finn, *We Must Take Charge*, 181–182, 190–195.

98. Allen, *Schools for a New Century*, 141.

99. Harry Wray, "Significance, Change, and Continuity in Modern Japanese Educational History," *Comparative Education Review* 35, no. 3 (1991): 453.

100. Leonard James Schoppa, *Education Reform in Japan* (London: Routledge, 1991), 61.

101. Shimahara, "Teacher Education," 271–272.

102. Jacobson and Takemura, "Science Education in Japan," in *Japanese Educational Productivity*, ed. R. Leestma and H. J. Walberg (Ann Arbor: University of Michigan Press, 1992), 156, 158.

103. Schoppa, *Education Reform*, 67.

104. Communication of August 1994 with Sadao Tokui, a retired junior high school teacher, who acted as a part-time supervisor for one intern.

105. Shimahara, "Teacher Education," 271–272.

106. Shimahara and Sakai, *Learning to Teach*, 235; Shimahara and Holowinsky, *Teacher Education*, 34.

107. Nobuo K. Shimahara and Akira Sakai, "Teacher Internship and the Culture of Teaching in Japan," *British Journal of Sociology of Education* 13, no. 2 (1992): 147–162.

108. U.S. DOE, *Japanese Education Today*, 19; Nancy Sato and Milbrey W. McLaughlin, "Context Matters: Teaching in Japan and in the United States," *Phi Delta Kappan* 73, no. 5 (January 1992): 359–366.

109. Lois Peak, *Learning to Go to School in Japan* (Berkeley and Los Angeles: University of California Press, 1991), 51; Joseph J. Tobin, David Y. W. Wu, and Dana H. Davidson, *Preschool in Three Cultures: Japan, China, and the United States* (New Haven: Yale University Press, 1973), 68–70.

110. Shimahara and Holowinsky, *Teacher Education*, 32; Shimahara, "Teacher Education," 264.

111. A former teacher in the Japan Education Teacher program, Mark Fishbein's comment on an earlier draft. Bruce Feiler, *Learning to Bow* (New York: Ticknor and Fields, 1991).

112. Peak, *Learning in Japan*, 52; Tobin, Wu, and Davidson, *Preschool*, 69.

113. Benjamin Duke, *The Japanese School: Lessons for Industrial America* (Westport, Conn.: Praeger, 1986), 204.

114. "Vital Losses," *Asahi Evening News*, 28 February 1996.

115. Stevenson and Stigler, *Learning Gap*, 55–56, 164.

116. Lynn, *Educational Achievement*, 99–103.

117. Shimahara, "Teacher Education," 260; Japan, National Council on Education Reform (Japan, NCER), *Second Report on Educational Reform* (Tokyo: Government of Japan, 1986), 75; Feiler, *Learning to Bow*, 174–177; Gerald K. LeTendre, "*Shido*: The Concept of Guidance," in *Teaching and Learning in Japan*, ed. Thomas Rohlen and Gerald K. LeTendre (Cambridge: Cambridge University Press, 1996), 282–284.

118. Ivan Parker Hall, *Mori Arinori* (Cambridge: Harvard University Press, 1973); Harry Elmer Griffith, "Japanese Normal School Education," Ed.D. diss., Stanford University, 1950; Benjamin C. Duke, ed., *Ten Great Educators of Modern Japan: A Japanese Perspective* (Tokyo: University of Tokyo Press, 1989), 173–174, 207, 209–210.

119. Lynn, *Educational Achievement*, 95.

120. Japan, NCER, *Second Report*, 26; Central Council of Education, *Kongo ni okeru gakko kyoiku no sogoteki kakuju seibi no tame no kihonteki shisaku ni tsuite* (Basic plan for the comprehensive expansion and improvement of school education in the future) (Tokyo: Mombusho, 1971), 54; Japan, NCER, *Second Report*, 2–7, 53–54.

121. From 1978 to 1981, 387 teachers committed suicide. Shimahara, "Teacher Education," 260.

122. Wray, "Significance, Change, and Continuity," 456–458.

123. Donald R. Thurston, *Teachers and Politics in Japan* (Princeton, N.J.: Princeton University Press, 1973), 40–50; Benjamin Duke, *Japan's Militant Teachers* (Honolulu: University Press of Hawaii, 1973); Theodore Cohen, *Remaking Japan: The American Occupation as a New Deal*, ed. Herbert Passin (New York: Free Press, 1987), 202–204.

124. Thomas Rohlen, *Japan's High Schools* (Berkeley and Los Angeles: University of California Press, 1984), 210–221; Thomas Rohlen, "Conflicts in Institutional Environments: Politics in Education," in *Conflict in Japan*, ed. Ellis S. Krauss, Thomas P. Rohlen, and Patricia G. Steinhoff (Honolulu: University of Hawaii Press, 1984), 136–170; Editorial, "Time for Dogmatism is Past," *The Japan Times*, 5 August 1990.

125. Feiler, *Learning to Bow*, ch. 14.

126. Kawakami Fujiko, as cited in William K. Cummings, *Education and Equality in Japan* (Princeton, N.J.: Princeton University Press, 1980), 69–70; Wray, "Significance, Change, and Continuity," 451–453, 455–458.

127. Theodore R. Sizer, *Horace's Compromise: The Dilemma of the American High School* (Boston: Houghton Mifflin, 1983), 155–157; Powell, Farrar, and Cohen, *The Shopping Mall*, 67–76, 110–111, 277.

128. Finn, *We Must Take Charge*, 105–107.

129. Mortimore et al., *School Matters*, 250–251, 288–289.

130. U.S. DOE, NCES, *Digest 1992*, 78.

131. U.S. DOE, NCES, *Condition 1991*, 92–93.

CHAPTER 7

American and Japanese Curricular Differences

JAPAN'S NARROW AND RIGID CURRICULUM

Japan's centralized education system maintains higher academic standards than American schools at the precollege level because the content of national courses of studies for every subject and every grade is composed systematically and in some detail by the Mombusho and its appointed Curriculum Council, composed of expert teachers, administrators, and scholars.[1] The Ministry of Education has designed a curriculum as if all students were university bound. Concretely, that means a narrow academic curriculum that concentrates on mastery of basic skills through senior high school. At most schools electives are almost entirely academic. In addition, all Japanese textbooks must meet Mombusho's standards for courses of studies. Demanding (but dull) textbooks complete with sophisticated charts, maps, and statistics prepare students for difficult college entrance examinations. Students' mastery of their content means an absorption of two to three grade levels more by graduation time than most American public and private school students.

POST-1992 JAPANESE CURRICULUM

The pre-1992 curriculum came under severe criticism in the late 1970s and 1980 for being excessively narrow, uniform, centralized, and entrance examination oriented. Three reports of the NCER (1984–1987) and four reports (1991–1993) of the Central Council of Education Reform[2] recommended paying more attention to individuals and promoting "more diversified and flexible structures of education." These recommendations recognized to a limited extent that a student body of the post 1970s in which almost 100 percent of junior high school graduates enter senior high school, is a far different one in abilities, needs, and interests than in 1950 when only 10 percent went to high school. Accordingly, the Ministry revised slightly the courses of study and curriculum at the elementary level in 1992, at the junior high school in 1993, and undertook slightly broader reforms at senior high school in 1994.

The Ministry of Education's new Courses of Study for elementary and secondary schools states the following idealistic curricular objectives:

1. To encourage the development of young people who possess richness of heart and strength of mind through every facet of the educational activities that take place at school, while taking into account children's levels of development, as well as of the characteristics of the respective subject areas and subjects.

2. To attach more importance to the nurturing of children's capacity to cope positively with changes in society, as well as to the provision of a sound base for fostering children's creativity. Children's willingness to learn independently is also to be stimulated.

3. To place more emphasis on the essential knowledge and skills required of every citizen of our nation, and to enhance educational programs that enable each child to give full play to his or her individuality.

4. To put more value on developing in children an attitude of respect for Japanese culture and traditions, as well as an increased understanding of the cultures and histories of other countries. Thus children should be helped to develop the qualities required of Japanese living in the international community.[3]

As we have seen in Chapters 3 and 4 the Ministry's curricular reforms have fallen far short of achieving these four goals. Individuality, diversity, citizenship, internationalism, and creativity, are not being nurtured adequately for helping children "cope positively with changes in society."

Nonetheless, the post-1992 curricula reflects a stronger consensus on the purpose of schools and "places more emphasis on the essential knowledge and skills" required for a productive life in adult society than currently exists in the United States. The curricula are still too narrow, but their strengths over America's are that they (a) challenge all students to develop self-discipline and diligence; (b) imbue students with the attitude that it is their responsibility to achieve quality work and good conduct; and (c) nurture attitudes conducive to becoming a cooperative member of society.[4]

Dissimilarities in the two nations' curriculum reflect differing expectations. Japanese education reflects a society that expects school and life to be difficult and students to agonize and endure to achieve basic academic competencies and develop character. Conversely, the American system's emphasis is on developing self-esteem, creativity, independence, self-identity, social skills, and citizenship.[5] The Japanese curriculum is less sentimental and indulgent than America's and is based on the assumption that society knows best what is needed for students long-range welfare. Its premise is that technical skills can be learned on the job or through experience (consumer education, practical arts) as in the case of driver education, auto mechanics, computer education, and English conversation. It can be learned at technical schools and at personal expense. Emphasis on good character formation from preschool days is thought to negate the need for such American life adjustment courses as marriage and family relations and drug, alcohol, and sex education.

If we focus more specifically on the qualitative differences in Japanese and American high school curriculums, we should note that in 1993, 74.1 percent of 5,211,627 Japanese high school students were enrolled in the "general" schools (I prefer the designation "academic" hereafter to avoid misunderstanding with the general track in the United States and with the new Japanese comprehensive course and comprehensive school), 24.1 percent in vocational schools, and the other 1.8 percent in special schools.[6] Secondary school students in the academic track take twenty-six academic class hours, more than any American school.[7]

JAPAN'S ACADEMIC CURRICULUM

New Elementary School Curriculum as of 1992

Table 7.1 shows the new curriculum for Japanese elementary schools instituted in 1992 and Table 7.2 shows the weekly timetable for a typical fifth grade class. There are several contrasts with the American elementary school curriculum and timetable. First, Japanese schools' weekly schedule runs 2,161 minutes, compared to the 1,850 minutes of the school Shimahara and Sakai researched, New Jersey's Westville Upper Elementary School. This longer schedule gives Japanese schools greater flexibility to teach a more diversified curriculum. American schools at all levels have no scheduled time for cleaning, assemblies, meetings, and reflection.

Second, as we saw in Chapter 2, Japanese elementary school teachers work very hard at whole person education, that is children's moral, aesthetic, emotional, physical, and cognitive aspects.[8] These goals are achieved by providing weekly 70 minutes each for music and art and handicraft, 35 minutes for moral education, 100 minutes for cleaning, 135 minutes for special activities such as assemblies, meetings, and reflections, and 315 minutes for breaks and recesses, as compared to 250 minutes for American schools. Although the stereotype is one of Japanese students studying incessantly, Komori students spend 30 minutes less a week in academic classes and 9 minutes less in nonacademic classes than American students, despite attending schools two Saturdays a month.[9]

One American practice that slights whole person education is overspecialization. Specialists often teach physical education, art, and music.[10] Specialization may even lead two teachers to teach their academic strengths by exchanging classes for one or two subjects. At the elementary school Shimahara and Sakai

Table 7.1
The New Curriculum for Japanese Elementary Schools of 1992 and the Prescribed Subjects and Number of School Hours

Grade:	1	2	3	4	5	6
Japanese Language	306*	315	280	280	210	210
Social Studies	—	—	105	105	105	105
Arithmetic	136	175	175	175	175	175
Science	—	—	105	105	105	105
Life Environment Studies**	102	105	—	—	—	—
Music	68	70	70	70	70	70
Art and Handicraft	68	70	70	70	70	70
Homemaking	—	—	—	—	70	70
Physical Education	102	105	105	105	105	105
Moral Education	34	35	35	35	35	35
Special Activities***	34	34	34	34	34	34
Total	850	910	980	1015	1015	1015

*A one unit school hour is a class period of forty-five minutes.

**A new course replacing and combining social studies and science for first and second graders.

***Special activities include classroom activities, student council, club activities, and school events (ceremonies, presentation programs, events related to health/safety/ physical education, school excursions, and productive and community service activities).

observed that one fifth-grade teacher was teaching only reading, writing, spelling (English), and arithmetic as a result of these arrangements. These practices reduce teacher–student contact and explicitly indicate that expertise is more important than working with children's physical and socioemotional aspects. To lighten a teacher's heavy daily class load it may be appropriate to reduce one subject, but from fiscal and holistic considerations, it seems desirable for elementary school teachers to teach all other subjects, at least for the first four grades.

Third, elementary school art and music education provide for a higher level of achievement. It is common for preschoolers aged four and five to be able "to play simple tunes on various instruments, ranging from glockenspiels and snare drums to small, two-octave keyboard flutes . . . [and to be able to] play one or two simple tunes on percussion and keyboard instruments in part harmony and then to change parts."[11] By grade four their artwork in color, design, technique, line, and form is equivalent to that of an American seventh or eighth grader. Fourth graders can read music notations, and most can play a recorder and a wind instrument, and sometimes three simple musical instruments. At that age they are usually formed into orchestras.

Table 7.2
Weekly Timetable for a Fifth Grade Class at Komiro Elementary School

	Monday	Tuesday	Wednesday	Thursday	Friday	Saturday
8:30 – 8:45	School assembly		Sports assembly		Student assembly	
8:45 – 8:50	Short meeting	Short meeting	Short meeting	Short meeting	Short meeting	Short meeting
8:50 – 9:35	Lang. arts	Math	Lang. arts	Math	Lang. arts	Arts & crafts
9:35 – 9:40	Break	Break	Break	Break	Break	Break
9:40–10:45	Math	Lang. arts	Math	Lang. arts	Lang arts	Arts & crafts
10:25–10:45	Recess	Recess	Recess	Recess	Recess	Recess
10:45–11:30	Science	Social studies	Home econ.	Social studies	Math	Social studies
11:30–11:35	Break	Break	Break	Break	Break	Break
11:35–12:20	Science	Math	Home econ.	Science	Homeroom	Gym
12:20–13:10	Lunch	Lunch	Lunch	Lunch	Lunch	Reflection
13:10–13:30	Cleaning	Cleaning	Cleaning	Cleaning	Cleaning	
13:30–13:50	Recess	Recess	Club activity	Recess	Recess	
13:50–14:35	Moral ed.	Gym	Music	Gym		
14:35–14:50	Reflection	Reflection	Break	Reflection		

Source: Nobuo K. Shimahara and Akira Sakai, *Learning to Teach in Two Cultures: Japan and the United States* (New York: Garland, 1985), 141–142; Sho Takakura and Yokuo Murata, *Education in Japan 1989: Teaching Courses and Subjects* (Tsukuba: University of Tsukuba Institute of Education, 1989), 16.

Note: Once a week there is a meeting of the student committee.

Fourth, Japanese children are also able to exercise their muscles and clear their minds by having ten-minute recesses after every forty- to fifty-minute period of the school day, a twenty- to twenty-five-minute play period following the second period in the morning (during which teachers usually play with students), and a twenty-minute cleaning time and twenty-minute play period after lunch.[12] During the physical education period, teachers also take part in the activities with their pupils. Japanese educators realize that small children need frequent free play periods to let off steam and exercise their muscles. During class they encourage group student activity. Many preschool and lower elementary school teachers use a piano, organ, or chimes to begin and close the school day and to create a transition from one class period to another. By the time students have spent three months in the first grade, teachers can switch students quickly from boisterous, loud play to disciplined behavior and study.[13] Stevenson's team thought these practices resulted in greater student satisfaction, faster transition from one subject to another, and keener student attention to subject matter.[14]

Conversely, at many American elementary schools where students are bussed, pupils are almost totally confined to a classroom environment from the time they arrive until their dismissal. Children proceed from their buses to classrooms in the morning and at the end of the school day line up again to get on their school buses. Although it was customary thirty or more years ago for American elementary school pupils to play on school grounds before and after school and to enjoy at least one recess a day, at schools Shimahara and Sakai studied pupils only enjoyed a twenty-minute play time after lunch and physical education classes twice a week. Teachers find it energy consuming and stressful to establish classroom control under these conditions.[15]

Fifth, if we examine only mathematics and science, the areas where Japan has excelled, virtually all such concepts, such as conversion of decimals to fractions and construction of materials, are introduced two semesters or more earlier (and even earlier in China and Taiwan) than in America.[16] Japanese children learn more science because the curriculum is more systematic, and they have more hands-on experiences with science equipment (the latter is less true at the high school level to the dissatisfaction of science educators and scholars).[17] Stevenson and Stigler's research showed that Japanese students have a math set filled with colorful, well-developed materials for teaching mathematical concepts: tiles, a clock, a ruler, a checkerboard, colored triangles, beads, and many other attractive objects.[18] They also used almost twice as many concrete objects as American teachers.

Japanese try to provide continuity in the elementary and secondary curricula by revising them only every ten years. Pedagogical methods remain basically the same. Since 1957, however, American teachers have become jaded from faddish changes in curricula or teaching of subject matter. This practice of changing curricula is often unsound and destructive of teacher morale. California's radical change of its reading curriculum in 1987 to deemphasize phonics, spelling, vocabulary development, and other "skill-based" programs and to emphasize a "literature-based" approach focusing on whole words and the "wonder of literature" is one reason that the state now ranks at the bottom in national reading tests.[19] Shimahara and Sakai's study of two elementary school districts that adopted a somewhat similar "whole language" teaching experiment without adequate teacher involvement, advance planning, and previous experimentation revealed teacher discontent and half-hearted staff cooperation.[20] Similarly, faddish experiments in mathematics such as the New Math adopted by California in 1985 that deemphasize work sheets, drills, paper-and-pencil computations (such as long division), and memorization in favor of problem solving, debating, "valuing," and learning how children learn rather than what they learn have resulted in California students placing in the bottom third of the fifty states in NAEP tests.[21]

The New Junior High School Curriculum of 1993

Japanese junior high schools continue to deal with the moral, emotional, academic, work, and aesthetic aspects of children by allocating more curricular time for field trips, clubs, ceremonies, homeroom, art, music, and moral education than American schools. Table 7.3 lists the new curriculum for jun-

Table 7.3
The Junior High School Curriculum of 1993 and the Prescribed Number of School Hours

Grade:	7	8	9
Japanese Language	175*	140	140
Social Studies	140	140	70-105
Mathematics	105	140	140
Science	105	105	105-140
Music	70	35-70	35
Fine Arts	70	35-70	35
Health and Physical Education	105	105	105-140
Industrial Arts & Homemaking	70	70	70-105
Moral Education	35	35	35
Special Activities	35-70	35-70	35-70
Elective Subjects [English is listed as an "elective"]**	105-140	105-210	140-280
Total	1050	1050	1050

Source: Ministry of Education, Science, and Culture, *Education in Japan 1994: A Graphic Presentation* (Tokyo: Gyosei, 1994), 58–59.

*One unit school hour is a class period of fifty minutes. Note that these are only minimum requirements. In practice, ambitious schools will exceed the minimum requirement for academic subjects. That flexibility is explained in number 2 below, regarding electives.

**Electives include foreign language (English), but in fact English is not a true elective because it is required for at least 105 minutes. In academic and upward-bound schools English will be taught more during class hours. Thus, the amount of time for true electives is severely limited at the seventh and eighth grades. Schools are free to apply the extra time allotted for electives to required subjects.

ior high school students. Nine subjects are taught rather than the six taught in the American curriculum. All students will have studied music history, theory, conducting instrumental and choral performance, and reading and writing of music; hence most Japanese can read music and "possess the historical and theoretical tools to enjoy it."[22] Two and one-third class periods a week are in vocational education. In theory, elective subjects have been increased slightly for seventh and eighth graders, and ninth graders can spend five and one-half hours a week taking them. In fact, however, since the standard number of school hours for taking foreign languages (English) at each of the three grade levels is 105 to 140 minutes, a regrettable lack of time for taking electives at junior high schools exists. Although schools are held accountable by the Ministry of Education for observing minimum requirements, the number of academic courses taken may be much greater because that is a matter left to the discretion of the local school principal, a point that needs to be stressed strongly at the senior high school level.

As a transition between elementary and senior high school, the middle school curriculum focuses both on teaching group life and knowledge. It is characterized by no skipping of grades, mainstreaming, or tracking, except for ninth grade mathematics. By this curriculum students experience both the severe academic pressure of passing entrance examinations for entering ranked high schools, controlled education, and the greater expectations to learn hierarchy and behavior appropriate to group life.

The New 1994 Senior High School Curriculum

At the senior high school level there are three curricular courses: academic, specialized (vocational), and comprehensive.[23] Table 7.4 lists the required curriculum for senior high school students.

Four points can be made about the academic high school curriculum. First, no life adjustment courses are offered; available elective courses are severely limited to traditional courses related to entrance examinations. Second, with the exception of classes in home economics for girls and boys, no courses are truly vocational in nature. Third, a literary or a science preference can be elected by students in their junior year. For example, literary students will take four credits of World History A, four credits of Japanese Language 1, and three credits of Math, Physics, Biology, and English 1. Fourth, science and literary majors will be able to exercise slightly more choice than before because of more diversification. The Education Ministry's survey of senior high schools in 1994 showed that 61 percent of them were offering forty or more subjects, an increase from 26.7 percent in 1992.[24] As a result, literary students may select optional courses in Japanese language; science majors may choose from several different courses within math and science. All schools must teach in sequence the basic content of Math 1, 2, and 3, and they may also select and teach topics from Math A, B, and C. More than one course in a subject area may be elected in the same school year. Greater emphasis is to be placed on "thinking skills," use of computers, and recognition of differing students' ability.[25]

In fact, because the new academic curriculum is only slightly more individualized than before, it fails to achieve individuality. Its strength, however, is that it is far more demanding than 80 percent of American students will face. Academic-track students who choose the literary option still are required to study four units (three years) each of science and math; students who choose the science and math curriculum option will take a minimum of four units in integral and differential calculus, probability and statistics, and physics and chemistry.[26] All Japanese tenth grade students must take Science I, an integrated, general science course for four credit hours. A larger percentage of Japanese students (primarily those who elect the science option) than American students will take physics (25 versus 16%), chemistry (42 versus 35%), biology, and earth science in the eleventh and twelfth grades. International tests demonstrate that at both the elementary and secondary levels Japanese teachers are more effective in teaching science process skills, logical thinking, and in achieving smaller differences in science knowledge between males and females than in the United States.[27] The cumulative result is to develop a greater sensitivity to nature.

The level of math prior to high school in Japanese schools far exceeds that in American schools. Duke contends that a Japanese sixth or seventh grader studies mathematics at a level commensurate with a ninth grader in the United States.[28] Bruce Vogeli found that for most American students in junior high school, math courses were merely a review of elementary school arithmetic, but that those students in the fast track (approximately 15%) were working at almost the same level as the Japanese students and at grade nine were already studying basic algebra and geometry. Geometry usually is studied by American high school juniors. In the Math 1 course that must be taken by all Japanese students, quadratic functions, geometry, and measurement, and counting methods of cases and probability are taught.[29]

Japanese mathematics education goals are more comprehensive than at most American schools. They are to (a) provide necessary knowledge for other subjects such as science and the social sciences, where advanced mathematical knowledge and skills are considered essential; (b) teach all students to learn mathematical thinking because math is believed to teach a logical and systematic thinking process; and (c) cultivate a system of reasoning that maximizes the accuracy of conclusions reached.[30]

Vocational or Specialized Schools

Approximately 25 percent of Japanese high schools are vocational schools. They are low status and attract primarily the bottom 25 percent of junior high school students. Nonetheless, students are expected to take three years of English, three years of Japanese, three years of social studies, and two years each of science and math courses—a more demanding program than that required in most of our public schools for all but the top 25 percent. Students study mathematics at least nine hours a week, as well as health, physical education, homeroom, club activities, physical education, home economics, and music or art.[31] The Ministry of Education attempted to prevent the curriculum from being too academic by explicitly stipulating that in vocational schools at least thirty of the required eighty high school credits must be obtained in vocational or specialized subjects. Even in highly specialized vocational schools a student may select only a maximum of forty-five vocational credits from the total of eighty credits required.

As a result of reforms begun in the 1980s there are now 224 vocational schools engaged in new, distinctive programs covering such areas as biotechnology, information technology, electronic mechanics, and international economics. Another seventy-four schools are planning to offer similar specialized

Table 7.4
**New High School Curriculum for the Academic School Course
and the Standard Number of Credits for Each Subject**

Subject areas	Subjects	Credits
Japanese Language	Japanese Language 1 (a)	4
Required: a	Japanese Language 2	4
	Japanese Lang. Expression	2
	Contemporary J'se Language	4
	Contemp. J'se Use and Usage	2
	Classics 1	3
	Classics 2	3
	Appreciation of Classics	2
Geography and	World History A (a)	2
History	World History B (b)	4
Required: a *or* b; *and*	Japanese History A (c)	2
c, *or* d, *or* e, *or* f	Japanese History B (d)	4
	Geography A (e)	2
	Geography B (f)	4
Civics	Contemporary Society (a)	4
Required: a; *or* b *and* c	Ethics (b)	2
	Politics and Economics (c)	2
Mathematics	Mathematics 1 (a)	4
Required: a	Mathematics 2	3
	Mathematics 3	3
	Mathematics A	2
	Mathematics B	2
	Mathematics C	2
Science	Integrated Science (a)	4
Required:	Physics 1 A (b)	2
one subject each from	Physics 1 B (b)	4
two subject groups a,	Physics 2	2
b, c, d, or e	Chemistry 1 A (c)	2
	Chemistry 1 B (c)	4
	Chemistry 2	2
	Biology 1 A (d)	2
	Biology 1 B (d)	4
	Biology 2	2
	Earth Science 1 A (e)	2
	Earth Science 1 B (e)	4
	Earth Science 2	2

programs.[32] These are important innovations in offering greater diversity, but it is unlikely that the new programs can recruit students of sufficient ability to benefit greatly. Vocational schools are ranked low and have not been able to attract good students. By emphasizing the basics, even Japan's poorest students achieve a significantly higher performance in math and science than

Table 7.4 (*continued*)

Subject areas	Subjects	Credits
Health and	Physical Education (required)	7–9
Physical Education	Health (required)	2
Art	Music 1 (a)	2
Required: a, *or* b, *or* c,	Music 2	2
or d. Students who	Music 3	2
take further classes	Fine Arts 1 (b)	2
usually continue with	Fine Arts 2	2
the same subject	Fine Arts 3	2
	Crafts Production 1 (c)	2
	Crafts Production 2	2
	Crafts Production 3	2
	Calligraphy 1 (d)	2
	Calligraphy 2	2
	Calligraphy 3	2
Foreign Languages	English 1 (a)	4
Not "required" but all	English 2 (b)	4
usually take a, b, c	Oral Communication A (c)	2
and either d *or* e	Oral Communication B	2
	Oral Communication C	2
	Reading (d)	4
	Writing (e)	4
Home Economics	General Home Economics (a)	4
Required: a, *or* b, *or* c	Home Life Techniques (b)	4
	General Home Life (c)	4

Source: Ministry of Education, Science, and Culture, *Education in Japan 1994: A Graphic Presentation* (Tokyo: Gyosei, 1994), 60–61.

Note: Thirty-five school hours (one school hour lasts fifty minutes) of lessons per school year are counted as one credit. For special activities schools must provide not less than one school hour per week for each of "homeroom" and "club" activities. Student council activities and school events must be given an appropriate allocation of time.

America's bottom 50 percent of students. But except for the new vocational schools, they are too academic, difficult, and standardized.

Comprehensive Course

In modern Japan's educational history the new comprehensive program and comprehensive high school are the first radical departures from the heavy academic emphasis. Ironically, this school restructuring can be viewed as a revival of the Occupation force's effort to create comprehensive schools combining vocational, academic, and elective courses.[33] Professor Nobuo Shimahara is cautiously optimistic that these two structural reforms will offer greater diversity, individualization, and specialization. (I am less enthusiastic.) The discussion in this section is heavily indebted to him.[34]

Comprehensive schools include a very wide assortment of vocational and academic courses. They allow students a choice from among specialized fields such as economics, information science, international studies, foreign languages, arts, math and science, or humanities. They are open to students throughout a given prefecture, and they provide an opportunity to specialize from the junior year. There are now forty-two comprehensive high schools in twenty-three of Japan's forty-three prefectures. They resemble universities by their size, the breadth of offerings, and the specialization they allow. One large comprehensive school high school, Ina Gakuen, allows its 3,300 students to choose one-half of their courses from a curriculum of 164 courses covering seven disciplines. Another public school in Chiba City will allow its 2,100 students to finish all required courses in the sophomore year and choose from other courses within five different specializations.[35]

In contrast to the experimental comprehensive schools that began in the 1980s, the comprehensive programs are a product of four reports by the Central Council of Education from 1991 through 1993. Schools adopting comprehensive programs are expected to synthesize academic and vocational curricula to link academic work to future career goals (whether that means college or immediate employment after graduation), offer a broad variety of courses, offer a credit system allowing students to graduate on the basis of credits taken (eighty) rather than a fixed number of years and required courses, and, at least in theory, collaborate with other schools to allow students to earn credits from other schools. Significantly, comprehensive programs select students on the basis of interviews, recommendations, and school reports rather than relying primarily on entrance examinations. Comprehensive programs include minimum common course requirements for all students, clusters of elective courses covering such diverse areas as industrial management, biotechnology, art and culture, regional development, and optional studies, and three common fields: industrial society and human life, information technology, and independent study of selected problems. According to Shimahara, "This program would meet needs of a large proportion of students" because 30 to 35 percent of all high school students currently attending academic high schools end up seeking employment after graduation and about 10 percent of vocational students hope to attend college."[36] Fourteen high schools in as many prefectures began comprehensive programs in 1994 and 1995; all prefectures are currently planning comprehensive programs.

These changes potentially hold great promise for individualizing the curriculum for a diverse high school student body. Students attending them could receive a quality education. But very few of Japan's 4,181 public high schools are adopting the comprehensive programs because most high school principals, parents, and college-bound students are not enthusiastic about them. Most of the top 35 to 40 percent of students will not choose the new comprehensive schools because school ranking and university entrance examinations will discourage them. On the advice of their parents and teachers, students will choose highly ranked schools.

SYSTEMATIZED, SEQUENTIAL, AND PRIORITIZED LEARNING

In Japan every parent can find out what a grade level and subject's educational content will be by examining the systematic and sequential national courses of study for each subject. The merit of this type of curriculum is that it requires teachers to cover a specified level of concepts, problems, learning steps, and content within a specified amount of time for each subject. For an example of systematic education, let us look at the teaching of the Japanese language to elementary school children. They must learn 76 Chinese characters in grade 1, 145 in grade 2, 195 in grade 3, 195 in grade 4, 195 in grade 5, and 190 in grade 6. By the time students graduate from junior high school they must know approximately 1900 characters. Teachers are guided by the courses of study to help students master them. Curriculum priority requires Japanese language to be studied 50 percent longer than any other subject for the first four grades; thereafter, no other subject is stressed more in terms of time.[37]

Several studies over the last decade are demonstrating the success of the more scientific nature of the Japanese curriculum. The Japanese curriculum is based on subject prioritization; the American one on the assumption that one subject is as good as another. Japanese elementary school students will study mathematics twice as many hours a week as American students. Art, music, home economics, physical education, and moral education at all levels are offered only one to three times a week. Japanese secondary students will take ten to eleven courses a week per semester, but some courses will meet only one to three times a week.[38] American secondary school students usually will take only five or six courses daily each semester for approximately the same number of hours a week. At larger schools where more scheduling flexibility and a longer school day may exist, ambitious students can take six to seven courses a semester, but each subject will be studied approximately equally in terms of time. For many secondary students there is less sequential building on skills and learning, and less indication that any courses in the curriculum or courses within a discipline have academic priority over others. American students trying to satisfy the English requirement in some schools can elect courses from a smorgasbord of courses ranging from Remedial English and Applied Communications to Honors English, Science Fiction, Business English, and Shakespeare.

Two separate international studies of mathematics and science achievement by Husen (1967) and Comber and Keeves (1973) were based on an international panel's judgment of what should be taught to thirteen-year-olds in math and fourteen-year-olds in science. Teachers in fifteen countries were then asked to determine how much of this content was covered in their syllabi. Japan had the highest index score for science (63.1) and second highest for mathematics (296), but the United States was second from the bottom in math and 98 points behind Japan in science.[39] The TIMSS revealed that the five topics most emphasized by American eighth grade math teachers accounted for less than 50 percent of the teaching year; however, key topics occupied 75 percent of the school year's lessons in Japan and as many as one-third of American seniors were not taking mathematics, and nearly half were not taking any science in the same study.[40] Students in most countries studied between two or three hours a day, but in America, students studied less than one hour a day. TIMSS also showed that a Japanese seventh-grade math textbook had a six-week long chapter on the algebraic concept of variables, but the American curriculum allocated two- to three-day lessons on the concept during the elementary years, and delayed thorough discussion of the topic until the eleventh grade. Most amazingly, the TIMSS study showed that American eighth graders spent 143 hours studying math, but Japanese students spent only 117 hours and their teachers gave less homework. The higher qualitative performance of Japanese students is related to two important facts. Japanese students spend 80 percent of their lessons on developing math concepts, while American teachers spend 80 percent of their time stating math concepts, but only 20 percent developing them. Seventy-eight percent of Japanese eighth grade students are in classes where for "most of every lesson" they "work together as a class"; and the teacher teaches the whole class, compared to 49 percent of American students. Somewhat similar statistics prevail for science.[41] Nancy Whitman noted that Japanese teachers spent more than 90 percent of the time with students as a class. By contrast, Stevenson and Stigler observed that American elementary teachers were the leaders of pupils' activity only 51 percent of the time, and that "no one was leading instruction 9 percent of the time in Taiwan, 26 percent of the time in Japan, and an astonishing 51 percent of the time in the United States."[42]

Independent content analysis of Japanese and American mathematics textbooks by Whitman, Stevenson's research team, and TIMSS analysis demonstrates conclusively that Japanese textbooks are more systematized, sequential, and methodologically sound. Their conclusions can be roughly applied to textbooks for other subjects. Japanese textbooks

1. Are less than half the length of American textbooks but introduce many more concepts—and at least a year earlier. This methodology allows students greater opportunities for practice.
2. Are more abstract and less personalized, that is, they do not provide much information discussing the everyday world or biographies of famous mathematicians.
3. Assume teacher competence will provide elaboration and supplementary materials to make concepts understood. They engage children's active participation in the derivation and development of mathematical concepts.

4. Are more complex. They build rapidly from simple problems to more difficult ones and include problems that only a few students will be able to answer. American textbooks taught too many math and science concepts and did so too superficially.

5. Contain no answer books, few drills, exercises, or examples.

6. Obtain children's active participation in the mastery of understanding concepts by reading and inferring information from graphs, charts, and tables and requiring them to actively bridge gaps between steps in an argument.[43]

Other characteristics of American textbook and curricular process have been noted by analysts of all subjects. There is a greater emphasis upon repetition and review. Topics reappear in successive years at more and more advanced levels. Stevenson and Bartsch criticized this methodology as an inefficient "spiral" approach. In the contrasting "concentric" Japanese curriculum, "there is an ever-increasing expansion of knowledge that is dependent upon, but not repetitive of what has been taught earlier."[44] They concluded on the basis of the above findings that many American teachers are overwhelmed by the length of textbooks and assume that perfunctory attention to some concepts is acceptable because they will be taught again at a later grade. Moreover, textbook writers hold lower expectations of students' ability to handle difficult concepts and to work independently in solving problems.

America's decentralized educational system makes schools too responsive to local prejudices and vagaries. Textbooks and educational content suffer from special interest groups' censorship in some states and communities. Because Christian fundamentalists or very conservative political pressure groups are politically active, some schools still do not teach about evolution, communism, or sex education. Libraries either do not buy books believed to be morally offensive, or do not place them on open shelves. Over the last forty years factual content, analysis, and accuracy in American history and social studies textbooks steadily decreased. Simple graphs, pictures, and cartoons abound, but add little depth and sophistication.[45] Social studies textbooks at all school levels offer factual content that is less difficult and accurate and more politically and religiously safe than thirty years ago.[46] Recently, however, some improvement has occurred.[47]

Stevenson and Stigler's international team have spent more than eighteen years in comparing Asian and American elementary schools. They learned from their survey of Chinese and Japanese teachers that the most important attributes for a good teacher were the ability to explain things clearly and possessing enthusiasm. For American teachers the emphasis was on sensitivity to the needs and personality characteristics of individual children and having enthusiasm and patience.[48] Although there is much drill and rote learning, especially at the secondary level, Japanese elementary school pupils and secondary school math and science students do not learn only by painful rote. They also learn by inquiry, creating, and sharing shapes, models, natural objects, and solutions to problems with other students; by developing flexibility in mathematical thinking; and, very important, by the teacher addressing the lesson to the whole class rather than individual students.

An Asian lesson is also more coherent. Teachers move through an introduction, a consistent theme, and a conclusion more skillfully than their American counterparts. They also introduce new activities to achieve mastery of a unit or problem rather than skipping to new units before mastery has been accomplished (and then returning to them repeatedly in the same year or in later classes). Stevenson and Stigler reported that some Minneapolis teachers spent 40 percent of their time teaching mathematics, but others were never observed teaching it during twenty class observations. Japanese teachers often develop a solution to only one problem rather than many, avoid the American practice of long seatwork at the end of the period in favor of short, frequent periods of seatwork, and hold discussion and lesson evaluations after each period of seatwork to make sure that all students have understood the exercise. The same authors noted that seatwork for American fifth graders was never evaluated or discussed during 48 percent of lessons, this figure is less than 3 percent for Japanese classes.[49]

Japanese mathematics teachers focus first on interpreting and defining a concrete problem. Then they present ways it can be solved by mathematical notation. They usually do not define terms and state rules immediately (as American teachers do) before the students have experienced concrete problems. For example, only after students had experienced fractions by concrete representations did teachers define terms, state rules and use the words "fractions," "numerators," and "denominators." At that point Asian teachers are more likely to discuss math concepts with their students.[50] Similarly, Japanese elementary school teachers asked questions to stimulate thought, while Americans asked to get answers. Because of the entrance examinations, however, the opposite is more common in Japanese secondary schools.

The Japanese curriculum works as hard to teach positive attitudes toward learning as teaching content. Catherine C. Lewis thought a remarkable feature of the official Course of Study for Elementary Schools in Japan is the amount of pedagogical emphasis on developing good attitudes rather than just performance, fostering attention on process, and nurturing internal motivation to study and to understand. Japanese teachers think the American emphasis upon external rewards, punishments, and evaluation rather than children's identification and charting of progress on individual goals undermines children's intrinsic motivation and creativity.[51]

Separate studies by David Berliner and the Stevenson team demonstrate a marked difference in the length of time American elementary teachers devote to each subject. The Stevenson team noted that "children in one-third of the American classrooms spent less than 10 percent of their time on mathematics; at the fifth grade, children in three classrooms were *never* seen engaged in mathematics during the many days observers were present."[52] First-grade Minneapolis students spent over 50 percent of their class time in reading and

15 percent in math; fifth graders spent 42 percent of their time studying reading and only 18 percent of their time studying math. Even though reading is the most emphasized subject in the Japanese elementary school curriculum, Sendai first grade teachers only spent 38 percent of their time studying reading and 25 percent on math. At the fifth-grade level Japanese students spent a more balanced 24 and 23 minutes each for the two subjects. Some Minneapolis teachers spent 40 or 50 minutes teaching reading; others devoted three to four times that much to the subject. Some teachers taught no fractions, but others devoted thirty-two hours to them. Berliner was so critical of the lack of systematized learning that he wrote critically, "What is seen in classrooms more often resembles baby sitting than it does education."[53]

THE AMERICAN DIVERSIFIED CURRICULUM

Although American high schools for the academic track have moved away from a curriculum that in 1983 was almost 50 percent elective, sufficient mastery of the basics does not occur; many courses still remain elective and lack academic rigor.[54] State and local standards vary from high to low. National curriculum standards do not exist beyond the 1987 James Madison High School curriculum, offered as a model by the U.S. Department of Education.

From the American point of view, schools in a democracy should offer a comprehensive curriculum that serves *all* students needs, interests, and abilities. It should also be innovative and responsible to local needs and teachers' special competencies. These are good ideals when not carried to excess. To achieve them, middle to large American high schools have three tracks: academic, general, and vocational.

Academic Track

The academic track prepares 43 percent of students for college through requiring a large number of traditional academic courses each year.[55] In contrast with Japanese college-bound students, however, American students will usually take a full year or semester of practical courses such as typing, noncomputating computer science, manual education (primarily boys), home economics (primarily girls), and many elective courses corresponding to their academic, avocational, or vocational interests.[56]

General Track

The general track is for the approximately 45.3 percent of students who either do not plan on or are undecided about attending college.[57] Students in this track generally will take a large number of nonacademic elective courses, only one year of required science and mathematics, one solid course in English and history, usually U.S. History, and no foreign language.

The availability of the general track demonstrates three markedly different attitudes. First, most Japanese children are subjected to a college preparatory curriculum to master the basics. Second, Japanese students do not delay a decision to attend a university until their junior or senior year or after graduation. Third, the American curriculum mistakenly assumes students will make mature choices to develop their own long-range needs and identities. The last two assumptions are unrealistic.

Vocational Track

The vocational track offers commercial, industrial, and agricultural courses to the 11.7 percent of students who plan a working career immediately upon graduation from high school. Vocational student enrollment has declined 15 percent since 1962. Most of them have selected the general track. Only 20 percent of students in the vocational track in 1987 took a geometry course, compared to 80 percent of students in the academic track. And even though biology and chemistry might make them more marketable, only 4 percent of them took such a science sequence, as compared with 66 percent in the academic program.[58]

The vocational track has been strongly criticized on different aspects by many authors since 1983. Recent scholarship maintains that vocational education does not improve students' long-term employment prospects.[59] A California study concluded that "on the whole, vocational classes as currently offered . . . are not demonstrably effective in helping students find jobs after they graduate, or in retaining would-be-dropouts."[60] It also noted that employers complain that vocational track students lack basic skills in reading, writing, and arithmetic and are deficient in attitudes favorable to a solid work ethic. Scholars view many vocational courses as too primitive, outdated, and expensive. Given the state of today's advanced technologies, vocational courses have limited value for the student who wants to find a technical job in industry or to learn a trade. To make the vocational courses truly "relevant" to the technology of the 1990s, schools would have to expend enormous monies on equipment and staff. They also would need to demand a curriculum so rigorous in the sciences and math fields that the current group of students selecting vocational courses would avoid them. Many students over the past fifty years have not taken vocational courses from an overwhelming interest or belief that the courses had career relevance, but rather because they are easy. The dedicated vocational education teachers I knew were interested in high standards for their courses, and they resented being dumping grounds.

Enrollment Trends

From the early 1960s to 1983 a dramatic enrollment shift from the academic to the general track occurred. By 1983, the enrollment ratio in the academic track was 37.9 percent, the general track 35.2 percent, and the vocational track 26.9 percent.[61] Students electing the general track had increased from only 12 percent in 1962. The number of curricula and courses offered at more affluent, medium and larger public high schools had mushroomed dramatically. Schools looked like universities without the rigor. Typically, an urban American high school in 1983 offered 200 different courses.[62] Individual states or communities contributed to this proliferation of courses by mandating several nonacademic courses such as physical education, driver education, health education, consumer education, and practical arts. "Relevant" courses, that is, life-adjustment, vocational, and avocational courses proliferated. Even more shocking, 25 percent of the credits earned by the "general track" students were in remedial English and mathematics, physical and health education, "work–study" programs outside the school, and personnel service and development courses, such as training for adulthood and marriage.[63] These trends were major reasons for the declining performance of American high school students.

Enrollment trends since 1983 are a mixed bag. The bad news is that the percentage of high school seniors in the general track increased to 45.3 percent in 1992. Furthermore, 48.9 percent of black, 56.4 of Hispanic, 40.3 of Asian, and 60.8 percent of Native Americans, the very groups that *should* be challenging the academic track in larger numbers, were choosing the general track. Much more encouraging is the increase in high school graduates electing the more demanding "New Basics" academic program recommended by *A Nation At Risk*—from 12.1 to 23.3 percent between 1982 and 1992.[64] If foreign languages are dropped from the New Basics, 29.4 percent of high school graduates were enrolled—up sharply from 21 percent in 1982, and if computer science is dropped the increase from 1982 to 1992 was 12.7 to 46.8 percent respectively. The average number of Carnegie units earned by public high school graduates had increased from 21.44 in 1982 to 23.76 in 1992.[65] The biggest increase in credits occurred in foreign languages, science, and mathematics, especially in the "algebra or higher" category. However, students have not significantly increased their enrollments in the more difficult science subjects of chemistry and physics.[66]

Perspective on this improved performance is necessary because there has not been a significant increase in actual academic performance. More basic courses do not automatically mean higher academic performance if the same poor attitudes and practices are continued. Ensuring that students master a higher level of content in core courses is more fundamental. If the new version of the ACT introduced in 1990 is adjusted for estimated average composite scores, the ACT test score of 18.4 for 1982 had risen only to 20.6 in 1992.[67] In fact, the mean SAT verbal score for college bound seniors has dropped from 453 in 1972 to 423 in 1994, and the math score from 484 to 479. The composite score of the SAT test for college-bound seniors rose a mere 9 points from 893 in 1983 to 904 in 1994.[68]

Individualized Curriculum Offerings

Most large American public schools go beyond academic, general, and vocational tracks by offering an honors track of demanding courses for the highly motivated student and a special education track for the physically and mentally handicapped, practices Japanese schools should not duplicate. But because the former go to excess, Powell, Farrar, and Cohen aptly labeled public schools of medium to large size as "shopping malls" where student–customers may avoid courses, browse, hang out, sample, or choose whatever they might like to study in a variety of shops (curricula).[69] The proprietors (administrators and teachers) attempt to woo students into classes and curriculum with a variety of courses and showmanship. The "shopping mall" high school can be divided into four curricula: horizontal, vertical, extracurriculum, and services curriculum. The horizontal curriculum offers everything from "Honors" and "Advanced Placement" courses at a sophisticated level in every academic subject such as environmental studies, ethnic studies, and psychology; life adjustment courses; recreation-oriented courses such as photography and weight lifting; interest courses designed for special groups such as Great American Women Authors, business education courses, guitar and glass making; and special education courses.

The vertical curriculum provides a variety of courses within each subject area. Hence in mathematics such courses as Remedial Algebra, Introductory Algebra, General or Regular Algebra, Accelerated Algebra, Advanced Placement Algebra, and Honors Algebra prevail. If properly taught all these courses can be rigorous, but students know which subjects and teachers are easy and which ones to avoid. Even if they plan to attend college, some may feel it does not matter what courses in math or English they take, but only that they satisfy the colleges' minimum requirements for a certain subject. A course on "comic books as literature" may carry the same credit as one on nineteenth-century English literature.[70] Furthermore, courses may have the same title, but content may vary according to teachers' standards and conformity to the proscribed content of state and district's courses of study.

America's best students in the postwar period have greatly benefited from schools' efforts to challenge them, but for most students, the proliferation of practical courses has produced a watered-down curriculum. On the plus side, U.S. schools could proudly note that by 1961 enrollments in Honors English had reached 2,381 courses in 1961, and 7 percent of students were electing programs for the gifted and talented. "College-level English" courses had increased from 1,450 in 1949 to more than 9,000 courses in 1961.[71] On the debit side, 11 percent of students were taking remedial reading in 1991 and 7 percent remedial mathematics in 1992.[72] Worse, many schools gave them the same credit as required courses.[73]

The same leveling-down trend could be seen in the third American curriculum, the extracurriculum or cocurriculum. Progressive educators conceived of it as a noncredit-bearing program to meet students' interests outside the curriculum. Administrators regard extracurriculum as important for retaining students and for obtaining community support. In Japan, extracurricular activities thrive only as true noncredit club activities geared to students' interests. In America, however, the extracurricular program now grants academic credit for courses such as band, debate, yearbook, student council, and journalism. Busy teacher–advisors of these activities now act as a lobbying group to preserve these credit-bearing courses in order to make student recruitment easier.[74]

The fourth curriculum is the services curriculum, the "fastest growing component of educational variety" in the 1970–1983 period.[75] In 1991, 8.81 percent of all public school students were enrolled in diagnostic and prescriptive courses compared to 4.57 percent of private school students.[76] This therapeutic curriculum directly addresses social and psychological problems of students through counseling programs for drug and alcohol education, pregnant teenagers, teenage prostitutes, and unmarried teenage fathers. Hamilton High School became a social service center, with its number of school nurses, guidance counselors, security personnel, and health services directors. Grant wrote, "There were free breakfast and lunch programs for children on welfare, sex education programs, drug counseling, suicide prevention programs, medical advice and counseling for pregnant teenagers, an in-school nursery for children of students, and after-school child care."[77] Grant complained that social service staff disperse the school's objectives because their loyalties often lie outside the school to parent agencies.

Elective courses carry merits and demerits. On the one hand, they meet individual interests and abilities when counselors, administrators, and teachers (and parents and students) use them appropriately to challenge students to achieve their potential. Approximately twenty percent of students will select highly challenging advanced academic courses from a genuine desire for greater knowledge and to improve their chances of gaining admission to selective colleges. On the other hand, elective courses crowd out core academic courses needed to ensure adequate basic student competencies, and may not demand effort.[78]

This diversified curricula and tracking system is a marvel to students from other countries because it answers to so many interests, needs, and abilities. It is a tragedy because it costs too much money, many students take the easiest courses possible, and low academic achievement standards result.

DIFFERING VALUES SHAPING AMERICAN AND JAPANESE CURRICULUM

Permissiveness, Structural Problems, and Academic Neutrality

Current American attitudes demonstrate a search for instant gratification, but learning requires patience, perseverance, effort, and self-discipline; it is not always fun. It becomes interesting once you have memorized the basic steps that provide a plateau from which you can learn more things. Increasingly, students (and adults) give up difficult tasks. Effort, agony, and self-discipline are required to learn, but too many American schools' attitudes are "Here are the courses. Choose what you want. We won't push you. Don't push us."[79] By acquiesing to these attitudes, parents, teachers, and schools are contributing to lower academic standards, but also equally important, to a dangerous weakening of the American character. Viewing this condition, the sociologist Martin Trow wrote, "In no other country is the difference between secondary and higher education as great . . . as . . . in the United States. . . . Public secondary education is among the least successful institutions in American life, whereas our system of higher education is among the most successful."[80] Burton Clark argues that the structural nature of the American secondary public school results in a "bias against excellence."[81]

Relevance

Another disturbing attitude that bedevils America's curriculum is the demand for "relevance." In the late 1960s, schools responded to the charge that they were isolating the students from the real world by becoming more "relevant." Additional pressure on the schools reduced academic programs, the length of the school day, and increased courses or content within already existing courses to emphasize relevance, self-esteem, and self-identity. Courses such as Apartment and Income Properties Management, Consumer Economics, Applied Communication, Driver Education, Search for Self, and Business English were adopted by school boards throughout the nation.

This leads to several questions: What is "relevant"? What contributes most to self-esteem? Do the majority of students really know as teenagers what courses they should pursue to maximize their personal identity? Why should youth be the judge? Do children know that the drills required in memorizing multiplication tables in the third or fourth grade are essential for becoming intelligent adult consumers? Do youth realize that understanding U.S. and World History will make them a better citizen of their own country and of the world, and will provide them with a more objective perspective for making judgments? Do students know that rigorous math and science courses and perseverance in mastering basic skills may be important for preparing for employment and college as well as for developing strength of character? Do elementary and secondary school students know that learning to read and to write well will provide them with leisure enjoyment for the rest of their lives and give them the capacity to communicate their thoughts at work and in personal correspondence? The answers are no! Adults must assume greater responsibility and courage for making choices that are important for students' and society's long-range interests.

Sports and the Extracurriculum

Although I enjoy sports greatly, I believe they are so overemphasized in American schools that they confuse priorities and lower academic expectations. Athletic teams and school bands flourish for a minority of the students and the booster clubs. The majority of students spectate, and academic studies languish. Students want recognition. They get it in sports; they fail to receive it sufficiently in individual academic subjects, art and music, or overall academic performance. Weekly attention is given to the athlete by pep rallies and school and community newspapers, but only once at graduation do ten or fifteen students receive perfunctory recognition for their scholarly achievement.[82]

Japanese schools have not overemphasized interscholastic athletic competition, or male sports over female sports, with the exception of baseball and soccer (primarily a phenomenon connected with a minority of private high schools). They get a much larger number of students to be participants rather than spectators and place much more emphasis upon a balanced program for both boys and girls.[83] The variety of clubs—sometimes fifty at the secondary school level—reflect a much wider range of interests and skills than American schools' extracurricular activities. Very few students (or even parents of athletes) attend major school sporting events because they do not recognize the superiority of any other program to their own. Most gymnasiums' or bleachers' seating capacity will not exceed one hundred.

Japanese school club activities are largely run by students and do not receive financial support. Students raise club money by school festivals, bazaars, and other activities. Large scale, smooth operation of elementary and secondary school and university festivals by students are awe inspiring. The annual Culture Day festival features good plays, debates, musical performances, tea ceremony, and various exhibitions of art and photographs. The record keeping, mutual support, and enthusiasm of the various clubs are amazing. Because clubs are largely administered by the students at the junior high, senior high, and college level, they need not spend a large amount of money on coaches or directors of their athletic, drama, or music programs. If American schools borrowed these practices, sports and cultural activities would increase students' sense of responsibility and avoid overemphasis upon professionalized competition.

Japanese elementary and secondary schools also include a category called "Special Activities" as an integral part of the curriculum. Progressive educators in the Occupation forces introduced this concept into Japanese schools via the first Course of Studies in 1947. It specifically stated, "Special Education Activities should be planned, organized, and carried out by the students themselves. . . . Through these activities, students learn how to live a democratic life and enhance their citizenship." Although Special Activities have not sufficiently achieved the latter goal, they have been more successful in attaining the former objective in Japan than in the United States. They include such items as classroom assemblies, student councils, club activities, ceremonial events, study-related events, physical education–related events, pupil guidance, and, at the senior high level, homeroom.[84]

Japanese schools place a much greater emphasis on intramural activities than American schools. One example is the *undo kai*, an all-day sports activity in which all students are required to participate. Parents, teachers, and especially students look forward to this event, in early October and/or late spring. Taped and live music are supplied by the school music club and band. Dignity is added at the opening ceremonies by pep talks to the student body by the principal and heads of the alumni and parent–teachers' associations. Students are generally organized into four groups, and activities center around various running games and a final tug-of-war.

Excessive Interpretation of Democracy

As an ideal, one objective of American elementary and secondary curricula is to produce active, critical citizens, a desirable goal. But other goals to diversify education to fit every need, interest, and ability; to aid each student's search for self-identity, self-esteem, and growth; and to respond to every pressure and special interest group and societal need all are an excessive abuse of curriculum. Fundamentalist religious groups want creationism taught; ethnic and minority groups want their achievements extolled; African Americans want courses on black history; chambers of commerce want content extolling capitalism. If society has problems with juvenile delinquency, traffic casualties, divorces and single families, sex, or use of drugs, schools are expected to offer units or courses on all these problems. The results are a curriculum lacking rigor, coherence, and priorities.

Pragmatism and Progressive Education

Pragmatism is a way of thinking influenced by the American frontier experience, where a person's ability to create practical solutions to cope with a difficult life were valued. For the pragmatist, the ultimate test of any idea, institution, or product is how well it works. Historically, Americans have sought immediate results from an idea or an institution. Americans also tend to revere most highly those who produce inventions of practical utility. Today, many students avoid modern foreign languages, music, art, world history, and advanced studies in science and mathematics because they do not see immediate, practical payoffs.

Two famous philosophers of pragmatism were William James (1842–1910) and John Dewey (1859–1952). Dewey's Progressive Educational philosophy dominated American educational thought and practice from 1930 to 1960. It is painful to criticize because of its laudable emphasis on democracy and insights on child growth. Dewey placed emphasis on the concept that children "learn by doing."[85] A "good" teacher worked closely as a facilitator with students through functional-unit activities to encourage their socialization, effective living, and active citizenship. Dewey thought education should focus more on the present to play a reconstructive role in changing society.[86]

Dewey's disciples exaggerated his thoughts; they were less interested in social reform. They saw the child as a social animal who has no real existence by himself. Educators should *adjust* the individual to his society rather than changing it.[87] They considered traditional educators to be old-fashioned, unscientific, and authoritarian and held a low regard for traditional academic subjects, drill, rote learning, and competition for grades. Later, progressive educators emphasized the joy of education, not its effort, and made children's self-esteem and self-identity the ultimate standards of children.

Progressive educators thought students should be evaluated on the basis of their IQ, family background, cooperation on group projects, and by their own self-evaluation of how well they realized their own potential rather than report cards. Pushing children beyond their level was thought to produce undesirable frustrations and overachieving that was psychologically harmful. The more useful a subject, the greater its superiority over traditional academic subjects.[88] By its romantic idealism, excessive child-centered focus, and slighting of academics, progressive education contributed to a neglect of excellence, rigorous standards, and effort.[89]

Utilitarianism

Utilitarianism is a major influence shaping and bloating the American curriculum.[90] Ironically, one of the latest examples of utilitarian education comes from Boyer. In addition to recommending a common core of academic courses to occupy about half a student's study load during the last two years of high school, he advocated that the other half be a program of elective clusters. One group of clusters would include five or six courses of advanced study in selected academic subject areas, a strong encouragement of more academic rigor. But other students could choose from an elective cluster of five or six subjects related to career options such as health services, computers, and office management.[91] Boyer's proposal has great merit, but only if the preceding ten years of school have been qualitative. It resembles Japan's new comprehensive schools and course.

Extreme Individualism

In Chapter 4, I discussed the benefits for Japanese schools of adopting individualism selectively, but in Chapter 6, I examined briefly some negative aspects of its excessive implementation on American schools. Here again I want to stress the negative aspects of it when applied excessively to the American curriculum. Two recent studies of American and Japanese school practices demonstrate that in American schools, because of teacher individualism, complacent school districts, and independent textbook publishers' practices, teachers skip topics and whole chapters of textbooks and allocate time for individual subjects according to whim and individual strengths.[92]

CONCLUSION

The American school curriculum suffers from a lack of clarity regarding goals and realistic view of students. This lack of focus reflects the fundamental ambiguity in American thought over the relationship between the individual and society. Because of sentimental and permissive views about the nature of students, the curriculum overemphasizes development of individual identity, growth, and self-esteem. This approach neglects a deep consideration of educational and ethical standards that take into account both children's and society's long-range interests. It needs to be emphasized that most elementary and secondary students have only a limited idea of their future needs and the future handicap they will suffer from if they are not diligent and persevering. They need greater adult guidance and more rigorous standards.

More core courses and structural and curricular reforms are not deep-seated solutions to reducing dropout rates, raising academic achievement, and shaping character. The crucial measurements are how much classroom time is devoted to learning, how much academic achievement teachers will demand, and how much rigor parents will support.

Although some experts on Japanese elementary education have come to the conclusion that tracking is not desirable because of the greater losses than gains, I think it is desirable that at least one core subject in American junior and senior high schools—other than Advance Placement and Honors courses—should be grouped according to student aptitude, ability, and zeal. Utmost care, however, must be exercised to prevent tracking that would work deeply to the disadvantage of minority groups by taking into account students' aptitude, teachers' recommendations, and the student's interest in a given subject. Further, since some students with poor study habits or grade point averages may possess a strong ability in one subject, grouping according to ability means that they will not always be placed in classes of lower level students. Also, the academically gifted will not hide their ability, but rather feel challenged by their peers to excel. If, however, grouping results in a teacher attitude that students in the lesser ability classes can only achieve at a certain level, the experiment should be abandoned forthwith, or teachers should be reassigned.

The curriculum's lack of focus and failure to impart to children basic cultural information in the earliest grades of elementary school led E. D. Hirsch, Jr., to condemn schools for their "fragmented curriculum" and "romantic formalism." He believes current history and social studies textbooks fail to pay attention to transmitting culturally significant information. Hirsch is correct in his belief that "cultural illiteracy" results in African Americans, Hispanic, and whites from low socioeconomic homes scoring significantly lower on standardized achievement tests because they lack the information that more literate Americans share. The loss of cultural literacy lowers their intellectual self-esteem and desire to challenge new materials. He complains that the more incoherent the curriculum becomes, the more literacy has declined even among students from literate families.[93] Hirsch, however, seriously errs in ignoring the importance of learning of the non-Western world for students in the twenty-first century.

In his book, *More Like Us*, James Fallows argued that the virtue of the American educational system over the Japanese "lies in its ability to deal with chaos."[94] He believes the Americans have the better system because it is created to adapt to diversity. Curriculum diversification, however, has been carried to such an extreme at the secondary level to cope with chaos and diversity that education lacks coherence and identity. By pursuing diversity at the expense of greater focus and priorities, American schools lack a clear sense of direction and rigor.

NOTES

1. Richard Lynn, *Educational Achievement in Japan* (Armonk, N.Y.: M. E. Sharpe, 1988), 21. Lynn is in error. Courses of study for each academic subject and grade do not run two-hundred pages.

2. Central Council of Education, *Educational Reforms for a New Age* (Tokyo: Gyosei, 1991), 21–26, 89–96.

3. Japan, Ministry of Education, Science, and Culture (Japan, MESC), *Education in Japan 1994: A Graphic Presentation* (Tokyo: Gyosei, 1994), 58–59.

4. Ezra Vogel, *Japan as Number One: Lessons for America* (Tokyo: Charles E. Tuttle, 1979), 160–161; William K. Cummings, *Education and Equality in Japan* (Princeton, N.J.: Princeton University Press, 1980), 119–129.

5. Joseph J. Tobin, David Y. H. Wu, and Dana H. Davidson, *Preschool in Three Cultures: Japan, China and the United States* (New Haven: Yale University Press, 1989), 190–191.

6. Japan, MESC, *Education in Japan 1994*, 14, 24.

7. Thomas Rohlen, *Japan's High School* (Berkeley and Los Angeles: University of California Press, 1984), 156–167.

8. Nobuo K. Shimahara and Akira Sakai, *Learning to Teach in Two Cultures: Japan and the United States* (New York: Garland, 1985), 68, 84–85. R. D. Hess and Azuma Hitoshi, "Cultural Support for Schooling: Contrasts between Japan and the United States," *Educational Researcher* 20, no. 9: 2–8; Nancy Sato and Milbrey W. McLaughlin, "Context Matters: Teaching in Japan and in the United States," *Phi Delta Kappan* 73, no. 5 (January 1992): 359–366; Catherine C. Lewis, *Educating Hearts and Minds* (Cambridge: Cambridge University Press, 1995), ch. 3; Harold S. Stevenson and James W. Stigler, *The Learning Gap: Why Our Schools Are Failing and What We Can Learn from Chinese and Japanese Education* (New York: Summit, 1992), 144–145.

9. Lewis, *Educating Hearts and Minds*, 32; 45; Stevenson and Stigler, *Learning Gap*, 75–78; Ryoko Tsuneyoshi, *Ningen keisei no Nichi-Bei hikaku* (A comparison of Japanese and American character formation) (Tokyo: Chuo Koron, 1992), 41–48.

10. Shimahara and Sakai, *Learning to Teach*, 27–30.

11. Lois Peak, *Learning to Go to School in Japan* (Berkeley and Los Angeles: University of California Press, 1991), 66.

12. Sho Takakura and Yokuo Murata, *Education in Japan 1989: Teaching Courses and Subjects* (Tsukuba: University of Tsukuba, Institute of Education, 1989), 16; Peak, *Learning in Japan*, 78, 84, 87, 96.

13. Tobin, Wu, and Davidson, *Preschool*, 12–13, 16–18, 56.

14. Stevenson and Stigler, *Learning Gap*, 26, 143, 148.

15. Shimahara and Sakai, *Learning to Teach*, 25, 28–32, 74.

16. J. W. Stigler, S. Y. Lee, G. W. Lucker, and H. W. Stevenson, "Curriculum and Achievement in Mathematics: A Study of Elementary School Children in Japan, Taiwan and the United States," *Journal of Educational Psychology* 74 (1982): 315–322; Harold W. Stevenson and Karen Bartsch, "An Analysis of Japanese and American Textbooks in Mathematics," in *Japanese Educational Productivity*, ed. R. Leestma and H. J. Walberg (Ann Arbor: University of Michigan, 1992), 110–111; Stevenson and Stigler, *Learning Gap*, 140–141.

17. Williard J. Jacobson and Shiekazu Takemura, "Science Education in Japan," in *Japanese Educational Productivity*, ed. R. Leestma and H. J. Walberg (Ann Arbor: University of Michigan, 1992), 139.

18. Stevenson and Stigler, *Learning Gap*, 186.

19. "Betrayal in California," *The New York Times*, 10 February 1997; Charles J. Sykes, *Dumbing Down Our Kids* (New York: St. Martin's Press, 1995), 101–102.

20. Shimahara and Sakai, *Learning to Teach*, 48–52, 54, 112.

21. Sykes, *Dumbing Down*, 115–117.

22. Leigh Brustein and John Hawkins, "An Analysis of Cognitive, Noncognitive, and Behavioral Characteristics of Students in Japan," in *Japanese Educational Productivity*, ed. R. Leestma and H. J. Walberg (Ann Arbor: University of Michigan, 1992), 217.

23. Japan, Ministry of Education (Japan, MOE), *Outline of Japanese Education 1989* (Tokyo: Government of Japan, 1989), 106–107.

24. "Schools Failing to Cut Classes," *Asahi Evening News*, 25 June 1994.

25. Nancy C. Whitman, "Teaching of Mathematics in Japanese Schools," in *Windows on Japanese Education*, ed. Edward R. Beauchamp (Westport, Conn.: Greenwood Press, 1991), 171–172.

26. Ibid.

27. Jacobson and Takemura, "Science Education," 136–138, 144–147, 150–152, 166.

28. Benjamin Duke, *The Japanese School: Lessons for Industrial America* (New York: Praeger, 1986), 99.

29. Takakura and Murata, *Education in Japan*, 51–60.

30. Japan, MOE, *Outline*, 29–35.

31. Ibid.

32. Nobuo Shimahara, "Restructuring Japanese High Schools: Reforms for Diversity," *Educational Policy* 9, no. 2 (June 1995): 17.

33. Harry Wray, "Significance, Change, and Continuity in Modern Japanese Educational History," *Comparative Education Review* 35, no. 3 (1991): 448–450.

34. Shimahara, "Restructuring Japanese High Schools," 15, 19–21.

35. Fourteen more of such schools will open by 1999. Ibid., 17–18.

36. Ibid., 19–21.

37. Japan, MOE, *Outline*, 27–28. Harold W. Stevenson, Shin-ying Lee, and James Stigler, "Learning to Read Japanese," in *Child Development and Education in Japan*, ed. Harold W. Stevenson, Hiroshi Azuma, and Kenji Hakuta (New York: W. H. Freeman, 1986), 209.

38. Japan, MESC, *Education for Japan, 1989*, 61–63.

39. Lynn, *Educational Achievement*, 98–99; William K. Cummings, "Patterns of Academic Achievement in Japan and the United States," in *Educational Policies in Crisis*, ed. William K. Cummings, Edward R. Beauchamp, Shogo Ichikawa, Victor N. Kobayashi, and Morikazu Ushiogi (Westport, Conn.: Praeger, 1986), 125–131; T. Husen, *International Study of Achievement in Mathematics* (New York: Wiley, 1967); L. C. Comber and J. Keeves, *Science Achievement in Nineteen Countries* (New York: John Wiley & Sons, 1973).

40. Elaine Woo, "Study Points out Shortcoming of Science Education in U.S.," *The Japan Times*, 21 October 1996.

41. U.S. Department of Education, National Center for Education Statistics (U.S. DOE, NESC), *Digest of Education Statistics, 1997* (Washington, D.C.: U.S. Government Printing Office, 1997), 444–445; U.S. Departments of Education, National Center for Education Statistics (U.S. DOE, NCES), *Pursuing Excellence*, ed. Lois Peak (Washington, D.C.: U.S. Government Printing Office, 1996), 10–12, 27, 39, 63–64.

42. Whitman, "Teaching of Mathematics," 155–161, 165–166; Stevenson and Stigler, *Learning Gap*, 145–146, 182.

43. Stevenson and Bartsch, "An Analysis," 100–110; 124–132; Whitman, "Teaching of Mathematics," 155–161; U.S. DOE, NCES, *Pursuing Excellence*, 35–48.

44. Stevenson and Bartsch, "An Analysis," 110.

45. Paul A. Gagnon, *Democracy's Untold Story: What World History Textbooks Neglect* (Washington, D.C.: American Federation of Teachers, 1987), 137; Gilbert T. Sewall, *American History Textbooks: An Assessment of Quality* (New York: Educational Excellence Network, 1987), 72; Frances Fitzgerald, *America Revised: History Schoolbooks in the Twentieth Century* (Boston: Little, Brown, 1979), 213.

46. Diane Ravitch and Chester E. Finn, Jr., *What Do Our 17-Year-Olds Know* (New York: Harper & Row, 1987), 6–8, 55–58, 61; Sewall, *American History*, 7, 132.

47. Harry Wray, "Civics Education in the United States," in Tuk-Chu Chun, ed. *Understanding the World Civic Education, Globalization and the Korean Response* (Seoul: Hak Mun, 1994). The late Judith Huffman's observations were made in commenting on an earlier draft by the author.

48. Stevenson and Stigler, *Learning Gap*, 166–167.

49. Ibid., 149–150, 183.

50. Ibid., 177–185.

51. Catherine C. Lewis, "Creativity in Japanese Education," in *Japanese Educational Productivity*, ed. R. Leestma and H. J. Walberg (Ann Arbor: University of Michigan Press, 1992), 251–252.

52. Stevenson and Stigler, *Learning Gap*, 149–150; Harold W. Stevenson, James W. Stigler, and Shin-yang Lee, "Achievement in Mathematics," in *Child Development and Education in Japan*, ed. Harold W. Stevenson, Hiroshi Azuma, and Kenji Hakuta (New York: W. H. Freeman, 1986) 208.

53. D. C. Berliner, "Effective Classroom Teaching," in *Research on Exemplary Schools*, ed. G. R. Austin and H. Garber (New York: Academic Press, 1985).

54. U.S. DOE, NCES, *Digest 1994*, 132; Chester Finn, Jr., *We Must Take Charge* (New York: Free Press, 1991), 45.

55. U.S. DOE, NCES, *Digest 1994*, 132.

56. Japan, National Commission in Excellence in Education (Japan, NCEE), *A Nation at Risk: The Imperative for Educational Reform* (Washington, D.C.: U.S. Government Printing Office, 1983), 18.

57. U.S. DOE, NCES, *Digest 1994*, 132. General track enrollment in 1982 was 35.2 percent.

58. William Bennett, *American Education: Making It Work* (Washington, D.C.: U.S. Government Printing Office, 1988), 17.

59. U.S. DOE, NCES, *Digest*, 132; Patricia Alberg Graham, *S.O.S.: Sustain Our Schools* (New York: Hill and Wang, 1992), 25–26.

60. Bennett, *Making It Work*, 27–28.

61. U.S. DOE, NCES, *Digest 1994*, 132; Bennett, *Making It Work,* 14; Clifford Adelman, "Devaluation, Diffusion and the College Connection: A Study of High School Transcripts, 1964–1981." Prepared for the Japan, National Commission on Excellence in Education, March 1983, 12–14.

62. Henry J. Perkinson, *The Imperfect Panacea: American Faith in Education, 1865–1990* (New York: McGraw-Hill, 1991), 108–109; Arthur G. Powell, Eleanor Farrar, and David K. Cohen, *The Shopping Mall High School* (Boston: Houghton Mifflin, 1985), 252, 291, 295; Ernest L. Boyer, *High School* (New York: Harper Colophon Books, 1983), 76–78; Rohlen, *Japan's High Schools*, 157; Victor N. Kobayashi, "Japanese and U.S. Curricula Compared," in *Educational Policies in Crisis*, ed. William K. Cummings, Edward R. Beauchamp, Shogo Ichikawa, Victor N. Kobayashi, and Morikazu Ushiogi (Westport, Conn.: Praeger, 1986), 70.

63. U.S. National Commission on Excellence in Education (U.S. NCEE), *A Nation at Risk* (Washington, D.C.: U.S. Government Printing Office, 1983), 8–9, 19–22.

64. U.S. DOE, NCES, *Digest 1992*, 131, 133, 143–147; U.S. Department of Education, National Center for Education Statistics (U.S. DOE, NCES), *Condition of Education 1995* (Washington, D.C.: U.S. Government Printing Office, 1995), 263. Asian students averaged 2.17 Carnegie credits of foreign language compared to a national average of 1.46 in 1987.

65. U.S. DOE, NCES, *Condition 1995*, 78–79, 262, 263.

66. U.S. DOE, NCES, *Digest 1994*, 133.

67. This was only 0.7 percent higher than in 1969. U.S. DOE, NCES, *Digest 1994,* 132.

68. U.S. DOE, NCES, *Condition 1995,* 68–69; U.S. DOE, NCES, *Digest 1994*, 128–133.

69. Powell, Farrar, and Cohen, *Shopping Mall High School*, 8–10, 12–13.

70. Gerald Grant, *The World of Hamilton High* (Cambridge: Harvard University Press, 1988), 86–87.

71. U.S. DOE, NCES, *Condition 1995*, 80.

72. U.S. DOE, NCES, *Digest 1992*, 69; U.S. DOE, NCES, *Digest 1994*, 70.

73. Powell, Farrar, and Cohen, *Shopping Mall High School*, 287–288, 295.

74. Ibid., 138.

75. Ibid., 33.

76. U.S. DOE, NCES, *Digest 1994*, 70.

77. Grant, *Hamilton High*, 65–66.

78. Ibid., 38–39, 67.

79. Powell, Farrar, Cohen, *Shopping Mall High School*, 69–70, 180–182, 191–192; Boyer, *High School*, 33.

80. Martin Trow, "The State of Higher Education in the United States," in *Educational Policies in Crisis*, ed. William K. Cummings, Edward R. Beauchamp, Shogo Ichikawa, Victor N. Kobayashi, and Morikazu Ushiogi (Westport, Conn.: Praeger, 1986), 392.

81. Burton R. Clark, "The High School and the University: What Went Wrong," Part I, *Phi Delta Kappan* 66, no. 6 (1985): 391–397.

82. James Coleman, *Adolescents and the Schools* (New York: Basic Books, 1965), 35.

83. Fifty to 80 percent of junior high and 30 to 50 percent of senior high students participate in various sports or cultural clubs. Takakura and Murata, *Education in Japan*, 98.

84. Ibid., 146.

85. Dianne Ravitch, *The Troubled Crusade: American Education 1945–1980* (New York: Basic Books, 1983), 44–50.

86. Lawrence A. Cremin, *The Transformation of the School: Progressivism in American Education, 1876–1957* (New York: Alfred A. Knopf, 1961), vii–x, 22–28.

87. Ravitch, *Troubled Crusade*, 55, 60–61; Harry Wray, "Shusen chokugo no Nihon ni okeru 'Shakaika' sosetsu no haikei (Problems and controversies in the creation of social studies in occupied Japan)" 1945–1947, *Shakaika kyoiku kenkyu* (The journal of social studies) 52 (1984): 28, 31.

88. A famous 1918 report entitled "The Cardinal Principles of Secondary Education" called upon schools to stress health, citizenship, and worthy home-membership. As an afterthought they added the "command of fundamental processes." Boyer, *High School*, 48, 51; Ravitch, *Troubled Crusade*, 64–66.

89. Japan, NCEE, *A Nation at Risk*, 18–21; Boyer, *High School*, 51; Ravitch, *Troubled Crusade*, 59–72.

90. Boyer, *High School*, 72–73, 57; Arthur Bestor, *Educational Wastelands: The Retreat from Learning in Our Public Schools* (Urbana: University of Illinois Press, 1953), 75.

91. Boyers, *High School*, 85–117.

92. Shimahara and Sakai, *Learning to Teach*, 49, 91, 119; Stevenson and Stigler, *Learning Gap*, 140–141, 150, 182–191.

93. E. D. Hirsch, Jr., *Cultural Literacy* (New York: Vintage, 1987), iii–12, 115, 126.

94. James Fallows, *More Like Us*.

Chapter 8

Conclusion

American education and society are at a crossroads. If there is a chance to prevent further decline of the individual, economic productivity, citizenship, and social order, it lies in society and schools demanding higher intellectual and ethical standards and improved attitudes. Poor schools and poor student performances *will not* disappear by requiring more of the basic subjects and increasing the number of years they are studied, by raising teacher salaries, by lengthening the school year, by reducing classroom numbers, by establishing model schools, or by implementing the use of national examinations. All these actions will help, but poor academic performance will no more disappear by these measures than building new factories, increasing the length of the work week, and improving workers' fringe benefits will fundamentally increase nationwide factory productivity. Within the schools a correction of attitudes toward study, toward effort, and toward a disciplined and good learning climate must be made to accomplish results, just as good attitudes toward work, toward the factory, and toward factory performance are important to raise productivity. Without these student and societal changes in attitudes, national goals will founder and result ultimately in only superficial short-range achievements.

American education must challenge all its students at all levels—preparing its best students for future leadership and its less gifted students for reaching to and beyond their limits and living more productive and self-fulfilling lives. Students should learn the pleasure of having accomplished academic work to the best of their ability. Their characters should be steeled as Japanese students are by the self-discipline, diligence, perseverance, and responsibility necessary to achieve a satisfactory academic performance. The permissive attitudes that an average grade is good enough, the easiest curriculum track is the best choice, and a half-done job is adequate cannot produce good citizens and communities, productive, self-fulfilled individuals, a disciplined society, a vigorous economy, or a strong democracy.

Instead of concerning themselves primarily with correcting the problem of low academic standards and poor attitudes at the high school and university levels, American schools need to undertake annual skill tests from the lowest grades through high school to measure whether a satisfactory performance level has been achieved. If it has not, students must spend an extra month at school. If that expedient still does not achieve the necessary competence, students must repeat the same subject or subjects until they do. Society must make schools more demanding, and quality education for all children a central concern. Some American philanthropies have recognized these needs and are donating resources to correct existing conditions. But altered attitudes and greater effort are much more important than money.

It needs to be underlined, however, that wholesale American adoption of the Japanese secondary schools' practice of frequent objective examinations that sacrifice understanding for memorization is not recommended. Selective adaptation of some Japanese attitudes and practices that I have recommended throughout this book, however, would result in better student academic performance and significant savings that could be used for improving teacher salaries, extending the school year a month, assigning teachers for an eleventh month for such things as in-service workshops and teaching the gifted students and the students who need help achieving competence in the basic skills, development of curriculum and teaching resources, and attendance to take approved summer school courses. By these measures America can raise academic standards and literacy levels.

At the turn of the twenty-first century Japanese and American societal and educational attitudes and practices saddle both countries with serious deficiencies. They undermine the capacity of both nations to provide informed, caring, and active citizens and to maintain orderly and harmonious communities. Constructive societal attitudes infused into the educational system in the past allowed both nations to meet the challenges of the nineteenth and first half of the twentieth century. But today both countries face new challenges, and dealing with them is hindered by obsolete attitudes or good ones carried to extremes.

JAPANESE ATTITUDES CARRIED TO EXTREMES

Modern Japan has been characterized by the goals of protecting its national identity and economic interests, homogeneity, and hierarchical societal attitudes. These goals have led to excessively bureaucratic and centralized controls over education for the purpose of achieving high academic standards and an orderly, harmonious society.[1] Because of the Ministry of Education's bureaucratic and paternalistic attitude that it knows best for the people, and because of its distrust of teachers, local autonomy, and popular initiative, it fails to create independent, private organizations with the power to impose autonomous educational standards and penalties.[2] An elitist leadership's materialistic and utilitarian motivations mean that neither education nor students are ends in themselves, but rather a means to satisfy societal order and to achieve national and economic goals. These objectives and motivations result in a standardization and conformity in the educational system that neglect individual differences and human dignity, slight the cultivation of critical judgment and local autonomy, limit civic education and textbook authors' academic freedom, and frustrate the objective of producing more community-minded and international-minded citizens.

To produce a competent work force modern Japan created entrance examination systems, school ranking, and a centralized, standardized education system for sorting, selecting, and shaping human resources. By 1941, all these measures had produced a major military power. By 1990, they supported an economic giant and a more orderly society than the West can match, but the costs are too great. These preferences have resulted in a distortion of true education and the ranking of individuals not on the basis of their intrinsic dignity and personal excellence, but their success in entering the most prestigious educational institutions and the rank of corporate organization or government bureaucracy that employs them. Even mothers are evaluated on the basis of their children's success in academic achievement.

At the dictate of the state and private industry, schools offer a curriculum that by the secondary school level confuses education with university entry, memorizing massive amounts of subject matter, and answering mock examinations that produce the belief there is only one correct answer to a problem. Because entrance examinations test students in limited subject areas, aesthetic subjects and curriculum diversity suffer, and students learn to become manipulative of the system. With the exception of students seeking recommended status for university entry, most university and college-bound students undertake serious study on only those subjects for which they will sit for examinations. Their focus is narrowly on the goal of getting into the best secondary schools and universities possible to ensure future material goals. In addition, since cram schools and private schools have programmed their educational content to teach courses in the most effective manner, an increasing number of students in metropolitan areas such as Honshu are bypassing public secondary schools in favor of private schools or slight the public schools by giving priority to study at cram schools. Today, approximately 70 percent of secondary students in metropolitan areas are attending cram schools or are being privately tutored at the end of the school day. This process is slowly but surely undermining the public school system. In other areas ambitious public schools eager for higher rank and prestige hold extra classes daily in the morning and afternoon and during vacations to help students pass examinations, and, not so incidentally, to raise the school's prestige. To compensate for the reduced number of school days due to the abolition of two Saturdays a month, many schools at all levels are instituting compensatory classes for a week or more during the short summer vacation.

Such practices have a serious effect on students. First, students tend to evaluate one another on the same materialistic criteria as adult society. Second, many students become politically apathetic and physically harmed by inadequate sleep, and exercise and improper diet; some become stressed, demoralized, self-centered, and lacking in human compassion. Businessmen complain that students lack initiative and creativity and cannot apply knowledge to specific tasks because they are too manually oriented. The attitudes and practices generated by education have contributed to Japan's present economic recession. Students possess a limited knowledge as citizens of Japan's modern foreign policy, Occupation reforms, controversial domestic problems, and alternate lifestyles because the Ministry of Education's textbook authorization system omits or sanitizes shameful historical events and rejects themes that do not conform to orthodox interpretations of the national ethic. Third, fourteen-year-old students' humanity is sacrificed by a selection system that prematurely labels them as "losers" and sorts them into lower-ranking academic, vocational, and night schools; even the "winners" are placed in a curriculum not designed to meet their differing needs, abilities, or interests. Some students then pass on the bullying they experience from controlled education and a seemingly unsympathetic establishment to weaker classmates or underclassmates.

Fourth, other "winners," mainly males, find themselves passively accepting the role that society will expect of them on the completion of their schooling, that of sacrificing their individual preference, leisure, and families to the needs of the corporation, the bureaucratic structure, and national ethic. Boys, an increasing number of whom are from single-parent families, are continually reminded by parents that they have serious responsibilities to study hard to maintain their future family and, eventually, the household. Parents and teachers emphasize the need to avoid risk, narrow their interests, and cram large amounts of factual data so that they may be successful when taking entrance examinations. Some parents counsel against or refuse to allow them to select a college major that will not bring financial security. The harsh reality of such a socialization results in a loss of dreams, a lack of resolution, and academic apathy later at the university level and diminished individual initiative, imagination, and creativity in the business and political sectors. I believe the intensification of pressure on students in current Japan, from the increase of single-parent families, the hell of examination, and secondary school pedagogy, is increasingly making many students, particularly males, cautious, passive, pessimistic, insecure, and indecisive. This tendency is stronger for both males and females at national universities because they must prepare to sit for five difficult examination subjects rather than two or three at private universities.

Female coeds experience their own individual pressure because they must compete in a business environment that discriminates against them, especially those who plan to become career women and working mothers. This handicap challenges them to be slightly stronger and more outgoing, adventurous, decisive, and assertive than males. Females are willing to take greater risks, to study and work abroad, and to interact more freely and openly with foreigners. (Many younger females complain that males are too insecure, too indecisive, and too passive. Males, however, complain that the females are too demanding and too aggressive.) As one example of these gender trends, for the volunteer U.N. training programs in Kenya, in 1995, women applicants outnumbered men three to one, and of the twenty-nine people accepted by 1995, twenty were women. The selection process bypasses many Japanese males because the United Nations seeks persons of vitality, broad vision, individual creativity, and decisive character.[3]

There is a striking paradox here that raises significant questions about current Japanese education and parental rearing. It deserves reflective thought by Japanese concerned about the future direction of Japanese education and society. Does it not seem odd that in spite of the relative absence of pressure on females to study and enter good universities, they develop the more positive qualities noted above? Does it not seem strange that, despite lower societal expectations of them, female students achieve a higher academic performance than boys at all levels of education? Accordingly, would not a relaxation of societal pressures on males create just as good an academic performance and produce more flexible, assertive, and positive youth? Young men and women need more trust from their teachers, parents, and society.

Fostering democratic values and practices suffer in the Japanese educational climate because students have been taught little of their human rights and roles as active citizens. Having experienced limited recognition of their human dignity and individuality, they understand adult life and democracy to mean avoiding conflict and self-interest; enduring discomfort and indignity; and surrendering one's identity to the group or corporate structure for the purpose of order, harmony, efficiency, or profit. The secondary school system's narrow focus on passing entrance examinations means that teachers do not have the time, or students the opportunity, to develop methodologies important to a vibrant democracy such as class discussion, panel discussion, debate, and the testing of individual views by vigorous dialogue.

As a result of mothers' and the Ministry of Education's demands that the schools teach public ethics and character formation to preserve classroom order and to achieve group consciousness, students learn that there is one way to dress, eat, act, sit, and participate in class and society. Middle schools' efforts to achieve order result in potentially damaging confidential teacher evaluations, a rigid system of excessive rules, and the use of upper classmates to enforce student compliance and effective school management. School administrators, feeling pressure from their demanding cultural tasks, learn to be conservative and to protect themselves from criticism and legal liability by imposing rules on correct ways to dress and behave. Authoritarianism, standardization, and rigidity breed conformity, bullying, and inflexibility. Early schools' admirable attention to detail and forms disciplines character and achieves a higher academic and art and music performance for all students, but continued emphasis on these practices by secondary schools produces rigidity, uniformity, and conformity, so much so that many high school students no longer like art and music. Gradually, students learn that conforming to uniformity becomes "easy" and "comfortable"; they complain of an inability to make independent decisions on behavior. Denied their own individuality and humanity by this daily conformity to "correct" forms eventually leads to students internalizing rigid attitudes, and intolerance of their peers' (and foreigners') behavior and of values that deviate from the norm.

National goals of creating order and harmony through groupism result in schools excessively emphasizing values of exclusivity, loyalty, conformity, and shame at the expense of cultivating human dignity, diversity, risk taking, and more internationally minded students. Students are reluctant to assert themselves and to differ with others in class discussion for fear of hurting the other party or of themselves being hurt. When these school practices are combined with the pressures of academic emphasis, entrance examinations, and school ranking, they lead to students' resentment, refusal to attend school, or a search for an alternative school where individuality is recognized. In 1994, the number of primary and junior high school students who were absent from school for thirty consecutive school days or more was about 77,000, the highest number ever recorded by the Ministry of Education. Approximately 270 alternative schools have developed nationwide to serve students who have opted out of the regular school system.[4]

Japan needs active, assertive, risk-taking citizens who have the backbone and independence to judge for themselves when government policies, social fads, business practices, and crass materialism are wrong. By today's education, however, they are ill-equipped to resist uniformity and conformity, to demand a higher ethical performance from politicians, businessmen, and an increasingly corrupt bureaucracy, and to stand up for their rights and beliefs. They (and adult Japanese) do not understand the real significance of the precious value of human dignity, because schools have stressed excessively the attitudes that endurance, self-restraint, submission, and sacrifice of self to transcending group needs are ultimate virtues. A society that fails to value individuality, diversity, assertiveness, and true human dignity when confronted with power, rank, prestige, custom, trends, and age is at the mercy of corporate groups, fads, and arbitrary authority. Individuals only become sheep following the latest collectivist trend.[5]

A newly emerging generation of students demanding more easygoing acceptance of diversity and attitudes is healthy and positive. Such students are demonstrating that they reject the present hothouse educational system and corporate and bureaucratic establishment way of running Japan. For them the end-all-and-be-all of life is not attending a famous university, working in a prestigious corporation or bureaucracy, or sacrificing personal and future family life for the goals of corporate Japan. They want more from life than the uniformity, conformity, stress, and loss of personal and family life from cram schools, entrance examinations, and corporations' dehumanizing pressure. Part of the reason for current youth's interest in volunteerism, mysticism, escapism, hedonism, and cults is the desire to transcend self and materialism for higher ideals. Being corrupted by the affluence of contemporary Japanese society, children surrounded by comforts and bribed by material rewards are enjoying them to the extent that they are less willing to sacrifice than their parents and ancestors were. Whether the Japanese leadership will be more successful than leaders in advanced Western countries have been in motivating students who are increasingly surrounded by affluence to make short-range sacrifices for a better long-range future, remains a moot question. But today's youth are much less motivated by repetitious exhortation of Confucianistic virtues than by their own self-interest.

These new attitudes challenge the nation's ability to create diligent and responsible citizens to shoulder the blue collar, technical, and professional jobs needed to continue Japan's growth and prosperity. Japan's lack of natural resources does mean that Japan will continue to need a competent, hard-working, and imaginative population. Japan does need to diversify its curriculum, relax school rules, and foster greater humanity in the schools, but it must also continue good character formation at all levels to avoid the lack of discipline and order present in American schools and society.

Changes are not likely to happen, however, as long as the upper and upper-middle classes and the well-educated oppose reforms that weaken their present advantages. To achieve fundamental educational reform will require changes in attitudes.

This summary characterization of Japanese education exaggerates Japan's deficiencies and neglects the very positive features I have written about throughout this volume. It is, however, I believe, an accurate picture of the direction in which Japanese education and society are moving. These trends do not bode well for the future of Japanese society, economy, or democracy. To correct them Japan can selectively borrow from the positive attitudes and practices to be found in American society and education and those of other nations. But Japan must be careful not to borrow harmful ones.

AMERICAN ATTITUDES CARRIED TO EXCESS

American education also reflects overriding societal and educational attitudes that have been carried to excess. In the American experience decentralization and a laissez-faire attitude have encouraged experimentation, local autonomy, and fiscal responsibility for schools. But in the last quarter of the twentieth century, it has become increasingly evident that the continuation of such practices produces curriculums that lack focus and prioritization, and such gross differences in fiscal support and academic standards across states and within individual states exist that many children are denied equal educational opportunity. And because America has enjoyed world military power and an affluent standard of life, the attitude of students and society is that Americans need not fret about poor academic performance. These complacent attitudes accompanying decentralization have meant that state boards of education and local school districts fail to produce courses of study and a curriculum at each grade level that will (1) impose upon schools and teachers high minimum standards and adherence by teachers to time schedules designated for each subject; and (2) be based on sequential, systematized, and prioritized content that does not perpetuate the practice of "one subject is as good as another." They must institute standards and procedures for discipline and removal of incompetent teachers as well as those engaged in "teacher–pupil conspiracies" that bargain with students to obtain orderly behavior in exchange for mediocre academic performances.

Though today Americans live in a much more competitive world, many political, business, and education leaders still retain outdated attitudes that human and physical resources are unlimited and that the same old educational attitudes and practices and market economics will result automatically in supplying qualified labor to meet economic and societal demands. State and local governments roughly maintain the same curriculum, teacher recruitment, training, and entry standards, short school day, and nine-month school year of eight decades ago. By the superior practices of paying salaries 10 percent higher than those of civil service workers of the same qualifications and years of service, of providing teachers nearing retirement salaries three times that of beginning teachers, and of offering good retirement benefits, Japan's schools attract and retain good teachers. But America continues to give the molders of its youth inadequate salaries. If Japan's positive steps were taken, teacher associations' and unions' opposition to a ten-month school year for all students and an eleven-month teaching year could be overcome. Studies demonstrate that poor classroom discipline and management result in inadequate time on task and academic achievement.

State legislatures, local school districts, and society should insist on greater emphasis from preschool through high school on good character formation as an end in itself and on the achievement of more orderly classrooms for higher academic achievement. Schools, parents, and society should reduce student disciplinary and academic problems by discouraging premature adult activities and independence. Japanese practices that delay adult behavior and emphasize students' responsibility for their own conduct, cleaning of schools, and for maintaining class order and loyalty should be selectively adapted. Educators must reduce emphasis on aptitude and IQ, because these practices neglect the impact that a good school environment, student effort, and teachers' focus on an entire class can have on student performance.

Cultivation of individualism, independence, and democracy in American schools has been excessively and erroneously interpreted. Democracy is confused with education centered on the least common denominator, permissive college entry standards, compensating remedial math and English courses, and a nonprioritized curriculum that satisfies every pressure group. Democracy and individualism have been interpreted to mean that the individual is the norm, and his or her identity, personal growth, and self-esteem are the ultimate end of all education. But where are the needs of society and the individual's long-range interest? The curriculum has been excessively diversified to meet every student's need, interest, and ability—an absolute impossibility. Furthermore, because every ethnic group wants its uniqueness extolled, insufficient attention is paid to fostering the common values and interests that bind a community and a nation together. The results are division, diffusion, lack of curriculum prioritization, and mediocrity.

Most damaging are the complacent, permissive, and unrealistic attitudes and low expectations that characterize current American society and schools. These attitudes hinder the long-range welfare of students and society and contribute to a total educational outcome that is in the bottom half in almost every subject area in comparative international examination studies among advanced nations. Complacency, superiority, a mediocre work ethic, and low expectations are fed by educators' misleading statistics that indicate to parents that their schools are better than average; it is only other schools that are inferior. The total impact is a learning climate that ignores reality: Today's students live in a more competitive world, and they cannot fulfill their identity unless they develop greater self-discipline, diligence, and perseverance. Japanese parental and teacher expectations are much higher and a greater interest is shown in children's education. For them, a school is a place to learn as well as a place to develop character; it is the duty and the role of students to fulfill these expectations. And students understand it.

American parents and society show limited interest in education and associate the school with a place where youth develop socially and have fun. They show more interest in sports and television and their own lives than in reading to their children, taking them to the library, establishing good TV viewing habits, enforcing study hours, and engaging them in lively discussions. Instead, many parents allow children excessive part-time work and even the purchase of cars at age sixteen. Too much spending money, free time, boredom from lack of achievement, and laxity encourage children to take up smoking, drinking, drugs, and sexual pursuits at an early age because these activities are associated with adulthood; moreover, students lack the tough discipline and negotiating skills with peers to refrain from these activities. If you think Americans don't lack discipline, look around you at the increasing number of parents and youth who are overweight, smoking and drinking too much, taking drugs, and consuming goods beyond their means. If you think Americans have not lost their work ethic, you would be amazed at the differences between McDonald's and other fast-food establishments in America and in Japan. Quick, friendly service, clean tables, and no litter on floors characterize Japan's McDonald's and America's 1960s ones.

A turnaround in American attitudes can only come from dedicated leadership at all levels, public recognition, and rewards for good student performance, for caring students and teachers, and for principals who create a good school climate that fosters academic behavior and character formation. Attitudes must be based on new priorities recognizing excellence of mind and the arts. Instead of presidents who congratulate victorious athletes and individual athletic teams, America needs presidents, governors, mayors, and outstanding civic and cultural leaders who telephone and write to honor students, teachers, and principals at all levels who have distinguished themselves by their academic, artistic, cultural, and service achievements.

To change attitudes and to give greater prestige to scholarship and character, Americans need to send successful African Americans, Hispanics, Asians, Caucasians, and handicapped teachers and children into the schools. The mass media must teach a message both of inspiration and reality. It must discipline itself by deemphasizing the materialistic, sensational, notorious, dysfunctional, and freakish violators of common values and mores. They need to give less attention to the Dennis Rodmans, the Madonnas, and the Howard Sterns. Instead, the mass media should extol the positive virtues of heroes and heroines and ordinary people who, by their actions and sacrifices, make better families and communities, and by their child-rearing practices, create caring children and positive attitudes toward schools, learning, and community. The media need to support unifying values and to honor community and church groups that sustain schools and community.[6]

American policy makers and citizens must have the courage and self-discipline to consider students' and communities' long-range interests, to support priorities needed to overcome educational deficiencies, and to prevent the continued decline in the quality of social life and work ethic.

FINAL REMARKS

I cannot stress too much that the failure of Americans to overcome racist attitudes and to provide true social justice to minorities will prevent effective reform. Minorities that are discriminated against daily will not see any reason for embracing common, unifying American values and correcting negative or indifferent attitudes toward attending school and academic performance. Mine is not an alarmist's call to reactionary methods and values; it is a challenge to Americans to put their individual and collective lives in order by living up to their democratic, humane, and spiritual values.

It is also a warning to the Japanese to avoid complacency as a result of the generally favorable attention they are receiving today for educational achievement. The Japanese have sacrificed much over the last 130 years to achieve a qualitative and quantitative expansion of their educational system. Although they may be proud of these accomplishments, many current educational attitudes and practices are rapidly becoming obsolete as a result of swift domestic and international changes. Given the present affluence of Japanese society, their schools have for the first time in the modern era the luxury and leisure to develop an educational system that will better serve the long-range interests of society and individuals.

Japanese need not adopt American individualism, but they should foster more individualized education and diversity. They can adopt American educational practices to overcome some of the rigidity, standardization, and conformity in their own system and place greater emphasis upon citizenship, diversity, and human dignity to achieve a more democratic, humane society. A failure to create more active, internationally minded, assertive, and positive youth with critical judgment skills will severely limit Japan's ability to cope with pressing local, national, and international needs.

How will Japanese and American societies accomplish the necessary changes? New blue ribbon committees in both societies can help point the way, but what is more important is the creation of citizen groups in every school district, community, and prefecture or state to engage in a year-long grassroots dialogue about what kind of schools and society they really want. Ultimately, it is our role as Japanese and American citizens to fashion the schools and communities we need to give direction to policy makers. That is what democratic citizenship is all about. Our children and the future of our two societies demand such a call to dialogue, action, and shared values.

For the sake of all American and Japanese students I strongly recommend that both societies arrive at a consensus regarding the following:

1. What old cultural and civic values and attitudes should be preserved or adapted and which new ones should be forged and taught? Upon reaching that consensus, a qualitative, academically rigorous morals–civics course should be introduced in the United States and improved in Japan.
2. What should curriculum priorities be?
3. What are the high minimum academic standards our schools should demand?
4. What can parents and the general public do to help teachers and schools improve educational achievement, time on task, character formation, and sense of community?
5. What kind of schools do we need for our students and societies, particularly in the last two years of high school?

Japanese particularly should focus on needs one, two, and five; Americans need to emphasize all five of them. To increase children's humanity and moral judgment, strengthen their character, and create a more vibrant democracy I strongly recommend that Japanese and American schools strengthen the teaching of human rights, civic rights, and moral education.[7] Children need ideals and models; let us give them more. By making the effort to implement these five goals, we shall regenerate our schools, our communities, and ourselves.

The greatest satisfaction that we can have as persons is in working creatively with others to build better schools and better communities. Our children will be the beneficiaries.

Finally, in relation to item five, I believe it is time for both Americans and Japanese to consider the advisability of creating a diversified, comprehensive, and multitrack curriculum for the last two years of secondary school. The present assumption of high school curriculum in both societies, especially Japan, is that most students are planning to attend university. This prioritization exceeds the interests and the abilities of most students. It does not meet their or society's long-range needs. Not everyone has the ability, the desire, or the need to go to a two-year college or a four-year university. Such unrealistic expectations create student frustration, resentment, and a needless loss of self-respect. More important, it denies society skilled electricians, plumbers, carpenters, computer operators, technicians, secretaries, farmers, and unskilled manual laborers who know their work, take pride in it, and receive public recognition for it. Both societies need to give students the recognition they deserve by sending them to neighborhood, comprehensive public schools where they will not feel individual demoralization and social discrimination. Simultaneously, those students who plan on attending a university may benefit from an individualized and diversified curriculum that offers them a greater selection of languages, advanced courses, and specialization.

Japanese students have reached a level of competence in the basic skills for the first ten grades that would allow them to institute immediately a diversified curriculum for career and university-bound students in the last two years of high school. But to prevent those last two years from being wasted and ineffective, the curriculum should be focused, qualitative, and systematic. If the curriculum is as individualized and systematic at all schools as the newest vocational schools and experimental comprehensive schools that I have written about in the previous chapter, Japan could adequately meet students' and societal needs for the twenty-first century.

The transition of Americans to a final two-years-of-school-style curriculum will take at least five years because they have not reached the academic standards nor the discipline of study of Japanese students. America cannot implement a new diversified, comprehensive curriculum at the eleventh grade until schools raise academic standards enough to justify it. American schools need to create a curriculum until the eleventh grade that is rigorous enough in the basic courses to ensure that all students, except the mentally handicapped, achieve competence in the basic skills of reading, writing, computing, science, civics, and mathematics. Such priorities and goals require a longer school year and school day, altered attitudes toward learning and teaching, and persistent effort. Schools and society will promote excellence for all, greater discipline of character, and higher ideals. At that point, and only when societal and students' *long-range interests* are met, American students can enjoy a diversified, individualized curriculum that meets their personal needs, interests, and abilities. Greater humanity, more integrated communities, civic participation, and a more qualitative life will be individuals' and society's rewards.

Low expectations beget uninvolved, bored, disenchanted, and mediocre students. High expectations produce the rewards of involvement and the satisfaction of having achieved something worthwhile. It is in the art of adults giving of themselves to nobler causes that we transcend our narrow concerns of self, and create humanity and community. It is in the act of students extending themselves that they learn the basic skills and character for becoming better citizens and building more orderly, harmonious, and civic-minded communities. The time to start is now. The most important reasons for American and Japanese failure to overcome their educational deficiencies are the harmful attitudes and practices within and outside the schools. To put it bluntly, Americans and Japanese are in need of some attitude adjustment to improve the quality of their schools and society. Are Japanese and Americans capable of rising to the challenges? I optimistically believe so. If they do, future generations will be the winners.

NOTES

1. "Panel Calls on Government to Lighten Up on the Locals," *Asahi Evening News*, 30 March 1996.

2. Editorial, "Complete Educational Reform Requires Full-Time 5-Day Week," *Asahi Evening News*, 1 April 1996.

3. Editorial, "U.N. Volunteer Training Shows What Japan Needs," *Asahi Evening News*, 1 April 1996.

4. Mariko Akamoto, "Alternative Schools Listed," *Asahi Evening News*, 1 April 1996.

5. Hitoshi Abe, Muneyuki Shindo, and Sadafumi Kawato, *The Government and Politics of Japan*, trans. James W. White (Tokyo: University of Tokyo Press, 1994), 233.

6. William Damon, *Greater Expectations: Overcoming the Culture of Indulgence in Our Homes and Schools* (New York: Free Press, 1995), 22–25.

7. Hideharu Tajima, "Moral Education Lacking in Today's Schools," *Asahi Evening News*, 15 April 1996.

Selected Bibliography

Abe, Hitoshi, Muneyuki Shindo, and Sadafumi Kawato. *The Government and Politics of Japan*, translated by James W. White. Tokyo: University of Tokyo Press, 1994.

Allen, Dwight. *Schools for a New Century*. Westport, Conn.: Praeger, 1992.

Amagi, Isao, ed. *Sogo ni mita Nichibei kyoiku no kadai* (Mutually observed tasks of Japanese and American education). Tokyo: Dai Ichi Hoki Shuppan, 1987.

Amano, Ikuo. "The Dilemma of Japanese Education Today." *The East* 86 (January–February 1989).

August, Robert L. "*Yobiko*: Prep Schools for College Entrance in Japan." In *Japanese Educational Productivity*. Edited by R. Leestma and H. J. Walberg. Ann Arbor: University of Michigan Press, 1992.

Azuma, Hiroshi. "Why Study Child Development in Japan?" In *Child Development and Education in Japan*. Edited by Harold W. Stevenson, Hiroshi Azuma, and Kenji Hakuta. New York: W. H. Freeman, 1986.

Beauchamp, Edward R. "The Development of Japanese Educational Policy 1945–1985." In *Windows on Japanese Education*. Edited by Edward R. Beauchamp. Westport, Conn.: Greenwood Press, 1991.

Beauchamp, Edward R., and James M. Vardaman, eds. *Japanese Education since 1945: A Documentary Study*. Armonk, N.Y.: M. E. Sharpe, 1994.

Benjamin, Gail R. *Japanese Lessons*. New York: New York University Press, 1997.

Benjamin, Gail R., and Estelle James. "Public and Private Schools and Educational Opportunity in Japan." In *Japanese Schooling*. Edited by James J. Shields, Jr. University Park: Pennsylvania State University Press, 1989.

Bennett, William. *American Education: Making It Work*. Washington, D.C.: U.S. Government Printing Office, 1988.

Berliner, D. C. "Effective Classroom Teaching." In *Research on Exemplary Schools*. Edited by G. R. Austin and H. Garber. New York: Academic Press, 1985.

Bestor, Arthur. *Educational Wastelands: The Retreat from Learning in Our Public Schools.* Urbana: University of Illinois Press, 1953.

Bishop, John. "Incentives for Learning: Why American High School Students Compare so Poorly to Their Counterparts Overseas." Unpublished paper for the U.S. Department of Labor, Commission on Workforce Quality and Labor Market Efficiency. February 1989.

———. "Is the Test Score Decline Responsible for the Productivity Growth Decline?" *American Economic Review* 79 (March 1989).

Blinco, Priscilla N. "Task Persistence in Japanese Elementary Schools." In *Windows on Japanese Education.* Edited by Edward R. Beauchamp. Westport, Conn.: Greenwood Press, 1991.

Bloom, Alan. *The Closing of the American Mind.* New York: Simon & Schuster, 1987.

Boocock, Sarane Spence. "The Japanese Preschool System." In *Windows on Japanese Education.* Edited by Edward R. Beauchamp. Westport, Conn.: Greenwood Press, 1991.

Boyer, Ernest L. *High School.* New York: Harper Colophon Books, 1983.

Brown, J.H.U., and Jacqueline Comolo. *Educating for Excellence: Improving Quality and Productivity in the 90s.* New York: Auburn House, 1991.

Brustein, Leigh, and John Hawkins. "An Analysis of Cognitive, Noncognitive, and Behavioral Characteristics of Students in Japan." In *Japanese Educational Productivity.* Edited by R. Leestma and H. J. Walberg. Ann Arbor: University of Michigan Press, 1992.

Central Council of Education. *Kongo ni okeru gakko kyoiku no sogoteki kakuju seibi no tame no kihonteki shisaku ni tsuite* (Basic plan for the comprehensive expansion and improvement of school education in the future). Tokyo: Mombusho, 1971.

———. *Educational Reforms for a New Age.* Tokyo: Gyosei, 1991.

Cheyney, Lynne V. *Tyrannical Machines.* Washington, D.C.: National Endowment for the Humanities, 1990.

Chubb, John E., and Terry M. Moe. *Politics, Markets, and America's Schools.* Washington, D.C.: The Brookings Institution, 1990.

Clark, Burton. "The High School and the University: What Went Wrong, Part I." *Phi Delta Kappan* 66, no. 6 (1985).

Coleman, James. *Adolescents and the Schools.* New York: Basic Books, 1965.

Conant, James B. *The American High School Today.* New York: McGraw-Hill, 1959.

Cremin, Lawrence A. *The Transformation of the School: Progressivism in American Education, 1876–1957.* New York: Alfred A. Knopf, 1961.

Cummings, K. William. *Education and Equality in Japan.* Princeton, N.J.: Princeton University Press, 1980.

———. "Patterns of Academic Achievement in Japan and the United States." In *Educational Policies in Crisis.* Edited by William Cummings, Edward R. Beauchamp, Shogo Ichikawa, Victor N. Kobayashi, and Morikazu Ushiogi. Westport, Conn.: Praeger, 1986.

———. "Japan's Science and Engineering Pipeline." In *Windows on Japanese Education.* Edited by Edward R. Beauchamp. Westport, Conn.: Greenwood Press, 1991.

Cutts, Robert L. *An Empire of Schools: Japan's Universities and the Molding of a National Power Elite.* Armonk, N.Y.: M. E. Sharpe, 1997.

Damon, William. *Greater Expectations: Overcoming the Culture of Indulgence in Our Homes and Schools.* New York: Free Press, 1995.

DeCoker, Gary. "Japanese Preschools: Academic or Nonacademic." In *Japanese Schooling*. Edited by James J. Shields, Jr. University Park: Pennsylvania State University Press, 1989.

———. "'Internationalization' in Japan's Elementary School Social Studies Textbooks: First Lessons in Government Ideology." The International Content of Japanese Elementary School Social Studies Textbooks. Unpublished paper presented at the Midwest Japan Seminar, 23 September 1995.

DeVos, George A. "Achievement Orientation, Social Self-Identity, and Japanese Economic Growth." *Asian Survey* 15, no. 12 (1965).

Dore, Ronald. *Education in Tokugawa Japan*. Berkeley and Los Angeles: University of California Press, 1965.

Doyle, Denis P., Bruce S. Cooper, and Roberta Trachtman. *Taking Charge: State Action on School Reform in the 1980s*. Indianapolis, Ind.: Hudson Institute, 1991.

Dozier, Theresa Kneckt. "Restructuring Student and Parent Attitudes: The Next Education Reform." *Paideia* (Winter 1993).

Duke, Benjamin. *Japan's Militant Teachers*. Honolulu: University Press of Hawaii, 1973.

———. *The Japanese School: Lessons for Industrial America*. Westport, Conn.: Praeger, 1986.

———. *Education and Leadership for the Twenty-First Century: Japan, Britain, and America*. Westport, Conn.: Praeger, 1991.

Educational Testing Service. *America's Challenge: Accelerating Academic Achievement: A Summary of Findings from 2 Years of NAEP*. Princeton, N.J.: Educational Testing Service, 1990.

———. *The Civics Report Card*. Washington, D.C.: U.S. Department of Education, 1990.

———. *The Geography Learning of High-School Seniors*. Princeton, N.J.: National Assessment of Educational Progress, 1990.

Enloe, Walter, and Philip Lewin. "The Cooperative Spirit in Japanese Primary Education." *The Educational Forum* 51, no. 3 (Spring 1987).

Fairbank, John K. *The United States and China*. Cambridge: Harvard University Press, 1958.

Fallows, D. "The Lifetime Lessons of Japan's Schools." *Washington Post*, Outlook Section, 9 September 1990.

Feiler, Bruce. *Learning to Bow*. New York: Ticknor and Fields, 1991.

Feistritzer, C. Emily. *Teacher Crisis: Myth or Reality?* Washington, D.C.: National Center for Education Information, 1986.

Finn, Chester E. A., Jr. *We Must Take Charge*. New York: Free Press, 1991.

Fitzgerald, Frances. *America Revised: History Schoolbooks in the Twentieth Century*. Boston: Little, Brown, 1979.

Fleury, Bernard. *Reform of Schooling*. New York: University Press of America, 1995.

Fujimura-Faneslow, Kumiko, and Anne E. Imamura. "The Education of Women in Japan." In *Windows on Japanese Education*. Edited by Edward R. Beauchamp. Westport, Conn.: Greenwood Press, 1991.

Fujita, Mariko. "It's All Mother's Fault: Child Care and the Socialization of Working Mothers in Japan." *The Journal of Japanese Studies* 15, no. 1 (1989).

Fukuzawa, Rebecca Irwin. "The Path to Adulthood: According to Japanese Middle Schools." In *Teaching and Learning in Japan*. Edited by Thomas P. Rohlen and Gerald K. LeTendre. Cambridge: Cambridge University Press, 1996.

Gardner, John. *Excellence*. New York: Norton, 1987.

Goodlad, John. *A Place Called School: Prospect for the Future*. New York: McGraw-Hill, 1984.

Goodman, Roger. *Japan's "International Youth."* Oxford: Oxford University Press, 1990.

Graham, Patricia Alberg. *S.O.S.: Sustain Our Schools*. New York: Hill and Wang, 1992.

Grant, Gerald. *The World of Hamilton High*. Cambridge: Harvard University Press, 1988.

Hall, Ivan Parker. *Mori Arinori*. Cambridge: Harvard University Press, 1973.

Hendry, J. *Becoming Japanese: The World of the Japanese Preschool Child*. Honolulu: University of Hawaii Press, 1986.

Hess, R. D., and Azuma Hitoshi. "Cultural Support for Schooling: Contrasts between Japan and the United States." *Educational Researcher* 2, no. 9 (1991).

Hess, Robert D., Susan Holloway, Teresa McDevith, Hiroshi Azuma, Keiko Kashiwagi, Shigefumi Nagano, Kazuo Miyake, W. Patrick Dickson, Gary Price, and Giyoo Hatano. "Family Influences on School Readiness and Achievement in Japan and the United States: An Overview of a Longitudinal Study." In *Child Development and Education in Japan*. Edited by Harold W. Stevenson, Hiroshi Azuma, and Kenji Hakuta. New York: W. H. Freeman, 1986.

Hirose, T., and T. Hatta. "Reading Disabilities in Modern Japanese Children." *Journal of Research in Reading* 11, no. 2 (1988).

Hirsch, E. D., Jr. *Cultural Literacy*. New York: Vintage Books, 1987.

The Holmes Group. *Tomorrow's Schools*. East Lansing, Mich.: The Holmes Group, 1990.

Horio, Teruhisa. *Educational Thought and Ideology in Modern Japan*, edited and translated by Steven Platzer. Tokyo: University of Tokyo Press, 1988.

Ichikawa, Shogo. "Financing Japanese Education." In *Windows on Japanese Education*. Edited by Edward R. Beauchamp. Westport, Conn.: Greenwood Press, 1991.

————. *Nihon no kyoiku, kyoiku kaikaku no riron to kozo* (Japanese education: The structure and theory of educational reform). Tokyo: Kyoiku Kaihatsu Kenkyujo, 1991.

International Association for the Evaluation of Educational Achievement. *Mathematics and Science Achievement in the Final Year of Secondary School: IEA's Third International Mathematics and Science Study*. By Ina V. S. Mullis, Michael O. Morton, Albert E. Beaton, Eugenia Gonzalez, Dana L. Kelly, and Teresa A. Smith. Boston: Center for Study of Testing, Evaluation, and Educational Policy, Boston College, 1998.

Irvine, Jacqueline Jordan. *Black Students and School Failure: Policies, Practices, and Prescriptions*. Westport, Conn.: Praeger, 1990.

Itzkoff, Seymour. *The Decline of Intelligence in America*. Westport, Conn.: Praeger, 1994.

Jacobson, Willard J., and Shigekozu Takemura. "Science Education in Japan." In *Japanese Educational Productivity*. Edited by R. Leestma and H. J. Walberg. Ann Arbor: University of Michigan Press, 1992.

James, Estelle, and Gail Benjamin. *Public Policy and Private Education in Japan*. London: Macmillan, 1988.

Japan, Ministry of Education. Mombusho kyoiku kaikaku jitchi honbuhen. *Kokusai rikai to kyoryoku no shinten* (The development of international cooperation and understanding). Tokyo: Gyosei, 1988.

Japan, Ministry of Education, Bureau on Elementary and Middle Grades Education. Mombusho shoto chuto kyoikukyoku. *Toko kyohi (futoko) mondai ni tsuite* (On the problem of school phobia [school refusal]). Tokyo: Mombusho, 1992.

Japan, Ministry of Education, Science, and Culture. *Development of Education in Japan, 1981–84.* Report for submission to the 39th session of the International Conference on Education. Tokyo: The Ministry, 1984.

―――. *Outline of Education in Japan 1989.* Tokyo: The Ministry, 1989.

―――. *Japanese Government Policies in Education, Science, and Culture 1991.* Tokyo: The Ministry, 1991.

―――. *Statistical Abstract of Education, Science, and Culture.* Tokyo: The Ministry, 1992.

―――. *Education in Japan 1994: A Graphic Presentation.* Tokyo: Gyosei, 1994.

Japanese Study Group. "Educational Reform in the United States." *A Report of the Japan–United States Cooperative Study on Education in Tokyo,* January 1987.

Kaigo, Tokiomi, and Naka Arata. *Nihon kyokasho taikei kindai hen* (A compilation of Japanese textbooks: Modern edition). Tokyo: Kodansha, 1962.

―――. *Nihon no kyoiku* (Japanese education). Tokyo: Tosho Sensho, 1979.

―――. *Kindai nihon no kyoiku* (Modern Japanese education). Tokyo: Tokyo Shosen, 1983.

Karasawa, Tomitaro. *Kyokasho no rekishi* (A history of textbooks). Tokyo: Sobunsha, 1962.

―――. *Nihon kyoiku shi* (History of Japanese education). Tokyo: Sobunsha, 1962.

Kataoka, T. "Class Management and Student Guidance in Japanese Elementary and Lower Secondary Schools." In *Japanese Educational Productivity.* Edited by R. Leestma and H. J. Walberg. Ann Arbor: University of Michigan Press, 1992.

Kida, Hiroshi. *Sengo kyoiku no tenkai to kadai* (Postwar educational developments and tasks). Tokyo: Kyoiku Kaihatsu Kenkyujo, 1976.

Kobayashi, Victor N. *John Dewey in Japanese Educational Thought.* Ann Arbor: University of Michigan School of Education, 1964.

―――. "Japanese and U.S. Curricula Compared." In *Educational Policies in Crisis.* Edited by William K. Cummings, Edward R. Beauchamp, Shogo Ichikawa, Victor N. Kobayashi, Morikazu Ushiogi. Westport, Conn.: Praeger, 1986.

Kozol, Jonathan. *Illiterate America.* New York: Doubleday, 1985.

―――. *Savage Inequalities.* New York: Crown, 1991.

Kuhlman, Edward L. *Agony in Education.* New York: Bergin & Garvey, 1994.

Lebra, Takie Sugiyama. *Japanese Patterns of Behavior.* Honolulu: University of Hawaii Press, 1976.

―――. *Japanese Women.* Honolulu: University of Hawaii Press, 1984.

LeTendre, Gerald K. "Shido: The Concept of Guidance." In *Teaching and Learning in Japan.* Edited by Thomas Rohlen and Gerald K. LeTendre. Cambridge: Cambridge University Press, 1996.

Lewis, Catherine C. "Cooperation and Control in Japanese Nursery Schools." *Comparative Education Review* 28 (1984).

―――. "Creativity in Japanese Education." In *Japanese Educational Productivity.* Edited by R. Leestma and H. J. Walberg. Ann Arbor: University of Michigan Press, 1992.

―――. *Educating Hearts and Minds.* Cambridge: Cambridge University Press, 1995.

Linicome, Mark. "The Historical Context of Japanese Education to 1945." In *Windows on Japanese Education.* Edited by Edward R. Beauchamp. Westport, Conn.: Greenwood Press, 1991.

Linn, Robert L. *Profile of School Administrators in the U.S.* Washington, D.C.: National Center for Education Information, 1988.

Lynn, Richard. *Educational Achievement in Japan.* Armonk, N.Y.: M. E. Sharpe, 1988.

Marcus, Philip N. "Evidence of Decline in Educational Standards." In *Education on Trial.* Edited by William Johnston. San Francisco: Institute for Contemporary Studies, 1985.

Mortimore, Peter, Pamela Sammons, Louise Stoll, David Lewis, and Russell Ecob. *School Matters.* Berkeley and Los Angeles: University of California Press, 1988.

National Commission on Excellence in Education. *A Nation at Risk: The Imperative for Educational Reform.* Washington, D.C.: U.S. Government Printing Office, 1983.

National Council on Educational Reform. *First Report on Educational Reform.* Tokyo: Government of Japan, 1985.

————. *Second Report on Educational Reform.* Tokyo: Government of Japan, 1986.

————. *Third Report on Educational Reform.* Tokyo: Government of Japan, 1987.

National Research Council. *Everybody Counts: A Report to the Nation on the Future of Mathematics Education.* Washington, D.C.: National Academy Press, 1989.

Odden, Allan. "Class Size and Student Achievement: Research Based Policy Alternatives." *Education Evaluation and Policy Analysis* 12, no. 2 (Summer 1990).

Ohanian, Susan. "Notes on Japan from an American School-Teacher." *Phi Delta Kappan* 68, no. 5 (January 1987).

Otsu, Kazuko. "Shakaika ni okeru gurobaru kyoiku no 4 tsu no apurochi" (Four possible approaches to global education in social studies). *Kyoikugaku kenkyu* 61, no. 3 (September 1994).

Passin, Herbert. *Society and Education in Japan.* New York: Teachers College Press, Columbia University, 1965.

Peak, Lois. *Learning to Go to School in Japan.* Berkeley and Los Angeles: University of California Press, 1991.

————. "Formal Pre-Elementary Education in Japan." In *Japanese Educational Productivity.* Edited by R. Leestma and H. J. Walberg. Ann Arbor: University of Michigan Press, 1992.

Perkinson, Henry J. *The Imperfect Panacea: American Faith in Education, 1865–1990.* New York: McGraw-Hill, 1991.

Phillip, Mary-Christine. "Trying to Save a Generation at Risk." *Black Issues in Higher Education,* 12 August 1993.

Powell, Arthur G., Eleanor Farrar, and David K. Cohen. *The Shopping Mall High School.* Boston: Houghton Mifflin, 1985.

Purpel, David. *The Moral and Spiritual Crisis in Education.* New York: Bergin & Garvey, 1989.

Ravitch, Diane. *The Troubled Crusade: American Education 1945–1980.* New York: Basic Books, 1983.

Ravitch, Diane, and Chester E. Finn, Jr. *What Do Our 17-Year-Olds Know?* New York: Harper & Row, 1987.

Rohlen, Thomas. "The Juku Phenomenon: An Exploratory Essay." *Journal of Japanese Studies* 6, no. 2 (1980).

————. "Conflicts in Institutional Environments: Politics in Education." In *Conflict in Japan.* Edited by Ellis S. Krauss, Thomas P. Rohlen, and Patricia G. Steinhoff. Honolulu: University of Hawaii Press, 1984.

————. *Japan's High Schools*. Berkeley and Los Angeles: University of California Press, 1984.

Rohlen, Thomas P., and Gerald K. LeTendre, eds. *Teaching and Learning in Japan*. Cambridge: Cambridge University Press, 1996.

Rubinger, Richard. *Private Academies of Tokugawa Japan*. Princeton, N.J.: Princeton University Press, 1982.

————. "Continuity and Change in Mid-Nineteenth-Century Japanese Education." In *Japanese Schooling*. Edited by James J. Shields, Jr. University Park: Pennsylvania State University Press, 1989.

Sato, Nancy, and Milbrey W. McLaughlin. "Context Matters: Teaching in Japan and in the United States." *Phi Delta Kappan* 73, no. 5 (January 1992).

Schlesinger, Arthur M., Jr. *The Disuniting of America*. New York: W. W. Norton, 1992.

Schoolland, Ken. *Shogun's Ghost: The Dark Side of Japanese Education*. New York: Bergin & Garvey, 1990.

Schoppa, Leonard James. *Education Reform in Japan*. London: Routledge, 1991.

————. "Education Reform in Japan: Goals and Results of the Recent Reform Campaign." In *Windows on Japanese Education*. Edited by Edward R. Beauchamp. Westport, Conn.: Greenwood Press, 1991.

Sewall, Gilbert T. *American History Textbooks: An Assessment of Quality*. New York: Educational Excellence Network, 1987.

Shimahara, Nobuo. "Teacher Education in Japan." In *Windows on Japanese Education*. Edited by Edward R. Beauchamp. Westport, Conn.: Greenwood Press, 1991.

————. "Restructuring Japanese High Schools: Reforms for Diversity." *Journal of Educational Policy* 9, no. 2 (June 1995).

————. "Teacher Education Reform in Japan: Issues of Ideology and Control." In *Teacher Education in Industrialized Nations: Issues in Changing Social Contexts*. Edited by Nobuo K. Shimahara and Ivan Holowinsky. New York: Garland, 1995.

Shimahara, Nobuo K., and Akira Sakai. *Learning to Teach in Two Cultures: Japan and the United States*. New York: Garland, 1985.

————. "Teacher Internship and the Culture of Teaching in Japan." *British Journal of Sociology of Education* 13, no. 2 (1992).

Shipler, David K. "Why Black Men Identify with O.J." *Asahi Evening News*, 15 February 1997.

Simmons, Cyril. *Growing Up and Going to School in Japan*. Philadelphia: Open University Press, 1990.

Singleton, John. "Gambare: A Japanese Cultural Theory of Learning." In *Japanese Schooling*. Edited by James J. Shields, Jr. University Park: Pennsylvania State University Press, 1989.

Sitzer, Sage. *Sociology of American Sport*. Dubuque, Iowa: William C. Brown, 1980.

Sizer, Theodore. *Horace's Compromise: The Dilemma of the American High School*. Boston: Houghton Mifflin, 1983.

Stevenson, Harold W. "Learning to Read Japanese." In *Child Development and Education in Japan*. Edited by Harold W. Stevenson, Hiroshi Azuma, and Kenji Hakuta. New York: W. H. Freeman, 1986.

————. "Achievement in Mathematics." In *Child Development and Education in Japan*. Edited by Harold W. Stevenson, Hiroshi Azuma, and Kenji Hakuta. New York: W. H. Freeman, 1986.

Stevenson, Harold W., and Karen Bartsch. "An Analysis of Japanese and American Textbooks in Mathematics." In *Japanese Educational Productivity*. Edited by R. Leestma and H. J. Walberg. Ann Arbor: University of Michigan Press, 1992.

Stevenson, Harold W., and James Stigler. *The Learning Gap: Why Our Schools Are Failing and What We Can Learn from Japanese and Chinese Education*. New York: Summit, 1992.

Stigler, J. W., S. Y. Lee, G. W. Lucker, and H. W. Stevenson. "Curriculum and Achievement in Mathematics: A Study of Elementary School Children in Japan, Taiwan and the United States." *Journal of Educational Psychology* 74 (1982).

Sugihara, Seishiro. "Educational Expenditure in Japan and the United States." *East West Education* 11 (Spring 1990).

Sykes, Charles. *Dumbing Down Our Kids*. New York: St. Martin's Press, 1995.

Takahashi, Shiro, and Harry Wray. *Senryoka kyoiku kaikaku to kenetsu* (Educational reform and censorship under the Allied Occupation of Japan). Tokyo: Nihon Kyoiku Shimbunsha, 1987.

Takakura, Sho, and Yokuo Murata. *Education in Japan: Teaching Courses and Subjects, 1989*. Tsukuba: University of Tsukuba Institute of Education, 1989.

—. *Education in Japan: A Bilingual Text—Present System and Tasks/Curriculum and Instruction*. Tokyo: Gakken, 1998.

Thompson, Scott D. "Report Card USA: How Much Do Americans Value Schooling?" *National Association of Secondary School Principals (NASSP) Bulletin* (October 1989).

Thurston, Donald. *Teachers and Politics in Japan*. Princeton, N.J.: Princeton University Press, 1973.

Tobin, Joseph J., David Y. H. Wu, and Dana H. Davidson. *Preschool in Three Cultures: Japan, China, and the United States*. New Haven: Yale University Press, 1989.

Trainor, Joseph C. *Educational Reform in Occupied Japan: Trainor's Memoir*. Tokyo: Meisei University Press, 1983.

Trow, Martin. "The State of Higher Education in the United States." In *Educational Policies in Crisis*. Edited by William K. Cummings, Edward R. Beauchamp, Shogo Ichikawa, Victor N. Kobayashi, Morikazu Ushiogi. Westport, Conn.: Praeger, 1986.

Tsuchida, Ineko. "Teachers' Motivational and Instructional Strategies." Ph.D. diss., School of Education, University of California at Berkeley, 1993.

Tsukada, Mamoru. "A Factual Overview of Japanese and American Education." In *Educational Policies in Crisis*. Edited by William K. Cummings, Edward R. Beauchamp, Shogo Ichikawa, Victor N. Kobayashi, Morikazu Ushiogi. Westport, Conn.: Praeger, 1986.

—. "Institutionalized Supplementary Education in Japan." *Comparative Education* 24, no. 3 (1988).

—. *Yobiko Life: A Study of the Legitimation Process of Social Stratification in Japan*. Berkeley: Institute of East Asian Studies, University of California, 1991.

Tsuneyoshi, Ryoko. *Ningen keisei no Nichi-Bei hikaku* (A comparison of Japanese and American character formation). Tokyo: Chuo Koron, 1992.

Turner, E. W. "The Effect of Long Summer Holidays on Children's Literacy." *Educational Research* (June 1972).

Ushiogi, Morikazu. "Transition from School to Work: The Japanese Case." In *Educational Policies in Crisis*. Edited by William K. Cummings, Edward R. Beauchamp, Shogo Ichikawa, Victor N. Kobayashi, Morikazu Ushiogi. Westport, Conn.: Praeger, 1986.

U.S. Department of Education. *Japanese Education Today*. Washington, D.C.: U.S. Government Printing Office, 1987.

U.S. Department of Education, National Center for Education Statistics. *Digest of Education Statistics*. Annual, 1989–1997. Washington, D.C.: U.S. Government Printing Office.

———. *Dropout Rates in the United States: 1991*. Washington, D.C.: U.S. Government Printing Office, 1992.

———. *America's Teachers: Profile of a Profession*. Washington, D.C.: U.S. Government Printing Office, 1993.

———. *Pursuing Excellnce*. Washington, D.C.: U.S. Government Printing Office, 1996.

———. *The Condition of Education 1991–1997*. Washington, D.C.: U.S. Government Printing Office, 1991–1997.

Vogel, Ezra. *Japan As Number One: Lessons for America*. Tokyo: Charles E. Tuttle, 1979.

White, Merry. *The Japanese Educational Challenge*. New York: Free Press, 1987.

———. *The Japanese Overseas*. New York: Free Press, 1988.

White, Merry, and R. Levine. "What Is an Ii Ko Good Child?" In *Child Development and Education in Japan*. Edited by Harold W. Stevenson, Hiroshi Azuma, and Kenji Hakuta. New York: W. H. Freeman, 1986.

Whitman, Nancy. "Teaching of Mathematics in Japanese Schools." In *Windows on Japanese Education*. Edited by Edward R. Beauchamp. Westport, Conn.: Greenwood Press, 1991.

Wray, Harry. "Change and Continuity in Images of the *Kokutai* and Attitudes and Roles towards the Outside World: A Content Analysis of Japanese Textbooks, 1903–1945." Ph.D. diss., University of Hawaii, 1971.

———. "Decentralization of Education in the Allied Occupation of Japan, 1945–1952." *The Occupation of Japan: Educational and Social Reform*. Edited by Thomas Burkman. Norfolk, Va.: Gatling Printing, 1981.

———. "*CIE, Mombusho, and kyoiku sasshin iinkai* (The connection between the CIE, Ministry of Education, and educational reform committee)." In *Tenno ga Baiburu o Yonda hi* (The day the emperor read the Bible). Edited by Ray Moore. Tokyo: Kodansha, 1982.

———. "*Amerika kara mita Shinjuwan* (Pearl Harbor seen from America)." In *Shinjuwan moeru* (Pearl Harbor enflamed). Edited by Hata Ikuhiko. Tokyo: Hara Shobo, 1991.

———. "Significance, Change, and Continuity in Modern Japanese Educational History." *Comparative Education Review* 35, no. 3 (1991).

———. "Civics Education in the United States." In *Understanding the World Civic Education, Globalization and the Korean Response*. Edited by Tuk-Chu Chun. Seoul: Hak Mun, 1994.

Wray, Harry, and Shiro Takahashi. *Obei kara mita Nihon no kyoiku* (Japanese education viewed from Europe and the United States). Tokyo: Kyodo Shuppan, 1989.

Yamada, Carol Linda Susan. "Family Culture and Educational Attainment in Japan." Ph.D. diss., University of Tsukuba, 1988.

Yamamura, Yoshiaki. "The Child in Japanese Society." In *Child Development and Education in Japan*. Edited by Harold W. Stevenson, Hiroshi Azuma, and Kenji Hakuta. New York: W. H. Freeman, 1986.

Index

Ability, 54–57, 287, 294. *See also* Aptitude, message to students; Effort
Ability grouping, tracking, 280
Absenteeism, 14, 17, 26–27, 67, 84, 177, 209
Academic achievement: African American, 206; classroom management and discipline, 14, 16–17, 20–21; compared in Japan and the United States, 1–2, 10–12, 49–50, 111, 275–276, 278–280, 294–296, 299; diffused American curriculum, 274–276, 279–281; discrimination, 188–190, 209; economic competitiveness, 49, 288–289; longer school year, 4–8; obstacles, 106; parental support in Japan and the United States, 60–62, 65–67; part-time work, 23–25, 294–295; post-1984 American, 184, 200; pre-1984 American, 194–195, 273; relationship to character formation, 16–17, 20–21; relationship to self-esteem, 31, 64, 180–182; school rules, 111; state and national government responsibility, 184–189, 194, 203–204, 294–296; teacher competence, 230–233

Accountability, assessment and choice, 204–205; minimum competency tests, 288
Achievement tests: American College Test (ACT), 56–57, 273; Educational Testing Service Achievement, 67; excessive emphasis on aptitude, 18–19; International Assessment for Evaluation of Education Achievement (IEA), 195; International Assessment of Educational Progress, 295–298; National Assessment of Educational Progress, 196–200; recommendations, 67–68, 268; Scholastic Aptitude Test, 56–57; Third International Mathematics and Science Study (TIMSS), 1–2, 268
Administration and administrators, comparing Japan and the United States, 91–95; cautious attitude, 91–93, 113; complacency, 179, 192–193, 237–238; flexibility, 92–93, 95, 113; innovation, 93; Japan service education, 92–93, 95, 113, 239–240, 291–292; loss of good teachers to, 241–242; policy making, 224–225, 245; practices on absenteeism, 14; salaries, 227–238;

ABOUT THE AUTHOR

Harry Wray is Professor of Japanese History and International Relations in the College of Foreign Studies, Nanzan University, Nagoya, Japan.

ISBN 0-89789-652-1

90000>

HARDCOVER BAR CODE